D0987409

PERSPECTIVES ON BEHAVIORAL SELF-REGULATION

Advances in Social Cognition
Volume XII

PERSPECTIVES ON BEHAVIORAL SELF-REGULATION

Advances in Social Cognition
Volume XII

Edited by

Robert S. Wyer, Jr.
University of Illinois, Urbana–Champaign

Lead Article by
Charles S. Carver
and
Michael F. Scheier

LAWRENCE ERLBAUM ASSOCIATES, PUBLISHERS
1999   Mahwah, New Jersey   London

Copyright © 1999 by Lawrence Erlbaum Associates, Inc
All rights reserved. No part of this book may be reproduced in
any form, by photostat, microfilm, retrieval system, or any
other means, without prior written permission of the publisher.

Lawrence Erlbaum Associates, Inc., Publishers
10 Industrial Avenue
Mahwah, NJ 07430

Cover design by Kathryn Houghtaling Lacey

Library of Congress Cataloging-in-Publication Data

Stereotype Activation and Inhibition: Advances in Social Cognition,
Volume XII
    ISSN: 0898-2007
    ISBN: 0-8058-2588-6 (cloth)
    ISBN: 0-8058-2589-4 (paper)

Books published by Lawrence Erlbaum Associates are printed on
acid-free paper, and their bindings are chosen for strength and dura-
bility.

Printed in the United States of America
10 9 8 7 6 5 4 3 2 1

Contents

Preface

This is the twelfth volume of the *Advances in Social Cognition* series. From its inception, the purpose of the series has been to present and evaluate new theoretical advances in all areas of social cognition and information processing. An entire volume is devoted to each theory, allowing the theory to be evaluated from a variety of perspectives and permitting its implications for a wide range of issues to be examined.

The series reflects two major characteristics of social cognition: the high level of activity in the field and the interstitial nature of the work. Each volume contains a target chapter that is timely in its application, novel in its approach, and precise in its explication. The target chapter is followed by a set of companion chapters that examine the theoretical and empirical issues the target chapter has raised. These latter chapters are written by authors with diverse theoretical orientations, representing different disciplines within psychology and, in some cases, entirely different disciplines. Target authors are then given the opportunity to respond to the comments and criticisms of their work and to examine the ideas conveyed in the companion chapters in light of their own. The dialogue created by this format is both unusual and extremely beneficial to the field.

An understanding of the cognitive and motivational determinants of behavioral self-regulation is unquestionably one of the most important goals of social and personality psychology and has far-reaching practical as well as theoretical implications. No two people have contributed more to this understanding than Charles Carver and Michael Scheier, the authors of the target chapter. Their feedback model of self-regulation has been one of the most successful theoretical formulations of regulatory processes yet to emerge and has stimulated empirical research for several years. In the course of refining and extending this formulation, the authors now identify and discuss a number of unresolved issues, including the role of affect in self-regulation, the interplay of intentionality and automaticity, and the determinants of persistence in and disengagement from goal-directed activity. The range of phenomena to which their theoretical framework potentially applies is evident from its ability to incorporate implications of other conceptualizations as diverse as catastrophe theory and dynamic systems theory. The target chapter represents a major conceptual advance in our understanding of self-regulatory processes. Moreover, its focus on the interplay of motivational and cognitive influences on overt behavior exemplifies a general perspective that has only begun within the 1990s to predominate social cognition theory and research.

The diversity of theoretical and empirical issues identified by Carver and Scheier is matched by the companion chapters. These chapters, by eminent scholars in the field, are written from perspectives ranging from developmental psychology to cognitive science, clinical psychology, and organizational decision making. The topics they address include the role of affect in goal-directed activity, the development of self-regulation, a comparison of cybernetic and organismic paradigms of motivation, and the various roles played by confidence and expectancy biases, autonomy, and action identification.

This volume is the last edition of the *Advances in Social Cognition* to be published by Lawrence Erlbaum Associates. In its 12-year history, the series has presented major theoretical contributions in virtually every area of social cognition and permitted them to be evaluated from a number of perspectives. This could not have been accomplished without the support and commitment of Lawrence Erlbaum and his staff to publishing a high-quality set of volumes. It has been a pleasure to work with them.

—Robert S. Wyer, Jr.

1

Themes and Issues in the Self-Regulation of Behavior

Charles S. Carver
University of Miami

Michael F. Scheier
Carnegie Mellon University

We are interested in the structure of behavior. The questions that lie behind this interest are very abstract: What concepts are most useful in thinking about how people create overt action from intentions and desires? Once people have decided to do something, how do they stay on course? What processes account for the existence of feelings, as people make their way through the world? An idea that's been at the fore of our thinking since the 1970s is that behavior is a self-regulatory event.[1] It's an attempt to make something happen that's already in mind, even if only vaguely so. This idea spawns several distinct themes, which are the core topic of this chapter.

---

[1] A brief note on terminology: Block (1996) has argued that *autoregulation* is preferable to self-regulation, because it avoids the implication that the self is always involved in the regulatory process, an implication that often isn't intended. For example, most people wouldn't want to argue that processes such as blood pressure control are managed by the self. Although Block's point is well taken, the term *self-regulation* is so entrenched in multiple literatures that it seems impractical at this point to try to enforce a shift in label.

This chapter differs in several respects from most previous target chapters of this series. For one thing, we've written a lot more here about theory than about data. Much of this chapter is a statement of ideas we think are important in conceptualizing behavior. Other parts of it address potential bridges across literatures and unresolved questions and problems. Data are mentioned in both cases, but ideas rather than a particular body of research findings take center stage.

Another thing that makes this chapter a little unusual is that a lot of the ideas we're going to argue are important have been noticed by other people as well as by us. We're not describing a new theory. We're not making an integrative presentation of a broad program of research. Very little of what's in this chapter is unique. We would like to think this doesn't mean we're just reinventing the wheel, however. Our intent is to recast several ideas from a slightly different angle than may be familiar to readers. One thing we've done throughout our careers is to juxtapose ideas that hadn't been juxtaposed before, which on occasion has led to a pulling together of disparate threads in an interesting way. That has been one of our goals here as well.

The chapter is organized in terms of a series of conceptual themes that we've found useful and important in our own thinking. Some of these themes have been central in our thinking for some time; others are newer and more tentative. With only a couple of exceptions, each statement of a theme is followed directly by a section in which we raise a series of issues pertaining to the theme. We've done this because one of the explicit goals of this chapter is to point to issues that are far from settled and to questions that remain unexplored. The organizational format of themes and issues is intended to facilitate dialogue on these issues and questions.

We start simple and build from there. We begin with basic ideas about the nature of behavior and the organization of some of the processes by which we believe behavior is regulated. We then turn to a consideration of emotion—how it's created and how classes of affects differ from each other. This is followed by a consideration of the fact that people sometimes are unable to do what they set out to do and what follows from that problem. The next theme stems from questions that have been raised about top-down models of behavior and suggestions that thinking occurs in two distinguishable modes. The next two sections, the most speculative of the chapter, concern dynamic systems and catastrophe theory as models for understanding behavior and how these models may contribute to the ways in which people such as ourselves think about self-regulation. We conclude with a brief consideration of problems in behavior and the therapy process.

THEME: BEHAVIOR IS GOAL DIRECTED AND FEEDBACK CONTROLLED

The view we take on behavior begins with the concept of goal and the process of feedback control. We see these ideas as intimately linked. Our focus on goals is very much in line with a growing re-emergence of goal constructs in today's personality–social psychology (Austin & Vancouver, 1996; Elliott & Dweck, 1988; Miller & Read, 1987; Pervin, 1982, 1989). A variety of labels are used in this literature, reflecting differences in emphasis among various writers.

For example, Klinger (1975, 1977) used the phrase *current concern* to describe goals with which a person is now engaged. The sense of engagement is also conveyed by *personal strivings* (Emmons, 1986) and *life task* (Cantor & Kihlstrom, 1987). A construct that tends to convey a more restricted scope than these is the *personal project* (Little, 1983, 1989). It resembles Klinger's current concern, though its label doesn't convey quite the same sense of urgency.

In all these conceptualizations, one can point to overall goals and subgoals. There is also room for a great deal of individualization. That is, a life task or striving can be achieved in many ways, and people choose paths compatible with other aspects of their life situation (many current concerns must be managed simultaneously) and other aspects of their personality.

Two goal constructs that differ somewhat from those named thus far are the *possible self* (Markus & Nurius, 1986) and the *self-guide* (Higgins, 1987, 1996). These constructs are intended to bring a dynamic quality to conceptualization of the self-concept. In contrast to traditional views, but consistent with other goal frameworks, possible selves are future oriented. They concern how people think of their as-yet-unrealized potential, the kind of person they might become. Self-guides similarly reflect dynamic aspects of the self-concept.

Theorists who use these various terms—and others—have their own emphases (for broader discussions, see Austin & Vancouver, 1996; Carver & Scheier, 1998), but many points are the same. All include the idea that goals energize and direct activities (Pervin, 1982), that goals serve to engage the activities of the people who adopt them. These views implicitly (and sometimes explicitly) convey the sense that goals give meaning to people's lives (cf. Baumeister, 1989). In each theory, there's an emphasis on the idea that understanding the person means understanding the person's goals. Indeed, in the view represented by these theories, it's often implicit that the self consists partly of the person's goals and the organization among them.

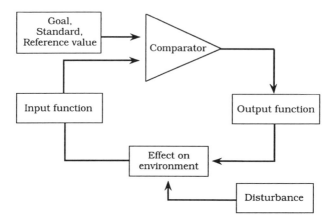

FIG. 1.1. Schematic depiction of a feedback loop, the basic unit of cybernetic control. In such a loop, a sensed value is compared to a reference value or standard and adjustments are made in an output function (if necessary) to shift the sensed value in the direction of the standard.

Feedback Loops

How are goals used in acting? Most people discuss this question in terms of decomposition of goals into subgoals. That's part of our answer too, but only part of it. Another part is that goals serve as reference values for feedback loops. A feedback loop, the unit of cybernetic control, is a system of four elements in a particular organization (cf. Miller, Galanter, & Pribram, 1960). These elements are an input function, a reference value, a comparator, and an output function (Fig. 1.1).

An input function is a sensor. It brings information in. We'll treat this input function as equivalent to perception. The reference value is a second source of information (i.e., besides the information from the input function). We'll treat the reference values in the loops we're interested in as goals. The comparator is a device that makes comparisons between input and reference value. The comparison yields one of two outcomes: either the values being compared are discriminably different from one another or they're not. The comparison can vary in sensitivity, however, leading it to detect either very small discrepancies or only much larger ones.

Following this comparison is an output function. We'll treat this as equivalent to behavior, though sometimes the behavior is internal. If the comparison yields a "no difference," the output function remains whatever it was. This may mean no output, or it may mean that the ongoing output continues. If the comparison yields "discrepancy," however, the output function changes.

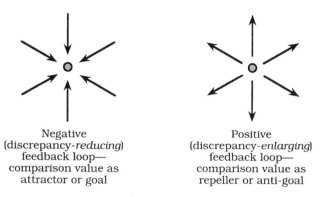

Negative
(discrepancy-*reducing*)
feedback loop—
comparison value as
attractor or goal

Positive
(discrepancy-*enlarging*)
feedback loop—
comparison value as
repeller or anti-goal

FIG. 1.2. Negative feedback loops cause sensed qualities to shift *toward* positively valenced reference points. Positive feedback loops cause sensed qualities to shift *away* from negatively valenced reference points.

There are two kinds of feedback loops, corresponding to two kinds of goals (Fig. 1.2). In a negative, or discrepancy-reducing, loop the output function is aimed at diminishing or eliminating any detected discrepancy between input and reference value. This sort of conformity is seen in the attempt to approach or attain a valued goal.

Keep in mind that this isn't behavior for the sake of behavior, but behavior in the service of creating and maintaining conformity of input to a standard. That is, the value sensed by the input function depends on more than the output (see Fig. 1.1). Disturbances from outside can change present conditions, either adversely (increasing a discrepancy with the reference value) or favorably (diminishing a discrepancy). In the first case, the recognition of a discrepancy prompts a change in output, as always. In the second case, though, the disturbance preempts the need for an output adjustment because the system sees no discrepancy. Thus, no output adjustment occurs.

The second kind of feedback loop is a positive, or discrepancy-enlarging, loop (Fig. 1.2). The value here isn't one to approach, but one to avoid. It may be simplest to think of this as an "anti-goal." A psychological example of an anti-goal is a feared possible self. Other, more concrete examples would be traffic tickets, public ridicule, and being fired from your job. A positive loop senses present conditions, compares them to the anti-goal, and tries to enlarge the discrepancy between the two. For example, a rebellious adolescent who wants to be different from his parents senses his own behavior, compares it to his parents' behavior, and tries to make his own behavior as different from theirs as possible.

The action of discrepancy-enlarging processes in living systems is typically constrained in some way by discrepancy-reducing loops (Fig. 1.3).

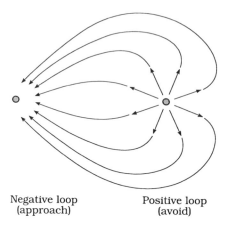

Negative loop   Positive loop
(approach)   (avoid)

FIG. 1.3. The effects of positive feedback systems are often bounded or constrained by negative feedback systems. A value moves away from an undesired
condition in a positive loop, and then comes under the influence of a negative
loop, moving toward its desired condition.

To put it differently, avoidance behaviors often lead into approach behaviors. An avoidance loop creates pressure to increase distance from
the anti-goal. The movement away occurs until the tendency to move
away is captured by the influence of an approach loop. This loop then
serves to pull the sensed input into its orbit. The rebellious adolescent,
trying to be different from his parents, soon finds a group of other adolescents to conform to, all of whom are remaining different from their
parents.

Our use of the word orbit in the previous paragraph suggests a metaphor that may be useful for readers to whom these concepts don't feel
terribly intuitive. You might think of feedback processes as meta-
phorically equivalent to gravity and antigravity. The negative feedback
loop exerts a kind of gravitational pull on the sensed input it's controlling, pulling that input closer to its ground zero. The positive loop has a
kind of antigravitational push, moving sensed values ever farther away.
Don't forget, though, that this is a metaphor. More is involved here than
a force field.

It's worth noting that the situations people confront are often more
complex than the one shown in Fig. 1.3. Often, there are several potential
values to move toward (Fig. 1.4). For this reason, one positive value won't
always capture or constrain all the avoidance attempts. Thus, if several
people are trying to deviate from a mutually disliked reference point,
they may diverge wildly from one another. For example, one disgrun-
tled adolescent trying to escape from his parents' values may gravitate

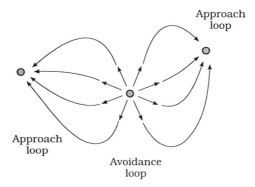

FIG. 1.4. Sometimes more than one desired value is available when an avoid-ance loop is operating. In such a case, efforts to escape the undesired value may be captured by one of the desired values, or it may be captured by the other desired value. It seems likely that which desired value constrains the moving-away-from process is determined in part by which value is closer to a person's preexisting values, and in part by the direction in which the person initially moves to avoid the undesired value.

to membership in a rock band, another may gravitate to the army. Pre-sumably what direction is chosen to approach will depend in part on the fit between the available reference values and the person's preexisting values and in part on the direction the person took initially to escape from the anti-goal.

Some years ago we argued that the comparator of a psychological feedback loop is engaged by increases in self-focused attention (Carver, 1979; Carver & Scheier, 1981, 1990a). Indeed, the similarity in function between experimental manipulations of self-focus and the elements of the feedback loop was one thing that attracted us to the feedback model in the first place. Self-focused attention leads to more comparisons with salient standards (Scheier & Carver, 1983) and it enhances behavioral conformity to salient standards. The standards have ranged from explicit instructions, to personal attitudes, to subjective norms (for reviews, see Carver & Scheier, 1981, 1998). On the avoidance side, self-focus has led to more rejection of attitudinal positions held by a negative reference group (Carver & Humphries, 1981) and to stronger reactance effects (Carver & Scheier, 1981).

The literature of self-awareness isn't the only one that fits the picture of feedback loops, however (Carver & Scheier, 1998). For example, social comparison processes can easily be viewed in these terms: Upward com-parisons help you pull yourself toward desired reference points. Down-ward comparisons help you force yourself farther away from (upward from) those who are worse off than you are. We have also discussed self-verification processes in these terms: People try to force the social feedback they receive from others in their lives into closer conformity with the images they have of themselves (Swann, 1990).

ISSUES

By this point, a couple of issues will have arisen in at least some readers' minds. One issue concerns the relatively automatic quality of the processes we've outlined. We've made these processes sound as though they just *happen*. Where's the place in this model for will?

Will and Self-Determination

Locke and Latham (1990a), whose research focuses on work motivation, have a theory that greatly resembles the feedback model just described, that is, "Goal setting is ... usually only effective when feedback allows performance to be tracked in relation to one's goals" (Locke & Latham, 1990b, p. 241). Despite this, they recoil at the idea that the functions embedded in their theory reflect the operation of feedback processes. The crux of the objection seems to be that a feedback model is too mechanistic. Feedback models don't portray behavior as a series of willful choices.

A similar issue emerges in the writings of Deci and Ryan (e.g., 1985, 1991; Ryan, 1993; Ryan, Sheldon, Kasser, & Deci, 1996), although apart from this particular similarity, Deci and Ryan's approach to motivation has very little in common with that of Locke and Latham (see Deci, 1992, for a critique of the latter, including the objection that *it* is mechanistic). Deci and Ryan emphasize the importance of personal autonomy or self-determination in behavior, arguing that behavior done autonomously is fundamentally different from behavior that's done for other reasons. This emphasis raises the question of whether the occurrence of a feedback process can be thought of as autonomous and self-determined. Although this question involves many issues, one issue it involves is that of will.

We have never taken a strong position on will, partly because we don't have a strong opinion on it. Maybe the web of feedback processes about which we're writing operates in service to some other process we haven't identified. If so, our account would be even more incomplete than it is anyway. It would, nonetheless, remain a reasonable portrayal of the various functions that are engaged by whatever is the missing function. As such, it would seem to remain useful.

On the other hand, maybe what people recognize from introspection as effortful decision making and planning—the sort of things that make it obvious to you that you have your own will—is actually self-delusional. Perhaps these patterns of thought are the product of processes behind the scenes, outside awareness, drawing us toward images of who we might be. Pervin (1992), writing about the Locke and Latham model, expressed skepticism about its rational, volitional view, based partly on his years of clinical experience. His skepticism derived from the trouble people have in exercising will, doing things they wish to do and refraining from things they wish not to do. We share some of this skepticism.

Reemergent Interest in Approach and Avoidance

Another issue relates to the existence of two kinds of feedback processes. Our interest in the embodiment of these two kinds of feedback processes in behavior is echoed in the reemergence of interest in two kinds of regulation in several other literatures (Carver, 1996a).

Biological Theories. One of these literatures derives from a group of theories that are biological in focus. Their research base ranges from animal conditioning and behavioral pharmacology (Gray, 1972, 1977, 1978, 1982, 1987b) to neuropsychological studies of brain activity (Davidson, 1992a, 1992b; Tomarken, Davidson, Wheeler, & Doss, 1992).

These theories all incorporate the idea that two systems (sometimes more) are involved in the regulation of behavior (cf. Konorski, 1967; Schneirla, 1959; Thayer, 1989). One system, dealing with approach behavior, is variously called the behavioral activation system (Cloninger, 1987; Fowles, 1980), the behavioral approach system (Gray, 1981, 1987a, 1990), the behavioral engagement system (Depue, Krauss, & Spoont, 1987), or the behavioral facilitation system (Depue & Iacono, 1989). The other, dealing with withdrawal or avoidance, is usually called the behavioral inhibition system (Cloninger, 1987; Gray, 1981, 1987a, 1990), although it's sometimes termed a withdrawal system (Davidson, 1992a, 1992b). The two systems are generally regarded as independent, because they're believed to be regulated by different brain mechanisms.

Self-Discrepancy Theory. Another literature with a dual-motive theme derives from self-discrepancy theory (Higgins, 1987, 1996; Higgins, Bond, Klein, & Strauman, 1986). This theory holds that people relate their perceptions of their actual selves to several self-guides, particularly ideals and oughts. Ideals are qualities the person desires to embody—aspirations, hopes, and positive wishes for the self. Living up to an ideal means attaining something desired. An ideal is clearly an approach goal. We believe it is *purely* an approach goal.

Oughts, in contrast to ideals, are defined by a sense of duty, responsibility, or obligation. An ought is a self that one feels compelled to be, rather than intrinsically desires to be. The ought self is a positive value, in the sense that people try to conform to it. However, living up to an ought also implies acting to avoid a punishment—self-disapproval or the disapproval of others. In our interpretation, this makes oughts more complex structurally than ideals. Oughts intrinsically imply both an avoidance process and an approach process. Their structure thus resembles what was illustrated earlier in Fig. 1.3.

Recent work has explored more fully the avoidance aspect of the dynamics behind the ought self. Higgins and Tykocinski (1992) showed that people whose self-structure reflects discrepancies between actual and oughts (but not between actual and ideals) process information differently from people whose self-structure reflects the opposite pattern. In an incidental memory task, those with self-structures dominated by actual-ought discrepancies seemed to be focused on avoiding negative goals. Subjects with self-structures dominated by actual-ideal discrepancies gave evidence of being focused on positive goals.

Further evidence comes from Higgins, Roney, Crowe, and Hymes (1994). In one study, subjects chose friendship strategies from among six options. All options were positive, but three had an approach ("do") orientation ("be generous and willing to give of yourself") and three incorporated an avoidance ("don't") orientation ("try to make time for your friends and *not neglect them*" [emphasis added]). Subjects whose self-structure was dominated by actual-ought discrepancies chose more strategies with an avoidance orientation than subjects whose self-structure was dominated by actual-ideal discrepancies. Once again, then, the data showed distinct influences of approach and avoidance modes of action.

Self-Determination Theory. Another literature that seems to have echoes of this approach versus avoidance theme is that of self-determination theory (Deci & Ryan, 1985, 1987, 1991, 1995; Ryan, 1993; see also Vallerand, 1997). This literature begins with the idea that some actions (*self-determined* behaviors) are undertaken out of belief that the activity is intrinsically valuable. Other actions (*controlled* behaviors) are undertaken to satisfy pressures or demands. Behaviors can be controlled even if the control occurs entirely inside your own mind. If you engage in an action because you know you'd feel guilty if you didn't, you're engaging in controlled behavior.

What's key is the extent to which the activities are integrated into the structure of the self. Although there are multiple levels of integration, there's a functional split between what's called *introjected* regulation and *identified* regulation. Introjected regulation means the behavior is done for controlling reasons, although the control happens intrapsychically (e.g., the behavior is done to avoid a sense of guilt or to please someone else). In identified regulation, in contrast, the person has accepted the behavior as important and meaningful. It thus is self-determined.

It should be apparent that self-determined behavior is approach behavior. Because introjected behavior is done in order to avoid a sense of guilt, however, it closely resembles what Higgins calls ought-regulated behavior. It involves approach, but approach in the service of avoidance. Thus, it seems to involve the functioning of both approach and avoidance processes.

More Than Homeostasis?

Another issue concerns the question of whether a control-theory approach is useful for anything other than homeostasis. That is, some have argued that feedback processes are limited to creation and maintenance of steady states (Bandura, 1989). This, however, is a very limited view, which presumes that all reference values are fixed and constant.

Such is not the case, and such a view has never been a part of feedback-based models of self-regulation (see Pribram, 1990; Waddington, 1957). Many of the goals that underlie human behavior represent specifications of entire programs of activity (e.g., take a month's vacation in Europe, write a book chapter). As such, the goal at any given moment is fluid and constantly changing as the person traverses the path of activity. Other goals are recurrent (do the laundry). They are re-evoked for regulatory activity as the situation changes (you run out of clean socks) across the passage of time and events. In short, human behavior is aimed at a variety of moving targets. This apparent issue is really a nonissue.

THEME: GOALS ARE HIERARCHICAL

Another theme in the translation of goals into behavior reflects the obvious fact that some goals are broader in scope than others. How to think about the difference in breadth isn't always easy to put your finger on. Sometimes it's a difference in temporal commitment. For example, the personal project of being well prepared for a test may be multifaceted, but this is a goal with a fairly short life span. In contrast, the life task of being well prepared for business meetings has longer relevance. Sometimes, though, a difference in breadth is more than that. It's a difference in the goal's level of abstraction.

Premise: Goals Can Be Differentiated by Levels of Abstraction

The notion that goals differ in their level of abstraction is easy to illustrate. You might have the goal of being an honorable person, or a self-sufficient person, or a person who always comes out on top in dealing with others. These goals are at a relatively high level of abstraction. You may also have the goal of avoiding a person at work who gossips, or of making dinner for yourself, or of getting a good price on a car. These are all at a lower level of abstraction. The first set concern being a particular kind of *person*, the second set concern completing a particular kind of *action*.

You could also think of goals that are even more concrete than the latter set, such as the goal of walking quietly to your office and closing the door without being heard, or the goal of cutting vegetables into a pan, or of keeping your face blank while naming a dollar figure to a salesman. These goals (which some would call plans or strategies instead of goals) are closer to specifications of individual acts than were the second set, which were more summary statements about the desired outcomes of intended action patterns.

How should we think about this difference in abstraction among goals? As you may have noticed, the examples used to illustrate concrete goals (and more-concrete goals) relate directly to the examples of abstract goals. We did this to point out that abstract goals are linked to concrete goals. We consider here the idea that these links form a hierarchy of levels of abstraction.

In a 1973 book, William Powers argued that a hierarchical organization of feedback loops underlies the self-regulation of behavior. Because feedback loops imply goals, this argument also constituted a model of hierarchical structuring among the goals involved in creating action. His general line of thinking ran as follows: In a hierarchical organization of feedback systems, the output of a high level system consists of the resetting of reference values at the next lower level of abstraction. To put it somewhat differently, higher order or superordinate systems "behave" by providing goals to the systems just below them.

The reference values specified as behavioral outputs become more concrete and restricted as one moves from higher to lower levels of the hierarchy. Control at each level reflects regulation of a quality that contributes to the quality controlled at the next higher level. Each level monitors input at a level of abstraction that's appropriate to its own functioning and each level adjusts output so as to minimize discrepancies at that level. It's not assumed that one processor handles functions at various levels of abstraction, but that structures at various levels handle their separate concerns simultaneously.

Powers focused particularly on low levels of abstraction. He said much less about the levels of abstraction that are of most interest to us, except to suggest labels for several levels whose existence makes intuitive sense. *Programs* are activities involving conscious decisions at various points. *Sequences*, the next level down, run off directly once cued. The level above programs is *principles*, qualities that are abstracted from or, alternatively, implemented by programs. These are qualities that are represented by trait labels. Powers gave the not-very-euphonious name *system concepts* to the highest level he considered, but goal representations at this level reduce essentially to the idealized overall sense of self, relationship, or group identity.

A simple way of portraying this hierarchy is illustrated in Fig. 1.5. This diagram omits the loops of feedback processes assumed here, using lines to indicate only the links among goal values. The lines imply that moving toward a particular lower level goal contributes to the attainment of some higher level goal (or even several at once). Multiple lines leading to a given goal indicate that several lower level action qualities can contribute to its attainment. As indicated previously, there are goals

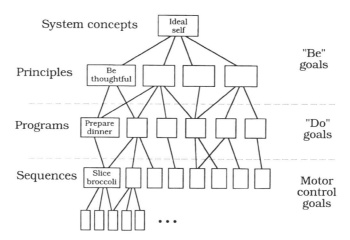

FIG. 1.5. A hierarchy of goals (or of feedback loops). Lines indicate the contribution of lower level goals to specific higher level goals. They can also be read in the opposite direction, indicating that a given higher order goal specifies more-concrete goals at the next lower level. The hierarchy described in text involves goals of being particular ways, which are attained by doing particular actions.

to "be" a particular way and goals to "do" certain things (and at lower levels, goals to create physical movement).

Action Identification

Although the Powers hierarchy per se hasn't been studied empirically, another theory that strongly resembles it—Vallacher and Wegner's (1985, 1987) action identification theory—has been. This model is framed in terms of how people think about the actions they're taking, but it also conveys the sense that how people think about their actions is informative about the goals by which they're guiding the actions.

People can identify a given action in many different ways, and the act identifications can vary in level of abstraction. High-level identifications are abstract (e.g., becoming more cultured), lower level identifications get more and more concrete (e.g., attending a ballet; listening to sounds and watching people move around while you sit quiet and still). Low-level identifications tend to convey a sense of how an activity is done, whereas high-level identifications tend to convey a sense of why.

Vallacher and Wegner posited a natural tendency for people to drift upward to higher levels of identification, as long as they can success-fully maintain those identities. When there's difficulty in carrying out an activity at the higher level identification the person drops down to a lower level identification. Consistent with this line of thought is ev-idence that easy and familiar actions occur more smoothly when the person holds a high-level orientation and that more difficult and un-familiar actions are facilitated by holding a lower level orientation (Vallacher, Wegner, McMahan, Cotter, & Larsen, 1992; Vallacher, Wegner, & Somoza, 1989).

In considering the relation between the action identification model and the Powers hierarchy, we make two more points. First, although the Vallacher and Wegner (1985, 1987) model is hierarchical, it doesn't spec-ify what qualities define various levels. It simply assumes that where there's a potential emergent property, there's the potential for differing levels of identification. On the other hand, the examples used to illustrate the theory tend to map onto the levels of the Powers hierarchy: sequences of acts, programs of actions (with variations of smaller scale and larger scale programs), and principles of being. Thus, work on action identifi-cation tends to suggest the reasonableness of these particular levels of abstraction in thinking about behavior.

The notion of hierarchicality is perhaps clearest in action identification theory, but other models in personality–social psychology also have this character, at least by implication. For example, many theories assume that people are motivated to maintain positive self-evaluation (Steele, 1988). People bask in the accomplishments of those who are close to them when it reflects well on them, but avoid such information when it creates unflattering comparisons (Tesser, 1980a, 1986, 1988; Tesser & Campbell, 1983). These literatures appear to reflect efforts to prevent discrepancies between a desired sense of self and present perception of self. In each case, people try to protect a quality that's important and central to them by taking concrete and overt steps of some sort. This principle thus seems compatible with the logic of hierarchical organization.

ISSUES

The notion of hierarchicality raises a number of questions and issues. Here are just a few of them.

Which Level Is Functionally Superordinate Can Vary

We've described a model in which abstract qualities such as the integrated sense of an idealized or hoped for self (or relationship or society) are superordinate goals for behavior. This doesn't mean that such goals are always directing behavior. Although they're used sometimes, behavior is often guided by goals at lower levels—for example, the level of program control.

To put it differently, lower levels of control are *functionally* superordinate when the person's current concern is at a lower level of abstraction (cf. Klinger, 1975; Shallice, 1978; Vallacher & Wegner, 1985, 1987). This would appear to be the case, for example, when people do activities such as shopping for groceries, washing dishes, or driving to work. During such activities (aimed at do goals) people may lose sight of higher order aims (be goals), as they focus on the concrete realities of the situations confronting them (cf. Norman, 1981).

We've tended to assume that self-regulation at any level higher than the one that's functionally superordinate is discontinued until attention refocuses on reference values at the higher level. This does *not* mean that actions taken while under low-level control have no relevance to goals at the higher levels. When behavior is being controlled at lower levels, the behavior still contributes to reduction—or creation—of discrepancies at higher levels. Whether higher level discrepancies decrease, increase, or remain unchanged depends on the consequences of the lower level activity. The links between the goal qualities at various levels haven't ceased to exist just because the higher levels aren't being used to guide action. Presumably, the higher order effects of the lower order actions become apparent when attention is refocused on the higher order goals.

Multiple Paths to High-Level Goals, Multiple Meanings in Concrete Action

Although the hierarchy we are discussing is in some ways very simple, it has implications for several issues in thinking about behavior. It's implicit here that goals at any given level can often be achieved by a variety of means at lower levels. This flexibility is particularly apparent at upper levels of the hierarchy, where the goals are more abstract. This permits one to address the fact that people sometimes shift radically the manner in which they try to reach a goal when the goal itself has not changed appreciably. This happens when the emergent quality that constitutes the higher order goal is implied in several distinct lower order activities. For example, a person can be helpful by writing a donation check, picking up discards for a recycling center, volunteering at the Special Olympics, or holding a door open for someone else.

Just as a given goal can be obtained via multiple pathways, so can a specific act be performed in the service of diverse goals. For example, you could buy someone a gift to make her feel good, to repay a kindness, to put her in your debt, or to satisfy part of your perceived holiday-season role. Thus, a given act can have strikingly different meanings, depending on the purpose it is intended to serve. This is an important subtheme of this view on behavior: Behavior can be understood only by identifying the goals to which behavior is addressed, which isn't always easy to do from either an observer's point of view (cf. Read, Druian, & Miller, 1989) or an actor's point of view.

Goal Importance; Goals and the Self

Another point made by the notion of hierarchical organization concerns the fact that goals are not equivalent in their importance. The higher you go into the organization, the more fundamental to the overriding sense of self are the qualities encountered. Thus, goal qualities at higher levels would appear to be intrinsically more important than those at lower levels.

Goals at lower levels aren't necessarily equivalent to one another in importance, however. Just as it's sometimes hard to tell what goal underlies a given behavior, it can also be hard to tell from a behavior how important is the goal that lies behind it. In a hierarchical system, there are at least two ways in which importance accrues to a concrete goal. The more directly a concrete action contributes to attainment of some highly valued goal at a more abstract level, the more important is that concrete action. Second, an act that contributes to the attainment of several goals at once is more important than an act that contributes to the attainment of only one goal.

Relative importance of goals brings us back to the concept of self. In contemporary theories, the self-concept has several aspects. One is the structure of knowledge about your history; another is knowledge about who you are now. These can both be conceptualized as working models, accepted and used for the present but in constant evolution (even your sense of the past is amenable to reconstruction). Another aspect is the self-guides or images of potential selves used to guide movement from the present into the future (which may also be working models). A broad implication of this sort of theory is that the self is partly the person's goals.

A question that's interesting to pose but hard to answer is, How many layers of a person's goals should be considered to fall under the label *self?* Most would certainly agree that a person's idealized self belongs there, and many would probably say the same for an ought self (although not all would agree about this, a point to which we return momentarily). Because these values so readily translate into principles of conduct, it seems likely that most people would agree that one's guiding principles are also elements of the self.

But where are the limits? How far down the hierarchy of goals can you go and have it still be sensible? Are the goals that define programs of activity part of the self? Certainly each person individualizes the pattern of goals that make up even such a commonly held program of action as doing the laundry or taking a holiday trip. Furthermore, people differ from one another in terms of the programs in which they engage. But does that make these goal structures part of the self? We have no clear answer to this question.

There is some precedent, however, for equating reduction in self-focus (via alcohol use or deindividuation) with suspension of self-regulation at the program level and higher. Does this mean there's no self at lower levels? The answer to this question may be a matter of definition. The sequences programmed into people's repertoires differ from one person to another, implying a distinctiveness that may connote selfhood. On the other hand, these bits of information are so concrete and minimal that it may not be useful to think of them as elements of the self.

Self-Determination Theory and the Self

Although the viewpoint we've just outlined will probably seems reasonable to many, we suspect that not all will agree with it. Recall that self-determination theory views some actions as undertaken out of intrinsic interest or the belief that the activity is valuable, whereas others are undertaken to satisfy some pressure or demand. The critical issue is the extent to which goals are integrated into the structure of the self. In introjected regulation, the goal is taken as a goal but not incorporated into the self. The behavior thus is controlled, although the controlling is intrapsychic. As we said earlier, introjected values appear similar to oughts (Higgins, 1987, 1996)—they involve moving *toward* a goal to *avoid* disapproval or self-disapproval.

Identified regulation occurs when the behavior has been accepted by the individual as personally important and meaningful. Although it may not be intrinsically enjoyable, the person sees authentic value in it. At this stage, the goal has begun to be integrated within the person's sense of self. These behaviors are self-determined and authentic, reflecting the total involvement of the self.

This view suggests a limitation on the content of the self. In self-determination theory, the term *self* is limited to the identified and integrated values that represent the true self. Deci and Ryan probably wouldn't agree that the ought self is part of the true self. The ought self is a coercive and controlling force, because the person lives up to its values to avoid disapproval or self-disapproval. The feared self is even more coercive, for obvious reasons.

The true self, in this view, is restricted to ideals that are integrated with whatever is the person's intrinsically motivated self. Even the role of ideals can be a little tricky here, because what a person thinks of as an ideal can actually be controlling, if the person uses it in a self-coercive way. That is, if you hold this ideal as a condition of self-worth, it is no longer acting as part of the true self. The key is whether the behavior is done with freedom and authenticity (which, in some measure, returns us to the question of will).

Given these considerations, it appears that the essence of a controlling force on behavior is that it involves the engagement of an avoidance loop. The critical difference between goals that connect to the true self and goals that don't seems to be whether they engage only an approach system or whether they also engage an avoidance system. If so, it it would seem that any activity that's done to avoid an antigoal fails to involve the true self, by definition.

The avoidance system is the part of the organism that evolved to help us stay out of danger—to stay alive. It's critically important. In this light it seems odd, or at least arbitrary, to say that the avoidance system isn't part of the self. However, that seems to us to be an inescapable implication of the position that Deci and Ryan have taken. We can think of no case in which a value of the true self as they discuss it incorporates an avoidance tendency.

THEME: AFFECT ARISES FROM A PROCESS OF FEEDBACK CONTROL

We shift our attention now to another important aspect of human self-regulation: emotion. In this section, we add a layer of complexity to the basic feedback model which differs greatly from the complexity represented by hierarchicality. Again, the fundamental organizing principle is feedback control. But now the control is over a different quality.

What are feelings, and what makes them exist? Many theorists have analyzed the information that feelings provide and the situations in which affect comes to exist (see, e.g., Frijda, 1986; Izard, 1977; Lazarus, 1991; Ortony, Clore, & Collins, 1988; Roseman, 1984; Scherer & Ekman, 1984). The question we address here is slightly different: What's the internal mechanism by which feelings come to arise? Not to be retrieved from memory, but to arise in the first place?

Theory

We've suggested that feelings arise as a consequence of a feedback process (Carver & Scheier, 1990b). This process operates simultaneously with the behavior-guiding function and in parallel to it, whenever it's operating. This second system serves what for lack of a better term we called a *meta-monitoring* function. How to describe this function? One way is to say it's checking on how well the action loop is doing at reducing its discrepancies. More precisely, the perceptual input for the meta loop is a representation of the *rate of discrepancy reduction in the action system over time*. (We focus first on discrepancy-reducing loops, turning later to enlarging loops.)

We find an analogy useful here. Because action implies change between states, consider behavior analogous to distance (construed as a vector, because perception of action incorporates the difference between successive states and the direction of the difference). If the action loop deals with distance, and if the meta loop assesses the progress of the action loop, then the meta loop is dealing with the psychological equivalent of velocity (also as a vector), the first derivative of distance over time. To the extent the physical analogy is meaningful, the perceptual input to the meta loop should be the first derivative over time of the input used by the action loop.

TABLE 1.1
Five conditions of behavior over time

Behavioral Situation	Construal at Action Loop	Construal at Meta Loop	Affect
1. Progress toward goal at a rate equal to the standard	Discrepancy reduction	No discrepancy	None
2. Progress toward goal at a rate lower than the standard	Discrepancy reduction	Negative discrepancy	Negative
3. Progress toward goal at a rate higher than the standard	Discrepancy reduction	Positive discrepancy	Positive
4. No progress toward goal	No discrepancy reduction	Negative discrepancy	Negative
5. Movement away from goal	Discrepancy enlargement	Negative discrepancy	Negative

We don't believe this input is responsible for affect by itself, because a given rate of progress has different affective consequences under different circumstances. As in any feedback system, this input is compared against a reference value (cf. Frijda, 1986, 1988). In this case, the reference is an acceptable or desired rate of behavioral discrepancy reduction. As in other feedback loops, the comparison checks for a deviation from the standard. If there is a deviation, an output function engages.

We suggest that the outcome of the comparison process at the heart of this loop (the error signal generated by the comparator) is manifest phenomenologically in two forms. One is a hazy and nonverbal sense of expectancy—confidence or doubt. The other is affect, feeling, a sense of positiveness or negativeness.

From our perspective, the size of the discrepancy at the action loop doesn't determine the input to the meta loop (see Table 1.1). A large discrepancy at the action loop can relate to either abundant progress or little progress. A large behavioral discrepancy thus can be tied to either positive or negative affect. The same point applies to cases in which behavioral discrepancies are small. If the meta system senses an abundant rate of movement forward, there should be positive affect (and confidence). If it senses inadequate movement, there should be negative affect (and doubt).

Progress Toward a Goal Versus Completion of a Series of Subgoals

Our view emphasizes progress toward goals across time and rejects the idea that affect arises from goal attainment per se. We took this position partly because affect can arise on the way to goals, rather than simply at goal attainment. It's reasonable to ask, though, why not assume that affect arises from the attainment of subgoals. If a subgoal has been attained,

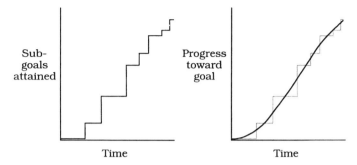

FIG. 1.6. One might think of affect as arising from the attainment of subgoals, but ultimately the passage of time must be taken into consideration. An analysis in terms of subgoal attainment (left panel) then represents a first approximation of an analysis in terms of continually assessed progress toward the overall goal (right panel).

there's a cause for positive affect, even though the ultimate goal hasn't been reached. The more subgoals attained, the more positive the affect (cf. Wyer & Srull, 1989, chap. 12).

We have two reactions to this view. First, it seems to provide little guidance about what experience should exist in the absence of attaining a subgoal. Should there be negative affect, because the subgoal hasn't yet been attained? If so, when is there ever a condition of neutral affect when there's a goal in mind? Affect would always be either positive or negative with respect to that goal, and we don't think that's correct.

Second, and maybe more important, even this view ultimately must take into account the passage of time. That is, attainment of a subgoal in 30 seconds must generally be more pleasing than attainment of the same subgoal in 30 minutes. Absence of subgoal attainment across an hour must generally be more distressing than absence of attainment across 10 minutes. As the time dimension is taken into account, however, the subgoal analysis becomes a first approximation of our model, just as a difference equation is a first approximation to a differential equation (Fig. 1.6).[2] As subgoals are sliced thinner and thinner (it is somewhat arbitrary, after all, what constitutes a subgoal), the subgoal analysis becomes a closer and closer approximation of a derivative across time.

---

[2]Our mention of a difference equation also suggests a link between these models and the idea that people retrospectively evaluate affectively relevant experiences in terms of the peak intensity and the end intensity of the experience (Kahneman, Fredrickson, Schreiber, & Redelmeier, 1993). The duration of the experience is given little weight in these judgments. Thus, if a very painful period has an added period of lesser pain as its ending, the entire experience is seen as having been less aversive than if the final period was omitted (this is true despite the fact that the final period contributed additional time in pain, albeit less intense pain). Thus, people's affective judgments seem particularly sensitive to changes—changes which in our view signify progress, in this case progress toward absence of pain.

The models ultimately reduce to the same thing. The difference between them pertains primarily to one's assumption about whether affect comes in chunks according to a step function (due to attainment of subgoals) or whether it is created continuously.

Evidence

At least a little evidence has accumulated that supports the idea that affect originates in a rate or velocity function. Hsee and Abelson (1991), who came independently to this idea, reported two studies of velocity and satisfaction. In one, subjects read descriptions of paired hypothetical scenarios and indicated which one they would find more satisfying. For example, they chose whether they'd be more satisfied if their class standing had gone from the 30th percentile to the 70th during the past 6 weeks, or if it had done so during the past 3 weeks.

Some comparisons were of positive outcomes, some negative. Given positive outcomes, subjects preferred improving to a high outcome over having a constant high outcome; they preferred a fast velocity over a slow one; and they preferred fast, small changes to slower, larger changes. When the change was negative (e.g., salaries got worse, a downward velocity) subjects preferred a constant low salary to a salary that started high and fell to the same low level; they preferred slow falls to fast falls; and they preferred large slow falls to small fast falls.

In a second study, subjects viewed an outcome actually changing in time. They watched as a computer displayed a bar moving vertically on a scale portraying changes in hypothetical outcome (e.g., the price of a stock). This time subjects had a reference scenario with a satisfaction level of 5 on a 9-point scale in comparison to which they were to make ratings. Study 2 also yielded a velocity effect. Subjects preferred a fast velocity when outcome was improving and a slow velocity when outcome was declining.

We conducted a study that conceptually replicates aspects of these findings, but with an event that was personally experienced rather than hypothetical (Lawrence, Carver, & Scheier, 1997). We manipulated success feedback on an ambiguous task over an extended period. Participants received varying patterns of feedback, converging such that Block 6 was identical for all subjects at 50% correct. Subjects in a neutral condition had 50% on the first and last blocks, and 50% average across all blocks. Other subjects had positive change in performance, starting poorly and gradually improving. Others had negative change, starting well and gradually worsening. All rated their mood before starting and again after Block 6 (which they didn't know ended the session). Those whose performances were improving reported better moods and those whose performances were deteriorating reported worse moods compared to those with a constant performance.

Another study that appears to bear on this view of affect, although not having this purpose in mind, was reported by Brunstein (1993). It examined subjective well-being among college students over the course of an academic term, as a function of several perceptions, including perception of progress toward goals. Of particular interest, progress at each measurement point was strongly correlated with concurrent well-being.

Cruise Control Model

It took us a while to realize it, but this is essentially a "cruise control" model. That is, the system we've postulated functions in much the same way as the cruise control on your car. If you're going too slowly toward some goal in your behavior, negative affect arises. You respond to the situation by putting more effort into your behavior, trying to speed up. If you're going faster than you needed to, positive affect arises, and you coast. The car's cruise control is very similar. You come to a hill, which slows you down. Your cruise control responds by feeding the engine's cylinders more gas, which brings the speed back up. If you come across the crest of a hill and are rolling downhill too fast, the system pulls back on the gas and drags the speed back down.

The analogy is intriguing in part because it concerns an electromechanical regulation of the very quality we believe the meta system is regulating: velocity. It's also intriguing to realize that this analogy incorporates a similar asymmetry in the consequences of deviating from the set point. That is, both in your car's cruise control system and in your behavior, going too slow requires investment of greater effort and resources. Going too fast does not. It requires only pulling back on resources. That is, your cruise control doesn't apply your brakes, it just cuts back on the gasoline. In this way, it permits you to coast back to your velocity set point. In the same fashion, you don't respond to positive affect by trying to make it go away, but just by easing off.

Does positive affect actually lead people to withdraw effort? There is a little information on this, but not much. Melton (1995) found that people in a good mood performed worse than control subjects on syllogisms. A variety of ancillary data led him to the conclusion that people in good moods did worse because they were expending less effort. To us, this looks like coasting.

Acceleration, Deceleration, and Surprise

This model addresses rates of progress. It should be obvious, however, that the rate itself can change. Change in rate is subjectively manifest not as affect per se, but as change in affect. Increases in rate cause shifts toward more positive feelings. Shifts in rate can be gradual or abrupt. The more abrupt an increase in progress, the more the subjective experience includes a rush of exhilaration, reflecting the sharpness of the contrast between the more negative feeling and the more positive one (cf. the description of "sentimentality" by Frijda, 1988, p. 350). The more abrupt a decrease in progress, the more the experience incorporates a kind of "deexhilaration"—the well known "sinking feeling."

We said earlier the quality of experience the meta loop senses as input is analogous to velocity. To carry the analogy a step further, what we're now addressing is acceleration, the second derivative of distance over time. The analogy suggests that some neural processor is computing a second derivative over time of the information input to the action loop.

We've held that the sense of exhilaration–deexhilaration from an abrupt change in rate is distinct from the affective tone of positiveness versus negativeness. The literature of emotion holds suggestive support for this position. The concept in this literature that's closest to the quality we're discussing is surprise. Surprise constitutes a special case in this literature, for at least two reasons.

First, historically there has been a lack of consensus as to whether to consider surprise an emotion. For example, although Izard (1977) included surprise as a fundamental emotion, he also said "Surprise is not an emotion in the same sense as joy or sadness is" (p. 277), and "In some respects surprise is not a real emotion like the other fundamental emotions considered in this book" (p. 281). Tomkins (1984, p. 171) said that surprise "is ancillary to every other affect." Second, at least two projects (Fehr & Russell, 1984; Shaver, Schwartz, Kirson, & O'Connor, 1987) have found that words indicating surprise aren't treated by adults the same as other emotion-relevant words. This led Shaver et al. (1987) to express reservations about surprise as an affect.

Also of interest is evidence that surprise in itself may be neither positive nor negative (e.g., Izard, 1977, p. 283; Ortony et al., 1988, p. 32). Rather, its tone may be a product of the experiences associated with it. Roseman (1984, p. 31) identified surprise as co-occurring with both positive and negative emotions. Several studies have found empirically that surprise either is unrelated to a pleasantness dimension (e.g., Ellsworth & Smith, 1988; Tesser, 1990) or is related equally well to independent dimensions of positive and negative affect (Moffitt & Singer, 1994). Such findings suggest that surprise is free of positiveness or negativeness, but is instead combinable with either of these tones.

This pattern is much what one would see from a quality that's related to affect but not quite the same as affect. This is essentially what we're proposing about the quality resulting from the perception of acceleration or deceleration (which may *be* surprise). That is, we're arguing that it is derived from the experience of affect change, though not an affect itself.

We think the subjective quality tied to the experience of acceleration and deceleration is important. We believe it's created simultaneously with new affect when it's created at all (it arises when affect is shifting). We believe, however, that what it contributes to the experience is different from what's contributed by affect per se (cf. Izard, 1977; Tomkins, 1984).

Affect From Discrepancy-Enlarging Loops

When we began this section, we said we'd restrict ourselves at first to discrepancy-reducing loops. Thus far we've done that, dealing only with issues that arise in the context of approach. Now we turn to attempts to distance oneself from a point of comparison, attempts to "not-be" or "not-do," discrepancy-enlarging loops.

It should be apparent from our earlier discussion that behavior toward avoidance goals is just as intelligible as behavior toward approach goals. But what about the affective accompaniments to avoidance loops? Our view of this derives from several sources, including insights provided by Higgins and his colleagues (Higgins, 1987, 1989, 1996). For clarity, we present our own position now and compare it to the ideas of Higgins later.

The affect theory described here rests on the idea that positive affect results when a behavioral system is making rapid progress in *doing what it's organized to do*. The systems considered thus far are organized to close discrepancies. There's no obvious reason, however, why the principle shouldn't apply just as well to systems with the opposite purpose. If the system is making rapid progress doing what it's organized to do, the result should be positive affect. If the system is doing poorly at what it's organized to do, the result should be negative affect.

That much would seem to be fully comparable across the two types of systems. We see, however, a difference in the affective qualities involved (see Fig. 1.7). In each case, there's a positive pole and a negative pole, but the positives aren't quite the same, nor are the negatives quite the same.

Following the lead of Higgins, we suggest that the affect dimension relating to discrepancy-reducing loops is (in its purest form) the dimension that runs from depression to elation. The affect dimension that relates to discrepancy-enlarging loops is (in its purest form) the dimension that runs from anxiety to relief or contentment. As Higgins and his colleagues note, dejection-related and agitation-related affect may take several forms, but these two dimensions capture the core qualities behind the forms. The connections drawn in Fig. 1.7 between affect quality and type

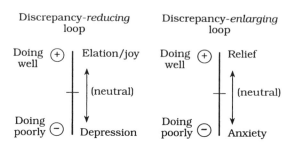

FIG. 1.7. Two sorts of metalevel systems and the affective dimensions we believe arise from the functioning of each. Discrepancy reducing systems are presumed to yield affective qualities of sadness or depression when progress is below standard and happiness or elation when progress is above standard. Discrepancy-enlarging systems are presumed to yield anxiety when progress is below standard and relief or contentment when progress is above standard.

of system are compatible not just with the Higgins model, but also with certain other theories. For example, Roseman (1984, p. 31) argued that joy and sadness are related to appetitive (moving-toward) motives, whereas relief and distress are related to aversive (moving-away-from) motives.

It's of interest that the two dimensions in Fig. 1.7 are asymmetrical regarding the degree of activation in the affects at the opposing poles. Anxiety is an energized affect, relief (the opposite pole) is not. Joy and enthusiasm are energized, sadness (the opposite pole) is not.

This asymmetry fits the idea that the two affect dimensions arise from functioning of systems with different types of goals (the argument we've made). In effect, the pole with activation is the one tied to the "business end" (the reference value) of the behavioral system to which it relates. Activation in an approach loop occurs when, by doing well, one is closing in on a desired goal—when the situation invites pouncing. Activation in an avoidance loop occurs when, by doing poorly, one is slipping toward a match to an anti-goal—when the situation is dire (cf. Riskind, Kelley, Harman, Moore, & Gaines, 1992). Pouncing and escaping dire straits are, in effect, what these two kinds of behavioral systems are all about.

These observations regarding activation fit the idea that the two affect dimensions relate to two different kinds of behavioral tendencies (approach and escape), which have different dynamics and thus different energy mobilization needs. The notion that there are ties between particular qualities of affect and functioning of systems that regulate behavioral approach versus avoidance has been suggested for varying reasons by a number of theorists (e.g., Davidson, 1992a, 1992b; Depue & Iacono, 1989; Gray, 1981, 1990; Tomarken et al., 1992). We examine this work more closely a bit later.

Merging Affect and Action

Thus far, we've said little about how the mechanism creating affect influences behavior. This is an important issue. After all, affect matters in large part because it serves as a signal pertaining to the current consequences of action. How, then, does the affect loop influence *action*?

A more basic question (which takes us to the same end) is this: We've treated affect as the error signal of a feedback loop, but what's the *output function* of that loop? If the input function is a perception of rate of progress, the output function must be an adjustment in rate of progress. In some cases, an adjustment is straightforward—go faster. Sometimes it's less straightforward. The rates of many "behaviors" we're interested in (higher order activities) aren't defined in terms of literal pace of physical action. Rather, they're defined in terms of choices among potential actions, or even potential programs of action. For example, increasing your rate of progress on a reading assignment may mean choosing to spend a weekend working rather than playing. Increasing your rate of kindness means choosing to do an action that reflects that value. Thus, adjustment in rate must often be translated into other terms, such as concentration, or reallocation of time and effort.

It should be apparent, however, that the action system and the rate system work in concert with one another. Both are involved in the flow of action. They influence different aspects of the action, but both are always involved.

It's interesting that the functions that we've just been describing are roughly comparable to two functions typically ascribed to motivation. In effect, we seem to have arrived at saying that the action loop handles most of what's sometimes called the directional function of motivation (the choice of an action from among many options, keeping an action on the track intended) and that the affect loop is handling the intensity function of motivation (the vigor, enthusiasm, effort, concentration, or thoroughness with which the action is pursued). Our linking of affect with the intensity aspect of motivation is a consequence of structural assumptions we began with, rather than a principled decision. However, this link is certainly consistent with statements of many theorists who have emphasized the intimate connection between emotion and motivation.

A Precedent

The idea that two kinds of feedback loops (position and velocity) can work in concert has at least one precedent, in a literature very different from this one. McIntyre and Bizzi (1993) made a related argument about the controlling of arm movements. They were addressing a point of dispute in the motor-control literature about whether pure feedback models were adequate to account for the execution of rapid movements. They argued that if separate control loops are assumed for position and velocity, the system works as well as alternative (more complex) models. Simulation data supported this argument.

What's of particular interest at present is the property that rendered this position-plus-velocity model useful to McIntyre and Bizzi in the first place. They said the addition of the velocity signal serves to increase the "command following" performance of the system as a whole. It allows the system to produce faster movements and do so in a stable manner. This isn't so far from what affect does to the regulation of behavior.

This description suggests a similarity in function between the coupling of systems discussed by McIntyre and Bizzi (1993) and the coupling between affect and action systems we've suggested here. In both cases, the second (velocity) system manages rapid adjustment and does so in a way that ensures stable overall functioning. We're not going to suggest that velocity systems handling motor movements generate affect. However, the conceptual parallel causes us to wonder whether systems at those lower levels create sensations analogous to affect (perhaps the sense of sharpness versus sluggishness in movement control), which we recognize but rarely think about further.

ISSUES

This view of the nature and origin of affect raises a number of issues— indeed, far more than we can address here. We limit ourselves to a few of the more provocative and interesting ones.

Is This Really a Feedback System?

Our view on affect is that it results from a comparison process in a feedback loop. This view has a counterintuitive implication. If affect is created the way we say it is, it's a signal that the rate of progress isn't right and should be adjusted. This implies that, although the organism tries to minimize pain, it does not in general try to maximize pleasure.

Minimizing pain is straightforward. Negative feelings reflect a negative discrepancy in rate, indicating a problem. Things aren't moving forward fast enough. The normal response is to try harder. If this happens, the negative affect ceases to exist. Thus, people try to minimize pain.

Maximizing pleasure is trickier. Positive feelings reflect a positive discrepancy in rate. This is good in at least two senses: It means things are going better than they need to, and the experience feels good subjectively. To a system whose goal is controlling sensed rate, however, a discrepancy is still a discrepancy, and discrepancies are to be reduced. If what we're discussing really is a feedback loop of the sort we've proposed, neither negative *nor* positive affect is a state the system wants to see. Either quality of affect (either deviation from the standard) would represent an error and lead to changes in output that would reduce it.

If the meta loop were truly a feedback system, an overshoot of the reference value should lead to a self-corrective attempt to return to the reference value. Put more concretely, this view argues that people who exceed the desired rate of progress will slow subsequent effort in this domain. They're likely to coast for a while. The result in the person's subjective experience would be that the positive affect from the overshoot isn't sustained for very long. This is particularly true if the person turns to another arena of behavior (Erber & Tesser, 1992).

Why should there be a natural tendency that would cause positive affect to be short-lived? A plausible basis lies in the idea that behavior is hierarchically organized and has multiple current concerns. People typically are working toward several goals more or less simultaneously. To the extent that movement toward goal attainment is more rapid than expected in one domain, it lets the person shift effort toward strivings in another domain, at no cost. To continue an unnecessarily rapid pace in the first domain may increase positive affect, but by diverting efforts from other goals it may increase the potential for negative affect in other domains.

Variations in Meta Level Standards

Standards for rate of progress can be lax or stringent. What influences the standard used? Obviously a critical determinant is the extent to which there's time pressure on the activity. Some actions are clearly time dependent (you have a presentation at 10 o'clock tomorrow), others are more vaguely so (it's about time to fertilize the lawn), and time dependency for others is even hazier (I want to go to China someday). When an activity has demanding time constraints, the meta-level reference value used is stringent. With a relative lack of time pressure, a lax standard is more likely.

Not only do meta-level reference values differ across categories of behavior, but they can also shift through time and experience (cf. Lord & Hanges, 1987). That is, as people accumulate experience in a given domain, adjustments can occur in the pacing they expect and demand of themselves. There's a kind of recentering of the system around the past experience, by changing the reference value.

Sometimes the adjustment is downward. For example, a researcher experiencing difficulty in meeting his personal timetable for career development may gradually use less stringent standards of pacing. One consequence of this is a more favorable balance of positive to negative affect across a given time span. In other cases, the adjustment is upward. Someone who gains work-related skills may undertake greater challenges, requiring quicker handling of action units. Upward adjustment of a rate criterion has the side effect of decreasing the potential for positive affect and increasing the potential for negative affect.

These changes don't happen quickly or abruptly. Shifting the reference value downward isn't the first response when you have trouble keeping up a demanding pace. First you try harder to keep up. Only more gradually, if this fails, does the meta standard shift to accommodate. Similarly, an upward shift in reference value isn't the immediate response when your rate exceeds the standard. The more typical response is to coast for a while. Only when the overshoot is frequent does the standard shift upward.

We believe that such adjustments in meta standard occur automatically, but slowly. Such adjustments themselves appear to reflect a self-corrective feedback process, as the person reacts to insufficient challenge by taking on a more demanding pace and reacts to too much challenge by scaling back (see Fig. 1.8). This feedback process is slower than the ones we've focused on thus far. Rather, there's a gradually accumulating shift.

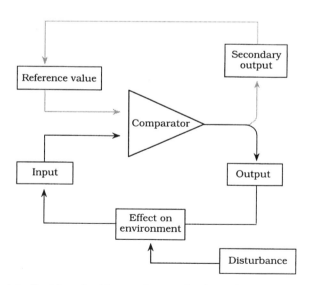

FIG. 1.8. A feedback loop (in this case, the postulated meta loop) acts to create change in the input function, to shift it toward the reference value. Sometimes an additional process is in place as well (gray lines), which adjusts the reference value in the direction of the input. This additional process is presumed to be weaker or slower; thus, the reference value is stable, relative to the input value.

Assume for the moment that a signal to change standard occurred every time there was a signal to change output, but it was much weaker. Given this, it would take a long time for the standard to change. Indeed, as long as the person deviated from the standard in both directions (under and over) with comparable frequency, the standard wouldn't change at all. It's only with repeated deviation in one direction that there would be an appreciable effect.

It's also of interest (and once again counterintuitive) that these shifts in reference value (and the resultant effects on affect) imply a mechanism within the organism that functions to actively prevent the too-frequent occurrence of positive feeling, as well as the too-frequent occurrence of negative feeling. That is, the (bidirectional) shifting of the rate criterion over time would tend to control pacing of behavior in such a way that affect continues to vary in both directions around neutral, roughly the same as it had before.

Such an arrangement for changing a meta-level standard thus wouldn't result in maximization of pleasure and minimization of pain. Rather, the affective consequence would be that the person experiences more or less the same range of variation in affective experience over extended periods of time and circumstances (cf. Myers & Diener, 1995). The organization as a whole would function as a gyroscope that serves to keep us floating along within the framework of the affective reality we're familiar with. It would provide for a continuous recalibration of the feeling system across changes in situation. To use a different image, it would repeatedly shift the balance point of a psychic teeter-totter, so that rocking in both directions remains possible. What we're describing here resembles in some respects what Solomon (1980; Solomon & Corbit, 1974) described as the long-term consequences of the operation of an opponent process system.

Comparison to Self-Discrepancy Theory

Let us turn now to a comparison between these ideas and self-discrepancy theory (Higgins, 1987, 1989, 1996; Higgins et al., 1986; Strauman, 1989), which holds that certain emotions occur as the result of two kinds of discrepancies within the self. The first is between the perceived actual self and the ideal self (actual-ideal discrepancies). The second is between the perceived actual self and the ought self (actual-ought discrepancies). According to self-discrepancy theory, discrepancies between ideal and actual yield depression or other dejection-related feelings (see also Finlay-Jones & Brown, 1981). Discrepancies between actual and ought yield anxiety or other agitation-related feelings.

Three differences between self-discrepancy theory and our model deserve brief mention. First, in self-discrepancy theory, affect comes from a discrepancy between two representations of the self. To us, the discrepancy that matters concerns rate of progress toward goals, including idealized representations of the self. Thus, from our point of view, a person who is discrepant from the ideal but has the perception of moving toward it rapidly enough should experience positive rather than negative affect.

A second difference is also implicit in this last statement. Our model readily addresses both positive and negative affect. Self-discrepancy theory originated to address negative affect. It's less clear how to think about positive affect within it in a way that permits the existence of positive, negative, and no affect under varying circumstances. Our model thus seems to add something in including a clear basis for the existence of positive feeling qualities as well as a basis for the existence of negative feelings.

The third comparison, the most interesting, concerns the distinction between ideals and oughts, the most novel and innovative aspect of the Higgins analysis. This distinction is what provides a conceptual basis for differentiating anxiety from depression. This is an important and difficult differentiation, made between two qualities that tend to co-occur. Self-discrepancy theory has been quite successful in predicting a unique association between actual-ideal discrepancies and dysphoria and a unique association between actual-ought discrepancies and anxiety.

As we said earlier, we think there is a structural difference between oughts and ideals. Ideals seem to require only approach goals (with discrepancy-reducing loops). In contrast, oughts seem inherently to involve two self-regulatory processes at once. Oughts seem to involve trying to move toward a positive goal and simultaneously trying to escape from an anti-goal (implying a discrepancy-enlarging loop).

Which of these loops matters most? Our viewpoint suggests that if an avoidance loop is doing poorly at avoiding, anxiety arises. This suggests that the source of anxiety in an actual-ought discrepancy may actually be an ineffective effort to avoid the feared self (cf. Ogilvie, 1987). We recently explored this idea empirically (Carver, Lawrence, & Scheier, in press). In the full sample, actual-feared discrepancies proved to preempt the role of actual-ought discrepancies in predicting agitation-related affects. Somewhat to our surprise, the feared self also played a role in prediction of dejection-related affects. It didn't preempt the role of the ideal self, but rather added to it.

Perhaps the most interesting findings, however, came from analyses in which we considered interactions involving proximity to feared self and proximity to ought self. Significant interactions emerged for the agitation-related affects anxiety and guilt. Among subjects relatively near their feared selves, discrepancy from the feared self strongly predicted anxiety and guilt, whereas discrepancy from the ought self played no predictive role. Among subjects farther from the feared self, however, anxiety and guilt were strongly predicted by actual-ought discrepancies and discrepancies from the feared self played no role. In contrast to this pattern, interactions between feared and ideal discrepancies did not approach significance with respect to the dejection-related affects (depression and happiness). This indicates that the dynamic behind these affects did not vary as a function of distance from the feared self.

In sum, the data appear to fit a picture in which being near the feared self causes people to orient to the feared self. In that region, actual-feared discrepancy is the only discrepancy that matters. This fits the notion that evolution places a great premium on avoiding danger. The second force (the move-toward force) is less pressing. When there's distance between the actual and the feared self, there's less reason for concern about danger. In this zone of self-regulation, people can attend more closely to the desired values that ultimately are important in guiding behavior, and they seem to do so.

Comparison With Positive and Negative Affectivity

Another comparison worth considering is between our position and that discussed under the labels *positive* and *negative affect* (Watson & Tellegen, 1985; Zevon & Tellegen, 1982; see also Diener & Emmons, 1984; Diener & Iran-Nejad, 1986; Warr, Barter, & Brownbridge, 1983).

The view identified with the terms positive and negative affect (and their dispositional counterparts positive and negative affectivity) has become quite prominent. We would argue, however, that these labels are misleading (see also Larsen & Diener, 1992). The labels convey the sense that these two dimensions are unipolar, running from neutral to positive feeling and from neutral to distress, respectively. In reality, despite the labels, each dimension has both positive and negative indicators. Each dimension thus has both positive and negative poles.

Indeed, Watson and Tellegen (1985) initially labeled them as bipolar. More specifically, they found two dimensions of affect, across multiple samples, but there often were negative indicators of "positive affect" and positive indicators of "negative affect." Of particular interest, the few descriptors of depression (e.g., blue, sad, downhearted) loaded on *positive* affect. The few terms reflective of relief (the closest being calm, carefree, placid, and satisfied) loaded on *negative* affect. These loadings are quite consonant with the model in Fig. 1.7, earlier. In sum, the data reviewed by Watson and Tellegen (1985) fit well to the dimensions we've argued for on different grounds.

This resemblance would be harder to discern, however, from later discussions of positive and negative affect. In developing scales to measure positive and negative affect, Watson, Clark, and Tellegen (1988) chose not to include any item implying either depression or relief/serenity. Their item choices ensured that each dimension was represented only by items with the valence matching the scale's label. In so doing, they evaded the question—left hanging by the earlier research—of why descriptors such as *sad* and *down* should be part of a dimension with the label *positive affect*.

Their measure, the Positive and Negative Affect Scales (PANAS) has become popular as a research tool, both in a situational format and in an individual-differences format. One consequence of its popularity and the labels of the scales is that many people have come to assume that all negative affect is more or less the same. This, we think, is an error, particularly regarding depression and anxiety (see also Endler, Cox, Parker, & Bagby, 1992). As noted above, Watson and Tellegen (1985) found that depression-related items relate to the positive affect dimension. There's also evidence that depression and anxiety have different cognitive concomitants (e.g., Ahrens & Haaga, 1993; Clark, Beck, & Brown, 1989; Dalgleish & Watts, 1990; Greenberg & Alloy, 1989; Greenberg & Beck, 1989; Mineka & Sutton, 1992; Strauman, 1989; Wickless & Kirsch, 1988). Further evidence that these qualities are differentiable comes from the entire literature of self-discrepancy theory.

Certainly there are many circumstances when an impending failure to attain a desired goal is confounded with an impending failure to avoid a punisher. For example, failing to have a desired romantic liaison may co-occur with receipt of rejection or disapproval. In such situations people may experience both sadness and anxiety, and in such situations the distinction may be of little practical importance. However, there's a conceptual difference between failure to attain something desired and failure to avoid something undesired. We believe it's important to note this difference, and we suspect there are circumstances in which the distinction is of practical value as well.

Comparison With Biological Models of Bases of Affect

Another useful theoretical comparison pertains to the group of biologically focused theories that we mentioned earlier in the chapter. The theories are quite similar to one another in many ways, but in other ways they differ. These theories all incorporate the idea that two systems (sometimes more) are involved in the regulation of behavior. Many assume further that the two systems underlie affect. In situations with cues of impending reward, the activity of the approach system creates positive feelings. In situations with cues of impending punishment, the avoidance system creates feelings of anxiety.

Data from a variety of sources fit this picture. Of particular interest are findings from Davidson and his collaborators. These findings are of interest partly because so many of them come from human subjects. This research typically examines electroencephalogram recordings, assessing changes in activation in response to affect-inducing stimuli and assessing the possibility of individual differences in susceptibility to the experience of particular affective qualities.

Among the findings are these: Subjects exposed to films inducing fear and disgust (Davidson, Ekman, Saron, Senulis, and Friesen, 1990) and confronted with possible punishment (Sobotka, Davidson, & Senulis, 1992) show elevations in right frontal activation. In contrast, subjects with an opportunity to obtain reward (Sobota et al., 1992), subjects presented with positive emotional adjectives (Cacioppo & Petty, 1980), and smiling 10-month-old children viewing their approaching mothers (Fox & Davidson, 1988) showed elevations in left frontal activation.

Resting asymmetries have been viewed as reflecting differential susceptibility to affect. Higher relative left frontal activation (at rest) has been related to reports of higher levels of trait positive affectivity (Tomarken et al., 1992) and to the tendency to experience stronger responses to films eliciting positive feelings (Wheeler, Davidson, & Tomarken, 1993). Higher relative resting levels of right frontal activation have been related to stronger negative affect in response to films eliciting anxiety and disgust. On the basis of findings such as these, Davidson (1992a, 1992b) concluded that neural substrates for approach and withdrawal systems (and thus positive and negative affect) are located in the left and right frontal areas of the cortex, respectively.

The logic of these models thus far resembles the logic of our model (and also the model associated with the dimensions of positive and negative affect). At this point, however, the theories begin to diverge. The question on which they diverge concerns the regulatory processes involved in and affects that result from, *failure to attain reward* and *successful avoidance of punishment*.

One clear statement on this question came from Gray (1977, 1978, 1981, 1987b, 1990). Gray held that the avoidance system is engaged by cues of punishment and cues of frustrative nonreward. It thus is reponsible for negative feelings in response to either of these types of cue. Similarly, he held that the approach system is engaged by cues of reward or cues of escape from (or avoidance of) punishment. It thus is responsible for positive feelings in response to either of these types of cue. In his view, then, each system creates affect of one hedonic tone (positive in one case,

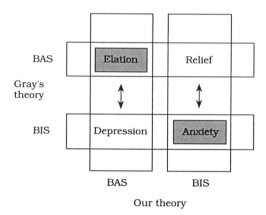

FIG. 1.9. Gray's view of affect (horizontal groupings) ties positive affects to the effects of a behavioral activation system (BAS), as results of occurrence of reward and avoidance of punishment. It ties negative affects to the effects of a behavioral inhibition system (BIS), as results of frustrative nonreward and occurrence of punishment. Our view (vertical groupings, as in Fig. 1.7) ties the dimension of elation–depression to an approach system and the dimension of anxiety–relief to an avoidance system, each of which thus has properties somewhat different from those assumed by Gray.

negative in the other), regardless of its source (see Fig. 1.9). This view is consistent with a picture of two unipolar affective dimensions, each linked to a distinct behavioral system. A similar position has been taken by Lang, Bradley, and Cuthbert (1992).

Our position on the nature of the systems is somewhat different. It argues for an approach system and an avoidance system, in which—in each case—affect is a product either of doing well or doing poorly. Thus, it implies two bipolar dimensions, one tied to approach, the other to avoidance (Fig 1.9). We think the disappointment and eventual depression that result from failure to attain desired goals involve the approach system (for similar predictions see Clark, Watson, & Mineka, 1994, p. 107; Cloninger, 1988, p. 103). Sadness and depression involve *reduced* activity in the approach system as the pursuit of goals diminishes. A parallel line of reasoning suggests that relief, contentment, tranquility, and serenity relate to the avoidance rather than the approach system, reflecting low levels of activity in that system.

Less information exists about neurophysiological bases of these affects than about anxiety and happiness. With regard to relief-tranquility, we know of no data at all. With respect to depression, limited evidence does exist. Henriques and Davidson (1991) found that clinically depressed persons had less activation in left frontal areas than nondepressed controls. In contrast, there was no evidence of a difference between groups in right frontal activation. This pattern was replicated by Allen, Iacono, Depue, and Arbisi (1993).

Recall that Davidson views baseline measures as representing susceptibility rather than ambient affect per se. Thus, this finding tentatively seems to suggest that depressed persons are vulnerable to depression through deficits in their approach system. This set of findings seems more compatible with our position than with that of Gray.

THEME: CONFIDENCE AND DOUBT, PERSISTENCE AND GIVING UP

In describing the genesis of affect, we suggested that one mechanism yields two subjective readouts: affect, and a hazy sense of confidence versus doubt. We turn now to a consideration of the latter, expectancies for the immediate future. These expectancies are more cognitive than is affect, but we're not saying that they're carefully thought out or that they emerge in consciousness as probability estimates. Rather, they're a nonverbal sense of optimism versus pessimism about the goal in mind.

Links Between Affect and Expectancy

The premise of a common origin implies a link in experience between feelings and expectancies. Several studies make a case—some directly, others indirectly—for such a link. Studies have found that being in a bad mood makes bad events seem more likely and being in a good mood makes good events seem more likely (Erber, 1991; Forgas & Moylan, 1987; Johnson & Tversky, 1983; MacLeod & Campbell, 1992; Mayer, Gaschke, Braverman, & Evans, 1992; Salovey & Birnbaum, 1989). There's also evidence that depressed people see bad outcomes as more likely than do nondepressed people (Beck, 1972; Lewinsohn, Larson, & Muñoz, 1982; Pietromonaco & Markus, 1985; Pietromonaco & Rook, 1987; Youngren & Lewinsohn, 1980).

A finding that makes a similar point, but with an interesting twist, comes from research by Martin, Ward, Achee, and Wyer (1993), who gave people an ambiguous task under varying instructional sets. In one experiment, some subjects were told to continue until they felt it was a good time to stop, others to continue as long as they still enjoyed it (subjects had specific questions to pose to themselves to help them decide). Of interest was how long subjects stayed engaged in the task. Among subjects asking themselves "Is this a good time to stop?," those who'd been put in good moods beforehand stopped sooner than those in bad moods. Among subjects asking themselves "Am I still enjoying the task?," those in bad moods stopped sooner than those in good moods.

The interpretation is that when people asked themselves the question they'd been given, the tendency to answer "yes" or "no" was influenced by their mood. Good mood biased toward saying yes, bad mood biased toward saying no. If the question is "Is it time to stop?," yes means stop. If the question is "Am I still enjoying the task?," yes means continue. Thus, a given mood causes the two sets to push behavior in opposite directions, but by the same mechanism: a link between good feelings and yes and between bad feelings and no (see also Clore, Schwarz, & Conway, 1994; Forgas, 1994; Hirt, Melton, McDonald, & Harackiewicz, 1996). This seems consistent with our assertion that affect and confidence (in this case, the sense of yes vs. no) are linked.

Indirect support for a link between expectancies and affect also comes from research on brain function and expectancies. As we said earlier, there's a good deal of evidence linking affective qualities to activation of the frontal lobes (Davidson, 1992a, 1992b). Greater activation of right frontal areas ties to the experience of negative affects such as anxiety and disgust. Greater activation of left frontal areas ties to the experience of positive feelings.

There's also evidence that links frontal asymmetry to expectations. This evidence, however, involves a manipulation of activation. This research derives from evidence that attending to the left or right causes greater activation of the opposite hemisphere. Drake (1984) used this manipulation to increase activation in one side or the other, then asked subjects to make ratings of the likelihood that various events would happen to them. Subjects in whom the manipulation aimed to activate the left hemisphere made ratings that were more optimistic about their future than subjects in whom the manipulation aimed to activate the right hemisphere. This finding was replicated using another manipulation of attention (Drake, 1987), and this difference in processing has also led people to make differentially optimistic recommendations about risky decisions (Drake, 1985).

These findings regarding expectancies display a strong parallel to the findings reported by Davidson and colleagues regarding affect. Left hemisphere activation induced optimism (whereas in the Davidson research it was related to positive feelings); right hemisphere activation induced pessimism (whereas in the Davidson research it was related to negative feelings). This parallel between findings hints that the expectancies and the affect were produced by similar mechanisms.

Interruption and Flow

We've often suggested that when people experience adversity in trying to move toward their goals, they periodically experience an interruption of their efforts, to assess the likelihood of a successful outcome (e.g., Carver & Scheier, 1981, 1990a, 1990b). In effect, people suspend the behavioral stream, step outside it, and evaluate in a more deliberated way than occurs while acting. This may happen once, or often. It may be brief, or it may take a long time.

What circumstances induce this interruption and assessment? Little evidence exists on this question, but it's easy to speculate. People often engage in deliberative assessment of outcome likelihood before undertaking actions (cf. Gollwitzer, 1990). This is particularly likely if the person knows ahead of time the task is going to be hard. Indeed, in such cases the person's evaluation of the likelihood of success may be a critical determinant of the decision to undertake the behavior.

Interruption can also occur in the midst of behaving, if the person encounters obstacles or impediments along the way. The experience of deceleration may play an important role in such cases. That is, it seems reasonable that a shift toward more negative feelings is often the cue that triggers interruption of ongoing action and causes people to consciously judge the chances of their eventual success. This is consistent with characterizations of the experience of surprise, which we argued relates to the acceleration–deceleration experience. For example, Tomkins (1984, p. 171) said that surprise represents sort of a "circuit breaker or interruptor mechanism."

One might contrast the experience of interruption with that of *flow* (Csikszentmihalyi, 1990). Flow seems to be a condition in which behavior is never interrupted for an expectancy assessment. Perhaps the flow experience reflects a velocity function that's smoothly tracking its reference value. This would fit with descriptions of the flow experience that emphasize the close fit between the demands of the environment and the person's competencies, such that the person is fully engaged in behaving, but is never pressed to wonder whether the behavior can be successfully maintained.

Conscious Expectancy Assessment

Interruption of action in the face of adversity is tied to a deliberative assessment of the likelihood of success, given continued efforts. In more consciously assessing the chance of the desired outcome, people presumably depend heavily on memories of prior outcomes in similar situations.

They may also consider such things as additional resources they might bring to bear (cf. Lazarus, 1966; MacNair & Elliott, 1992) or alternative approaches to the problem. People make use of social comparison information (e.g., Wills, 1981; Wood, 1989; Wood, Taylor, & Lichtman, 1985) and attributional analyses of prior events (Pittman & Pittman, 1980; Wong & Weiner, 1981) in anticipating the eventual outcome.

How do these thoughts influence the expectancies that emerge? In some cases, the mechanism is probably quite simple. When people retrieve chronic expectancies from memory in summary form, the information already *is* expectancies—accumulations or consolidations of products of previous behavior. When brought from memory, this information would contribute directly to subsequent confidence or doubt. Because they may also link to memories of an affective quality, they may also directly influence subsequent affect (cf. Mayer & Gaschke, 1988).

For some cases, however, a more complex process seems likely. In such cases, people bring to mind possibilities regarding the situation. For them to influence subsequent expectancies, their consequences must be evaluated. How? We suggest they are briefly played through mentally as behavioral scenarios (cf. Taylor & Pham, 1996). Playing through the scenarios should lead to conclusions that influence the expectancy. ("If I try approaching it this way instead of that way, it should work better." "This is the only thing I can see to do, and it will just make the situation worse.")

It seems reasonable that this mental simulation engages the same mechanism as handles the meta process during actual overt behavior. When your progress is temporarily stalled, playing through a scenario that's confident and optimistic yields a higher rate of progress than is currently being experienced. The meta loop thus yields a more optimistic outcome assessment than is being derived from current action. If the scenario is negative and hopeless, it indicates a further reduction in progress, and the meta loop yields further doubt.

Persistence Versus Giving Up

The processes of creating expectancies and locating expectancy-related information in memory are of interest in their own right. However, of even greater importance (in our view) is what follows.

Expectancies are reflected in behavior (Fig. 1.10). If expectations are for a successful outcome, the person returns to effort toward the goal. If doubts are strong enough, the result is an impetus to disengage from further effort and potentially to disengage from the goal itself (Carver & Scheier, 1981, 1990a, 1990b; see also Klinger, 1975; Kukla, 1972; Wortman

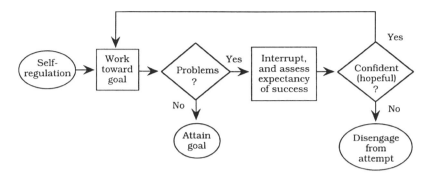

FIG. 1.10. Flowchart depiction of self-regulatory possibilities, indicating that action sometimes continues unimpeded toward goal attainment, that obstacles to goal attainment sometimes induce a sequence of evaluation and decision making, and that if expectancies for eventual success are sufficiently unfavorable the person may disengage from further effort.

& Brehm, 1975). This theme—divergence in behavioral response as a function of expectancies—is an important one, applying to a surprisingly broad range of literatures, well beyond what can be addressed here (see chap. 11, Carver & Scheier, 1998).

A subtle but important point is hidden within this principle. When people become frustrated or afraid, they don't always quit. Frustration and fear *are* signs of situational expectancies shifting toward the negative. But, as described above, this situational influence (lack of progress) isn't the only determinant of the expectancies that determine task responses. Situationally deteriorating expectancies can be overridden by a residual sense of confidence (cf. Carver, Blaney, & Scheier, 1979a). Thus, when negative affect goes up (and with it doubt), people sometimes overcome it to continue their efforts. This ability to rely on more well-established expectancies seems to be one way our elaborate cognitive capabilities can remove us from the press of the forces of the moment. Such effects aren't inevitable (cf. Duval, Duval, & Mulilis, 1992), but they do occur sometimes.

Mental Disengagement and Self-Oriented Rumination

Sometimes the disengagement that follows from doubt is overt, but sometimes it is precluded by situational constraints. In these cases, disengagement can take the form of mental disengagement—off-task thinking, daydreaming, and so on (cf. Diener & Dweck, 1978). Although this can sometimes be useful (self-distraction from a feared stimulus may permit anxiety to abate), it can also create problems. If there's time pressure, mental disengagement can impair performance, as time is spent on task-irrelevant thoughts. Consistent with this, interactions between self-focus and expectancies, similar to those shown emerging for persistence, have been shown for measures of performance (Carver, Peterson, Follansbee, & Scheier, 1983; Carver & Scheier, 1982).

Often mental disengagement can't be sustained, as situational cues force a reconfronting of the task. In such cases, the result is a phenomenology of repetitive negative rumination, which often focuses on self-doubt and perceptions of inadequacy. A number of writers—both from an earlier tradition of cognitive-attentional theories of anxiety (e.g., Sarason, 1975; Wine, 1971, 1980) and some more recent (Ingram, 1990)—have equated this phenomenology of negative rumination with the term *self-focus*. We think that label is a mistake, a misrepresentation of what's going on (see also Pyszczynski, Greenberg, Hamilton, & Nix, 1991).

Why is the label self-focus misleading here? Because self-focus doesn't always produce interference. As described earlier, self-focus is in many cases associated with *task* focus, as the experience of attention inward engages the feedback process underlying effort. Indeed, among confident subjects in the studies just mentioned, this is what occurred even under conditions of adversity. Self-focus led to more task effort, as manifest both in overt behavior and in contents of consciousness. Only among doubtful subjects did self-focus lead to performance impairment or to negative rumination.

ISSUES

The last part of our discussion of mental disengagement has begun to move us into a consideration of issues. Here are several more, including a few theoretical comparisons.

Is Disengagement Good or Bad?

One question that must be raised about the dichotomy between effort and giving up concerns the adaptive value of the two tendencies. Is the disengagement tendency good or bad? The answer is that it's both and neither. On the one hand, disengagement (at some level, at least) is an absolute necessity. Disengagement is a natural and indispensable part of self-regulation. If we are ever to turn away from efforts at unattainable goals, if we're ever to back out of blind alleys, we must be able to disengage, to give up and start over somewhere else.

The importance of disengagement is particularly obvious with regard to concrete, low-level goals: We must be able to remove ourselves from literal blind alleys and wrong streets, give up plans that have become disrupted by unexpected events, and spend the night in the wrong city if we've missed the last plane home. The tendency is also important, however, with regard to more abstract and higher level goals. A vast literature attests to the importance of disengaging and moving on with life after the loss of close relationships (e.g., Cleiren, 1993; Duck, 1982; Orbuch, 1992; Stroebe, Stroebe, & Hansson, 1993; Vaughan, 1986; Weiss, 1988). People sometimes must even be willing to give up values that are deeply embedded in the self, if those values create too much conflict and distress in their lives.

As with most processes in self-regulation, however, the choice between continued effort and giving up presents opportunities for things to go awry. It's possible to stop trying prematurely, thereby creating potentially serious problems for oneself (Carver & Scheier, 1998). It's also possible to hold on to goals too long and prevent oneself from taking adaptive steps toward new goals. But both continued effort and giving up are necessary parts of the experience of adaptive self-regulation. Each plays an important role in the flow of behavior.

Hierarchicality and Importance Can Impede Disengagement

We said earlier that disengagement sometimes is precluded by situational constraints. However, it's not just situational constraints that prevent disengagement. Another, broader aspect of this problem stems from the idea that behavior is hierarchically organized, with goals increasingly important being higher in the hierarchy. Presumably disengaging from concrete values is often easy. Indeed, the nature of programs is such that disengagement from subgoals is quite common, even while continuing to pursue the program's overall goal. For example, if you go to buy something and the store is closed for inventory, you're likely to leave this store and head for another one.

Lower order goals vary, however, in how closely they're linked to values at a higher level, and thus how important they are. To disengage from low-level goals that are tightly linked to higher level goals causes discrepancy enlargement at the higher level. These higher order qualities are important, even central to one's life. One cannot disengage from them, or disregard them, or tolerate large discrepancies between them and current reality, without reorganizing one's value system (Greenwald, 1980; Kelly, 1955; McIntosh & Martin, 1992; Millar, Tesser, & Millar, 1988). In such a case, disengagement from concrete behavioral goals can be quite difficult.

Now recall again the affective consequences of being in this situation. The desire to disengage was prompted by unfavorable expectancies.

These expectancies are paralleled by negative affect. In this situation, then, the person experiences negative feelings (because of an inability to make progress toward the goal) and is unable to do anything about the feelings (because of an inability to give up). The person simply stews in the feelings that arise from irreconcilable discrepancies (see also Martin & Tesser, 1989; Wyer & Srull, 1989, chap. 12). This kind of situation—commitment to unattainable goals—seems a sure prescription for distress.

Helplessness

Discussions of giving up inevitably touch on the concept of helplessness. This term came from the finding that exposure to painful and unavoidable shocks made it harder for dogs to learn avoidance responses when doing so became possible (Overmier & Seligman, 1967; Seligman & Maier, 1967). As analogous research was done on humans, the theory became more cognitive, involving expectations of future noncontingency (Abramson, Seligman, & Teasdale, 1978) or expectations of being unable to control outcomes (Wortman & Brehm, 1975). In simple terms, helpless people develop the idea they can't obtain good outcomes because the outcomes are unrelated to their actions.

The emphasis on expectancies in models of human helplessness (and in their successor, the hopelessness theory of depression by Abramson, Metalsky, & Alloy, 1989) resembles the emphasis we've placed on expectancies here. Although labels differ, one of the overall points is much the same from theory to theory: people who feel doubtful enough about being able to move toward their goals stop trying, whereas people with more confidence keep trying.

We make two brief points here about helplessness. First, phenomena termed *helplessness* are sometimes treated as though they represent a unique or special domain of behavior. They do not. Helplessness occupies one place (or more) in a more elaborate set of self-regulatory phenomena. Helplessness is a reflection of a giving-up response. Conceptually, it's related in important ways to other, more benign—even *necessary*—kinds of giving up.

The second point is perhaps more important. An understanding of helplessness is incomplete without including an element that's rarely if ever noted. The person displaying helplessness is manifesting a giving-up response in some ways (performance deficit, cognitive interference). But the expression of the giving-up response is incomplete. The critical element that's usually left out of the discussion is this: In cases of real helplessness, the goal for which the giving-up response is occurring is a goal that cannot easily be abandoned. Thus, it remains in place. There is a giving up of effort, but not a giving up of the goal (cf. Klinger, 1975).

Why? Because in cases of real helplessness, the goal is too important. If the goal is trivial, you'll give it up and turn to something else. If the goal is subjectively important, though, you can't disengage. The result of this combination of circumstances is much the same as in any instance of commitment to an unattainable goal: absence of goal-directed effort and presence of emotional distress. Unless the person remains committed to the goal, however, there's no obvious reason for the distress.

Efficacy Expectancy and Expectancy of Success

Two further theoretical comparisons deserve comment regarding the effect of expectancies on behavior. The first concerns Bandura's (1977, 1982, 1986) analysis of efficacy expectancies. This theory began as a way of understanding behavior change. Bandura (1977) argued that people with problems generally know exactly what actions to do. Just knowing what to do, however, isn't enough. You must also be confident of your ability to *do* the behavior. This perceived ability to carry out a desired action is what Bandura terms self-efficacy. To Bandura, when therapy works, it's because the therapy restored the person's sense of efficacy, or confidence in the ability to carry out actions that earlier were troublesome.

We agree fully with aspects of that model. Bandura has argued persuasively that the bottleneck in behavior often is the lack of confidence about having the capacity to perform it. On the other hand, there are also situations in which personal capability is not the central issue. By emphasizing the role of personal capability to the exclusion of other factors, Bandura removed from the model's purview situations in which expectations of good or bad outcomes derive from other sources of influence. For example, if a cancer patient believes that a prescribed medical regimen will cause recovery, it hardly seems sensible to say that the optimism about survival (and the careful following of the doctor's instructions) rests on perceptions of self-efficacy.

In Bandura's efficacy model, expectations of personal efficacy are always the critical element. We have long felt this is misleading. Judgments about the probable impact of other causal forces also influence people's belief that continued action will yield good versus bad outcomes. In our view, perceptions not only of capabilities but also of causal factors outside the person matter in determining behavior. What ultimately matters is the emergent expectation of success or failure, which derives from assessment of both kinds of factors.

In some cases, the role of personal agency is paramount. In other cases, it's minimal. As we said earlier about feedback loops, sometimes the action of the output function is what produces the desired effect, but sometimes an external perturbation does so. Whether the role of personal agency is paramount or not, what matters is whether the person remains engaged with the behavioral goal.

We also feel, however, that Bandura's emphasis on the role of efficacy perceptions has clouded the extent to which he takes other factors into account implicitly. He has discussed alternative sources of futility (1982, pp. 140–141), but not comparable alternative sources of success expectancies. Clearly these influences matter, as well. Consider an example: Imagine an amateur wrestler who knows he is moderately good at offensive maneuvers, very good at defensive ones, and moderately good at evoking his best efforts in the heat of competition. From these and other considerations, he derives a sense of self-efficacy with respect to wrestling (or even specific efficacy expectancies for different situations in a match). He has a particular vision of his capabilities, his competencies. Given a specific opponent (with a given set of perceived capabilities), he also has a sense of the likelihood of prevailing.

Now imagine he learns this opponent has severely sprained an ankle, cannot use it without enormous pain, and therefore cannot even attempt certain important maneuvers. Surely this news will increase his confidence of success. Is that because his sense of self-efficacy has increased? Some would say yes. Yet how can that be? His knowledge of the extent of his own skills hasn't changed. How could the sense of self-efficacy increase if self-efficacy is a self-judgment of one's capability?

We think self-efficacy researchers often measure more than people's judgments of their capabilities. The measures used to assess the influence of the self often assess other influences indirectly, though the result is always labeled *self*-efficacy. Thus, although the discussions always focus on the self, the situations the self confronts are a partner in the assessment.

The Sense of Personal Control

A related construct that merits mention here is personal control. Many people believe that the sense of control is an important element in successful adjustment to stressful events (Baltes & Baltes, 1986; Heckhausen & Schulz, 1995; Skinner, 1996; Taylor, 1983, 1990; Taylor & Brown, 1988; Thompson & Spacapan, 1991; Weiner, 1985). Indeed, the idea that people deal better with stressors when they have a sense of control is a recurring theme in the stress literature.

Does the sense of control really confer benefits? The answer isn't as simple as it might seem. Some studies indicate that having a sense of control is beneficial. There also appear to be situations in which personal control is detrimental. In a review of research on the sense of control, Burger (1989) identified several conditions that might cause people to relinquish control or to experience distress when having control. Of particular interest is his assertion that control is undesirable when it reduces the likelihood of a desired outcome (or increases the chances of an undesired outcome). This assertion is of particular interest because it implies that what matters most is the anticipated outcome rather than the path by which the outcome will occur.

As a group, the studies Burger reviewed (and newer studies) hint strongly that control is desirable (and may diminish distress) when it makes a desired outcome more likely, but that having control is undesirable (and may exacerbate distress) when it makes a desired outcome less likely. This conclusion, however, challenges the importance of the sense of control per se. The powerful factor instead would be expectancies about the desired or undesired outcomes, consistent with our conceptualization (see Fig. 1.11).

Unfortunately, a good deal of research on the effects of control confounds the perception that good or bad outcomes *depend on what you do* (personal control) with the anticipation that good outcomes *will occur* (positive outcome expectancies; for a discussion of issues in conceptualizing control, including this one, see Thompson & Spacapan, 1991). For example, a study by Thompson, Sobolew-Shubin, Galbraith, Schwankovsky, and Cruzen (1993) appears to indicate the value of perceived control. However, subjects' ratings of the amount of control they perceived in a given domain were combined with their ratings of the effectiveness of their control efforts in that domain (i.e., successes). This

Sense of personal causal responsibility

		Yes	No
Good outcome	Yes	A	B
	No	C	D

FIG. 1.11. If perceptions of control are beneficial, people in the left column should experience less distress than people in the right column. If perceptions of control are beneficial when associated with good outcomes but detrimental when associated with bad outcomes, A should be better off than B and C should be worse off than D. The effect of perceived control per se can not be evaluated, however, by comparing cell A with cell D, which is what many studies have done.

makes it impossible to know whether it was the control perception that mattered or the perception of success. As another example, items measuring the general sense of internal locus of control often also imply greater confidence of good outcomes (Carver, 1997c).

A final note on the concept of control. Some suggest that control can be exerted vicariously. Thus, the perception that others (e.g., medical caregivers) have control over aspects of a stressful event is presumed to work in the same way as the expectation of personal control. That is, if someone working for your benefit has control, you should have less distress. In our opinion, this stretches the concept of personal control past recognizability. Invoking the concept of vicarious control is a virtual admission that what matters is the expected outcome, not the perception of control over the outcome. It is interesting that Thompson and Spacapan (1991) concluded that vicarious control yields positive effects when good outcomes are expected and adverse effects when poor outcomes are expected, much as Burger (1989) argued for personal control. Such a pattern is consistent with the conceptualization presented here.

Watersheds, Disjunctions, and Bifurcations Among Responses

Another issue of interest concerns the divergence that is part of this model among the behavioral and cognitive responses to favorable versus unfavorable expectancies. We've long argued for a psychological watershed among responses to adversity, such that these responses tend to diverge (Carver, 1979; Carver & Scheier, 1981). One class of responses consists of continued comparisons between present state and goal and continued efforts. The other class consists of disengagement from comparisons and quitting. Just as rainwater falling on a mountain ridge ultimately flows to one or the other side of the ridge, so do behaviors ultimately flow to one or the other of these classes.

Our initial reason for taking this position stemmed largely from the several demonstrations that self-focused attention creates diverging effects on both information seeking and behavior, as a function of expectancies of success (Fig. 1.12). We aren't the only ones to have emphasized a disjunction among responses, however. A number of others have done so, for reasons of their own.

An early model that emphasized the idea of a disjunction in behavior was proposed by Kukla (1972). Another such model is the integration between reactance and helplessness by Wortman and Brehm (1975). They argued that threats to control produce an attempt to regain or reassert control. Perceptions that control is lost produce helplessless. Thus, there's

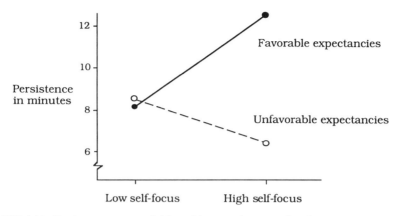

FIG. 1.12. Persistence at an insoluble problem as a function of performance expectancy regarding the target task and self-directed attention. Data from "Reassertion and Giving Up: The Interactive Role of Self-Directed Attention and Outcome Expectancy," by C. S. Carver, P. H. Blaney, and M. F. Scheier, 1979, *Journal of Personality and Social Psychology, 37*, 1859–1870. Copyright 1979 by the American Psychological Association. Adapted with permission. Combines data from Experiments 1 and 2.

a disjunction between reassertion of control and giving up. Brehm and his collaborators (Brehm & Self, 1989; Wright & Brehm, 1989) have more recently developed an approach to task engagement that resembles that of Kukla (1972), although their way of approaching the description of the problem was somewhat different.

Not all theories about persistence and giving up yield this dichotomy among responses. The fact that some do, however, is interesting. It becomes more so later on.

Does Disengagement Imply an Override Mechanism?

The idea that effort gives way to disengagement as expectancies become more negative raises another issue. How does this characterization of giving up mesh with the conceptualization presented in earlier sections? If behavior operates under the principle of feedback control, why shouldn't people try endlessly to reduce discrepancies, however ineffectively? Why should the distress and doubt not simply persist or intensify? What permits the person to disengage?

Our initial thought was that there must be an override of some sort that's capable of taking precedence over this feedback system, taking it out of gear, and causing disengagement from the reference value currently used to guide action (Carver & Scheier, 1990a). There's some basis for believing, however, that such an assumption isn't necessary.

An alternative view is that people always have many motives, desires, and goals in mind, all competing for access to consciousness (e.g., Atkinson & Birch, 1970; Murray, 1938). The level of each motive is subject to many influences. Most discussions of this sort of model focus on the passage of time since a given motive was satisfied. However, perhaps another influence is level of confidence or doubt regarding the desired outcome. Perhaps the tendency to exert effort toward the focal goal simply diminishes (compared to tendencies to exert effort toward other goals) as expectancies for success become lower. Indeed, it might be argued that this should be precisely the effect of a slow-acting feedback process that scales back goals when they aren't being met.

In this view, another behavior simply becomes prepotent at some point, and the person turns away from the previous behavior to the newly focal one. Disengagement would be isomorphic to engaging the newly focal goal. Indirect evidence from an analogous issue concerning the control of visual attention suggests that there is no need to assume a discrete disengage mechanism (Cohen, Romero, Servan-Schreiber, & Farah, 1994). Rather, disengagement may be attributable to the competitive nature of attention allocation: Attention devoted to one area creates an inhibition of attention elsewhere.

Thinking about disengagement in this way, and adding the further assumption of a spreading-activation model of memory (a commonly made assumption), suggests further implications. The idea that increased activation brings material closer to consciousness has led us occasionally to the homely metaphor of the mind as a soup pot (Carver, 1997a). As the pot is heated, bits in the soup rise to the surface. In the soup pot, rising is influenced by such issues as how fast various bits absorb and lose heat, how large the pieces are, how much interference with movement is created by a piece being oversized, and so on. In an analogous way, information activated in memory (by the many influences that produce activation, including spreading activation and deactivation from other active nodes, residual activation from primes that directly activated the information earlier) drifts higher in the soup pot of the mind. Whatever bits are at the top of the soup correspond to the information closest to the person's current content of consciousness.

In this metaphor, the pieces in the heating soup are all continuously active, to some degree or other, even if they are nowhere near the top of the pot. They are still absorbing activation, still bumping against each other—indeed, parts underneath are still supporting the parts of the soup that are at the surface. The analogy suggests that parts of the mind that are out of awareness similarly remain engaged in work, spreading activation among themselves and, in some cases, serving to support the edifice that's made it to consciousness, at the top of the pot. In such a model, many areas of partial activation compete continuously for access to consciousness, but of necessity only some small fragment of these competing elements can be in consciousness at any given moment.

Most discussions of information being in and out of consciousness focus on purely perceptual or cognitive events, but there's no obvious reason why such arguments can't be applied to goals and goal striving as well (Bargh, 1997; Wegner & Bargh, 1998). It seems likely that a variety of goals are partially active and engaged in people's minds most of the time (perhaps all the time), out of awareness but competing for access to attentional resources. Whichever goal has temporarily become active enough to reach the top of the pot is the one you are aware of.[3]

Presumably there is a range of variability in degree of engagement (and thus in degree of access to consciousness). A person who is struggling behaviorally to overcome an impediment to a goal has the goal and self-regulatory attempt fully in consciousness. A person who is experiencing ruminative intrusions about the goal (Martin & Tesser, 1996) has the goal near the top of the pot, but a bit below the level that keeps the person actively engaged in its pursuit. For the person who has gone on to other things and no longer experiences the intrusion, that goal has drifted yet lower. It may not be gone. Some part of the mind may still be grinding away at resolving the blockage. But this process is at present no longer sufficiently potent to obtain access to attentional resources.[4]

For many years, how to integrate the interrupt-and-disengage aspect of the conceptual model with the feedback part has been a vexing puzzle to us. The disengagement facet has always had something of an ad hoc feel to it. However, the assumption that people have multiple

---

[3]This depiction may strike some as portraying a process that's far too haphazard to be plausible. Certainly, we assume that there are systematic influences in the mental soup pot: Having a strong intention to go to the store helps keep that goal active. Entering a setting that has standing behavior patterns (Barker & Associates, 1978) tends to activate those linked behavioral tendencies (Carver & Scheier, 1981). But there are also many unexpected influences from moment to moment that cause people to abruptly change directions in their behavior. What appears haphazard may not be haphazard at all. It may simply reflect the operation of a very complex set of processes.

[4]We might speculate about what conditions might increase access to attentional resources for a goal pursuit that's far down on the priority list. One possibility is a sudden step toward resolution of the blockage. If the internal problem solver that's slowly picking at the problem suddenly lurches forward, doubt decreases. If, as speculated earlier, doubt is one factor causing a goal to drop in priority, a decrease in doubt may increase the goal's priority. Thus, an out-of-awareness partial resolution of the problem might cause the goal to rise in priority, even to pop into the person's mind unbidden.

current concerns, and that shifts in allocation of attention depend partly on confidence, would integrate these two aspects of the model more fully. The phenomenology of disengagement would not change, but the event would be construed more in terms of what goals retained what positions in a priority queue.

THEME *AND* ISSUE: CONTROLLED BEHAVIOR
VERSUS EMERGENT BEHAVIOR

The picture we've drawn of human behavior thus far is that of a person with goals and intentions, regulating efforts to move toward the realization of those goals in behavior. It has been a top-down picture, in the sense that the actions under discussion have been presumed to be guided by the attempt to attain goals that often are fairly abstract. Several literatures exist that raise questions about the accuracy of that picture. From consideration of this broad issue arises another theme: that behavior is guided both by bottom-up and by top-down influences.

Coordinations

One of the literatures bearing on this issue focuses on coordinations, largely (though not solely) coordinations of physical movement (e.g., Kugler & Turvey, 1987; Turvey, 1990). An influential idea in that literature is that complexity on the surface of behavior can emerge from the action of very simple processes. The complexity need not be either represented or controlled centrally. A related point is that a lot less has to be managed by active controllers than you may think.

Work on these themes has focused in large part on the study of rhythmicities, oscillatory movements. As such movements begin, after a brief period of variability they settle into a regular pattern. Several potential patterns may exist in a given movement domain, and sometimes abrupt transitions occur from one pattern to another, as some variable changes. An easy example is the shift in a horse's gait from walk to trot to canter as the horse moves faster and faster.

Another example (in human behavior) is what happens if you coordinate your index fingers in a table-tapping task in which the fingers are out of phase: one up, the other down. As you try to do this faster and faster, at some point your coordination will jump—abruptly and involuntarily—to an in-phase coordination: both up at once, both down at once (Kelso, Scholz, & Schöner, 1986). Apparently no higher mental controller requests this change in organization. It emerges from the nature of the task and your management of its simple elements.

The idea that patterns of coordination "fall out of" the structure of the body and the environment and the idea that complexity emerges from simple actions have also been taken up by people interested in more social aspects of behavior. For instance, Newtson (1993, 1994) argued that the organization in dyadic interaction also has emergent properties, qualities that aren't represented in the goals of either interactant. He says a good metaphor for interaction is a wave. Waves can be portrayed by the very simple parameters of intensity, frequency, and phase. In interacting, each person creates a wave, which affects the other's wave, so that they acquire a relationship to one another. Newtson says that people don't have internal wave-generating mechanisms; rather, the wave pattern is emergent and self-organizing from the interaction itself.

Two Modes of Influence?

The idea that coordinations are a surface complexity that emerges from the concurrent action of simple systems is interesting (a separate literature in robotics makes a similar case—see Carver & Scheier, 1998). Does this idea imply that *all* complex behavior takes that form? Some people seem to draw that conclusion, but it seems unlikely to be correct.

For example, Kelso, a prominent theorist on self-organization and emergent coordinations, devoted a chapter of his 1995 book to intentions, doing so largely to show that intentions aren't as important as people think. He noted, for example, that a body's coordinations constrain intentions (it's hard to form the intention to do something for which your body doesn't have the needed action coordinations). He also pointed out the ironic fact that carrying out an intention to do a behavior can take longer than it takes to do the same behavior as a reaction (which makes it seems as though intentions are more detrimental than helpful).

Nonetheless, it's clear from his discussion that Kelso believes that intentions *can* influence action. Describing an experiment in which subjects tried to resist the self-organizing tendency to tap in-phase at higher speeds, he wrote that " . . . all subjects were able to intentionally maintain the anti-phase pattern . . . even at frequencies well beyond each subject's *spontaneous* transition frequency. Thus, [the person] is able to intentionally sustain a pattern that is intrinsically unstable" (1995, pp. 151–152). This appears to indicate that the conceptualization of emergent coordinations is not intended to supplant models in which executive control plays a role (see also Aslin, 1993, p. 393). Rather, Kelso is emphasizing that intentions are not *everything*, that other forces are at work, interweaving with, and constraining, intentional processes.

Surely there is good reason to suspect there are interesting rhythmicities and cycles in human behavior that haven't yet come to light, which may have important influences on human experience that haven't yet been well appreciated. There is also reason to suspect there's merit to the idea that patterns in behavior self-organize in the initial stages of their emergence (Smith & Thelen, 1993). Yet it also seems reasonable to suggest that emergent patterns eventually stabilize and that information about their nature is coded into memory in a form in which the patterns can then be invoked for re-creation by a higher order intentional process. To put it differently, it makes sense to us to assume that there are two modes of influence on the patterning of these behaviors.

Connectionism

Another literature that raises questions about the role of central control processes is the literature of connectionism. Connectionists model thought in networks of simple neuron-like units, in which "processing" consists of passing activation among units. As in neurons, the signal can be excitatory or inhibitory. Energy passes in only one direction (though some networks incorporate feedback links). Processing proceeds entirely by the spread of activation. There's no higher order executive to direct traffic or control processing. Further, in a distributed connectionist network, knowledge is not represented centrally or as nodes of information. Rather, knowledge is represented in terms of the pattern of activation of the network as a whole. Information thus is distributed (Smith, 1996).

In networks containing feedback relations, the pattern of weights and activations is updated repeatedly—thus modifications are made iteratively throughout the network, clarifying the pattern. In such a network, processing occurs dynamically across a large number of iterations or cycles. The activation of each node is updated many times, as are the weighting functions involved in summing the activation. Gradually these values asymptote and the system "settles" into a configuration. This settling reflects the least amount of overall error the system has been able to create, given its input and the weights with which it began.

A useful way to think about this process is that the system simultaneously satisfies multiple constraints that the elements create on each other (Thagard, 1989). For example, two mutually inhibitory nodes can't both be highly active at the same time. These constraints among the nodes are settled out during the iterative updating of activation levels. This idea of *parallel constraint satisfaction* is now having a substantial impact on how people in social psychology think about a variety of topics (Kunda & Thagard, 1996; Read, Vanman, & Miller, 1997; Schultz & Lepper, 1996).

For our present purpose, however, what's most important about connectionist models is the part that's had the *least* impact in personality–social psychology (although see Smith, 1996, for a different view): the idea that knowledge is distributed, represented by a pattern rather than in any central form. At least some connectionist theorists would argue that it's a mistake to assume a top-down executive process with access to consolidated knowledge, because that's not how knowledge is stored.

Two-Mode Models of Thought

Cognitive psychologists have worked hard to deal with issues raised by differences between the so-called symbolic approach (which tends to assume an executive function) and the connectionist approach. In so doing, several theorists have come to argue that thinking takes two forms, rather than one.

For example, Smolensky (1988) argued that a top-level *conscious processor* is used for effortful reasoning and following of programs of instructions. An *intuitive processor*, which manages intuitive problem solving, heuristic strategies, and skilled or automatic activities, relies on connectionist processes. This general idea recurs in several other theories (Holyoak & Spellman, 1993; Shastri & Ajjanagadde, 1993; Sloman, 1996). What Smolensky called a conscious processor, Sloman (1996) called *rule-based* and Shastri and Ajjanagadde (1993) called *reflective*, implying that it's deliberative and effortful. What Smolensky called an intuitive processor, Sloman called *associative* and Shastri and Ajjanagadde called *reflexive*, implying that it's quick and spontaneous.

How do the two processing modes relate to one another? The connectionist, multiple constraint satisfaction mode seems to reflect something akin to what Kelso (1995) thinks of as pattern emergence. Patterns emerge because there are constraints—physical and environmental—that mutually settle into a pattern that takes them into account. The other mode of processing seems to reflect intentions, a purposeful seeking out of regularities in memory to apply to the case at hand.

Two-Mode Models in Personality–Social Psychology

The idea that people connect to the world through two different modes of processing is not unique to these cognitive theories. It also appears in the literature of personality and social psychology. At least two contemporary models from that literature have enough resemblance to the two-mode models in cognitive psychology to warrant mention.

One of them is Epstein's (1985, 1990, 1994) cognitive–experiential self-theory. This model assumes the existence of two systems for processing information. The *rational* system operates primarily consciously, functions according to logical rules of inference, and operates relatively slowly. The *experiential* system is intuitive, crudely differentiated, and works by generalization, providing a "quick and dirty" way of assessing and responding to reality. As such, it relies on heuristics and readily available information. It functions automatically and in an experientially determined manner. Epstein argues that the more emotionally charged a situation is, the more a person's thinking is dominated by the experiential system.

Epstein holds that both systems are always at work in normal humans and that they jointly determine behavior. Each can be evoked to a greater or lesser degree under the right circumstances. For example, asking people to give strictly logical responses to hypothetical events tends to place them in a rational mode, whereas asking them how they would respond if the events happened to them tends to place them in experiential mode (Epstein, Lipson, Holstein, & Huh, 1992).

In Epstein's view, the experiential system is the default response resulting from eons of evolution. It's invoked whenever speed is needed. You can't be thorough when you need to act fast (e.g., when the situation is emotionally charged). Maybe you can't even wait to form an intention. Recall our earlier mention of the observation that it seems to take longer to form and execute an intention to act than to act in reaction to another stimulus (Kelso, 1995, p. 141). This observation is very much in the spirit of Epstein's distinction between processing modes.

Another theory that assumes two processing modes was proposed by Heckhausen and Gollwitzer (1987; Gollwitzer, 1990, 1996). This theory holds that there are important differences between the mind-set that people have when deciding whether to adopt a goal and the mind-set they have once that decision is made. The *deliberative* mind-set is characterized by careful examination of competing goals and the objective weighing of pros and cons of each. It's assumed to foster accurate and open-minded appraisal of evidence and thorough judgment processes.

The *implemental* mind-set, taken up only after the decision has been made to commit oneself to attaining some goal, is aimed at serving movement toward the goal. It's oriented toward moving quickly and expeditiously to a positive outcome. It's assumed to have a determined, close-minded, self-serving focus, biased toward thinking about success (Beckmann & Gollwitzer, 1987). There's evidence that people in implemental mind-sets exhibit a variety of heuristic biases: They are more likely to perceive themselves as in control of their outcomes (Gollwitzer &

Kinney, 1989) and are more likely to display positive illusions more generally (Taylor & Gollwitzer, 1995) than people in deliberative mind-sets.

These two-mode models differ from each other in several ways. For example, the Heckhausen–Gollwitzer theory doesn't seem to assume a way for the implemental mind-set to operate on its own except when a decision has been made to attain a goal, whereas the Epstein theory assumes that the experiential system is always at work. Another difference is that the Heckhausen–Gollwitzer theory describes mutually exclusive mind-sets, whereas the Epstein theory assumes two systems that are always functioning in parallel.

There are also striking similarities between theories, however, including the characteristics that the theorists assume for the two processing modes. The rational (Epstein) and deliberative (Heckhausen–Gollwitzer) models are very much like each other and very much like the symbolic systems in two-mode models in cognitive psychology. The experiential (Epstein) and implemental (Heckhausen–Gollwitzer) modes are both prone to shortcuts and biased processing, and both resemble the connectionist systems in two-mode models in cognitive psychology.

A Side Issue: Two Sources of Automaticity

These various theories tend to view the functioning of one system as involving greater automaticity than the other (this is less true of Heckhausen and Gollwitzer's model than others). They also seem to allow for two distinguishable sources of automaticity. Sometimes automaticity is inherent in the activity. Either the process is hardwired, or it's newly (thus automatically) self-organizing. For example, Epstein sees the experiential system as embodying primitive, built-in reaction tendencies, the adaptive responses that are part of infrahuman species as well as humans. Similarly, implicit in connectionist thinking is the idea that patterns emerge on their own, arising from the (automatic) constraint satisfaction process.

The other source of automaticity is repetition (see Bargh, 1997). Given enough repetition, an activity that was effortful and conscious may drop out of consciousness altogether. Having reached that point, the activity is now under the management of the experiential system. Smolensky (1988) argued similarly that when a behavior becomes automatic, responsibility for its management is being transferred from the conscious processor to the intuitive processor.

In this view, many behavior qualities may have a life history that moves from one mode of processing to the other and then back again. That is, perhaps dynamic connectionist processes at a low level automatically produce emergent patterns. After repeated emergence of a type of pattern, it begins to coalesce. After yet further recurrences, it's easier to get into without excess variability or noise (cf. Kelso's, 1995, discussion of the loss of variability in professionals).

This acquired ease of getting into the pattern implies that something is consolidating in memory. The consolidated pattern—the emergent quality at the higher level—may now be becoming recognizable to a rational or conscious mode of processing. At some point, it can be invoked by the conscious processor as a guide to behavior, even if the ability to execute it from the top down is at first poorly consolidated. With practice, the patterned information can be used top-down effectively, as well as re-emerge bottom-up from another recurrence of the connectionist (or emergent coordination) experience.

With further top-down use, the application of the "rule" (whatever the emergent quality consists of) becomes more accurate (matches more closely the patterns that were first induced bottom-up). Having become more accurate, it then begins to become more automatic. Gradually, the awareness of using it fades, as there's less and less need to invoke it explicitly. The more it fades, the more its use becomes a matter of management by the intuitive mode.

Presumably there would be differences between a pattern that's self-organizing and only in the early or middle stages of consolidation (and thus emerges intuitively if it exists at all) and a pattern that has been consolidated, made available to the conscious processor, and then rendered automatic by frequent use. Just what those differences might be is an interesting question.

Implications for Earlier Sections

In this section we described several two-mode models in cognitive psychology and in personality–social psychology, and inferred two modes of influence in coordinative systems as well. Each case we addressed here raises the suggestion that the picture presented in the earlier parts of this chapter is, at best, incomplete. There, we emphasized functioning from the top down and disregarded influences from the bottom up.

It does seem clear, however, that not all behavior is actively controlled. Sometimes apparent complexity and patterning occur for reasons that don't require explanation via internal mechanisms. Although this is true, it also seems clear that not *all* behavior occurs that way. An interesting set of problems will be to identify patterns arising from self-organizing tendencies and to assess how large a role this type of pattern emergence plays in human behavior. It seems clear as well that further study is warranted for the idea that people process the world in more than one way. This is a theme with its own set of unexplored issues.

We aren't entirely sure how to characterize the broad implications of these ideas for the principles presented in earlier sections. It isn't clear, for example, that they deny the usefulness of those ideas in any way. It seems reasonable to suggest that bottom-up emergence of patterns is one way in which goals are synthesized. That is, when the pattern becomes sufficiently consolidated to become accessible from the top down, it has become a behavioral goal. Such a view would imply the (perhaps) continuing development of new emergent patterns over the individual's life span, with these emergent patterns now becoming available for use in executing a variety of intended actions. This would be a very different view from a model in which all action patterns were presumed to be available initially, with some selected for retention because they were "reinforced." The question of where goals come from and how they are synthesized is one that hasn't been well explored, and these ideas suggest an interesting way of approaching it.

THEME: DYNAMIC SYSTEMS AND HUMAN BEHAVIOR

We turn now to another theme, which actually was hovering around the edges of the previous section. Recent years have seen the emergence in psychology of new (or at least newly prominent) ideas about how to conceptualize natural systems. Several labels attach to these ideas: Chaos, dynamic systems theory, complexity, catastrophe theory. A number of introductions to various aspects of this body of thought have been written, some of which include applications to psychology (e.g., Barton, 1994; Brown, 1995; Field & Golubitsky, 1992; Gleick, 1987; Ruelle, 1991; Stewart, 1990; Thelen & Smith, 1994; Vallacher & Nowak, 1994, 1997; Waldrop, 1992). In this section we address themes that are central to this way of thinking, then indicate places where we think the themes apply meaningfully to subjects of our own interest.

Dynamic systems theory, or chaos theory, is deterministic (despite the contrary implication of the word *chaos*). It holds that the behavior of a system reflects the forces operating on (and within) it. It also emphasizes that the behavior of a complex system over anything but a brief time is very hard to predict. Why? One reason is that the system's behavior may be influenced by the forces operating on and within it in nonlinear rather than linear ways. Thus, the behavior of the system—even though highly determined—can appear random. This determinism in principle but unpredictability in practice underlies the label *chaotic*.

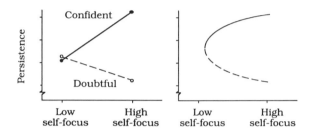

FIG. 1.13. Interactions indicate that the effect of one variable differs as a function of the level of another variable. On the left is the interaction between self-focus and expectancy that was shown in Fig. 1.12. This indicates that the effect of self-focus is nonlinear (right panel). Its impact reverses at some point along the distribution of the variable confidence–doubt.

Nonlinearity

Many people are used to thinking of relationships between variables as linear. That's the principle on which most of our statistical procedures are based (though nonlinear tests do exist). When you compute a correlation, you're looking for a linear relationship. Dynamic-systems thinking asserts that this is too simple, that many relationships are not linear.

Familiar examples of nonlinear relationships are step functions (ice turning to water and water turning to steam as temperature increases), threshold functions, and floor and ceiling effects. Other examples of nonlinearity are interactions (Fig. 1.13). In an interaction, the effect of one predictor on the outcome differs as a function of the level of a second predictor. Thus the effect of the first predictor on the outcome isn't linear. The second predictor is thereby acting as what the jargon of dynamic systems calls a *control parameter*—a factor "that hold[s] potential for changing the intrinsic dynamics of a system" (Vallacher & Nowak, 1997).

Obviously the interaction in Fig. 1.13 is far from unique. Indeed, many psychologists think in terms of interactions much of the time. To that extent, many psychologists already think in terms of dynamic systems, whether they realize it or not. Threshold effects and interactions are kinds of nonlinearity that many people take for granted, although perhaps not labeling them as such. Looking intentionally for nonlinearities, however, reveals others. For example, many developmental psychologists now think many developmental changes are dynamic rather than linear (Bertenthal, Campos, & Kermoian, 1994; Goldin-Meadow & Alibali, 1995; Ruble, 1994; Siegler & Jenkins, 1989; Thelen, 1992, 1995; van der Maas & Molenaar, 1992).

Sensitive Dependence on Initial Conditions

Nonlinearity of relations is one reason why it's hard to predict complex systems. Two more reasons why prediction over anything but the short term is difficult is that you never know all the influences on a system, and the ones you do know you never know with total precision. What you think is happening may not be quite what's happening. That difference, even if it's small, can be very important.

This theme is identified in the dynamic systems literature with the phrase *sensitive dependence on initial conditions* (see, e.g., Ruelle, 1991). This phrase means that a very small difference between two conditions of a system can lead to divergence and, ultimately, the absence of any correlation between the paths the system takes later on. The idea is (partly) that a small initial difference causes a difference in what the system encounters next, which yields slightly different influences on the systems, producing slightly different outcomes (Lorenz, 1963). Through repeated iterations of small differences, the systems diverge, eventually leading the two systems to very different pathways (Mandel, 1995). After a surprisingly brief period, they no longer have any noticeable relation to one another.

How does the notion of sensitive dependence on initial conditions relate to human behavior? Most generally, it suggests that a person's behavior will be hard to predict over a long period except in general terms. For example, although you might be confident that Joe usually eats lunch, you wouldn't be able to predict as well what time, where, or what he'll eat on the second Friday of next month. This doesn't mean Joe's behavior is truly random or unlawful (cf. Epstein, 1979). It just means that small differences between the influences you think are affecting him and the influences that actually are taking place will result in moment-to-moment behavior that's unpredicted.

This principle also holds for prediction of your own behavior. There's evidence that people don't plan very far into the future (J. R. Anderson, 1990, pp. 203–205), even experts (Gobet & Simon, 1996). People seem to have goals in which the general form of the goal is sketched out, but only a few program-level steps toward it have been planned. Even attempts at relatively thorough planning appear to be recursive and "opportunistic," changing—sometimes drastically—when new information becomes known (Hayes-Roth & Hayes-Roth, 1979; see also Payton, 1990).

The notion of sensitive dependence on initial conditions provides an explanation for this. It's pointless (and maybe even counterproductive) to plan too far ahead too fully (cf. Kirschenbaum, 1985), because chaotic forces in play (forces that are hard to predict because of nonlinearities and sensitive dependence) can render much of the planning irrelevant.

Thus, it makes sense to plan in general terms, chart a few steps, get there, reassess, and plan the next bits. This seems a perfect illustration of how people implicitly take chaos into account in their own lives.

Phase Space, Attractors, and Repellers

Another set of concepts important in dynamic-systems thinking are variations on the terms *phase space* and *attractor* (Brown, 1995; Vallacher & Nowak, 1997). A *phase diagram* is a depiction of the behavior of a system over time. The system's states are plotted along two (sometimes three) axes, with time displayed as the progression of the line of the plot, rather than on an axis of its own. A *phase space* is the array of states that a system occupies across a period of time. As the system changes states over time, it traces a *trajectory* within its phase space—a path of the successive states it occupies across that period.

Phase spaces often contain one or more regions called attractors. *Attractors* are areas the system approaches, occupies, or tends toward more frequently than other areas. Attractors seem to exert a metaphorical gravitational pull on the system, bringing the system into proximity to them. Each attractor has what's called a *basin*, the attractor's region of attraction. All trajectories that enter the basin move toward that attractor (Brown, 1995). The horse's gaits we mentioned earlier can be thought of as attractors. The behavior of a moving horse is drawn to one or another of those gaits, depending on the horse's speed.

There are several kinds of attractors, some simple, others more complex. In a *point attractor*, all trajectories converge onto some point in phase space, no matter where they begin (e.g., body temperature). In a *cyclical attractor* (also called a *periodic*, or *limit-cycle*, attractor), the system always settles into a cycle in phase space (e.g., the circadian rhythm). In both cases, no matter where in phase space the system begins, the end result is stability: a stable point, or a stable orbit.

Of more interest are *chaotic attractors* (or *strange* attractors). The pattern to which this term refers is an irregular and unpredictable movement around attraction points. The most widely known example is the Lorenz attractor, named for the meteorologist who first plotted it (Lorenz, 1963). The Lorenz attractor has two attraction zones (Fig. 1.14). Plotting the behavior of this system yields a tendency to loop around both attractors, but unpredictably. Shifts in trajectory from one basin to the other seem random.

The behavior of this system displays sensitivity to initial conditions. A small change in starting point changes the specific path of motion entirely. The general tendencies remain the same—that is, the revolving around

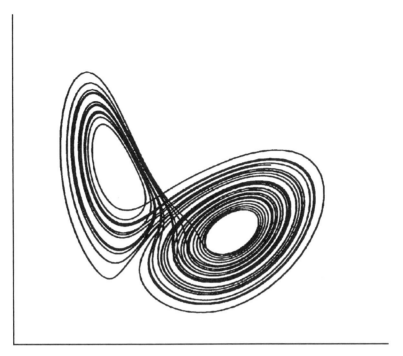

FIG. 1.14. The Lorenz attractor, an example of what is known as a chaotic attractor or strange attractor.

both attractors. But details, such as the number of revolutions around one before deflection to the other, form an entirely different pattern. The trajectory over time shows this same sensitivity to small differences. As the system continues, it often nearly repeats itself, but never quite does, and what appear to be nearly identical paths can diverge abruptly, with one path leading to one attractor and the adjacent path leading to the other.

A phase space also contains regions called *repellers*, regions that are hardly ever occupied. Indeed, these regions seem to be actively avoided. That is, a minimal departure from the focal point of a repeller leads to a rapid escape from that region of phase space. In a plot of attractors such as shown in Fig. 1.14, regions outside the areas of attraction are repellers.

Another Way of Picturing Attractors

The phase-space diagram gives a vivid visual sense of what an attractor "looks like" and how it acts. Another way that's often used to portray attractors is shown in Fig. 1.15. In this view, attractor basins are basins or

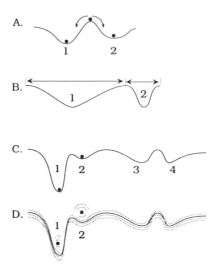

FIG. 1.15. Another way to portray attractors. A. Attractor basins as valleys in a surface (local minima). Behavior of the system is represented as a ball. If the ball is in a valley (point 1 or 2), it is in an attractor basin and will tend to stay there unless disturbed. If the ball is on a ridge (between 1 and 2), it will tend to escape its current location and move to an attractor. B. A wider basin (1) attracts more trajectories than a narrower basin (2). A steeply sloping basin (2) attracts more abruptly any trajectory that enters the basin than does a more gradually sloping basin (1). C. A system in which attractor 1 is very stable and the others are less stable. It will take more energy to free the ball from attractor 1 than from the others. D. The system's behavior is energized, much as the shaking of a metaphoric tambourine surface, keeping the system's behavior in flux and less than completely captured by any particular attractor. Still, more shaking will be required to escape from attractor 1 than attractor 2.

valleys in a surface (a more technical label for a basin is a *local minimum*). Repellers are ridges. This view assumes a metaphoric gravitational drift downward in the diagram, but other forces are presumed to be operative in all directions. (For simplicity, this portrayal usually is done as a two-dimensional drawing, but keep in mind that the diagram often assumes the merging of a large number of dimensions into the horizontal axis.)

The behavior of the system at a given moment is represented as a ball on the surface. If the ball is in a valley (points 1 and 2 in Fig. 1.15, A), it's in an attractor basin and will tend to stay there unless disturbed. If it's on a hill (between 1 and 2), any slight movement in either direction will cause it to escape its current location and move to an adjacent attractor.

A strength of this portrayal is that it does a good job of creating a sense of how attractors vary in robustness. The breadth of a basin indicates the diversity of the trajectories in phase space that are drawn into it. The broader the basin (B-1, in Fig. 1.15), the more trajectories will be drawn in. The narrower the basin (B-2), the closer the ball has to come to its focal point to be drawn to it. The steepness of the valley indicates how abruptly a trajectory is drawn into it. The steeper the slope of the wall (B-2), the more sudden is the entry of a system that encounters that basin.

The depth of the valley indicates how firmly entrenched the system is, once drawn into the attractor. Fig. 1.15 panel C represents a system of attractors with fairly low stability (the valleys are shallow). In Fig. 1.15 panel C, one attractor represents a stable situation (valley 1), whereas the others are less so. It will take a great deal more "energy" to free the ball from valley 1 than from the others.

There is a sense in which both breadth and depth suggest that a goal is important. Breadth does so because the system is drawn to the attractor from widely divergent trajectories. Depth does so because the system that's been drawn into the basin tends to stay there.

A weakness of this picture, compared to a phase-space portrait, is that it isn't as good at giving a sense of the erratic motion from one attractor to another in a multiple-attractor system. You can regain some of that sense of erratic shifting, however, if you think of the surface in Fig. 1.15 as a tambourine, with a certain amount of shaking going on all the time (Fig. 1.15 panel D). Even a little shaking causes the ball to bounce around in its well and may jostle it from one well to another, particularly if the attractors aren't highly stable. An alternative would be to think of the ball as a jumping bean, hopping and bouncing. These two characterizations would be analogous to jostling that comes from situational influences and jostling from internal dynamics, respectively.

Variability and Phase Changes

Another aspect of dynamic-systems thinking is the role of variability. It's been suggested that increases in variability herald, and may even promote, phase changes (Davies, 1988; Kelso, 1995; Siegler, 1994; Thelen, 1995; Thelen & Smith, 1994). One way to visualize the effect of variability on shifts from one attractor to another is to say that when the tambourine surface shown in Fig. 1.15 D is given a few hefty jolts instead of little shakes (imparting more energy), the ball bounces around more. Given enough shaking of the system—enough variability in movements within the current attractor basin—the chances of a shift to a new basin become greater. Another way to construe variability is to think of shifts in the contour of the landscape (something we haven't considered yet) as the system changes over time. If the landscape shifts in certain ways, variability also goes up (given a constant amount of shaking).

How is this variability manifest? Kelso (1995) pointed to two reflec-
tions of variability. *Critical fluctuations* refers to how far the bouncing ball
is displaced laterally from the center of the basin. If you think about variability caused by jolts to the tambourine, the energy of a larger jolt has
the potential of bouncing the ball farther laterally from the basin's center.
Critical slowing down is the time required for the system to return to its attractor after a perturbation. Other things being equal, the farther the ball
bounces from the basin's center, the longer it will take to return. If the ball
bounces around enough (producing increases in both of these indicators),
the chance of a shift to a new basin—a phase change—becomes greater.

If you think of the variability caused by changes in the surface configuration (rather than changes in the amount of jostling), you get a picture
that's a little different. Think of the basin the ball is in as flattening out.
The flatter it gets, the easier it is for the ball to roll away from the center
(critical fluctuations), and the slower is the ball to return to the center
(critical slowing down), because the basin's attraction is now weaker
(Fig. 1.16). The flatter the basin gets (given even minimal shaking of the
surface), the more likely is a phase change. The sense conveyed by this
portrayal is that of one attractor fading out of existence, leading the ball
to shift to another one.

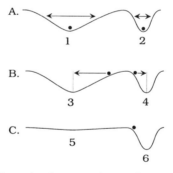

FIG. 1.16. A. Given a little random bouncing (energy from outside the system),
there is more potential for movement away from the center of an attractor that
has a broad, flat basin (1) than an attractor that has a narrower, steeper basin (2).
This is one marker of variability near a phase change, called critical fluctuation.
B. Given a perturbation away from the center of the basin (but not removal
from the basin), it will take longer for the system to return to the attractor with
a broad, flat basin (3) than an attractor with a narrower, steeper basin (4). This
is a second marker of variability near a phase change, called critical slowing
down. C. If the effective basin of one attractor becomes more shallow (5), so
that it no longer attracts (thus greatly increasing both markers of variability),
the system at some point shifts to an alternate attractor (6). Thus, variability
precedes a phase change.

Goals as Attractors

The themes of dynamic systems thinking outlined here have had several applications in personality–social and even clinical psychology. As Vallacher and Nowak (1997) pointed out, an easy and intuitive application of the attractor concept to human behavior is to link it with the goal concept. Goals are points around which behavior is regulated. Thus, people spend much of their time doing things that keep their behavior in close proximity to their goals. It seems reasonable to suggest, then, that goals represent a kind of attractor. Further, if an attractor represents a goal, it seems reasonable that a repeller would represent an anti-goal.

The idea of attractors and trajectories within phase space provides an interesting complement and supplement to the idea that behavior is guided by feedback processes regarding goals and anti-goals. However, we don't think the ideas about phase space *replace* the ideas about feedback and goals. Rather, the ideas mesh. Each provides something the other lacks.

Movement toward a goal isn't really an automatic gravitational drift, once the goal is identified (no matter how convenient that image). The feedback model provides a mechanism through which goal-directed activity is managed, a mechanism that isn't in the phase-space model. The phase-space model, however, suggests ways of thinking about how goals diverge and how people shift among multiple goals over time, issues that aren't dealt with as easily in terms of feedback processes.

That is, think of the landscape of chaotic attractors, but think about there being *many* different basins attracting behavior rather than just two or three. This seems to capture rather well the sense of human behavior. Since no attractor basin in this system ever becomes a point attractor or a cyclic attractor, behavior tends toward one goal then another, never being completely captured by any one goal. The person does one thing for a while, then something else. The goals are all predictable—in the sense that they all exist and influence the person over time, an influence that's highly predictable when aggregated across time (Epstein, 1979). But the shifts from one activity to another occur unpredictably (thus being chaotic).

In fact, let us join this characterization of goals with the soup pot model of mind we introduced earlier. To do this, we're going to take a three-dimensional attractor landscape and flip it on its vertical axis (fasten your seat belt). Instead of basins, we now have mounds, each representing an attractor (Fig. 1.17). In this example, each mound represents activity in the mind bearing on attaining a particular goal. Each mound rises closer to the surface as the activation of its elements increases (by spreading

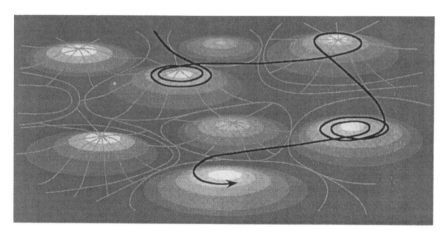

FIG. 1.17. Three-dimensional attractor landscape, with mounds instead of basins. As each mound rises closer to the surface (due to activation of its elements), the person's behavior shifts to that attractor, and effort toward that goal becomes focal. The result is a continuing shifting of overt activity from one target goal to another.

activation in memory). As a given mound (goal) reaches consciousness, the person's behavior shifts to that attractor, and effort toward that goal becomes focal (Fig. 1.17).

Other Simple Applications of Dynamic Systems

The themes of dynamic systems also suggest some other possibilities. We touch briefly on a few of them here (for broader treatments see Carver & Scheier, 1998; Nowak & Vallacher, 1999; Vallacher & Nowak, 1994).

Another example is Vallacher and Nowak's (1997) discussion of the nature of attitudes. They noted that social psychologists tend to treat attitudes as points on bipolar dimensions of like-versus-dislike, despite the fact we know this is an oversimplification. As Cacioppo and Berntson (1994) pointed out, most attitudes have a mix of positive and negative feelings embedded within them. It's misleading to average the positives and the negatives to create a summary score. Vallacher and Nowak go a step further, arguing that there's also a temporal variation in a subjective opinion. It occurs as a function of the continuously varying relative activation in memory of the affect-relevant nodes in memory that constitute the attitude's basis. (This view closely resembles a position that was articulated earlier, for different reasons, by Wyer, 1973.)

As seen from this view, an attitude might be viewed not as a point on a dimension (Fig. 1.18, A) but as a frequency distribution (Fig. 1.18, B). The distribution's mean (or mode or median) would correspond to the

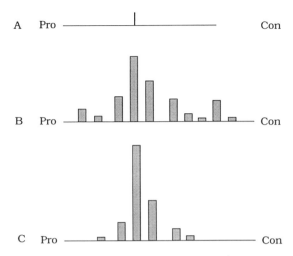

FIG. 1.18. Attitudes are often measured as points on a dimension ranging from strong approval of the attitude object to strong disapproval (A). They may, however, actually constitute accumulations of elements distributed along the dimension, with the elements forming a frequency distribution (B). An interesting aspect of this view is that people who report the same single-measure attitude may have very different frequency distributions from one another. Thus the persons portrayed in panels B and C may behave quite differently over time, though they both report the attitude portrayed in A. From "Dynamical social psychology: Chaos and Catastrophe for all," by C. S. Carver in *Psychological Inquiry, (8)* p. 117, 1997. Copyright Lawrence Erlbaum Associates.

single-point attitude that might be marked on an opinion scale ("How do you feel about professional basketball?"). The distribution around that value would reflect the extent of the diversity of the contributing elements, together with the relative frequency with which each is brought to mind when considering the attitude object (how often you feel very positive about professional basketball; how often you feel moderately positive about it; how often you feel totally neutral about it; how often you feel moderately negative about it; how often you feel very negative about it). A given attitude mark might even reflect distributions with very different ranges in different people. As Vallacher and Nowak (1997) suggested, how you feel at any moment may be a product of the chaotic dance among the elements in the frequency distribution.

The notion that attitudes represent frequency distributions of elements along a range of variability relates to the idea that traits represent not simple dimensions along which people differ, but rather a set of if-then contingencies, which are individualized to the person whose trait is being represented (Mischel & Shoda, 1995). Each of these contingencies may represent a frequency distribution of alternative actions, given a particular context. The resulting picture of traits (see also Buss & Craik, 1983) seems similar in some respects to Vallacher and Nowak's picture of attitudes.

Thus, it seems reasonable to imagine a person who acts in an extraverted manner much of the time but is introverted during another fairly large portion of time, either because of variations in context (Mischel & Shoda, 1995) or because of temporal cycles (cf. Vallacher & Nowak's, 1997, discussion of periodic attractors). A person can deeply enjoy the process of being engaged with groups of others and just as deeply enjoy being immersed—alone—in a book. This view of personality seems somewhat at odds with traditional trait theories, but it's in good accord with a view in which qualities of persons are not strictly dimensional but instead reflect chaotic variability.

Variability and Change

Several of the applications of dynamic systems ideas focus directly on the idea of variability as a harbinger of change. This is an idea that has proven useful enough in developmental psychology that it now appears there with some regularity. For example, Siegler (1994) noted that cognitive variability typically precedes changes that represent important steps in cognitive development. In studies of children's discovery of new strategies, the trials immediately before the discovery and the trial when the discovery is made often involve "especially variable behavior—disfluencies, unclear references, long pauses, and unusual gestures" (Siegler, 1994, p. 3). Thelen (1995) referred to this function of variability with the phrase "exploration and selection."

Another application of the variability notion comes from the work of Vallacher and Kaufman (1996), who studied what happens when people identify their behavior at low levels and are about to drift to a higher level. People construing their actions in low-level terms are understanding their behavior in terms of goals that are restricted in scope and are brief and transitory in use. In trying to reach a higher order understanding, they use the low-level information as raw material. This raw material can be packaged in many ways (using bits of what's available in different mixes), each of which would give a higher order identification. Vallacher and Kaufman (1996) argued that before adopting a higher order identification, many possible higher identifications come and go in brief bursts (thus a high degree of variability) until one emerges and takes hold in the person's mind. Results of a study they described were consistent with this reasoning.

ISSUES

In this section we raise two issues. One of them is quite narrow, extrapolating directly from the work that we just discussed. The other is much broader.

A Specific Issue: Variability and Switching of Attractors

Vallacher and Kaufman's argument, that when people move from a lower to a higher identification there's a burst of chaotic switching among images with one emerging as the adopted construal, raises some follow-up questions. For example, what happens when a person shifts from one high-level act identification to another? Such a lateral shift can happen either when a person reconstrues an ongoing activity in a new light (I'm not really in a policy discussion with my boss, I'm being told to spy on my office mates), or when a person stops one activity to take up another (that letter's done, now let me turn to this review I've been putting off). It's tempting to infer that a similar burst of mental turbulence should arise between the one construal and the other.

This inference seems particularly apt for cases in which a person's ongoing activity is reconceptualized while it's taking place. After all, a reconstrual presumably takes place precisely *because* information at a low level doesn't fit well the picture of the current construal. Perhaps an accumulation of inconsistent low-level information causes the person to drop briefly to the lower level, mentally re-shake the package of elements (now a package somewhat different from the one previously considered), and let the multiple possible higher level identities flash chaotically past until one identity fits the package well enough to emerge and lock in.

This portrayal of shifting construal of behavior is one in which periods of clear identification of one's goals are punctuated by brief bursts of what amounts to mental static. If so, these bursts of static must in many cases be quite brief, since people do sometimes shift abruptly from one activity to another. In other cases, the static may not be so brief at all. Using words such as *turbulence, static*, or *chaos* to refer to this experience is in a way very misleading. These periods may not feel subjectively like turbulence at all because their occurrence is quite familiar. The chaos may feel instead like "implicit decision making"—which it is, after all, even though the form Vallacher and Kaufman assume for the process isn't much like traditional views of decision making.

Thinking about consciousness from this point of view—as a process that jumps repeatedly from one construal to another—suggests an interesting possibility. In describing the hierachical model of goals that was outlined earlier in the chapter, we're often struck by the sense that self-regulation at the program level has a sequential or digital feel, whereas it has more of a continuous or analog feel at both higher and lower levels. We've often wondered why that should be so.

Conceiving of consciousness as jumping from level to level and from one construal to another provides an unusual angle on this question. Perhaps sequentiality is a property of consciousness, rather than of programicity. Consciousness often resides at the program level due to the many decisions that have to be made there. Perhaps our question about the nature of control at the program level arose because we've focused on the wrong part of what we were looking at. Perhaps consciousness provides a sequential readout of whatever is in its lens at that moment (which may itself be analog at all levels of abstraction).

Of some interest, in this regard, is Bargh's (1997) argument that consciousness serves the function of "fitting a parallel mind to a serial world." That is, many kinds of self-regulation are taking place simultaneously within the person, but the time line of reality is linear. Only one thing can be focal at any given moment. This characterization of the nature and role of consciousness seems quite consistent with the line of speculation we just advanced.

Is Dynamic Systems a Better View of Behavior?

Let us now turn briefly to a very broad issue. Proponents of dynamic-systems models sometimes imply (or even assert directly) that these models are superior to preexisting models for several reasons. For example, these models deal naturally with the idea that there are nonlinearities in relations among variables. However, as we noted earlier in this section, interactions also embody nonlinear relations. Thus, there perhaps has been more dynamic-systems thinking in contemporary social and personality psychology than was apparent (see also commentaries following Vallacher & Nowak, 1997).

Another argument that's sometimes made is that these models are explanatory, in contrast to other models, which are only descriptive. But is this really true? There's a great deal of emphasis in these models on the idea that attractors form and that the behavior of the system can be described in terms of movement from one attractor to another. But only occasionally is there any discussion of what the attractor really *is*, or why the system spends so much of its time in the attractor's vicinity, or why the movement from one attractor to another occurs (other than to say that variability makes it more likely to fall out of one basin into the next). Sometimes it's suggested that a self-organization tendency by itself is reason enough for these things to happen, but some of us find that not very satisfying (see also commentary by Aslin, 1993, especially p. 394). As these ideas gain currency in psychology, it will be important to keep straight what's descriptive and what's explanatory about them.

THEME: CATASTROPHE THEORY

Another set of ideas that's been around for a while but seems to be re-emerging in influence is catastrophe theory, a mathematical model focusing on creation of discontinuities, bifurcations, or splittings (Brown, 1995; Saunders, 1980; Stewart & Peregoy, 1983; Thom, 1975; van der Maas & Molenaar, 1992; Woodcock & Davis, 1978; Zeeman, 1976, 1977). A *catastrophe* occurs when a small change in one variable produces an abrupt (and usually large) change in another variable.

An abrupt change implies nonlinearity or discontinuity. This focus on nonlinearity is one of several themes that catastrophe theory shares with dynamic systems theory, though the two bodies of thought have different origins (and, indeed, some view them as quite different from each other—see chap. 2 of Kelso, 1995). You might think of the discontinuity that's the focus of catastrophe theory as reflecting "the sudden disappearance of one attractor and its basin, combined with the dominant emergence of another attractor" (Brown, 1995, p. 51).

Several types of catastrophe exist (Brown, 1995; Saunders, 1980; Woodcock & Davis, 1978). The one that's been considered most frequently regarding human behavior is the *cusp catastrophe*, in which two control parameters influence an outcome. Figure 1.19 portrays its three-dimensional surface. The control parameters are x and z, and y is the outcome. At low values of z, the surface of the figure expresses a roughly linear relationship between x and y. As x increases, so does y. As z (the second control parameter) increases, the relationship between x and y becomes less linear. It first shifts toward something like a step function. With further increase in z, the x–y relationship becomes even more clearly discontinuous—the outcome is either on the top surface or on the bottom. Thus, changes in z cause a change in the way x relates to y.

We said just earlier that the theme of nonlinearity was one notion that linked catastrophe theory to dynamic systems. Another is the idea of sensitive dependence on initial conditions. The cusp catastrophe displays this characteristic nicely. Consider the portion of Fig. 1.19 where z has low values and x displays a continuous relation to y, the system's behavior.

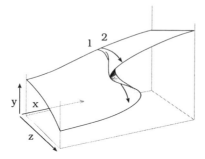

FIG. 1.19. Three-dimensional depiction of a cusp catastrophe. Variables x and z are control parameters, y is the system's behavior, the dependent variable. The catastrophe shows sensitive dependence on initial conditions. Where z is low, points 1 and 2 are nearly the same on x. If you project these points forward on the surface (with increases in z), you find that they move in parallel until the cusp begins to emerge. The lines are separated by the formation of the cusp and project to completely different regions of the surface.

Points 1 and 2 on x are nearly identical, but not quite. As z increases and we follow the movement of these points forward on the surface, for a while they track each other closely, until suddenly they begin to be separated by the fold in the catastrophe. At higher levels of z, one track ultimately projects to the upper region of the surface, the other to the lower region. Thus, a very slight initial difference results in a substantial difference farther along.

Hysteresis

The preceding description also hinted at an interesting and important feature of a catastrophe known as *hysteresis*. There are several ways to get a handle on what this term means. A simple characterization is that at some levels of z there's a kind of foldover in the middle of the x–y relationship. A region of x exists in which there's more than one value of y. Another way to characterize the hysteresis is that two regions of this surface are attractors and one is a repeller (Brown, 1995). This unstable area is illustrated in Fig. 1.20. The dashed-line portion of Fig. 1.20 that lies between values a and b on the x axis—the region where the fold is going backward—repels trajectories (Brown, 1995), whereas the areas near values c and d attract trajectories. To put it more simply, you can't *be* on the dashed part of this surface.

Yet another way of characterizing hysteresis is captured by the statement that the system's behavior depends on the system's recent history (Brown, 1995; Nowak & Lewenstein, 1994). That is, as you move into the

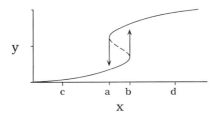

FIG. 1.20. A cusp catastrophe exhibits a region of hysteresis (between values a and b on the x axis), in which x has two stable values of y (the solid lines) and one unstable value (the dotted line that cuts backward in the middle of the figure). The region represented by the dotted line repels trajectories, whereas the stable regions (those surrounding values c and d on the x axis) attract trajectories. Traversing the zone of hysteresis from the left of this figure results in an abrupt shift (at value b on the x axis) from the lower to the upper portion of the surface (right arrow). Traversing the zone of hysteresis from the right of this figure results in an abrupt shift (at value a on the x axis) from the upper to the lower portion of the surface (left arrow). Thus, the disjunction between portions of the surface occurs at two different values of x, depending on the starting point.

zone of variable x that lies between points a and b in Fig. 1.20, it matters which side of the figure you're coming from. If the system is moving from point c into the zone of hysteresis, it stays on the bottom surface until it reaches point b, where it jumps to the top surface. If the system is moving from d into the zone of hysteresis, it stays on the top surface until it reaches point a, where it jumps to the bottom surface.

Another link between the ideas of dynamic systems and catastrophe theory concerns the notion of variability surrounding phase transitions (although see Kelso, 1995, for a different view). In the cusp catastrophe, the zone of hysteresis is a region in which two different states occur with equal frequency. Imagine you're studying a behavior displaying a cusp catastrophe. You're studying many subjects, and each subject contributes only one instance of the behavior (so you aren't getting information about the behavior's history over time). Imagine your subjects vary nicely on whatever variable is the x axis. Just to make it simple, assume you have perfect assessment of the behavior of interest, and assume the behavior is perfectly related to your predictor variables, so there's no error.

If the situation you're studying has a large enough value on the z variable, there will be huge variability in your behavioral (outcome) data in the region of hysteresis. There—but only there—you'll find both large and small values of the behavior. Some people will be on the top surface, others on the bottom surface. Both surfaces exist in that region, although nowhere else. The regions to the right and to the left of the hysteresis, which we earlier referred to as attractors, have little variability. Thus, between-subject variability appears to be large at points of bifurcation or phase transition between one attractor and another. A similar argument can be made for within-subject variability across multiple instances of behavior (Carver & Scheier, 1998).

Some Applications of Catastrophe Theory

How does catastrophe theory apply to the human behaviors of most interest to personality and social psychologists? Several applications of these ideas have been made during the 1990s, and several others seem obvious candidates for future study.

The first serious application of catastrophe theory by a social psychologist apparently came in an article published in 1980 by Abe Tesser (1980b). He described there two potential influences on a romantic relationship: attraction toward the partner and social pressures against the partner (e.g., when the partner is the "wrong" race, social class, or religion). When social pressures are low, dating-related behavior is at the back plane of the catastrophe figure. Extent of dating activity shows a generally linear increase with attraction.

When social pressures against the relationship are high, however, dating-related behavior is at the forward plane of the figure. When attraction is low to moderate, the social pressure keeps dating activity low. When attraction is high, the social pressure is resisted and dating activity is high. In the middle range of attraction, the behavior that emerges depends on the system's prior history. When attraction that once was high fades, the model predicts that dating-related behavior will continue until (and unless) attraction slips too low. When attraction that once was low increases, the model predicts that dating-related behavior will remain low unless attraction increases beyond the region of hysteresis.

Other treatments of relationships have also incorporated the sense of a discontinuous step function, if not actually a catastrophe. Consider the forming and ending of close relationships (Baron, Amazeen, & Beek, 1994; Brickman, 1987). On first exposure to a person, you may have little thought of developing a close relationship. The sense of separateness may exist for some time, even as the relationship grows closer. At some point, however, a sense of commitment to the relationship emerges—and may do so quite suddenly (thus people speak of "falling" in love with someone they've known for some time). Once there's a sense of commitment, people view things differently—tending, for example, to put a positive interpretation on subsequent events between them (Murray &

Holmes, 1993, 1997; Murray, Holmes, & Griffin, 1996). The view that's now held is that of a relationship.

Perhaps even clearer as an abrupt transformation is the ending of a relationship. De-commitment is a critical event. As long as the perception is one of a committed relationship, the person keeps viewing events in those terms. After the line is crossed and the commitment is gone, however, everything changes (cf. Gottman, 1993; Rusbult, 1980, 1983; Rusbult & Martz, 1995).

It seems likely that emergence of commitment and de-commitment often occur at different points on the continuum of satisfaction in the relationship (cf. Rusbult, 1983). A relationship can be quite satisfying before a sense of commitment to it arises. On the opposite side, people often will endure relationships that are quite dissatisfying—with lack of communication, infidelity, even emotional and physical abuse—before breaking off, particularly when the person sees the relationship as important (Rusbult & Martz, 1995). This difference illustrates the tendency to hold onto a given perceptual organization as long as possible, until it can no longer be sustained. Is there a region of hysteresis? The question is quite intriguing.

Gottman (1993) has developed a model of the process of marital dissolution that has a good deal of resemblance to this depiction, and indeed makes explicit use of the catastrophe concept. He argues that when the balance of negativity to positivity in a couple's interaction gets too high, a cascade of processes occur, in which the individuals create implicit barriers to communication, recast their understanding of the relationship, and ultimately move to separation. But in his view more negativity is required to begin this cascade than would have been tolerated in forming the relationship in the first place.

Other candidates for examination in terms of catastrophes are easy to find. Here are a few more: Consider latitudes of acceptance and rejection in persuasion (for broader statements on how these ideas might relate to attitudes and attitude change, see Kaplowitz & Fink, 1992; Latané & Nowak, 1994). When a persuasive message deviates from the recipient's opinion but remains within the opinion range that the recipient is willing to consider (the latitude of acceptance), it has a persuasive influence. If the message is too deviant from the recipient's opinion (the latitude of rejection), it will be rejected out of hand. The fact that there's a break between these two latitudes suggests a discontinuity. But is there also a region of hysteresis?

What would happen if a persuasive message began within the latitude of acceptance and then wandered beyond it? What would happen if a persuasion attempt began in the latitude of rejection and then eased back toward the latitude of acceptance? Would there be a hysteresis, in which the initially acceptable message continued to be seen as such (even when it actually had gone outside that range) and the initially rejected message continued to be taken as such (even when it was now within the acceptable range)?

Another application concerns perseveration of beliefs. Once a person forms a belief, it's hard to change it. Once people make up their minds, information that would have had an influence if known as the belief was forming tends to be disregarded (e.g., Anderson, Lepper, & Ross, 1980). To reverse the belief now takes a larger accumulation of information contradicting the belief than would have been necessary to form an opposing belief in the first place. Is there a region of hysteresis in this phenomenon?

Yet another potential application is suggested by Martin and Tesser's (1996) analysis of rumination. They argued that rumination constitutes implicit problem solving and that it occurs in the service of an eventual discrepancy reduction. This argument leads to the further idea that there's a balance between action and rumination (Carver, 1996b), such that they have the same eventual goal but tend to occur in different circumstances (see Fig. 1.21). Action dominates when there are no obstacles or when obstacles are manageable. Rumination dominates when the action is fully thwarted. Presumably there's a grey area in the middle where some of each probably goes on.

An interesting question is whether this grey area displays hysteresis. Is a person who's stuck in rumination more likely to remain there when the situation changes to a point where action is more effective? Is a person who's struggling behaviorally to overcome obstacles likely to keep struggling past the point where it would make more sense to step back and think things over?

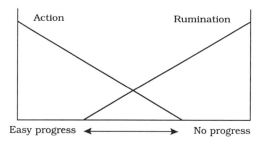

FIG. 1.21. When a person is self-regulating with respect to a goal and progress is relatively easy, action and the thoughts that accompany action dominate the discrepancy-reduction effort. When progress is thwarted, rumination dominates.

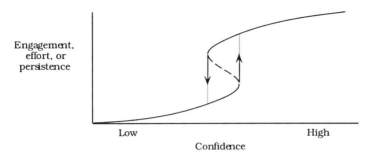

FIG. 1.22. A catastrophe model of effort versus disengagement.

Effort Versus Disengagement

What we think is another potentially important application of the catastrophe concept concerns the bifurcation between engagement in effort and giving up. Earlier, we pointed to a set of theories that assume such a disjunction (Brehm & Self, 1989; Kukla, 1972; Wortman & Brehm, 1975). In all those models (as in ours), there's a point at which effort seems fruitless and the person stops trying. Earlier, we simply emphasized that the models all assumed a discontinuity. Now we look at the discontinuity more closely and suggest that the phenomena addressed by these theories may embody a catastrophe.

Figure 1.22 shows a cross section of a cusp catastrophe seen earlier as Fig. 1.20. This figure displays a region of hysteresis in the engagement versus disengagement function. In that region, where task demands are close to people's perceived limits to perform, there should be greater variability in effort or engagement, as some people are on the top surface of the catastrophe, others on the bottom surface. Some people would be continuing to exert efforts, at the same point where others would be exhibiting a giving-up response.

Recall that the catastrophe figure also conveys the sense that the history of the behavior matters. A person who enters the region of hysteresis from the direction of high confidence (who starts out confident but confronts many cues indicating otherwise) will continue to display efforts and engagement, even as the situational cues imply less and less basis for confidence. A person who enters that region from the direction of low confidence (who starts out doubtful but confronts cues indicating otherwise) will continue to display little effort, even as the situational cues imply more and more basis for confidence.

This model helps indicate why it can be so difficult to get someone with strong and chronic doubts about success in some domain of behavior to exert real effort and engagement in that domain. It also suggests

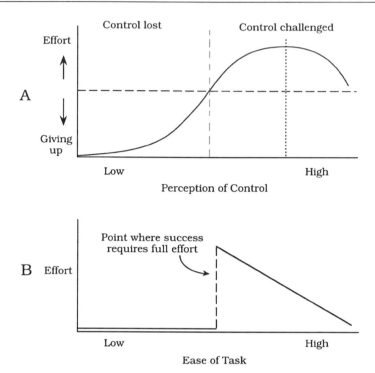

FIG. 1.23. Slightly modified depictions of (A) Wortman and Brehm's (1975) model of helplessness and reactance, and (B) Brehm and Self's (1989) model of effort (which for this purpose is essentially the same as Kukla's, 1972, model).

why a confident person is so rarely put off by encountering difficulties in the domain where the confidence lies. To put it in terms of broader views about life in general, it helps show why optimists tend to stay optimistic and pessimists tend to stay pessimistic, even when the current circumstances of the two sorts of people are identical (i.e., in the region of hysteresis).

Figure 1.23 shows a slightly simplified version of the Wortman and Brehm (1975) model (flipped horizontally to be on a scale that's directionally similar to that of Fig. 1.22) and the Brehm and Self (1989) model (which, for this discussion, is the same as the Kukla, 1972, model).[5] These functions both show bifurcations between two classes of response. As

---

[5]It should be noted that the x axes of these various models do not represent quite the same variables, although the variables are related to one another. Perceived task difficulty influences confidence (Brehm & Self, 1989), as does perceived facility at the task (Kukla, 1972) and extent of threat to control (Wortman & Brehm, 1975). Although none of these variables is a complete determinant of confidence, they all are related to confidence closely enough to warrant our treating them as equivalent for purposes of this exercise.

drawn by their authors, neither has a region of hysteresis. Is that feature—missing from the diagrams—present in the phenomena addressed by the theories? We think a plausible case can be made that it is.

The Wortman and Brehm model (panel A) is actually quite reminiscent of the middle stage of the development of the catastrophe surface, at the point where something like a step function has begun to emerge, but the region of hysteresis hasn't yet come to exist. If we clipped off the part of the graph to the right of the dotted vertical line, the resemblance would be even more striking. But what about the hysteresis? We suspect that a person who enters the situation with the belief of no control will continue to show little effort even when control begins to emerge. We also suspect that a person struggling with a threat to control will continue to struggle even when control goes. These effects of behavioral history would create a hysteresis, rendering this function very similar to the catastrophe.

The Brehm and Self model (panel B) differs in a number of ways from panel A and from Fig. 1.22, but we think a case can be made that a region of hysteresis may exist here as well. The critical issue may be the ambiguity of the situation the person is facing. The figure assumes the person knows the point at which maximum effort is required, but this is unlikely to always be true. A person who begins with a task that's far too hard to perform won't engage in serious effort. But if the task changes so that success is now possible, how will the person know it, if only minimal effort is being exerted? Not knowing, why would the person try harder? A person who begins with a task that's challenging but doable will exert strong effort. But how will this person know if the task demands change so that they exceed his maximum effort, unless he continues to try? In short, it appears there is good potential here for a region of hysteresis.

One remaining difference between both models in Fig. 1.23 and the catastrophe in Fig. 1.22 should be noted. The models in Fig. 1.23 both show a downturn at the right of the figures. The catastrophe does not. There are several possible reasons for this difference, and we aren't sure what interpretation is best. One way of thinking about this difference is to say that the catastrophe surface applies when the person confronts obstacles. If the person is confident about overcoming the obstacle, engagement is high. This view was implicit in our discussion regarding the Wortman and Brehm figure. In that figure, effort is high only when there's threat to control. If it were the case that the catastrophe surface depicts responses to adversity, rather than behavior in general, the far-right portion of Fig. 1.23 panel A would be irrelevant to the discussion, because there's no adversity there.

Two further points about these figures. First, no one has studied the processes of effort and disengagement in a truly parametric manner that would allow plotting the full range of the figures. Most work on the Wortman–Brehm (1975) model chose two points in the range of threat to control. Brehm, Wright, and coworkers have typically chosen three points on the range of task difficulty: easy, demanding but possible, and too hard to bother with. The exact shape of the function represented by these figures still isn't well known.

Second, keep in mind that the catastrophe cross section (Fig. 1.22) is the picture that emerges under catastrophe theory *only after a clear region of hysteresis has begun to develop* (Carver, 1997b). Farther back, the catastrophe model is more of a step function. An implication is that it's important to engage the control variable that's responsible for bringing out the bifurcation in the catastrophe surface. It may be that, in research bearing on this set of issues, this variable is at only a low-to-moderate level. If so, the hysteresis would be less observable, even if the research procedures were otherwise suitable to observe it.

What *is* the control variable that induces the bifurcation? We think that in the motivational models under discussion—and perhaps much more broadly—the control parameter is *importance*. Tesser (1980b) pointed to social pressure as a control variable. Social pressure is one force that can make a behavior or a decision important, but we think social pressure is only one of a broader set of pressures. Importance arises from several sources, but there's a common thread among events seen as important. They demand mental resources. We suspect that almost any strong pressure that demands resources (time pressure, self-imposed pressure) will induce similar bifurcating effects.

THEME: INSIGHTS INTO PROBLEMS IN SELF-REGULATION

A final theme of this chapter is that the principles used to examine the normal self-regulation of behavior can also give interesting insights into the nature of problems in self-regulation. Some of the insights are very simple: For example, people have to use the right channel of informational feedback or self-regulation will go awry. Others are more complex. We address here several such points (for broader treatment, see Carver & Scheier, 1998).

Behavioral Giving Up Without Full Disengagement

Many of people's problems have their roots in doubts. Doubt can cause scaling back of goals or giving up on goals. We argued earlier that giving up is an indispensable part of self-regulation, because people need to be able to retrace their steps, to back out of corners, free themselves to go elsewhere. Giving up, then, can be good. To be good, though, it must be appropriate to the circumstances and it must be thorough.

Some kinds of problems seem to reflect a failure to disengage when disengagement is the right response—when the goal is unattainable and the person knows it. Without disengaging, the person continues a cycle of sporadic effort (or mental effort), interruption from effort, the distress that comes from no progress, and confronting again the unattainable goal. It's important to be able to get past failures, to put them behind us, and move on. Sometimes moving on means disengaging from a demanding goal to take up a less demanding one. Sometimes it means giving up completely on something. Whichever the case, moving on isn't possible until the unattained goal fades into the background. The inability to give up a lost love is probably the easiest example of this problem, but there are many more.

We've frequently asserted that the surest prescription for distress is a continued commitment to a goal you believe you cannot attain. This highlights the importance of actually disengaging from a goal when it's out of reach. Sometimes people *appear* to have given up, but the quitting isn't complete (see also Snyder & Frankel, 1989). The behavioral effort has stopped, but the self-regulatory apparatus of the mind is still engaged with the lost goal. This, we think, is the source of depressed affect. If the goal can be relinquished, the source of the affect also goes away.

If it's bad to keep struggling toward goals that are unattainable, there are also drawbacks to giving up too quickly. A person who gives up whenever things get difficult is a person who will have trouble ever reaching any goal in life. Thus, persistence is important. Furthermore, if disengagement is premature and keeps you from trying your best, it's dysfunctional. It short-circuits performances that could otherwise succeed.

Sometimes people who want to quit early in the effort do quit—completely—and go on to something else. A person who moves endlessly from goal to goal to goal has a problem in life. Sometimes, however, people who want to quit stop making active efforts toward goals that are attainable, yet remain committed to the goal. This combination can be reflected in a variety of ways, including temporary self-distraction from the goal or even a temporary leaving of the scene. The goal hasn't been abandoned, but attempts to move forward are sporadic, disrupted repeatedly by withdrawal of effort and by mental disengagement. We think this pattern is nicely illustrated in literatures of test anxiety and social anxiety.

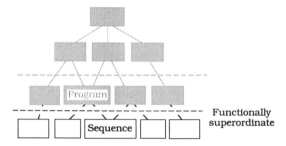

FIG. 1.24. When self-regulation at upper levels of a hierarchy have been temporarily suspended (the goals at those levels are not being attended to), goals at a lower level become functionally superordinate in guiding overt behavior. This doesn't mean that actions taken no longer have any relevance for the higher order goals, but that their impact on those higher goals won't be registered fully until attention is redirected to self-regulation at that level.

Lapses in Self-Control

Another angle on the nature of problems, suggested by the notion of hierarchicality, is that people sometimes create problems for themselves when they stop attending to the principles that define them as individuals (Fig. 1.24). Use of alcohol, for example, seems to disrupt self-regulation at principle and program levels (cf. Stuss, 1991), leaving people responsive to cues of the moment (Hull, 1981; Hull & Rielly, 1986; Ito, Miller, & Pollock, 1996; Steele & Josephs, 1990). Thus, sometimes intoxicated people do things that conflict with their principles, things they wouldn't do if they were sober.

Alcohol is one way of disrupting the functioning of the upper part of the hierarchy, but there are other ways as well. Baumeister (1988, 1991; Heatherton & Baumeister, 1991) has used the term *escape from the self* to refer to a variety of ways in which people remove themselves from higher order thought by immersing themselves in concrete sensory experiences. Typically they are prompted to do so by the realization of some failing or irreducible discrepancy at a high level of the hierarchy of the self. The immersion in the sensory experience doesn't make the problem go away, but it renders it temporarily less accessible to awareness.

Sometimes the situation is even more tangled than that. Sometimes the failure that the person is trying to avoid thinking about is the very activity that's producing the sensory immersion. Binge eating and drinking are two behaviors that serve these dual roles in many people's lives. As the person experiences a lapse in restraining the unwanted behavior, he or she experiences a sense of failure and continues the behavior as a way of obliterating the awareness of the failure. Baumeister and

Heatherton (1996) used the label *self-regulatory failure* to characterize situations such as this, in which the person simply abandons the attempt to remain focused on self-regulation at a high level of abstraction (see also Kirschenbaum, 1987).[6]

Baumeister and Heatherton focused particularly on cases in which a person gives up an effort to restrain or stifle a competing lower level impulse, such as the desire to eat or drink to excess. However, there appears to be a symmetry to this principle, in the sense that it applies to the overcoming of an inertia as well as to the restraint of an impulse (Carver & Scheier, 1998). That is, the person who has a comfortable but boring job, who wants a sense of fulfillment from work but hasn't taken steps to try to find a job that would provide it, needs to override the inertia by attending to the higher order goal. If the person fails to override the inertia, it looks like a case of self-regulatory failure.

Catastrophes and Problems in Behavior

We have come to conclude that the catastrophe principle can also be usefully applied to problems in behavior. Consider again the catastrophe surface and its meaning as a model of engagement versus giving up (Fig. 1.25, which is essentially the same as Fig. 1.19). When pressure is high, when the behavior's important (when z is large), the relationship isn't continuous. Engagement (on the top surface) yields abruptly to quitting, and quitting (on the bottom surface) yields abruptly (if at all) to engagement. For the person on the top, there's a cliff face, rather than a smooth slope—a slippery cliff to fall from, with a long drop. For the person on the bottom, effort's still possible, but for it to happen *now requires a high degree of confidence* (Fig. 1.26). That is, as importance increases, the region of hysteresis spreads wider and wider, causing its edge (where the shift to effort occurs) to be more extreme on the confidence dimension.

Many problems in living seem to fit this picture, including a variety of all-or-none, black-and-white thinking. As an obvious example, people who are crippled by doubts in an important domain of life would appear to live out that domain of life on the lower portion of the front edge of the catastrophe surface. Given their doubt, it's hard for them to make efforts at performing adequately in whatever domain the doubts exist

---

[6]Baumeister and Heatherton (1996) restricted the term *self-regulation* to instances in which the person (the self) acts to override or suppress another action tendency that has developed at a lower level of abstraction. The literature as a whole has used the term more broadly than this, to refer to a wide range of attempts to fit sensed qualities to reference values. In our view, the cases discussed by Baumeister and Heatherton are more appropriately labeled *self-control*, a term that has a long history of referring to the restraint of impulses.

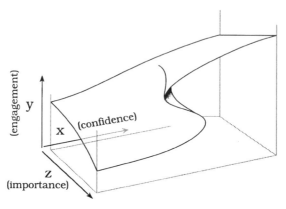

FIG. 1.25. The cusp catastrcphe (x and z are control parameters, y is the system's behavior).

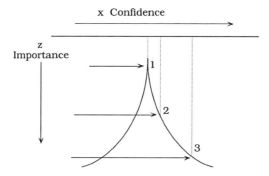

FIG. 1.26. The so-called *bifurcation* set of the cusp catastrophe in Fig. 1.25. This is essentially a "downward" projection of the two edges of the hysteresis onto a flat plane. It shows that as importance increases and the degree of hysteresis increases correspondingly, a person on the lower surface must move farther along the confidence dimension in order to shift to the top surface. With relatively low importance, the person must reach only point 1, but as importance increases, the confidence needed continues to increase (points 2 and 3).

precisely because that domain matters so much. That is, they're facing a huge challenge. To get to the point of real effort, they need to be *very* confident. Because they're not, the effort doesn't happen. They've lost the sense that they can make their lives better and feel stranded miles away from the possibility of re-engagement with life.

The catastrophe model suggests that the perceived importance of the outcome or behavioral domain is a key factor in keeping people who have this sort of outlook from taking chances. When something is seen as important, unless the person is very confident, the effort simply doesn't occur. This model thus suggests that a partial remedy for problems such as these would be to somehow move the person from the front plane of the surface farther toward the back.

Near the back, the relation between the other two variables is more gradual and more linear. When things don't matter so much, it's easier to experiment. At the back, a slight increment in confidence gains something in engagement; at the front, you have to be very, very confident before there's a real gain. At the back, the cost of doubt is gradual rather than precipitous. When it's a gentle hillside instead of a cliff, you can go up and down easily. You're able to stay engaged in the process of goal pursuit, and staying engaged is a critical determinant of success.

The key for some kinds of problems, then, may be to reduce the pressure, to get some psychological distance. We think that creating distance, taking pressure off, means (in part) moving toward the back wall of the catastrophe plane. This diminishes the emotion-evoking potential of the event. It also ameliorates the impact of doubts on actions, by making the impact of doubt less abrupt.

This line of thought has a disquieting implication, however. If the key to being able to deal with problems is to become less invested in them, the logical inference is that it's better to not care about things in your life. Many would find this idea rather disconcerting. What's the point of life, if you don't care about anything? Is it best to care a little, but not too much? Maybe there's a range of caring that's optimal, neither too much nor too little.

Another way of resolving this quandary joins the idea of catastrophe with the idea of chaotic processes. Always being at the forward edge of the catastrophe is dysfunctional; always being at the back edge may also be dysfunctional. A person who's always at the back is never really engaged in anything. Maybe, though, investment shouldn't be thought of as a constant. Maybe the reality is really a frequency distribution of moment-to-moment fluctuations among possible values, as Vallacher and Nowak (1997) argued about attitudes. With a behavior intensely important at some moments and unimportant at other moments, there would be a way to be invested but not overwhelmed.

Attractors, Minima, Stability, and Optimality

The ideas of dynamic-systems thinking also seem to have some interesting implications for thinking about problems and their alleviation. Several theorists have begun to apply these ideas to help understand the processes by which people change in response to therapeutic intervention.

Recall that in dynamic-systems models an attractor is a region of conceptual space to which a system is drawn. This concept can be used at a

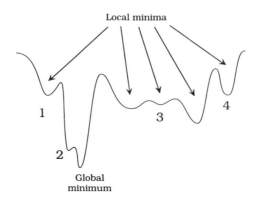

FIG. 1.27. A landscape portraying a surface in conceptual space may have several local minima: attractor basins that are less deep than the global minimum of the surface. Basins vary in depth, both overall and with respect to their immediate surround. Overall depth can be viewed as implying optimality of functioning, depth with respect to immediate bounds space as implying stability. Basin 3 is more shallow in terms of immediate surroundings than is either basin 1 or basin 4, but it's deeper overall. Thus, it's less stable but nearer the optimal. Basin 2 is even nearer the optimal, but the low ridge on one side implies that it's relatively unstable.

variety of levels of abstraction. Earlier, we used it at the level of a goal, saying that a person shifting goals could be viewed as moving from one attractor to another. In this discussion, we're going to apply the concept in a broader way. Now we're going to think of an attractor as a summary, or aggregation, of a person's overall adaptation to the world on all the dimensions of the person's life.

As we noted earlier, the stability of an attractor basin can be portrayed graphically as the depth of a basin in a surface (Fig. 1.27). A basin that's shallow compared to the ridges around it is unstable (if the landscape has other basins to shift to). A basin that's deeper is more stable. It may still be a local minimum rather than the global minimum, but it's more stable than the shallower one. Basin 3 in Fig. 1.27 is shallower than basins 1 or 4 and thus less stable than either of them. This is true despite the fact that basin 3 is at a lower level overall than is either basin 1 or 4.

The *local* stability of an attractor thus is indicated by its depth relative to the ridges on either side. There's also a way to think about the *overall* depth of a basin, which derives from thinking of the diagram in Fig. 1.27 in a different metaphor than we used earlier. Earlier, we treated it as an energy landscape, but it's sometimes viewed as an error landscape (see chap. 9 of J. R. Anderson, 1995). This latter view is particularly useful when thinking about adaptation. Thinking of the landscape as an error landscape implies that it's desirable to be in a lower basin. Thus, one might think of the overall depth of a basin (compared to the global minimum) as an index of the optimality of the pattern it represents.

Local stability and overall depth are at least partly independent. Thus, it's possible to be in a basin that's quite stable but far from optimal (basin 4). It's also possible to be in a basin that's nearly optimal but not very stable (basin 2).

The term *stability* applied to an attractor landscape refers to the likelihood of shifting from one basin to another. What psychological property corresponds to this? In a sense, it's much the same. Stability reflects the likelihood of shifting from one overall life pattern to another. A life pattern that's stable is one for which there's little tendency to change.

A life with stability is one in which the aggregate of behavior meshes with the person's life space as it's now structured. Stability may be something like the proportion of your thoughts and actions that are "adaptive and functional" with respect to your life space. If the proportion is high, the life pattern is stable and there's no tendency to change. If the proportion is lower (more actions fail to fit the constraints of the life space), the pattern is less stable. The less stable, the greater the potential for change.

Many people are poorly adapted to their niche. People feel anxiety or depression at least partly because their actions (and their mental orientations to their experiences) don't fit well into their life space. The local minima in which these people are living may be quite shallow. People in these situations may take steps to arrange their life space to minimize experienced error. A man who gets anxious whenever he's in a group, but who is able to avoid groups, is in a stable pattern. The stability is threatened only if something requires him to be with a group (e.g., his work forces him to attend a convention) or if a desire to feel a sense of belonging arises and causes a conflict with the desire to avoid the anxiety that comes from being with others. And often enough these situations do arise.

Many people are caught between the desire to hold onto a way of being that's moderately functional and a pressure to reorganize their lives in ways that will foster better adaptation. The idea of change can be threatening, partly because it means entering the unknown. So, for the most part, people cling to the existing pattern, trying to tune it a little so it works more smoothly rather than seeking fundamental change. To put it differently, they stay in their current attractor basin and try to dig it a little deeper, by changing their behaviors in small ways to fit their niche better, or by narrowing their life space to avoid situations that produce feelings of poor fit.

How can problem situations such as these be changed? The goal of therapy, broadly speaking, might be viewed as moving the person to a minimum closer to the optimal—to a new attractor, in which the problem is more fully resolved or in which global adaptation is more broadly positive than it now is. Doing this requires some reorganization of what now exists. It may require some extra-heavy shaking, maybe even jostling, of the tambourine of the person's lifespace.

It has been suggested that successful therapy involves just this sort of process (Hayes & Strauss, in press; Mahoney, 1991). Certain kinds of experiences in therapy jostle or destabilize the system (cf. Heatherton & Nichols, 1994; Miller & C'deBaca, 1994). If the system (the person) is sufficiently destabilized, it has the potential to bounce into a reorganization. The reorganization won't happen, though, unless the system is destabilized enough to get it free of the current attractor. Without enough variability within the basin, the person won't get over the borders of the local minimum he's in now.

Hayes and Strauss (in press) applied this line of reasoning to an analysis of the process and outcome of cognitive therapy for depression. They examined transcripts of therapy sessions of people in treatment, looking for evidence of destabilization. They assessed destabilization as variability in cognitive, affective, behavioral, and somatic aspects of participants' depressive patterns during the sessions. Consistent with the model, Hayes and Strauss found that periods of destabilization predicted subsequent reduction in depression.

Destabilization, Reorganization, and the Effects of Trauma

A line of thought very similar to the one underlying the Hayes and Strauss research emerges from Tedeschi and Calhoun's (1995) examination of the idea that many people—though certainly not all—experience positive consequences, even growth, after trauma. Tedeschi and Calhoun argued that the potential for growth is initiated by the traumatic event itself. They emphasized, however, that for this to occur, the event must be one "of seismic proportions," an event that shakes and partly destroys the person's world view (see also Janoff-Bulman, 1992). The choice of metaphor here is striking. Tedeschi and Calhoun weren't writing from a dynamic systems point of view, but their conceptualization shares much with it.

In their view, trauma creates (in addition to tremendous emotional distress, or perhaps even because of it) what in effect is a naturally occurring instance of the destabilization produced by therapy. Tedeschi and Calhoun suggest that growth begins with posttraumatic rumination, aimed at making sense of the world as it has just been experienced (cf. Martin & Tesser, 1996). Growth is reflected in the construction of a new, more meaningful, and more profound world view or self-view. This reconstructed viewpoint permits the person to interact with the world in a more effective and fulfilling way than before the traumatic event. The result thus is a better adaptation (an attractor basin closer to the global minimum) than existed before.

Obviously there are great differences between experiencing a trauma and entering a potentially unsettling therapy experience. However, it's remarkable how similar the models are to one another. The shaking of the system that promotes change can come from an event that the world delivers to you, it can come from a series of self-explorations, or potentially it can come from other sources. Wherever it comes from, the shaking seems to open the potential for a more adaptive reorganization of the self.

ISSUE

Attractor Landscape: Model or Only Metaphor?

The preceding discussion, in which we used an attractor landscape to represent a person's entire life space, raises another issue, although this issue could well have been raised earlier, in the section on dymanic systems. The issue is this: To what extent is this attractor landscape a useful model versus being simply an appealing metaphor?

As an image, the attractor landscape has an intuitive appeal: In the real world, things roll down hills and tend to settle into valleys, so why not here? These landscapes have been used by various people at widely differing levels of abstraction, so it seems a very flexible manner of representation. Yet its very flexibility raises a caution flag. How sure can one be about the meaning of the local stability of an attractor? When N variables have been aggregated into a single horizontal dimension, what exactly is the meaning of a shift from one basin to another? What's involved when the landscape's surface shifts in form (something we've largely avoided getting into here)?

We have found the image useful and the metaphor appealing, but it's hard to know how literally to view it. Remember that this depiction arose as a way of portraying a multiattractor system. It had a literal meaning. But the meaning has become more and more metaphoric as we travel farther and farther from the landscape's origins. This issue is not going to go away any time soon. Indeed, it's likely to become more pressing, as more and more people use these landscapes to illustrate their arguments.

CONCLUDING COMMENT

In this chapter, we have presented a series of themes that we think are important in conceptualizing human self-regulation. We argued first that behavior is goal directed and feedback controlled and that the goals underling behavior form a hierarchy of abstractness. We argued that the experience of affect also arises from a process of feedback control, but one that deals with a different aspect of the temporality within which all of life plays itself out. We argued that confidence and doubt yield patterns of persistence versus giving up and that these two responses to adversity form a dichotomy in behavior. These ideas have been part of our work for some time.

We then turned to ideas that are newer. We considered the theme of emergence of behavior, as opposed to controlled production of behavior, and concluded that both influences are important. We argued that the ideas of dynamic systems theory and catastrophe theory represent useful tools for the construal of behavior. In our view, they supplement rather than replace the tools now in use, and we see many ways in which those ideas mesh with the ideas presented earlier. We closed by considering the implications of some of the principles raised for conceptualizing problems in effective self-regulation.

All of these themes raise issues and questions for further consideration. The picture presented here is surely not complete. In a few cases, the issues that emerge were so intertangled with the themes themselves that we didn't even try to peel them apart. In some parts of the chapter, a good deal of what we've said reduces to educated speculation. But speculation is a useful starting point, and unresolved issues serve to make a body of thought interesting.

In developing the themes of this chapter, we've drawn on ideas from disparate sources. At the same time, however, we've tried to continue to follow the thread of the logical model from which we started. Along the way we've realized that good ideas sometimes can be found in what appear to be unlikely places. We've also realized how satisfying it is to discover similar insights in bodies of thought that have very different origins. We've enjoyed seeing ideas from divergent sources and perspectives come together and complement each other, and we hope you've been able to feel some of that satisfaction and enjoyment too.

ACKNOWLEDGMENT

Preparation of this article was facilitated by NCI grants CA64710 and CA64711.

All figures other than 1.1, 1.12, 1.17, 1.18, and 1.21 are from *On the Self-Regulation of Behavior*, by C. S. Carver and M. F. Scheier, 1998. Cambridge University Press. Reprinted with permission.

REFERENCES

Abramson, L. Y., Metalsky, G. I., & Alloy, L. B. (1989). Hopelessness depression: A theory-based subtype of depression. *Psychological Review, 96*, 358–372.

Abramson, L. Y., Seligman, M. E. P., & Teasdale, J. D. (1978). Learned helplessness in humans: Critique and reformulation. *Journal of Abnormal Psychology, 87*, 49–74.

Ahrens, A. H., & Haaga, A. F. (1993). The specificity of attributional style and expectations to positive and negative affectivity, depression, and anxiety. *Cognitive Therapy and Research, 17*, 83–98.

Allen, J. J., Iacono, W. G., Depue, R. A., & Arbisi, X. (1993). Regional EEG asymmetries in bipolar affective disorder before and after phototherapy. *Biological Psychiatry, 33*, 642–646.

Anderson, C. A., Lepper, M. R., & Ross, L. (1980). Perseverance of social theories: The role of explanation in the persistence of discredited information. *Journal of Personality and Social Psychology, 39*, 1037–1049.

Anderson, J. R. (1990). *The adaptive character of thought*. Hillsdale, NJ: Lawrence Erlbaum Associates.

Aslin, R. N. (1993). Commentary: The strange attractiveness of dynamic systems to development. In L. D. Smith & E. Thelen (Eds.), *A dynamic systems approach to development: Applications* (pp. 385–399). Cambridge, MA: MIT Press.

Atkinson, J. W., & Birch, D. (1970). *The dynamics of action*. New York: Wiley.

Austin, J. T., & Vancouver, J. B. (1996). Goal constructs in psychology: Structure, process, and content. *Psychological Bulletin, 120*, 338–375.

Baltes, M. M., & Baltes, P. B. (Eds.). (1986). *Aging and the psychology of control*. Hillsdale, NJ: Lawrence Erlbaum Associates.

Bandura, A. (1977). Self-efficacy: Toward a unifying theory of behavior change. *Psychological Review, 84*, 191–215.

Bandura, A. (1982). Self-efficacy mechanism in human agency. *American Psychologist, 37*, 122–147.

Bandura, A. (1986). *Social foundations of thought and action: A social cognitive theory*. Englewood Cliffs, NJ: Prentice-Hall.

Bandura, A. (1989). Self-regulation of motivation and action through internal standards and goal systems. In L. A. Pervin (Ed.), *Goal concepts in personality and social psychology* (pp. 19–85). Hillsdale, NJ: Lawrence Erlbaum Associates.

Bargh, J. A. (1997). The automaticity of everyday life. In R. S. Wyer, Jr. (Ed.), *Advances in social cognition* (Vol. 10, pp. 1–61). Mahwah, NJ: Lawrence Erlbaum Associates.

Barker, R. G., & Associates. (1978). *Habitats, environments, and human behavior*. San Francisco: Jossey-Bass.

Baron, R. M., Amazeen, P. G., & Beek, P. J. (1994). Local and global dynamics of social relations. In R. R. Vallacher & A. Nowak (Eds.), *Dynamical systems in social psychology* (pp. 111–138). San Diego: Academic Press.

Barton, S. (1994). Chaos, self-organization, and psychology. *American Psychologist, 49*, 5–14.

Baumeister, R. F. (1988). Masochism as escape from self. *Journal of Sex Research, 25*, 28–59.

Baumeister, R. F. (1989). The problem of life's meaning. In D. M. Buss & N. Cantor (Eds.), *Personality psychology: Recent trends and emerging directions* (pp. 138–148). New York: Springer-Verlag.

Baumeister, R. F. (1991). *Escaping the self*. New York: Basic Books.

Baumeister, R. F., & Heatherton, T. F. (1996). Self-regulation failure: An overview. *Psychological Inquiry, 7*, 1–5.

Beck, A. T. (1972). *Depression: Causes and treatment*. Philadelphia: University of Pennsylvania Press.

Beckmann, J., & Gollwitzer, P. M. (1987). Deliberative versus implemental states of mind: The issue of impartiality in pre- and postdecisional information processing. *Social Cognition, 5*, 259–279.

Bertenthal, B. I., Campos, J. J., & Kermoian, R. (1994). An epigenetic perspective on the development of self-produced locomotion and its consequences. *Current Directions in Psychological Science, 3*, 140–145.

Block, J. (1996). Some jangly remarks on Baumeister and Heatherton. *Psychological Inquiry, 7*, 28–32.

Brehm, J. W., & Self, E. A. (1989). The intensity of motivation. *Annual Review of Psychology, 40*, 109–131.

Brickman, P. (1987). *Commitment, conflict, and caring*. Englewood Cliffs, NJ: Prentice-Hall.

Brown, C. (1995). *Chaos and catastrophe theories* (Quantitative applications in the social sciences, no. 107). Thousand Oaks, CA: Sage.

Brunstein, J. C. (1993). Personal goals and subjective well-being: A longitudinal study. *Journal of Personality and Social Psychology, 65*, 1061–1070.

Burger, J. M. (1989). Negative reactions to increases in perceived personal control. *Journal of Personality and Social Psychology, 56*, 246–256.

Buss, D. M., & Craik, K. H. (1983). The act frequency approach to personality. *Psychological Review, 90*, 105–126.

Cacioppo, J. T., & Berntson, G. G. (1994). Relationship between attitudes and evaluative space: A critical review, with emphasis on the separability of positive and negative substrates. *Psychological Bulletin, 115*, 401–423.

Cacioppo, J. T., & Petty, R. E. (1980). The effects of orienting task on differential hemispheric EEG activation. *Neuropsychologia, 18*, 675–683.

Cantor, N., & Kihlstrom, J. F. (1987). *Personality and social intelligence.* Englewood Cliffs, NJ: Prentice-Hall.

Carver, C. S. (1979). A cybernetic model of self-attention processes. *Journal of Personality and Social Psychology, 37*, 1251–1281.

Carver, C. S. (1996a). Emergent integration in contemporary personality psychology. *Journal of Research in Personality, 30*, 319–334.

Carver, C. S. (1996b). Goal engagement and the human experience. In R. S. Wyer, Jr. (Ed.), *Advances in social cognition* (Vol. 9, pp. 49–61). Mahwah, NJ: Lawrence Erlbaum Associates.

Carver, C. S. (1997a). Associations to automaticity. In R. S. Wyer, Jr. (Ed.), *Advances in social cognition* (Vol. 10, pp. 95–103). Mahwah, NJ: Lawrence Erlbaum Associates.

Carver, C. S. (1997b). Dynamical social psychology: Chaos and catastrophe for all. *Psychological Inquiry, 8*, 110–119.

Carver, C. S. (1997c). The IE scale confounds internal locus of control with expectancies of positive outcomes. *Personality and Social Psychology Bulletin, 23*, 580–585.

Carver, C. S., Blaney, P. H., & Scheier, M. F. (1979a). Focus of attention, chronic expectancy, and responses to a feared stimulus. *Journal of Personality and Social Psychology, 37*, 1186–1195.

Carver, C. S., Blaney, P. H., & Scheier, M. F. (1979b). Reassertion and giving up: The interactive role of self-directed attention and outcome expectancy. *Journal of Personality and Social Psychology, 37*, 1859–1870.

Carver, C. S., & Humphries, C. (1981). Havana daydreaming: A study of self-consciousness and the negative reference group among Cuban Americans. *Journal of Personality and Social Psychology, 40*, 545–552.

Carver, C. S., Lawrence, J. W., & Scheier, M. F. (in press). Self-discrepancies and affect: Incorporating the role of feared selves. *Personality and Social Psychology Bulletin.*

Carver, C. S., Peterson, L. M., Follansbee, D. J., & Scheier, M. F. (1983). Effects of self-directed attention on performance and persistence among persons high and low in test anxiety. *Cognitive Therapy and Research, 7*, 333–354.

Carver, C. S., & Scheier, M. F. (1981). *Attention and self-regulation: A control-theory approach to human behavior.* New York: Springer-Verlag.

Carver, C. S., & Scheier, M. F. (1982). Outcome expectancy, locus of attributions for expectancy, and self-directed attention as determinants of evaluations and performance. *Journal of Experimental Social Psychology, 18*, 184–200.

Carver, C. S., & Scheier, M. F. (1990a). Principles of self-regulation: Action and emotion. In E. T. Higgins, R. M. Sorrentino (Eds.), *Handbook of Motivation and Cognition: Foundations of social behavior* (Vol. 2, pp. 3–52). New York: Guilford.

Carver, C. S., & Scheier, M. F. (1990b). Origins and functions of positive and negative affect: A control-process view. *Psychological Review, 97*, 19–35.

Carver, C. S., & Scheier, M. F. (1998). *On the self-regulation of behavior.* New York: Cambridge University Press.

Clark, D. A., Beck, A. T., & Brown, G. (1989). Cognitive mediation in general psychiatric outpatients: A test of the content-specificity hypothesis. *Journal of Personality and Social Psychology, 56*, 958–964.

Clark, L. A., Watson, D., & Mineka, S. (1994). Temperament, personality, and the mood and anxiety disorders. *Journal of Abnormal Psychology, 103*, 103–116.

Cleiren, M. (1993). *Bereavement and adaptation: A comparative study of the aftermath of death.* Washington, DC: Hemisphere.

Cloninger, C. R. (1987). A systematic method for clinical description and classification of personality variants. *Archives of General Psychiatry, 44*, 573–588.

Cloninger, C. R. (1988). A unified biosocial theory of personality and its role in the development of anxiety states: A reply to commentaries. *Psychiatric Developments, 2*, 83–120.

Clore, G. L., Schwarz, N., & Conway, M. (1994). Affective causes and consequences of social information processing. In R. S. Wyer, Jr. & T. K. Srull (Eds.), *Handbook of social cognition* (2nd ed., pp. 323–417). Hillsdale, NJ: Lawrence Erlbaum Associates.

Cohen, J. D., Romero, R. D., Servan-Schreiber, D., & Farah, M. J. (1994). Mechanisms of spatial attention: The relation of macrostructure to microstructure in parietal neglect. *Journal of Cognitive Neuroscience, 6*, 377–387.

Csikszentmihalyi, M. (1990). *Flow: The psychology of optimal experience.* New York: Harper & Row.

Dalgleish, T., & Watts, F. N. (1990). Biases of attention and memory in disorders of anxiety and depression. *Clinical Psychology Review, 10*, 589–604.

Davidson, R. J. (1992a). Anterior cerebral asymmetry and the nature of emotion. *Brain and Cognition, 20*, 125–151.

Davidson, R. J. (1992b). Prolegomenon to the structure of emotion: Gleanings from neuropsychology. *Cognition and Emotion, 6*, 245–268.

Davidson, R. J., Ekman, P., Saron, C. D., Senulis, J. A., & Friesen, W. V. (1990). Approach–withdrawal and cerebral asymmetry: Emotional expression and brain physiology I. *Journal of Personality and Social Psychology, 58*, 330–341.

Davies, P. (1988). *The cosmic blueprint: New discoveries in nature's creative ability to order the universe.* New York: Simon & Schuster.

Deci, E. L. (1992). On the nature and functions of motivation theories. *Psychological Science, 3*, 167–171.

Deci, E. L., & Ryan, R. M. (1985). *Intrinsic motivation and self-determination in human behavior .* New York: Plenum.

Deci, E. L., & Ryan, R. M. (1987). The support of autonomy and the control of behavior. *Journal of Personality and Social Psychology, 53*, 1024–1037.

Deci, E. L., & Ryan, R. M. (1991). A motivational approach to self: Integration in personality. In R. Dienstbier (Ed.), *Nebraska symposium on motivation: Vol. 38. Perspectives on motivation* (pp. 237–288). Lincoln, NE: University of Nebraska Press.

Deci, E. L., & Ryan, R. M. (1995). Human agency: The basis for true self-esteem. In M. Kernis (Ed.), *Efficacy, agency, and self-esteem* (pp. 31–49). New York: Plenum.

Depue, R. A., & Iacono, W. G. (1989). Neurobehavioral aspects of affective disorders. *Annual Review of Psychology, 40*, 457–492.

Depue, R. A., Krauss, S. P., & Spoont, M. R. (1987). A two-dimensional threshold model of seasonal bipolar affective disorder. In D. Magnusson & A. Öhman (Eds.), *Psychopathology: An interactional perspective* (pp. 95–123). Orlando, FL: Academic Press.

Diener, C. I., & Dweck, C. S. (1978). An analysis of learned helplessness: Continuous changes in performance strategy and achievement cognitions following failure. *Journal of Personality and Social Psychology, 36*, 451–462.

Diener, E., & Emmons, R. A. (1984). The independence of positive and negative affect. *Journal of Personality and Social Psychology, 47*, 1105–1117.

Diener, E., & Iran-Nejad, A. (1986). The relationship in experience between various types of affect. *Journal of Personality and Social Psychology, 50*, 1031–1038.

Drake, R. A. (1984). Lateral asymmetry of personal optimism. *Journal of Research in Personality, 18*, 497–507.

Drake, R. A. (1985). Lateral asymmetry of risky recommendations. *Personality and Social Psychology Bulletin, 11*, 409–417.

Drake, R. A. (1987). Conceptions of own versus others' outcomes: Manipulation by monaural attentional orientation. *European Journal of Social Psychology, 17*, 373–375.

Duck, S. W. (Ed.). (1982). *Personal relationships 4: Dissolving personal relationships.* London: Academic Press.

Duval, T. S., Duval, V. H., & Mulilis, J.-P. (1992). Effects of self-focus, discrepancy between self and standard, and outcome expectancy favorability on the tendency to match self to standard or to withdraw. *Journal of Personality and Social Psychology, 62,* 340–348.

Elliott, E. S., & Dweck, C. S. (1988). Goals: An approach to motivation and achievement. *Journal of Personality and Social Psychology, 54,* 5–12.

Ellsworth, P. C., & Smith, C. A. (1988). From appraisal to emotion: Differences among unpleasant feelings. *Motivation and Emotion, 12,* 271–302.

Emmons, R. A. (1986). Personal strivings: An approach to personality and subjective well being. *Journal of Personality and Social Psychology, 51,* 1058–1068.

Endler, N. S., Cox, B. J., Parker, J. D. A., & Bagby, R. M. (1992). Self-reports of depression and state–trait anxiety: Evidence for differential assessment. *Journal of Personality and Social Psychology, 63,* 832–838.

Epstein, S. (1979). The stability of behavior: I. On predicting most of the people much of the time. *Journal of Personality and Social Psychology, 37,* 1097–1126.

Epstein, S. (1985). The implications of cognitive-experiential self-theory for research in social psychology and personality. *Journal for the Theory of Social Behavior, 15,* 283–310.

Epstein, S. (1990). Cognitive-experiential self-theory. In L. Pervin (Ed.), *Handbook of personality: Theory and research* (pp. 165–192). New York: Guilford.

Epstein, S. (1994). Integration of the cognitive and the psychodynamic unconscious. *American Psychologist, 49,* 709–724.

Epstein, S., Lipson, A., Holstein, C., & Huh, E. (1992). Irrational reactions to negative outcomes: Evidence for two conceptual systems. *Journal of Personality and Social Psychology, 62,* 328–339.

Erber, R. (1991). Affective and semantic priming: Effects of mood on category accessibility and inference. *Journal of Experimental Social Psychology, 27,* 480–498.

Erber, R., & Tesser, A. (1992). Task effort and the regulation of mood: The absorption hypothesis. *Journal of Experimental Social Psychology, 28,* 339–359.

Fehr, B., & Russell, J. A. (1984). Concept of emotion viewed from a prototype perspective. *Journal of Experimental Psychology: General, 113,* 464–486.

Field, M., & Golubitsky, M. (1992). *Symmetry in chaos: A search for pattern in mathematics, art, and nature.* Oxford, England: Oxford University Press.

Finlay-Jones, R., & Brown, G. W. (1981). Types of stressful life events and the onset of anxiety and depressive disorders. *Psychological Medicine, 11,* 803–815.

Forgas, J. P. (1994). Sad and guilty? Affective influences on the explanation of conflict in close relationships. *Journal of Personality and Social Psychology, 66,* 56–68.

Forgas, J. P., & Moylan, S. (1987). After the movies: Transient mood and social judgments. *Personality and Social Psychology Bulletin, 13,* 467–477.

Fowles, D. C. (1980). The three arousal model: Implications of Gray's two-factor learning theory for heart rate, electrodermal activity, and psychopathy. *Psychophysiology, 17,* 87–104.

Fox, N. A., & Davidson, R. J. (1988). Patterns of brain electrical activity during facial signs of emotion in 10-month old infants. *Developmental Psychology, 24,* 230–236.

Frijda, N. H. (1986). *The emotions.* Cambridge, England: Cambridge University Press.

Frijda, N. H. (1988). The laws of emotion. *American Psychologist, 43,* 349–358.

Gleick, J. (1987). *Chaos: Making a new science.* New York: Viking Penguin.

Gobet, F., & Simon, H. A. (1996). The roles of recognition processes and look-ahead search in time-constrained expert problem solving: Evidence from grand-master-level chess. *Psychological Science, 7,* 52–55.

Goldin-Meadow, S., & Alibali, M. W. (1995). Mechanisms of transition: Learning with a helping hand. In D. Medin (Ed.), *The psychology of learning and motivation* (Vol. 33, pp. 115–157). San Diego, CA: Academic Press.

Gollwitzer, P. M. (1990). Action phases and mind-sets. In E. T. Higgins & R. M. Sorrentino (Eds.), *Handbook of motivation and cognition: Foundations of social behavior* (Vol. 2, pp. 53–92). New York: Guilford.

Gollwitzer, P. M. (1996). The volitional benefits of planning. In P. M. Gollwitzer & J. A. Bargh (Eds.), *The psychology of action: Linking cognition and motivation to behavior* (pp. 287–312). New York: Guilford.

Gollwitzer, P. M., & Kinney, R. F. (1989). Effects of deliberative and implemental mindsets on illusion of control. *Journal of Personality and Social Psychology, 56*, 531–542.

Gottman, J. M. (1993). A theory of marital dissolution and stability. *Journal of Family Psychology, 7*, 57–75.

Gray, J. A. (1972). The psychophysiological basis of introversion-extraversion: A modification of Eysenck's theory. In V. D. Nebylitsyn & J. A. Gray (Eds.), *The biological bases of individual behaviour* (pp. 182–205). New York: Academic Press.

Gray, J. A. (1977). Drug effects on fear and frustration: Possible limbic site of action of minor tranquilizers. In L. L. Iversen, S. D. Iversen, & S. H. Snyder (Eds.), *Handbook of psychopharmacology* (Vol. 8, pp. 433–529). New York: Plenum.

Gray, J. A. (1978). The 1977 Myers lecture: The neuropsychology of anxiety. *British Journal of Psychology, 69*, 417–434.

Gray, J. A. (1981). A critique of Eysenck's theory of personality. In H. J. Eysenck (Ed.), *A model for personality* (pp. 246–276). Berlin, Germany: Springer-Verlag.

Gray, J. A. (1982). *The neuropsychology of anxiety: An enquiry into the functions of the septo-hippocampal system.* New York: Oxford University Press.

Gray, J. A. (1987a). Perspectives on anxiety and impulsivity: A commentary. *Journal of Research in Personality, 21*, 493–509.

Gray, J. A. (1987b). *The psychology of fear and stress.* Cambridge, England: Cambridge University Press.

Gray, J. A. (1990). Brain systems that mediate both emotion and cognition. *Cognition and Emotion, 4*, 269–288.

Greenberg, M. S., & Alloy, L. B. (1989). Depression versus anxiety: Processing of self- and other-referent information. *Cognition & Emotion, 3*, 207–223.

Greenberg, M. S., & Beck, A. T. (1989). Depression versus anxiety: A test of the content-specificity hypothesis. *Journal of Abnormal Psychology, 98*, 9–13.

Greenwald, A. G. (1980). The totalitarian ego: Fabrication and revision of personal history. *American Psychologist, 35*, 603–618.

Hayes, A. M., & Strauss, J. L. (in press). Dynamic systems theory as a paradigm for the study of change in psychotherapy: An application to cognitive therapy for depression. *Journal of Consulting and Clinical Psychology.*

Hayes-Roth, B., & Hayes-Roth, F. (1979). A cognitive model of planning. *Cognitive Science, 3*, 275–310.

Heatherton, T. F., & Baumeister, R. F. (1991). Binge eating as escape from self-awareness. *Psychological Bulletin, 110*, 86–108.

Heatherton, T. F., & Nichols, P. A. (1994). Personal accounts of successful versus failed attempts at life change. *Personality and Social Psychology Bulletin, 20*, 664–675.

Heckhausen, H., & Gollwitzer, P. M. (1987). Thought contents and cognitive functioning in motivational versus volitional states of mind. *Motivation and Emotion, 11*, 101–120.

Heckhausen, J., & Schulz, R. (1995). A life-span theory of control. *Psychological Review, 102*, 284–304.

Henriques, J. B., & Davidson, R. J. (1991). Left frontal hypoactivation in depression. *Journal of Abnormal Psychology, 100*, 535–545.

Higgins, E. T. (1987). Self-discrepancy: A theory relating self and affect. *Psychological Review, 94*, 319–340.

Higgins, E. T. (1989). Knowledge accessibility and activation: Subjectivity and suffering from unconscious sources. In J. S. Uleman & J. A. Bargh (Eds.), *Unintended thought: The limits of awareness, intention, and control* (pp. 75–123). New York: Guilford.

Higgins, E. T. (1996). Ideals, oughts, and regulatory focus: Affect and motivation from distinct pains and pleasures. In P. M. Gollwitzer & J. A. Bargh (Eds.), *The psychology of action: Linking cognition and motivation to behavior* (pp. 91–114). New York: Guilford.

Higgins, E. T., Bond, R., Klein, R., & Strauman, T. J. (1986). Self-discrepancies and emotional vulnerability: How magnitude, accessibility and type of discrepancy influence affect. *Journal of Personality and Social Psychology, 41*, 1–15.

Higgins, E. T., Roney, C. J. R., Crowe, E., & Hymes, C. (1994). Ideal versus ought predilections for approach and avoidance: Distinct self-regulatory systems. *Journal of Personality and Social Psychology, 66,* 276–286.

Higgins, E. T., & Tykocinski, O. (1992). Self-discrepancies and biographical memory: Personality and cognition at the level of psychological situation. *Personality and Social Psychology Bulletin, 18,* 527–535.

Hirt, E. R., Melton, R. J., McDonald, H. E., & Harackiewicz, J. M. (1996). Processing goals, task interest, and the mood-performance relationship: A mediational analysis. *Journal of Personality and Social Psychology, 71,* 245–261.

Holyoak, K. J., & Spellman, B. A. (1993). Thinking. *Annual Review of Psychology, 44,* 265–315.

Hsee, C. K., & Abelson, R. P. (1991). Velocity relation: Satisfaction as a function of the first derivative of outcome over time. *Journal of Personality and Social Psychology, 60,* 341–347.

Hull, J. G. (1981). A self-awareness model of the causes and effects of alcohol consumption. *Journal of Abnormal Psychology, 90,* 586–600.

Hull, J. G., & Rielly, N. P. (1986). An information processing approach to alcohol use and its consequences. In R. E. Ingram (Ed.), *Information processing approaches to clinical psychology* (pp. 151–167). New York: Academic Press.

Ingram, R. E. (1990). Self-focused attention in clinical disorder: Review and a conceptual model. *Psychological Bulletin, 107,* 156–176.

Ito, T. A., Miller, N., & Pollock, V. E. (1996). Alcohol and aggression: A meta-analysis on the moderating effects of inhibitory cues, triggering events, and self-focused attention. *Psychological Bulletin, 120,* 60–82.

Izard, C. E. (1977). *Human emotions.* New York: Plenum. Janoff-Bulman, R. (1992). *Shattered assumptions: Towards a new psychology of trauma.* New York: The Free Press.

Johnson, E. J., & Tversky, A. (1983). Affect, generalization, and the perception of risk. *Journal of Personality and Social Psychology, 45,* 20–31.

Kahneman, D., Fredrickson, B. L., Schreiber, C. A., & Redelmeier, D. A. (1993). When more pain is preferred to less: Adding a better end. *Psychological Science, 4,* 401–405.

Kaplowitz, S. A., & Fink, E. L. (1992). Dynamics of attitude change. In R. L. Levine & H. E. Fitzgerald (Eds.), *Analysis of dynamic psychological systems, Vol. 2. Methods and applications* (pp. 341–369). New York: Plenum.

Kelly, G. A. (1955). *The psychology of personal constructs.* New York: W. W. Norton.

Kelso, J. A. S. (1995). *Dynamic patterns: The self-organization of brain and behavior.* Cambridge, MA: MIT Press.

Kelso, J. A. S., Scholz, J. P., & Schöner, G. (1986). Nonequilibrium phase transitions in coordinated biological motion: Critical fluctuations. *Physics Letters, 118,* 279–284.

Kirschenbaum, D. S. (1985). Proximity and specificity of planning: A position paper. *Cognitive Therapy and Research, 9,* 489–506.

Kirschenbaum, D. S. (1987). Self-regulatory failure: A review with clinical implications. *Clinical Psychology Review, 7,* 77–104.

Klinger, E. (1975). Consequences of commitment to and disengagement from incentives. *Psychological Review, 82,* 1–25.

Klinger, E. (1977). *Meaning and void: Inner experience and the incentives in people's lives.* Minneapolis: University of Minnesota Press.

Konorski, J. (1967). *Integrative activity of the brain: An interdisciplinary approach.* Chicago: University of Chicago Press.

Kugler, P. N., & Turvey, M. T. (1987). *Information, natural law, and the self-assembly of rhythmic movement.* Hillsdale, NJ: Lawrence Erlbaum Associates.

Kukla, A. (1972). Foundations of an attributional theory of performance. *Psychological Review, 79,* 454–470.

Kunda, Z., & Thagard, P. (1996). Forming impressions from stereotypes, traits, and behaviors: A parallel-constraint-satisfaction theory. *Psychological Review, 103,* 284–308.

Lang, P. J., Bradley, M. M., & Cuthbert, B. N. (1992). A motivational analysis of emotion: Reflex-cortex connections. *Psychological Science, 3,* 44–49.

Larsen, R. J., & Diener, E. (1992). Promises and problems with the circumplex model of emotion. In M. S. Clark (Ed.), *Review of personality and social psychology* (Vol. 13, pp. 25–59). Newbury Park, CA: Sage.

Latané, B., & Nowak, A. (1994). Attitudes as catastrophes: From dimensions to categories with increasing involvement. In R. R. Vallacher & A. Nowak (Eds.), *Dynamical systems in social psychology* (pp. 219–249). San Diego, CA: Academic Press.

Lawrence, J. W., Carver, C. S., & Scheier, M. F. (1997). *Velocity and affect in immediate personal experience*. Manuscript submitted for publication.

Lazarus, R. S. (1966). *Psychological stress and the coping process*. New York: McGraw-Hill.

Lazarus, R. S. (1991). *Emotion and adaptation*. New York: Oxford University Press.

Lewinsohn, P. M., Larson, D. W., & Muōz, R. F. (1982). The measurement of expectancies and other cognitions in depressed individuals. *Cognitive Therapy and Research, 6,* 437–446.

Little, B. R. (1983). Personal projects: A rationale and methods for investigation. *Environment and Behavior, 15,* 273–309.

Little, B. R. (1989). Personal projects analysis: Trivial pursuits, magnificent obsessions, and the search for coherence. In D. M. Buss & N. Cantor (Eds.), Personality psychology: Recent trends and emerging directions (pp. 15–31). New York: Springer-Verlag.

Locke, E. A., & Latham, G. P. (1990a). *A theory of goal setting and task performance*. Englewood Cliffs, NJ: Prentice-Hall.

Locke, E. A., & Latham, G. P. (1990b). Work motivation and satisfaction: Light at the end of the tunnel. *Psychological Science, 1,* 240–246.

Lord, R. G., & Hanges, P. J. (1987). A control system model of organizational motivation: Theoretical development and applied implications. *Behavioral Science, 32,* 161–178.

Lorenz, E. N. (1963). Deterministic nonperiodic flow. *Journal of Atmospheric Science, 20,* 130–141.

MacLeod, C., & Campbell, L. (1992). Memory accessibility and probability judgments: An experimental evaluation of the availability heuristic. *Journal of Personality and Social Psychology, 63,* 890–902.

MacNair, R. R., & Elliott, T. R. (1992). Self-perceived problem-solving ability, stress appraisal, and coping over time. *Journal of Research in Personality, 26,* 150–164.

Mahoney, M. J. (1991). *Human change processes: The scientific foundations of psychotherapy*. New York: Basic Books.

Mandel, D. R. (1995). Chaos theory, sensitive dependence, and the logistic equation. *American Psychologist, 50,* 106–107.

Markus, H., & Nurius, P. (1986). Possible selves. *American Psychologist, 41,* 954–969.

Martin, L. L., & Tesser, A. (1989). Toward a motivational and structural model of ruminative thought. In J. S. Uleman & J. A. Bargh (Eds.), *Unintended thought: The limits of awareness, intention, and control* (pp. 306–326). New York: Guilford.

Martin, L. L., & Tesser, A. (1996). Some ruminative thoughts. In R. S. Wyer, Jr. (Ed.), *Advances in social cognition* (Vol. 9, pp. 1–47). Mahwah, NJ: Lawrence Erlbaum Associates.

Martin, L. L., Ward, D. W, Achee, J. W., & Wyer, R. S., Jr. (1993). Mood as input: People have to interpret the motivational implications of their mood. *Journal of Personality and Social Psychology, 64,* 317–326.

Mayer, J. D., & Gaschke, Y. N. (1988). The experience and meta-experience of mood. *Journal of Personality and Social Psychology, 55,* 102–111.

Mayer, J. D., Gaschke, Y. N., Braverman, D. L., & Evans, T. W. (1992). Mood-congruent judgment is a general effect. *Journal of Personality and Social Psychology, 63,* 119–132.

McIntosh, W. D., & Martin, L. L. (1992). The cybernetics of happiness: The relation of goal attainment, rumination, and affect. In M. S. Clark (Ed.), *Review of personality and social psychology: Vol. 14. Emotion and social behavior* (pp. 222–246). Newbury Park, CA: Sage.

McIntyre, J., & Bizzi, E. (1993). Servo hypotheses for the biological control of movement. *Journal of Motor Behavior, 25,* 193–202.

Melton, R. J. (1995). The role of positive affect in syllogism performance. *Personality and Social Psychology Bulletin, 21,* 788–794.

Millar, K. U., Tesser, A., & Millar, M. G. (1988). The effects of a threatening life event on behavior sequences and intrusive thought: A self-disruption explanation. *Cognitive Therapy and Research, 12,* 441–458.

Miller, G. A., Galanter, E., & Pribram, K. H. (1960). *Plans and the structure of behavior*. New York: Holt, Rinehart, & Winston.

Miller, L. C., & Read, S. J. (1987). Why am I telling you this? Self-disclosure in a goal-based model of personality. In V. J. Derlega & J. Berg (Eds.), *Self-disclosure:* Theory, research, and therapy (pp. 35–58). New York: Plenum.

Miller, W. R., & C'deBaca, J. (1994). Quantum change: Toward a psychology of transformation. In T. Heatherton & J. Weinberger (Eds.), *Can personality change?* (pp. 253–280). Washington, DC: American Psychological Association.

Mineka, S., & Sutton, S. K. (1992). Cognitive biases and the emotional disorders. *Psychological Science, 3*, 65–69.

Mischel, W., & Shoda, Y. (1995). A cognitive-affective system theory of personality: Reconceptualizing the invariances in personality and the role of situations. *Psychological Review, 102*, 246–268.

Moffitt, K. H., & Singer, J. A. (1994). Continuity in the life story: Self-defining memories, affect, and approach/avoidance personal strivings. *Journal of Personality, 62*, 21–43.

Murray, H. A. (1938). *Explorations in personality.* New York: Oxford University Press.

Murray, S. L., & Holmes, J. G. (1993). Seeing virtues in faults: Negativity and the transformation of interpersonal narratives in close relationships. *Journal of Personality and Social Psychology, 65*, 707–722.

Murray, S. L., & Holmes, J. G. (1997). A leap of faith? Positive illusions in romantic relationships. *Personality and Social Psychology Bulletin, 23*, 586–604.

Murray, S. L., Holmes, J. G., & Griffin, D. W. (1996). The benefits of positive illusions: Idealization and the construction of satisfaction in close relationships. *Journal of Personality and Social Psychology, 70*, 79–98.

Myers, D. G., & Diener, E. (1995). Who is happy? *Psychological Science, 6*, 10–19.

Newtson, D. (1993). The dynamics of action and interaction. In L. D. Smith & E. Thelen (Eds.), *A dynamic systems approach to development: Applications* (pp. 241–264). Cambridge, MA: MIT Press.

Newtson, D. (1994). The perception and coupling of behavioral waves. In R. R. Vallacher & A. Nowak (Eds.), *Dynamical systems in social psychology* (pp. 139–167). San Diego, CA: Academic Press.

Norman, D. A. (1981). Categorization of action slips. *Psychological Review, 88*, 1–15.

Nowak, A., & Lewenstein, M. (1994). Dynamical systems: A tool for social psychology. In R. R. Vallacher & A. Nowak (Eds.), *Dynamical systems in social psychology* (pp. 17–53). San Diego, CA: Academic Press.

Nowak, A., & Vallacher, R. R. (1999). *Dynamical social psychology.* New York: Guilford.

Ogilvie, D. M. (1987). The undesired self: A neglected variable in personality research. *Journal of Personality and Social Psychology, 52*, 379–385.

Orbuch, T. L. (Ed.). (1992). *Close relationship loss: Theoretical approaches.* New York: Springer-Verlag.

Ortony, A., Clore, G. L., & Collins, A. (1988). *The cognitive structure of emotions.* Cambridge, England: Cambridge University Press.

Overmier, J. B., & Seligman, M. E. P. (1967). Effects of inescapable shock upon subsequent escape and avoidance learning. *Journal of Comparative and Physiological Psychology, 63*, 28–33.

Payton, D. W. (1990). Internalized plans: A representation for action resources. In P. Maes (Ed.), *Designing autonomous agents: Theory and practice from biology to engineering and back* (pp. 89–103). Cambridge, MA: MIT Press.

Pervin, L. A. (1982). The stasis and flow of behavior: Toward a theory of goals. In M. M. Page & R. Dienstbier (Eds.), *Nebraska Symposium on Motivation* (Vol. 30, pp. 1–53). Lincoln: University of Nebraska Press.

Pervin, L. A. (Ed.). (1989). *Goal concepts in personality and social psychology.* Hillsdale, NJ: Lawrence Erlbaum Associates.

Pervin, L. A. (1992). The rational mind and the problem of volition. *Psychological Science, 3*, 162–164.

Pietromonaco, P. R., & Markus, H. (1985). The nature of negative thoughts in depression. *Journal of Personality and Social Psychology, 48*, 799–807.

Pietromonaco, P. R., & Rook, K. S. (1987). Decision style in depression: The contribution of perceived risks and benefits. *Journal of Personality and Social Psychology, 52*, 399–408.

Pittman, T. S., & Pittman, N. L. (1980). Deprivation of control and the attribution process. *Journal of Personality and Social Psychology, 39*, 377–389.

Powers, W. T. (1973). *Behavior: The control of perception.* Chicago: Aldine.

Pribram, K. H. (1990). From metaphors to models: The use of analogy in neuropsychology. In D. E. Leary (Ed.), *Metaphors in the history of psychology* (pp. 79–103). Cambridge, England: Cambridge University Press.

Pyszczynski, T., Greenberg, J., Hamilton, J., & Nix, G. (1991). On the relationship between self-focused attention and psychological disorder: A critical reappraisal. *Psychological Bulletin, 110*, 538–543.

Read, S. J., Druian, P. R., & Miller, L. C. (1989). The role of causal sequence in the meaning of action. *British Journal of Social Psychology, 28*, 341–351.

Read, S. J., Vanman, E. J., & Miller, L. C. (1997). Connectionism, parallel constraint satisfaction processes, and Gestalt principles: (Re)introducing cognitive dynamics to social psychology. *Review of Personality and Social Psychology, 1*, 26–53.

Riskind, J. H., Kelley, K., Harman, W., Moore, R., & Gaines, H. S. (1992). The loomingness of danger: Does it discriminate focal phobia and general anxiety from depression? *Cognitive Therapy and Research, 16*, 603–622.

Roseman, I. J. (1984). Cognitive determinants of emotions: A structural theory. In P. Shaver (Ed.), *Review of Personality and Social Psychology* (Vol. 5, pp. 11–36). Beverly Hills, CA: Sage.

Ruble, D. N. (1994). A phase model of transitions: Cognitive and motivational consequences. In M. Zanna (Ed.), *Advances in Experimental Social Psychology* (Vol. 26, pp. 163–214). San Diego, CA: Academic Press.

Ruelle, D. (1991). *Chance and chaos.* Princeton, NJ: Princeton University Press.

Rusbult, C. E. (1980). Commitment and satisfaction in romantic associations: A test of the investment model. *Journal of Experimental Social Psychology, 16*, 172–186.

Rusbult, C. E. (1983). A longitudinal test of the investment model: The development (and deterioration) of satisfaction and commitment in heterosexual involvements. *Journal of Personality and Social Psychology, 45*, 101–117.

Rusbult, C. E., & Martz, J. M. (1995). Remaining in an abusive relationship: An investment model analysis of nonvoluntary dependence. *Personality and Social Psychology Bulletin, 21*, 558–571.

Ryan, R. M. (1993). Agency and organization: Intrinsic motivation, autonomy, and the self in psychological development. In J. Jacobs (Ed.), *Nebraska Symposium on Motivation* (Vol. 40, pp. 237–288). Lincoln: University of Nebraska Press.

Ryan, R. M., Sheldon, K. M., Kasser, T., & Deci, E. L. (1996). All goals are not created equal: An organismic perspective on the nature of goals and their regulation. In P. M. Gollwitzer & J. A. Bargh (Eds.), *The psychology of action: Linking cognition and motivation to behavior* (pp. 7–26). New York: Guilford.

Salovey, P., & Birnbaum, D. (1989). Influence of mood on health-relevant cognitions. *Journal of Personality and Social Psychology, 57*, 539–551.

Sarason, I. G. (1975). Anxiety and self-preoccupation. In I. G. Sarason & C. D. Spielberger (Eds.), *Stress and anxiety* (Vol. 2, pp. 27–44). Washington, DC: Hemisphere.

Saunders, P. T. (1980). *An introduction to catastrophe theory.* Cambridge, England: Cambridge University Press.

Scheier, M. F., & Carver, C. S. (1983). Self-directed attention and the comparison of self with standards. *Journal of Experimental Social Psychology, 19*, 205–222.

Scherer, K. R., & Ekman, P. (Eds.). (1984). *Approaches to emotion.* Hillsdale, NJ: Lawrence Erlbaum Associates.

Schneirla, T. C. (1959). An evolutionary and developmental theory of biphasic processes underlying approach and withdrawal. In M. R. Jones (Ed.), *Nebraska Symposium on motivation* (Vol. 7, pp. 1–42). Lincoln: University of Nebraska Press.

Schultz, T. R., & Lepper, M. R. (1996). Cognitive dissonance reduction as constraint satisfaction. *Psychological Review, 103*, 219–240.

Seligman, M. E. P., & Maier, S. F. (1967). Failure to escape traumatic shock. *Journal of Experimental Psychology, 74*, 1–9.

Shallice, T. (1978). The dominant action system: An information-processing approach to consciousness. In K. S. Pope & J. L. Singer (Eds.), *The stream of consciousness: Scientific investigations into the flow of human experience* (pp. 117–157). New York: Wiley.

Shastri, L., & Ajjanagadde, V. (1993). From simple associations to systematic reasoning: A connectionist representation of rules, variables, and dynamic bindings using temporal synchrony. *Behavioral and Brain Sciences, 16,* 417–494.

Shaver, P., Schwartz, J., Kirson, D., & O'Connor, C. (1987). Emotion knowledge: Further exploration of a prototype approach. *Journal of Personality and Social Psychology, 52,* 1061–1086.

Sherer, K. R., & Ekman, P. (Eds.). (1984). *Approaches to emotion.* Hillsdale, NJ: Lawrence.

Siegler, R. S. (1994). Cognitive variability: A key to understanding cognitive development. *Current Directions in Psychological Science, 3,* 1–5.

Siegler, R. S., & Jenkins, E. A. (1989). *How children discover new strategies.* Hillsdale, NJ: Lawrence Erlbaum Associates.

Skinner, E. A. (1996). A guide to constructs of control. *Journal of Personality and Social Psychology, 71,* 549–570.

Sloman, S. A. (1996). The empirical case for two forms of reasoning. *Psychological Bulletin, 119,* 3–22.

Smith, E. R. (1996). What do connectionism and social psychology offer each other? *Journal of Personality and Social Psychology, 70,* 893–912.

Smith, L. B., & Thelen, E. (1993). *A dynamic systems approach to development: Applications.* Cambridge, MA: MIT Press.

Smolensky, P. (1988). On the proper treatment of connectionism. *Behavioral and Brain Sciences, 11,* 1–23.

Snyder, M. L., & Frankel, A. (1989). Making things harder for yourself: Pride and joy. In R. C. Curtis (Ed.), *Self-defeating behaviors: Experimental research, clinical impressions, and practical implications* (pp. 131–157). New York: Plenum.

Sobotka, S. S., Davidson, R. J., & Senulis, J. A. (1992). Anterior brain electrical asymmetries in response to reward and punishment. *Electroencephalography and Clinical Neurophysiology, 83,* 236–247.

Solomon, R. L. (1980). The opponent-process theory of acquired motivation: The costs of pleasure and the benefits of pain. *American Psychologist, 35,* 691–712.

Solomon, R. L., & Corbit, J. D. (1974). An opponent-process theory of motivation: III. Temporal dynamics of affect. *Psychological Review, 81,* 119–145.

Steele, C. M. (1988). The psychology of self-affirmation: Sustaining the integrity of the self. In L. Berkowitz (Ed.), *Advances in Experimental Social Psychology* (Vol. 21, pp. 261–302). New York: Academic Press.

Steele, C. M., & Josephs, R. A. (1990). Alcohol myopia: Its prized and dangerous effects. *American Psychologist, 45,* 921–933.

Stewart, I. (1990). *Does God play dice?* London: Basil Blackwell.

Stewart, I. N., & Peregoy, P. L. (1983). Catastrophe theory modeling in psychology. *Psychological Bulletin, 94,* 336–362.

Strauman, T. J. (1989). Self-discrepancies in clinical depression and social phobia: Cognitive structures that underlie emotional disorders? *Journal of Abnormal Psychology, 98,* 14–22.

Stroebe, M. S., Stroebe, W., & Hansson, R. O. (Eds.). (1993). *Handbook of bereavement: Theory, research, and intervention.* Cambridge, England: Cambridge University Press.

Stuss, D. T. (1991). Self, awareness, and the frontal lobes: A neuropsychological perspective. In J. Strauss & G. R. Goethals (Eds.), *The self: Interdisciplinary approaches* (pp. 255–278). New York: Springer-Verlag.

Swann, W. B., Jr. (1990). To be adored or to be known? The interplay of self-enhancement and self-verification. In E. T. Higgins & R. M. Sorrentino (Eds.), *Handbook of motivation and cognition: Foundations of social behavior* (Vol. 2, pp. 408–448). New York: Guilford.

Taylor, S. E. (1983). Adjustment to threatening events: A theory of cognitive adaptation. *American Psychologist, 38,* 1161–1173.

Taylor, S. E. (1990). Health psychology: The science and the field. *American Psychologist, 45*, 40–50.

Taylor, S. E., & Brown, J. D. (1988). Illusion and well-being: A social psychological perspective on mental health. *Psychological Bulletin, 103*, 193–210.

Taylor, S. E., & Gollwitzer, P. M. (1995). Effects of mindset on positive illusions. *Journal of Personality and Social Psychology, 69*, 213–226.

Taylor, S. E., & Pham, L. B. (1996). Mental stimulation, motivation, and action. In P. M. Gollwitzer & J. A. Bargh (Eds.), *The psychology of action: Linking cognition and motivation to behavior* (pp. 219–235). New York: Guilford.

Tedeschi, R. G., & Calhoun, L. G. (1995). *Trauma and transformation*. Thousand Oaks, CA: Sage.

Tesser, A. (1980a). Self-esteem maintenance in family dynamics. *Journal of Personality and Social Psychology, 39*, 77–91.

Tesser, A. (1980b). When individual dispositions and social pressure conflict: A catastrophe. *Human Relations, 33*, 393–407.

Tesser, A. (1986). Some effects of self-evaluation maintenance on cognition and action. In R. M. Sorrentino & E. T. Higgins (Eds.), *Handbook of motivation and cognition: Foundations of social behavior* (pp. 435–464). New York: Guilford.

Tesser, A. (1988). Toward a self-evaluation maintenance model of social behavior. In L. Berkowitz (Ed.), *Advances in experimental social psychology* (Vol. 21, pp. 181–227). New York: Academic Press.

Tesser, A. (1990). Smith and Ellsworth's appraisal model of emotion: A replication, extension, amd test. *Personality and Social Psychology Bulletin, 16*, 210–223.

Tesser, A., & Campbell, J. (1983). Self-definition and self-evaluation maintenance. In J. Suls & A. G. Greenwald (Eds.), *Psychological perspectives on the self* (Vol. 2, pp. 1–31). Hillsdale, NJ: Lawrence Erlbaum Associates.

Thagard, P. (1989). Explanatory coherence. *Behavioral and Brain Sciences, 12*, 435–467.

Thayer, R. E. (1989). *The biopsychology of mood and arousal*. New York: Oxford University Press.

Thelen, E. (1992). Development as a dynamic system. *Current Directions in Psychological Science, 1*, 189–193.

Thelen, E. (1995). Motor development: A new synthesis. *American Psychologist, 50*, 79–95.

Thelen, E., & Smith, L. B. (1994). *A dynamic systems approach to the development of cognition and action*. Cambridge, MA: MIT Press.

Thom, R. (1975). *Structural stability and morphogenesis*. Reading, MA: Benjamin.

Thompson, S. C., Sobolew-Shubin, A., Galbraith, M. E., Schwankovsky, L., & Cruzen, D. (1993). Maintaining perceptions of control: Finding perceived control in low-control circumstances. *Journal of Personality and Social Psychology, 64*, 293–304.

Thompson, S. C., & Spacapan, S. (1991). Perceptions of control in vulnerable populations. *Journal of Social Issues, 47*, 1–21.

Tomarken, A. J., Davidson, R. J., Wheeler, R. E., & Doss, R. C. (1992). Individual differences in anterior brain asymmetry and fundamental dimensions of emotion. *Journal of Personality and Social Psychology, 62*, 676–687.

Tomkins, S. S. (1984). Affect theory. In K. R. Sherer & P. Ekman (Eds.), *Approaches to emotion* (pp. 163–195). Hillsdale, NJ: Lawrence Erlbaum Associates.

Turvey, M. T. (1990). Coordination. *American Psychologist, 45*, 938–953.

Vallacher, R. R., & Kaufman, J. (1996). Dynamics of action identification: Volatility and structure in the mental representation of behavior. In P. M. Gollwitzer & J. A. Bargh (Eds.), *The psychology of action: Linking cognition and motivation to behavior* (pp. 260–282). New York: Guilford.

Vallacher, R. R., & Nowak, A. (Eds.). (1994). *Dynamical systems in social psychology*. San Diego, CA: Academic Press.

Vallacher, R. R., & Nowak, A. (1997). The emergence of dynamical social psychology. *Psychological Inquiry, 8*, 73–99.

Vallacher, R. R., & Wegner, D. M. (1985). *A theory of action identification*. Hillsdale, NJ: Lawrence Erlbaum Associates.

Vallacher, R. R., & Wegner, D. M. (1987). What do people think they're doing? Action identification and human behavior. *Psychological Review, 94*, 3–15.

Vallacher, R. R., Wegner, D. M., McMahan, S. C., Cotter, J., & Larsen, K. A. (1992). On winning friends and influencing people: Action identification and self-presentation success. *Social Cognition, 10*, 335–355.

Vallacher, R. R., Wegner, D. M., & Somoza, M. P. (1989). That's easy for you to say: Action identification and speech fluency. *Journal of Personality and Social Psychology, 56*, 199–208.

Vallerand, R. J. (1997). Toward a hierarchical model of intrinsic and extrinsic motivation. In M. P. Zanna (Ed.), *Advances in experimental social psychology* (Vol. 29, pp. 271–360). San Diego, CA: Academic Press.

van der Maas, H. L. J., & Molenaar, P. C. M. (1992). Stagewise cognitive development: An application of catastrophe theory. *Psychological Review, 99*, 395–417.

Vaughan, D. (1986). *Uncoupling: Turning points in intimate relationships.* Oxford, England: Oxford University Press.

Waddington, C. H. (1957). *The strategy of the genes.* London: Allen & Unwin.

Waldrop, M. (1992). *Complexity: The emerging science at the edge of order and chaos.* New York: Simon & Schuster.

Warr, P., Barter, J., & Brownbridge, G. (1983). On the independence of positive and negative affect. *Journal of Personality and Social Psychology, 44*, 644–651.

Watson, D., Clark, L. A., & Tellegen, A. (1988). Development and validation of brief measures of positive and negative affect: The PANAS scales. *Journal of Personality and Social Psychology, 54*, 1063–1070.

Watson, D., & Tellegen, A. (1985). Toward a consensual structure of mood. *Psychological Bulletin, 98*, 219–235.

Wegner, D. M., & Bargh, J. A. (1998). Control and automaticity in social life. In D. Gilbert, S. T. Fiske, & G. Lindzey (Eds.), *Handbook of social psychology* (4th ed., pp. 446–496). Boston: McGraw-Hill.

Weiner, B. (1985). An attributional theory of achievement motivation and emotion. *Psychological Review, 92*, 548–573.

Weiss, R. S. (1988). Loss and recovery. *Journal of Social Issues, 44*, 37–52.

Wheeler, R. E., Davidson, R. J., & Tomarken, A. J. (1993). Frontal brain asymmetry and emotional reactivity: A biological substrate of affective style. *Psychophysiology, 30*, 82–89.

Wickless, C., & Kirsch, I. (1988). Cognitive correlates of anger, anxiety, and sadness. *Cognitive Therapy and Research, 12*, 367–377.

Wills, T. A. (1981). Downward comparison principles in social psychology. *Psychological Bulletin, 90*, 245–271.

Wine, J. D. (1971). Test anxiety and direction of attention. *Psychological Bulletin, 76*, 92–104.

Wine, J. D. (1980). Cognitive-attentional theory of test anxiety. In I. G. Sarason (Ed.), *Test anxiety: Theory, research, and application* (pp. 349–378). Hillsdale, NJ: Lawrence Erlbaum Associates.

Wong, P. T. P., & Weiner, B. (1981). When people ask "why" questions, and the heuristics of attributional search. *Journal of Personality and Social Psychology, 40*, 650–663.

Wood, J. V. (1989). Theory and research concerning social comparisons of personal attributes. *Psychological Bulletin, 106*, 231–248.

Wood, J. V., Taylor, S. E., & Lichtman, R. R. (1985). Social comparison in adjustment to breast cancer. *Journal of Personality and Social Psychology, 49*, 1169–1183.

Woodcock, A., & Davis, M. (1978). *Catastrophe theory.* New York: E. P. Dutton.

Wortman, C. B., & Brehm, J. W. (1975). Responses to uncontrollable outcomes: An integration of reactance theory and the learned helplessness model. In L. Berkowitz (Ed.), *Advances in Experimental Social Psychology* (Vol. 8, pp. 277–336). New York: Academic Press.

Wright, R. A., & Brehm, J. W. (1989). Energization and goal attractiveness. In L. A. Pervin (Ed.), *Goal Concepts in Personality and Social Psychology* (pp. 169–210). Hillsdale, NJ: Lawrence Erlbaum Associates.

Wyer, R. S., Jr. (1973). Category ratings as "subjective expected values": Implications for attitude formation and change. *Psychological Review, 80*, 446–467.

Wyer, R. S., Jr., & Srull, T. K. (1989). *Memory and cognition in social context.* Hillsdale, NJ: Lawrence Erlbaum Associates.

Youngren, M. A., & Lewinsohn, P. M. (1980). The functional relation between depression and problematic interpersonal behavior. *Journal of Abnormal Psychology, 89*, 333–341.

Zeeman, E. C. (1976). Catastrophe theory. *Scientific American, 234*, 65–83.

Zeeman, E. C. (1977). *Catastrophe theory: Selected papers 1972–1977.* Reading, MA: Benjamin.

Zevon, M. A., & Tellegen, A. (1982). The structure of mood change: An idiographic/nomothetic analysis. *Journal of Personality and Social Psychology, 43*, 111–122.

2

Emerging Goals and the Self-Regulation of Behavior

Mihaly Csikszentmihalyi
Jeanne Nakamura
The University of Chicago

We agree with the general thrust of Carver and Scheier's position on self-regulation and applaud their important effort to integrate complexity models in their synthesis. These models appear to be helping the authors think about a number of phenomena that lie beyond the scope of their original cybernetic model, such as the competing pulls exerted by multiple goals, the influence of nonlinear forces, and the impact of initial conditions on subsequent pathways. We will not delve into points of agreement, however, but focus instead on issues where we see things somewhat differently.

WHERE DO GOALS COME FROM?

Carver and Scheier—and the previous cybernetic theorists by whose work they were inspired (e.g., Miller, Galanter, & Pribram, 1960)—assume the existence of goals. Goals come into their models as a deus ex machina, something that needs no explanation. In the chapter, there is cursory consideration of new goals (e.g., in relation to emergent behavior; as reorganizations that occur when traumatic events destabilize existing patterns; also when, on p. 59, they remark that the formation of goals has not been well explored), but basically, they are taken for granted.

Such a strategy could be defended on the grounds that one cannot deal with every aspect of so complex an issue and that the authors felt that the question of how goals originate was irrelevant to their discussion. In our opinion, however, leaving the ontogenesis of goals out of the picture distorts everything that follows and detracts from the accuracy of their models.

The authors would presumably agree that early in life, goals are not the primary reference points against which feedback is evaluated. Instead, behavior is best seen as being regulated by the intent to optimize experiential states. The process consists of a feedback loop in which present experiences are compared to past experiences, and, depending on the affects generated, the goal becomes to either maintain or to change the quality of experience.

An infant begins to act not to reach goals, but because it has motor skills that make actions possible and because it has genetically programmed needs to take care of. If the actions of the infant produce a pleasurable experience, a positive emotion will arise and the infant may then develop the goal of repeating the experience. For instance, the first random strugglings of the infant may bring its mouth in contact with the mother's breast, activating a sucking response. Because feeding is pleasurable, it produces a feeling of contentment that the child will want to experience again when hunger returns. After repeated sequences of this sort, the infant will develop a dim mental representation of this feedback cycle. At that point, one might say that the infant has developed the goal of reaching the nipple when hungry, and from then on, that goal will regulate its feeding behavior.

EMOTIONS DETERMINE GOALS, NOT VICE VERSA

We would argue that such a developmental perspective helps to understand behavior not only at the first stages of infancy, but also all through life. To represent the feedback loop, in Fig. 1.1 of Carver and Scheier's chapter, we would substitute the legend "Past Experience" in the box that now says "Goal, standard, reference value" and "Present Experience" in the box now labeled "Input Function." The feedback loop then operates as follows: (a) I become aware of my present experience, including its emotional valence; (b) I compare present emotions to alternatives based on past experiences; and (c) if the comparison is in favor of my present experience, my goal becomes to maintain that state; if not, the goal becomes changing it in favor of one of the alternatives. Here, my current experience is evaluated not in terms of how rapidly it is moving me ahead toward some specified outcome but qua experience, against the reference provided by my earlier experiences (see Fig. 2.1).

Such a revised model has the advantage of being more dynamic, in that it accounts for the constant emergence of new goals. Traveling to a new country, hearing a song, meeting people, reading a book, or being exposed to a new sport, game, or skilled activity are all common events that bring about previously unimagined goals because they provide experiences that, in comparison to the person's baseline, are emotionally more positive.

As an example of how goals emerge in everyday life, consider the account of the origins of an interest in chemistry offered by the Nobel laureate, Linus Pauling, in our study of eminent creators:

> I don't think that I ever sat down and asked myself, "Now what am I going to do in life?" I just went ahead doing what I liked to do . . . first I liked to read. And I read many books . . . When I was 11, I began collecting insects and reading books in entomology. When I was 12, I made an effort to collect minerals . . . I read books on mineralogy and copied tables of properties . . . out of the books. And then when I was 13, I became interested in chemistry. I was very excited when I realized that chemists could convert certain substances into other substances with quite different properties. (Csikszentmihalyi, 1996, pp. 170–171)

The account conveys how one source of enjoyment succeeded another. Pauling presumably could have articulated the circumstances under which each of the interests emerged; for instance, he has described first encountering chemistry in the makeshift lab that a 13-year-old friend had set up at home.

In this sequence of events, a new encounter, more positive than prior positive experiences, is the matrix out of which a goal emerges. In a second possible pattern, the developmental course is more complex. Just as in the preceding case, the key fact is that the emergent goal is experientially based. However, the encountered (perhaps even actively sought) experience has a positive valence because it solves a preexisting problem that is attended by negative affective states. An example or two might help clarify this.

A distinguished writer described an early home life that was difficult and unhappy. Asked about his childhood interests, he recalled,

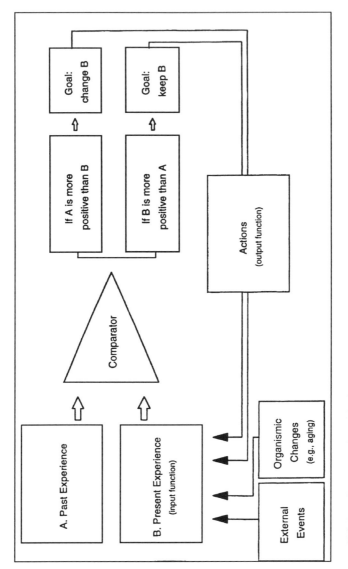

FIG. 2.1. Experience-based feedback loop (cf. Fig. 1.1, this volume).

110

Music was the first of these. Music precisely because among other things . . . it was abstract and therefore could be divorced from all the mess around me. I loved it. I used to listen to it all the time on the radio. I had a little record collection, and played things over and over again until I knew them really by heart. (Csikszentmihalyi, 1996, p. 250)

Because they are not thinking of experiential goals, Carver and Scheier are unable to envision how any activity "done to avoid an antigoal" could be intrinsically enjoyed (p. 18). Whereas they describe complex goals in which "approach" is "in the service of avoidance" (p. 11; e.g., practicing a musical instrument in order to avoid punishment), in the example just related, there was no external contingency to be evaded but rather an already existing negative experiential state to be escaped. The abstractness of music made it an attractive escape route.

Consider next a social activist who was interviewed for one of our projects and whose life exemplifies both patterns: first, formation of goals intended to continue an affectively positive experience; then, against the backdrop of negative experience, discovery of a satisfying activity and formation of new goals around it. First, family experiences in early life instilled in her an interest in social activism; as a child, she was caught up in her parents' intense caring about conditions in the wider society and strenuous efforts to help improve them. As a college student during the Vietnam War, however, events led her to conclude that the nation's social problems were much more fundamental than her parents, and she, had believed. This was deeply distressing; indeed "very, very, very traumatic." Against such a backdrop, she found new satisfaction in grassroots work toward radical change and committed herself to this. In response to new conditions, her goals thus changed; but in both cases, the goals were emergent, rooted in immediate experience.

One of the problems in understanding the function of goals in regulating behavior is that the word *goal* implies an end state that motivates a person's strivings. Yet, often goals are really means—they are pursued in order to achieve a positive affective state. For instance, let us consider why an amateur pianist might sit down to play a concerto. Is it to finish the piece as quickly as possible? Hardly. The goal of completing the piece is simply the means by which the pianist can experience the enjoyment of playing. Similarly, most mountain climbers set the goal of reaching the summit not because they want to get to the top, but because they want the experience of climbing. Contrary to the generally accepted view in psychology that behavior is directed to achieve consummatory ends, in many instances it is the means that justify the ends.

THE NATURE OF POSITIVE AFFECT

Given that the self-regulation loop we are proposing rests on optimizing experience, it is important to agree on what constitutes positive affect. We agree with Carver and Scheier that "positive affect results when a behavioral system is [making rapid progress in] doing what it is organized to do" (p. 25)—the square brackets indicate that we would prefer to dispense with the velocity argument implied by the bracketed material. (For example, we suspect that mountain climbers experience joy not because they sense that they are making good progress toward the peak, but because at a given moment they are meeting the challenges of the climb.)

The realization that people feel best when they fulfill their potentialities is at least as old as Aristotle. It was well expressed almost 700 years ago by Dante in one of his philosophical works:

> For in every action, whether caused by necessity or free will, the main intention of the agent is to express his own image; thus it is that every doer, whenever he does, enjoys (*delectatur*) the doing; because everything that is desires to be, and in action the doer unfolds his being, enjoyment naturally follows, for a thing desired always brings delight . . . therefore nothing acts without making its self manifest. (Alighieri, 1317/1921, Book I, chap. 13, translated by senior author)

But how do we know when a system is optimizing its organization? In the case of individuals, we operationalize optimal experience as a subjective event that a person describes as being simultaneously high on environmental opportunities or *challenges*, and high on personal abilities, or *skills* (Csikszentmihalyi, 1975; Csikszentmihalyi, 1990; Csikszentmihalyi, 1997; Csikszentmihalyi & Larson, 1987; Csikszentmihalyi & Rathunde, 1993; Hektner, 1996; Inghilleri, 1995, 1999; Massimini & Carli, 1988; Massimini, Delle Fave, & Carli, 1988; Massimini & Inghilleri, 1986; Moneta & Csikszentmihalyi, 1996).

The two axes of challenges and skills yield a set of ratios that describe the quality of experience in terms that are very similar to, but perhaps more parsimonious than, the models presented in Fig. 1.7 to 1.9 of the target chapter. For instance, we consistently find that when challenges are seen to be high and skills low, people report being anxious. When they see their skills as high but the challenges as low, they report a state of relaxation. When both challenges and skills are low, they report boredom and apathy. In those cases when both challenges and skills are high (or at least above the average, baseline level) they report a state of flow,

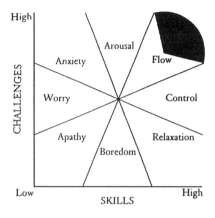

Sources: Adapted from Massimini & Carli 1988; Csikszentmihalyi 1990.

FIG. 2.2. Quality of experience as a function of the relation between challenges and skills. *Note:* From *Finding Flow*, by M. Csikszentmihalyi, 1997, New York: Basic Books, copyright 1997. Reprinted by permission.

or optimal experience. Because the model (Fig. 2.2) is explicitly interactionist, focusing on the balance of environmental challenge and personal capacities, it would seem to avoid problems ascribed to efficacy theory by the authors (p. 45).

In our studies also we find that anxiety and apathy (corresponding to "depression" in Carver and Scheier's models) are aversive states, the first high in activation and the second low; whereas flow (corresponding to "elation") and relaxation (corresponding to "relief") are both positive in feeling tone, the first being also high in activation, the second low.

Thus, we would conclude that an optimal experience obtains when a person is maximizing feeling states and is also fully active, which tends to occur when confronting the highest environmental challenge with the fullest use of personal skills. Whenever such an experience occurs, in comparison with past experiences it stands out as better than average, and we want to repeat it. Therefore, it becomes the nucleus of a goal.

THE NATURE OF GOAL-DIRECTED BEHAVIOR

We have suggested that leaving the ontogenesis of goals out of the picture distorts the authors' model of goal-directed behavior. One such distortion, mentioned earlier, is that it renders inconceivable an intrinsically enjoyed activity that is also an antigoal. We turn next to some additional examples of the problems that we perceive.

Carver and Scheier's model implies that people *cruise* (i.e., reduce rather than maintain or increase the effort that they expend) in response to the positive affect associated with making progress more rapidly than had been expected (p. 29). They envision a person juggling many goals; when one is under control, the person shifts attention to another. This scenario does not seem to fit the pursuit of experiential goals. An elated scientist, whose attention is riveted by the rapidly emerging solution to a problem, seems unlikely to ease up and deflect energies to another problem because things are going so well.

Again, if Carver and Scheier claim that people find it more difficult to make an effort when goals are important (p. 81), it may be because they have in mind desired outcomes that are not simultaneously experiential goals. People doing something that they enjoy (i.e., people with experiential goals) may be inspired, rather than deterred, by challenges that matter a lot. To put it another way, activity undertaken for its own sake often has outcomes that are subjectively important, without the sense of anxiety that the authors describe.

In addition to revealing possible problems with the dynamics of self-regulation proposed by the authors, the experiential model raises new issues about the self-regulation of behavior and focuses others in a new way. We might ask, for example, what conditions occasion formation of new goals. For instance, the emergence of new goals may be especially likely at certain points in the life course. During adolescence, hormonal changes often bring about a complete reorientation of goals due to the availability of pleasurable sexual experiences. At midlife, men and women may discover enjoyment in challenges that they have previously ignored, viewing them as the domain of the other gender (e.g., Levinson, Darrow, Klein, Levinson, & McKee, 1978).

We might ask many questions about the experiential model that we have proposed. What accounts for individual differences in attunement to the quality of one's experience, a factor central to operation of the feedback loop? For instance, what influences lead people to withdraw their attention from the flow of experience? One key factor is how frequently they shift their focus to a relatively distant future, whether doing so in order to monitor their rate of progress or for other reasons.

What other factors affect the consistency with which people are able to optimize the quality of their experience? Environmental conditions, characteristics of the activity, and autotelic personal qualities—a person's capacity to structure interactions with the environment in an experientially rewarding way (Csikszentmihalyi & Csikszentmihalyi, 1988; Hektner, 1996)—all play roles. An economist's observations during an interview in the Creativity in Later Life Project illustrate the autotelic person's deliberate, consistent structuring of daily activities so as to optimize experiential states:

> ... in the morning, that's when I really like intellectual activity; very, very finely focused intellectual activity .... And then after lunch is always a time where, you know, I like to slack off, maybe snooze for fifteen minutes, maybe take a bike ride. And it will be okay; you know, I do have chores so that I can justify taking a bike ride .... And then ... I'll be doing other things. Maybe I'll take off and garden for a little while, put a load of wash in the machine ... then it might feel really good to go and brush the bottom of the swimming pool and then top it off with jumping in and splashing around .... And then in the evening it's nice to have somebody over and have dinner. (Creativity in Later Life Project, June 19, 1990)

THE RELATIONSHIP BETWEEN GOALS AND THE SELF

We began by observing that Carver and Scheier do not discuss the ontogenesis of goals; no more do they account for the ontogenesis of the self. They write on p. 17: "A broad implication of this sort of theory is that the self is partly the person's goals." However, in the absence of a developmental account, this appears to create another deus ex machina, namely, the self.

In our model, action leads to experience, which leads to affect, which leads to goals. The goals help shape our subsequent experience by guiding how we channel our attention. When we become aware of our goals and their hierarchical relations to each other, we begin to develop a self. As Dante said, "nothing acts without making its self manifest." The self is the sum of the goals that a person constructs (on the basis of feedback to experiences and affects). It is that which we have learned to desire.

To the extent that a person's actions are not based on self-regulation oriented toward experiential goals one might say that the self is *inauthentic*. In other words, if a person consistently pursues goals that do not produce positive affect, but are chosen for other reasons, the self that is manifested is one that has been constructed by external forces. An *authentic* self, by contrast, is one built on goals chosen because they optimize experience. Such goals need not be lofty at all, as long as they reflect the person's actual experiences. For example, in a recent interview the Canadian novelist Robertson Davies described one of the fundamental principles of his life:

Well, you know, that leads me to something which I think has been very important in my life, and it sounds foolish and rather trivial. But I've always insisted on having a nap after lunch, and I inherited this from my father. And I one time said to him: "You know, you've done awfully well in the world. You came to Canada as an immigrant boy without anything and you have done very well. What do you attribute it to?" And he said, "Well, what drove me on to be my own boss was that the thing that I wanted most was to be able to have a nap every day after lunch." And I thought, "What an extraordinary impulse to drive a man on!" But it did, and he always had a twenty minute sleep after lunch. And I am the same . . . *If you will not permit yourself to be driven and flogged through life, you'll probably enjoy it more.* (Csikszentmihalyi, 1996, pp. 58–59)

By setting goals even as trivial as that of enjoying a nap every afternoon, it is possible to build a self that experiences itself as authentic because it knows that instead of being driven and flogged by external forces, it sets its own rules.

CONFLICT AMONG GOALS

We have been drawing attention to goal-directed behavior in which the goals emerge out of immediate experience. However, in everyday life, most of the time we are not consciously aware of our goals; and when we do think of them, they tend to be unclear and contradictory. In this sense, most of behavior is regulated by patterns of habit and necessity. Most people spend only about one third of their waking hours doing what they want to do. The rest they spend doing things because they feel they have to or because there is nothing else to do. Typically when studying, working, or doing maintenance work around the house, people wish they were doing something else and their affect is below average. At such times, there is a conflict between goals based on immediate experience and goals based on the anticipation of future experience.

It is in flow activities that full involvement in immediate experience tends to occur. These are activities that provide very clear goals moment by moment, immediate feedback, and an opportunity to match challenges with skills. Athletic contests, games, and musical performances have such a structure. Contrary to everyday life experiences with their vaguely defin ., shifting, sometimes conflicting demands, these self-contained worlds are clearly structured with unambiguous goals and feedback. In this sense, it is game-like flow activities rather than real life that most closely resemble the feedback loops of cybernetics. Our experiential states (e.g., anxiety; relaxation) provide information about the balance that currently exists between the challenges we encounter and our skills. The information can be used in the effort to adjust the balance and enter or reenter the flow state.

When involved in such activities, it is possible to forget ourselves and act with total abandon, yet at the fullest level of performance. In Mead's (1934) terms, when we are immersed in an activity, the *me*, the self as an object of awareness, disappears; the *I*, the unconscious actor, takes center stage. As the course of events unfolds, even from moment to moment, we may subtly modify our goals in response to our shifting experiential states. The authentic self is engaged; and because flow is experienced only if our capacities are being fully employed, growth of the self occurs.

In most cultures, it is assumed that a mature individual is one who can delay gratification—in other words, one who opts for investing energy in future goals in preference to present ones. Yet, it is arguable that the ideal situation is one where there is harmony between future and present goals, and the person is fully functioning and involved in the moment without sacrificing future goals. This happens in those circumstances in which externally motivated behavior that initially did not produce positive affect is later reinterpreted by the person so that the experience is now positive (cf. integrated self-regulation; e.g., Deci & Ryan, 1985). There is no distinction between what must be done and what one wishes to do. At that point, one achieves that *amor fati*, or love of fate, which philosophers such as Nietzsche and psychologists such as Maslow and Rogers have argued constitutes the fullest realization of an authentic self (Csikszentmihalyi & Rathunde, 1998).

For the social activist who both finds daily work absorbing and the long-term goal of social transformation inspiring or the scientist for whom the research process is fascinating and the long-term scientific enterprise compelling, future goals are joined to the immediate rewards of doing something deeply enjoyable. We are suggesting that organizing one's activity around this combination of goals is the optimal way of investing energy. Our primary reservation about Carver and Scheier's chapter concerns its silence on the ontogenesis of such goals, including the role of affective experience in their formation and pursuit. As a result, although their perspective is helpful in describing self-regulation in situations where goals are clear and stable, it may be less successful in illuminating everyday experiences where the affective evaluation of ongoing experience sets the stage for the feedback loops that control behavior.

ACKNOWLEDGMENT

The Creativity in Later Life Project was funded by a grant from the Spencer Foundation.

REFERENCES

Alighieri, D. (1317/1921). *De monarchia.* Florence, Italy: Rostagno.

Creativity in Later Life Project. (1990). [Interview]. Unpublished interview.

Csikszentmihalyi, M. (1975). *Beyond boredom and anxiety.* San Francisco: Jossey-Bass.

Csikszentmihalyi, M. (1990). *Flow: The psychology of optimal experience.* New York: Harper & Row.

Csikszentmihalyi, M. (1996). *Creativity: Flow and the psychology of discovery and invention.* New York: HarperCollins.

Csikszentmihalyi, M. (1997). *Finding flow.* New York: Basic Books.

Csikszentmihalyi, M., & Csikszentmihalyi, I. (Eds.). (1988). *Optimal experience: Psychological studies of flow in consciousness.* Cambridge, England: Cambridge University Press.

Csikszentmihalyi, M., & Larson, R. (1987). Validity and reliability of the experience sampling method. *Journal of Nervous and Mental Disease, 175* (9), 526–536.

Csikszentmihalyi, M., & Rathunde, K. (1993). The measurement of flow in everyday life. In J. Jacobs (Ed.), *Nebraska Symposium on Motivation* (Vol. 40, pp. 58–97). Lincoln: University of Nebraska Press.

Csikszentmihalyi, M. & Rathunde, K. (1998). The development of the person: An experiential perspective on the ontogenesis of psychological complexity. In R. M. Lerner (Series Ed.) & W. Damon (Vol. Ed.), *Handbook of child psychology: Vol. 1. Theoretical models of human development* (pp. 635–684). New York: Wiley.

Deci, E. L., & Ryan, R. M. (1985). *Intrinsic motivation and self-determination in human behavior.* New York: Plenum Press.

Hektner, J. M. (1996). *Exploring optimal personality development: A longitudinal study of adolescents.* Unpublished doctoral dissertation, University of Chicago.

Inghilleri, P. (1999). *From subjective experience to cultural evolution. (E. Bartoli, Trans.).* New York: Cambridge University Press. (Original work published 1995).

Levinson, D. J., Darrow, C. N., Klein, E. B., Levinson, M. H., & McKee, B. (1978). *The seasons of a man's life.* New York: Knopf.

Massimini, F., & Carli, M. (1988). The systematic assessment of flow in daily experience. In M. Csikszentmihalyi & I. S. Csikszentmihalyi (Eds.), *Optimal experience: Psychological studies of flow in consciousness* (pp. 266–287). New York: Cambridge University Press.

Massimini, F., Delle Fave, A., & Carli, M. (1988). Flow in everyday life: A cross-national comparison. In M. Csikszentmihalyi & I. S. Csikszentmihalyi (Eds.), *Optimal experience: Psychological studies of flow in consciousness* (pp. 288–306). New York: Cambridge University Press.

Massimini, F., & Inghilleri, P. (Eds.). (1986). *L'esperienza quotidiana: Teoria e metodi d'analisi* (Everyday experience: Theory and methods of analysis). Milan, Italy: Franco Angeli.

Mead, G. H. (1934). *Mind, self and society* (C. W. Morris, Ed.). Chicago: University of Chicago Press.

Miller, G., Galanter, E., & Pribram, K. (1960). *Plans and the structure of behavior.* New York: Holt, Rinehart, & Winston.

Moneta, G. B., & Csikszentmihalyi, M. (1996). The effect of perceived challenges and skills on the quality of subjective experience. *Journal of Personality, 64* (2), 275–310.

3

Affect, Goals, and the Self-Regulation of Behavior

Joseph P. Forgas
Patrick T. Vargas
University of New South Wales

Carver and Scheier present an impressively broad "grand theory" of the genesis and regulation of social behavior, placing particular emphasis on the role of goal-directed actions and feedback mechanisms in this process. The model draws on a wide-ranging and diverse sampling of the literature on behavior control; as they claim with admirable modesty, "very little of what is in this article is unique" (p. 2). Despite the avowedly eclectic nature of their enterprise, the magnitude of the topic—behavior— is so enormous that no single paper could do full justice to the task. As is the case with most such grand theories, the devil is often in the detail. Our objective with these comments is not to challenge the impressive overall conceptual scheme advanced. Rather, we hope to point out some of the problems and inconsistencies inherent in Carver and Scheier's treatment of constructs such as goals. Most of our comments focus on what we see as the model's less than adequate treatment of affective phenomena. We suggest a number of ways that the role of affective states as antecedent influences on goal setting, action plans, and behavior regulation could be more adequately covered in the theory.

The theory draws on a large number of competing ideas developed by psychologists. An integrative theory such as this needs to be rather specific in what it accepts and what it rejects and needs to provide clear criteria for those choices. The reasons for preferring and incorporating some explanations in the model while rejecting or ignoring others were not always as clear as one would like. Perhaps more emphasis could have been placed on how competing alternative explanations of purposive behavior could be empirically contrasted with, or integrated into, the present model. One example of this is Carver and Scheier's reliance on the concept of goals as the major latent construct to account for behavioral variance. In the first half of this chapter, we comment on some of the issues and problems that Carver and Scheier's treatment of goals as explanatory concepts leaves unanswered.

Of even greater interest to us is Carver and Scheier's treatment of affective phenomena, surely a key aspect of behavior regulation. They suggest that affective feelings are mediated by the monitoring of a feedback loop, signalling the rate of discrepancy reduction between goals and actual states. For the purposes of the theory, affect is considered to regulate the *intensity* function of motivation (p. 26), with far less emphasis on the influence of affect on the *direction* of the behavior control system. We suggest that this is an unduly limiting and restrictive conceptualization of the role of affect in behavior regulation. Carver and Scheier fail to consider voluminous evidence suggesting that affective states can also have a significant directional function, with a demonstrable influence of people's thoughts, judgments, and strategic social behaviors. We present a theoretical framework and review empirical evidence in the second half of this chapter indicating that affect should also be thought of as a significant antecedent and predictor of goal selection, goal setting, action plans, and behavior regulation.

GOALS AND BEHAVIOR REGULATION

It seems to us that a more functionally and behaviorally rooted definition of key concepts such as goals would serve the theory better than the current, largely a priori conceptualization emphasizing goal characteristics such as abstractness. Further, there are important and largely overlooked parallels between Carver and Scheier's treatment of goals and psychological work on other highly developed dispositional constructs that also regulate behavior such as attitudes and traits.

The Causal Status of Goals

Although goals are central to Carver and Scheier's conceptual scheme, they make inadequate reference to debates in psychology questioning the epistemological status of goals and the issue of human agency in general. Carver and Scheier conceptualize goals as if they had an independent causal status, capable of guiding and influencing what people do. This view is rooted in the dominant, rational view in psychology of human beings as internally controlled, goal-following creatures. However, several influential theorists queried this assumption, suggesting that personal goals may be no more than epiphenomena, with no causal status and no real influence on the regulation of behavior. This debate about our most fundamental beliefs about human agency also presents a major challenge to Carver and Scheier's approach. If behavior can be adequately explained as largely automatic and controlled by external contingencies (Skinner, 1953) and our ideas about free will and goal-directed action are no more than postbehavioral constructions (Wegner & Bargh, 1997), where does that leave a theory emphasizing purposive goal pursuit, as does Carver and Scheier's model? Some explicit consideration of these issues would help to better set the stage for Carver and Scheier's ambitious theorizing about purposive behavior.

Goal Abstractness, Goal Importance, and the Self

Carver and Scheier also suggest that the level of abstractness of a goal (e.g., motor control, do goals, and be goals) is strongly related to that goal's ultimate psychological importance (p. 15). This may not necessarily be true; more abstract goals need not be more important. For example, two different be goals (be fit and be tidy), although equally abstract, may well differ in psychological importance, one accounting for more behavioral variance than the other (p. 16). It is more critical that some do level goals may be more important than some be goals. Goal abstractness and goal importance are thus not necessarily isomorphic. Although goal abstractness seems to be largely a cognitive, representational feature, goal importance is a more functionally based, motivational construct. The subjective importance of a goal could be operationalized in a way analogous to concepts such as attitude strength: More important goals should be more accessible, more central to an individual's beliefs, and more resistant to change (Petty & Krosnick, 1995).

A more functional treatment of goals also has implications for Carver and Scheier's conceptualization of the self. Goal importance (unlike abstractness) can be empirically assessed (Wegener, Downing, Krosnick, & Petty, 1995), suggesting the possibility of a functional and empirically constructed goal hierarchy. More important but not necessarily more abstract goals should be more central to the self. In other words, importance and centrality should be more highly correlated than abstractness and centrality. This leads us to the question of "how many layers of a person's goals should be considered to fall under the label *self*," (p. 17)? An abstractness hierarchy does not offer a simple answer to this question, but an importance/centrality hierarchy may help in defining an empirical cutoff point for self/not-self goals.

People have some highly abstract, internalized goals that may not be part of their self-concept: Few people claim laziness as part of their self-concept, yet some people are undeniably lazy. Goal importance, rather than abstractness, could be a useful empirical criterion for marking a goal as integral to the self-concept. More frequently accessed goals that drive behavior with relatively little conscious effort should thus be considered part of the self (Fazio, 1987). Frequency of use as a criterion for a goal's inclusion in the self-concept also suggests a *process* by which goals may become internalized. The distinction between declarative and procedural knowledge may be a relevant metaphor for identifying goals that have or have not become part of an individual's self-concept (Anderson, 1982). Perhaps goals may be identified as part of the self-concept after they become proceduralized. When a goal is initially activated, it might be stored as declarative knowledge. An individual should frequently refer to the goal, note progress with respect to the goal, and actively monitor various aspects of that goal, as Carver and Scheier suggest. However, with repeated use, goals should come to be represented as procedural knowledge, become habitual, and require relatively little cognitive effort in guiding behavior. Such goals can be activated using direct access processing, as we shall argue later (Forgas, 1995a). Carver and Scheier only hint at this sort of distinction in their discussion on controlled and emergent behavior (p. 52) and do not link their ideas to processing differences in goal activation and to notions of self-concept.

Goals and Traits

Carver and Scheier rely on the goal construct as the primary dispositional variable that drives behavior. However, there are other psychological constructs, such as traits and attitudes, that function somewhat similarly. Personality traits are often manifested as goals, although not all goals can be described in terms of traits. It is a small step from trait to goal—the addition of a two-letter verb is all that is required to move from "honest" to "be honest," from "kind" to "be kind". The conceptual distinction is similarly narrow. Both traits and goals are about describing habitual patterns of behavior. Questions such as "What is Bob like?" can be equally well answered in trait terms ("Bob is kind") or in goal terms ("Bob tries to be kind"). Personality descriptions are suggestive about goal hierarchies and principal-level goals that are realized are similar to traits.

However, most of us also possess some unfulfilled goals (or, oughts according to Higgins, 1996) that do not find behavioral expression, and such goals are obviously not traits. So traits may, but need not be isomorphic with goals. Additionally, traits and goals may also differ in their relevance to the self. A trait that is unacknowledged or denied can still be an integral part of the self and be open to behavioral verification (e.g., laziness). In contrast, unacknowledged goals could not be verified as part of the self (e.g., observed laziness confirms the trait, but does not confirm a goal). Further, traits are closely linked to affectivity or temperament (Mayer & Salovey, 1988; Rusting, 1998a, 1998b; Salovey & Mayer, 1990), whereas goals do not necessarily have such an affective dimension. Carver and Scheier's inadequate treatment of affect is the focus of our comments in the second half of this chapter.

It also seems that the relationship between goals and behavior may be more tenuous and more dependent on inferences and attributions than is the link between traits and behaviors. This suggests that Carver and Scheier's overwhelming emphasis on goals as the dispositional origin of behaviors could be problematic, to the extent that goals are relatively more elusive, are less affective, and are more difficult to verify and measure than are competing dispositional constructs, such as traits. The model would clearly benefit from greater emphasis on the links between traits and goals as alternative psychological constructs capable of regulating behavior.

Goals and Attitudes

There are also some similarities between goals and attitudes. Functionally, goals and attitudes are both dispositional constructs used to explain behavior. In terms of Carver and Scheier's analysis, to the extent that most people seek to maintain internal consistency, attitudes are often synonymous with recurring "goals." Unlike goals, however, attitudes also comprise strong affective and evaluative feelings in regard to some topic. Attitudes are also linked to behavior dispositions producing approach and avoidance, analogous to Carver and Scheier's notion of approach and avoidance goals (or goals and antigoals). Further, both attitudes and goals can be either explicit or implicit. Attitude measurement relies on the fact that most attitudes can be consciously accessed (Thurstone, 1928), just as people can report on most of their goals. However, implicit attitudes are consciously inaccessible, and there may also exist goals that are outside of our awareness, as Carver and Scheier note.

Indeed, implicit goals may be some of the highest level and most fundamental goals there are, forming the basis of some of our most cherished theories: Be kind, get ahead, maintain internal consistency, hold correct attitudes, or do not exert more cognitive effort than seems necessary (Kruglanski, 1989). The existence of such powerful implicit goals is often documented by social psychological research and may present a problem for a theory of behavior regulation as proposed by Carver and Scheier. Such implicit goals are difficult to operationalize and to verify, and their behavioral consequences are not always readily observable, raising the spectre of unfalsifiability for theory relying on goals as the primary explanatory construct. Perhaps some attention to work on the measurement of implicit attitudes could provide a useful addition to Carver and Scheier's treatment of implicit goals.

Attitudes, just like goals, predict behavior better when both variables are assessed at the same level of specificity (Fishbein & Aizen, 1975). More specific goals and attitudes are better predictors of specific behaviors than are more general goals and attitudes. Attitude theory and the theory of planned action in particular (Aizen, 1991) have gone some way toward explaining the multiple contingencies that link attitudes to behavior. Much of that work is directly applicable to an understanding of how goals may or may not lead to specific behaviors, an issue of critical importance to Carver and Scheier's model. The concepts of attitude strength and attitude accessibility (Petty & Krosnick, 1995) are also directly relevant to goals: Goals that are stronger, more accessible, and more important should be more closely related to behavior than weaker goals. The operationalization of these variables in attitude research could thus provide a useful and relevant metaphor for Carver and Scheier's operationalization of goals as predictors of behavior.

Another point of similarity between attitude research and Carver and Scheier's goal theory is that both attitudes and goals influence, and also can be influenced by, behavior. People adjust their attitudes to fit their behavior (Festinger, 1957), and these processes are just as likely to apply to goals. This kind of reciprocal causality is not at present sufficiently recognized in Carver and Scheier's model. Although they do allow for the possibility that goals can be modified as a result of feedback based on behavioral information, they do not consider the possibility that goals themselves may be postbehavioral constructions (Nisbett & Wilson, 1977). If people can indeed infer their goals from their behaviors rather than the other way around (as they seem to do at least some of the time; see Wegner & Bargh, 1997), this would cast some doubt on the suggested causal status of goals as essential determinants of action. This point has direct bearing on our previous comments concerning the epistemological status of goals as causal antecedents of action.

We have argued in this section that there are several important unresolved issues about Carver and Scheier's treatment of goals as the key explanatory concept in behavior regulation. The theory seems to assume that goals have a necessary antecedent causal status and that a priori goal characteristics such as abstractness are the critical feature driving behavior regulation. Further, the theory could do more to clarify the relationship between goals and other dispositional constructs of behavior regulation, such as traits and attitudes. We proposed that greater attention to the functional, empirical aspects of goals and to past research on traits and attitudes would help to bridge some of the gaps in the theory. The second main question we want to address concerns the relatively inadequate treatment of affective processes and the lack of attention to the antecedent role of affect in behavior regulation in Carver and Scheier's theory. We turn to these issues next.

AFFECT AND BEHAVIOR REGULATION

The treatment of affect in Carver and Scheier's model is the focus of our remaining comments. We suggest that the model of behavior regulation proposed does not take sufficiently clear account of the multiple and interactive role that affective states can play in the initiation, performance, and evaluation of goal-directed behaviors. Specifically, we suggest here that (a) the status and definition of affect and its relationship to cognition and behavior need to be more clearly defined; (b) that a fuller understanding of how affect impacts on cognition and behavior regulation requires a detailed consideration of the kind of information-processing strategies people adopt in particular situations; and finally, (c) affective states can also play a critical role in triggering particular goals, influencing people's plans, and producing and specific goal-directed behaviors. Empirical evidence supporting these suggestions, including research from our lab, also is reviewed.

The Links Between Affect, Cognition, and Motivation

Carver and Scheier's theory suggests that affective states primarily arise as a consequence of a feedback process and are triggered by the rate of discrepancy reduction in the action system over time. This appears to be a fundamentally cognitivist conceptualization of affect, assuming that affective states are typically produced as a result of reasonably high-level inferential processes requiring the analysis and interpretation of external and internal information in relation to one's goals and behavior. It is not clear how Carver and Scheier's theory could accommodate evidence for the existence of precognitive affective reactions that may function as directional input to behavior management (Berkowitz, 1993; Blascovich & Tomaka, 1996; Forgas, 1995a; Zajonc, 1980). Yet it is still an unresolved conceptual issue whether affect should be treated as postcognitive and part of the cognitive-representational system or should be seen as an entirely separate, primary, mental faculty (Fiedler & Forgas, 1988; Hilgard, 1980; Salovey & Mayer, 1990). Several influential theorists argued that feelings may be external to and independent of cognition and can serve as input to subsequent cognitive and behavioral processes (Clore, Schwarz, & Conway, 1994; Damasio, 1994; De Sousa, 1987). Zajonc (1980) specifically proposed such a "separate-systems" view, suggesting that affect often precedes and is certainly distinct from cognitive processes. There is little allowance in Carver and Scheier's model for the notion that primary affective reactions can directly regulate and inform subsequent behavior (cf. Berkowitz, 1993) rather than affect arising as a consequence of a feedback loop concerned with the cognitive evaluation of goal performance.

The main input function Carver and Scheier assign to affect is as a determinant of the intensity of motivation, and as they acknowledge, this is a "consequence of structural assumptions we began with, rather than a principled decision" (p. 27). This seems to us a rather inadequate treatment of the role of affect in behavior regulation. There is extensive evidence that affective states can determine the content and direction of people's thoughts, plans, and behaviors and not merely the intensity of predetermined directed action, as suggested here. A comprehensive model of goal-oriented behavior may also need to consider the role of affective states as primary inputs into the behavior regulation process, an issue we return to shortly.

Affect, Mood, and Emotion

Carver and Scheier also do not adequately consider some of the fundamental problems encountered in defining and describing affective states. Several unresolved conceptual problems plague this field. There is little general agreement about how best to define terms such as *affect*, *feelings*, *emotions*, or *mood* (Fiedler & Forgas, 1988; Forgas, 1992a, 1995a), and

Carver and Scheier do not offer a clear definition of what exactly they mean by affect. We have argued elsewhere that *affect* may be used as a generic label to refer to both moods and emotions. *Moods* in turn could be described as "low-intensity, diffuse and relatively enduring affective states without a salient antecedent cause and therefore little cognitive content (e.g., feeling good or feeling bad)", whereas *emotions* "are more intense, short-lived and usually have a definite cause and clear cognitive content" (e.g., anger or fear; Forgas, 1992a, p. 230). This distinction may also be highly relevant to a model of behavior regulation. Considerable research now suggests that subtle, nonspecific moods may often have a potentially more enduring, subtle, and insidious influence on social cognition and social behaviors than do distinct and intense emotions that are subject to explicit cognitive monitoring (Forgas, 1992a, 1992b; 1994, 1995a, 1995b, in press-a, in press-b; Mayer, 1986; Mayer, Gaschke, Braverman, & Evans, 1992; Mayer, McCormicks, & Strong, 1995; Sedikides, 1992).

It is also not clear from Carver and Scheier's analysis whether it is specific, intense emotions rather than nonspecific, low-intensity moods that are most commonly triggered by perceived goal discrepancies and feed into the intensity function of motivation. This is a critical issue, because there is overwhelming evidence not only for mood effects on cognition, judgments, and behavior, but also for specific motivational effects associated with moods, and negative moods in particular (Forgas, 1991; Forgas & Ciarrochi, 1998; Forgas & Fiedler, 1996). Carver and Scheier's analysis would have benefitted from a more detailed discussion of the similarities and differences between different categories of emotional states and the role of these states as antecedents and consequences in the behavior regulation process. In particular, the influence of affective states on how people select, plan, and implement goal-oriented behaviors and how they evaluate and interpret feedback information about goal performance is insufficiently specified, as we see in the next section.

Affective Influences on Behavior Regulation: A Theoretical Framework

The behavior regulation model proposed by Carver and Scheier implicitly assumes that people employ a single, essentially rational and logical cognitive strategy in setting and pursuing their goals, collecting and acting on feedback information, and evaluating their progress and performance. However, the role of affect in the selection, direction, and implementation of goal performance and in the evaluation and use of feedback information receives relatively little attention in the model. Other than influencing the intensity of goal-oriented action, affective states are not considered as directly responsible for behavior regulation. We suggest that this represents an unnecessarily restrictive and limited approach to affective phenomena. Specifically, Carver and Scheier's model does not adequately deal with extensive evidence demonstrating the impact of affect on a wide variety of cognitive and behavioral processes that people employ in planning and executing goal-oriented behaviors and interpreting feedback about their performance.

Experiences of positive or negative affect accompany us throughout our daily lives. There is growing evidence that transient moods do have a significant influence both on the content of cognition and behavior (what people think and do), as well as the process of behavior production (how people think and act; Bower, 1981, 1991; Fiedler & Forgas, 1988; Forgas, 1995a, 1998a, 1998b, in press-a, in press-b; Forgas & Fiedler, 1996; Sedikides, 1992, 1995). For the purposes of this discussion, such *affect infusion* may be defined as an process whereby affectively loaded information exerts an influence on and becomes incorporated into a person's cognitive and behavioral processes, entering into their constructive deliberations and eventually coloring the outcome in a mood-congruent direction (Forgas, 1995a).

Affect infusion occurs because planning and executing complex social behaviors usually requires high-level, constructive, inferential cognitive processes. Social actors can only make sense of ambiguous situations and plan their actions and pursue their goals effectively by the constructive use of their preexisting thoughts, memories, and associations to create a meaningful cognitive representation of the social world. In many conditions, the prevailing affective state of a person can become part of the constructive informational base used when interpreting information, or planning and executing a behavior (Fiedler, 1991).

There is clear evidence that such affect infusion is most likely to occur in the course of *constructive processing* that involves the substantial transformation rather than mere reproduction of existing social knowledge. In other words, affect "will influence cognitive processes to the extent that the . . . task involves the active generation of new information as opposed to the passive conservation of information given" (Fiedler, 1990, pp. 2–3). Research shows, however, that affect infusion is not an invariable phenomenon. Frequently, the affective state of a person appears to have no influence on the content of cognition and action and may even have an inconsistent, mood-incongruent influence (Erber & Erber, 1994; Forgas, 1991; Sedikides, 1994). How can we explain these apparently contradictory findings?

The proposed Affect Infusion Model (AIM; Forgas, 1995a) argues that the nature and extent of affect infusion into behavior and cognition depends critically on what kind of processing strategy is adopted by a person in dealing with a particular task. This is in marked contrast to the single process assumptions of many social cognition theories, including the Carver and Scheier model proposed here. Affect infusion is most likely in the course of *constructive processing* that involves the substantial transformation rather than mere reproduction of existing cognitive representations and behavior patterns, requiring a relatively open information search strategy and a significant degree of generative elaboration of the preexisting knowledge (Fiedler, 1990, pp. 2–3). Some social cognitive tasks such as setting and monitoring routine, recurrent goals may require little constructive thinking (Fiedler, 1991) and should be relatively impervious to the infusion of affect. In contrast, other tasks such as executing complex or novel goals and monitoring ambiguous or indeterminate feedback about behavior may require highly constructive and generative processing strategies that can be readily influenced by prevailing affective states (Forgas, Bower, & Krantz, 1984).

The AIM distinguishes between four fundamental processing strategies that people might use when planning and executing purposive action of the kind considered by Carver and Scheier, each characterized by different affect infusion potentials. First, the *direct access* of a preexisting goal or response or second, the *motivated processing* in service of a preexisting goal both involve highly predetermined and directed information search and behavior patterns that require little generative, constructive processing, limiting the scope of affect infusion effects. In contrast, when the task requires a degree of constructive processing, judges may use either the third, a *heuristic*, simplified or a fourth, a *substantive*, generative processing strategy to plan their actions and produce a response. These are high-infusion strategies that require a degree of open, constructive thinking, where affect may either directly (Clore et al., 1994) or indirectly through primed associations (Forgas & Bower, 1987) inform the response.

According to the AIM, processing choices should be determined by three categories of variables associated with the *task*, the *person* and the *situation*, respectively. Familiarity, typicality, and complexity are the main task features of interest. Person features include traits, personal relevance, motivational goals, cognitive capacity, and affective state. Finally, situational factors such as need for accuracy, degree of external control, and social norms and expectations may also influence processing choices. A complete description of the AIM and the evidence supporting is presented elsewhere (Forgas, 1992a, 1995a), so it is not reviewed in detail here. The major relevance of the AIM to behavior regulation is that it provides a framework within which the presence or the absence of affect infusion into goal-oriented social behaviors can be predicted within an integrated theoretical model.

The AIM thus can provide answers to a variety of intriguing questions that are currently unspecified in Carver and Scheier's ambitious model of behavior regulation, such as: How can we account for the apparent context sensitivity of many mood effects on goal setting and goal evaluation? What sorts of behavior control strategies are most likely to be influenced by affect? What decisions about what kinds of goals are most and least likely to be open to affective distortions? What is the role of affect in the processing of more or less complex or ambiguous information about goal performance? Is more prolonged, systematic processing more or less likely to be subject to affect infusion? In particular, this model can also explain some nonobvious results, indicating that more prolonged and extensive processing recruited by more complex and ambiguous tasks often increases rather than decreases the degree of affect infusion into cognition and behavior (Fiedler, 1991; Forgas, 1992a, 1992b; 1994, 1995b; Sedikides, 1995).

Applying such a multiprocess framework to Carver and Scheier's model and the suggested distinction between different processing strategies when computing goal-oriented plans and evaluating feedback should have considerable benefits for a comprehensive theory of behavior regulation. For example, the *direct access* strategy is the simplest way of implementing a goal, based on the direct retrieval of preexisting, stored action plans. People possess a rich repertoire of such precomputed goals of various degrees of abstractness and generality, and this strategy is likely to be used whenever more extensive processing is not necessary. Direct access processing is a low-affect infusion strategy, as it involves little online constructive processing. It is interesting that this simple and probably very common strategy for behavior regulation has received relatively little attention in theories of social cognition and action.

Motivated processing is also a highly selective, guided, and targeted regulatory strategy, and, as such, it is also relatively impervious to affect infusion effects. Carver and Scheier's model pays relatively little attention to the possibility that emotions such as anger or fear, replete with cognitive content and appraisal qualities, often motivate specific goal-oriented thinking and behaviors (Berkowitz, 1993). Motivated processing may also be used to achieve mood maintenance as well as mood repair (Clark & Isen, 1982). Indeed, merely directing a person's attention to their affective seems sufficient to trigger deliberate, motivated behavior-regulation strategies (Berkowitz, 1993; Berkowitz & Troccoli, 1990). Affect-cognition research demonstrates that a number of specific goals can also elicit this kind of motivated processing, such as mood-repair and mood-maintenance, self-evaluation maintenance, ego-enhancement, achievement motivation, affiliation, and the like (Forgas, 1995a).

In contrast, *heuristic processing* may regulate behavior when people have no precomputed action plan nor a strong motivation to guide their actions, and they seek to produce a response with the least amount of effort, using whatever shortcuts or simplification are readily available. This strategy is common when the task is simple, typical, or of low personal relevance; when the actor has limited processing capacity; and when the context does not call for greater elaboration. Social behaviors are often regulated by heuristic cues such as irrelevant associations with environmental variables or a misinterpretation of a prevailing affective state (cf. Clore et al., 1994). Thus, heuristic processing can be responsible for some affect infusion into cognition and behavior in circumstances where more detailed processing is not employed.

Substantive processing is the most constructive and extended strategy for behavior management and occurs when people need to select, learn, and interpret new information about a task and link this information with preexisting memories and knowledge structures. Affect priming can account for significant affect infusion during substantive processing, as "activation of an emotion node also spreads activation throughout the memory structures to which it is connected" (Bower, 1981, p. 135). The selection and execution of goals and the monitoring of goal performance within the behavior regulation system outlined by Carver and Scheier can all be influenced by such affect infusion processes in the course of substantive processing, as we see later. In fact, affect infusion increases as more extensive and constructive processing is employed, a counterintuitive prediction that has been repeatedly confirmed in studies (Fiedler, 1991; Forgas, 1992b; 1994; Sedikides, 1995).

Affect Infusion Into Strategic Behaviors

Consistent with the theoretical arguments outlined, several experiments confirm that manipulated affective states can have a significant direct influence on the goals people set for themselves, the plans they make, and the way they actually behave in complex social situations (Forgas, in press-a, in press-b).

In one relevant series of experiments, we explored the effects of mood on strategic goal-oriented behavior: The way people formulate and use verbal messages such as requests. Requesting is an intrinsically complex behavioral task characterized by goal pursuit and psychological ambiguity, where requesters need to formulate their messages with the right degree of politeness so as to maximize compliance without the risk of giving offense. We expected that mood should significantly influence request goals and performance, with people adopting a more confident and direct requesting strategy when experiencing a positive mood, consistent with the greater availability of positively valenced thoughts and associations (Forgas, 1998a). Further, in terms of the AIM, these mood effects should be even greater when the situation is more complex and demanding and requires more substantive and elaborate processing strategies.

Mood was induced in an allegedly separate experiment by asking people to recall and think about happy or sad autobiographical episodes ($N = 112$; Forgas, 1998a, Exp. 1). In a subsequent task, participants selected a more or less polite request formulation that they would use in either an easy, or a difficult and demanding request situation. Results show that induced mood had a significant influence on request strategies. Happy participants preferred more direct, impolite requests, whereas sad persons used indirect, polite request alternatives. Further, these mood effects on requesting were significantly greater in the more difficult, demanding request situation that required more extensive, substantive processing strategies.

Very similar procedures were used in a follow-up experiment, but instead of prestructured requests, participants now formulated their own open-ended requests, which were subsequently rated for politeness by two independent raters (Forgas, 1998a, Exp. 2). Results again show that mood had a significant influence on these strategic behaviors. Happy persons produced significantly more impolite and less elaborate requests than sad individuals, and mood effects were again greater in the more problematic and difficult situational context (Fig. 3.1). These results confirm that moods can influence how people perceive and interpret strategic situations and how they formulate and execute goal-oriented behaviors such as requests. But why should mood effects be greater on requests in a more difficult and demanding situation? More difficult strategic tasks require more elaborate processing, and, according to the AIM, affect infusion should increase when more substantive processing is required to formulate a strategic behavior.

A third experiment predicted and found that mood also has a relatively greater influence on more unusual, unconventional behaviors that require more substantive processing such as producing an impolite, direct request (Forgas, 1998b, Exp. 1). Following an audiovisual mood induction (watching happy or sad films), participants selected more or less polite request forms in each of 16 different request situations. Results confirm that mood effects are greatest on decisions about using the most direct, unconventional requests that are most likely to violate cultural conventions of politeness and should recruit the most substantive, elaborate processing strategies. These findings indicate that mood

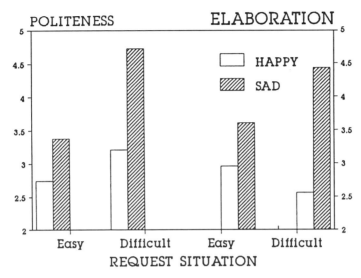

FIG. 3.1. Mood effects on goal-oriented behaviors: Negative mood increases and positive mood decreases request politeness and elaboration, and these mood effects are significantly greater in more difficult, demanding social situations that require more extensive processing. (After Forgas, 1998a)

effects on behavior regulation are indeed process-dependent, with affect infusion enhanced when more constructive processing is required by a more difficult strategic task (Fiedler, 1991; Forgas, 1995a).

Similar effects were also obtained in a fourth, unobtrusive experiment looking at naturally produced requests (Forgas, 1998b, Exp. 2). After an audiovisual mood induction, the experimenter casually asked participants to get a file from a neighboring office while the next experiment is set up. All participants agreed. Their words in requesting the file were recorded by a concealed tape recorder and subsequently were analyzed for politeness and other qualities. Results show a significant mood effect on these natural, unobtrusively elicited behaviors. Sad people used more polite, friendly, and more elaborate forms, and happy people used more direct and less polite forms. Negative mood also increased the latency of requests: Consistent with their more cautious, defensive behavioral strategies and the more extensive processing these unconventional behaviors presumably required, sad persons delayed making their requests significantly longer than did control or happy persons (Fig. 3.2). An analysis of the subsequent recall of these requests confirmed that unconventional requests were recalled significantly better. This confirms the predicted more elaborate, in-depth processing of these messages and

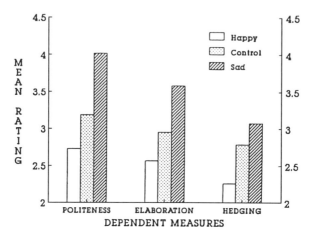

FIG. 3.2. Mood effects on naturally produced requests: Positive mood increases and negative mood decreases the degree of politeness, elaboration, and hedging in goal-oriented strategic communications. (After Forgas, 1998b).

supports the core prediction of the AIM that the greatest mood effects occur when more elaborate, substantive processing is used by a communicator.

These mood effects are not restricted to the production of requests. In another series of experiments (Forgas, in press-a), we looked at the role of temporary affective states in how people evaluate and behaviorally respond to more or less polite requests directed at them ($N = 96$). Again, an unobtrusive strategy was used. Students entering a library found pictures or text placed on their desks designed to induce good or bad moods. A few minutes later, they received an unexpected polite or impolite request from a stranger for several sheets of paper needed to complete an essay. Results showed that people in an induced negative mood were more likely to form a critical, negative view of requests and were less inclined to comply than were positive mood participants (Fig. 3.3). Further, these mood effects were significantly greater on the evaluation of impolite, unconventional requests that required more substantive processing, as confirmed by better recall memory for these messages later on.

These experiments show that affect infusion into the planning and execution of strategic behaviors is significantly mediated by the kind of processing strategy people employ. It is not entirely clear how such direct mood effects on the selection and execution of goal-oriented actions could be explained by Carver and Scheier's theoretical model. We believe that these findings indicate that a comprehensive theory of behavior regulation such as the one proposed by Carver and Scheier also needs to

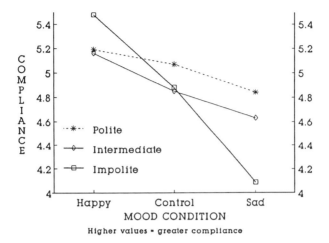

FIG. 3.3. The influence of unobtrusively elicited affect on responding to natu-ralistic requests: Positive mood increases and negative mood decreases compli-ance, and these mood effects are greatest in response to more impolite, uncon-ventional requests that require more extensive processing. *Note:* From "Asking Nicely? Mood Effects on Responding to More or Less Polite Requests," by J. P. Forgas, in press-b, *Personality and Social Psychology Bulletin*, p. 180, Copyright 1998, by Sage Publications, Adapted with permission.

incorporate a detailed consideration of how temporary affective states can influence people's goals, action plans, and strategic behaviors. The production of more complex, multiaction behavior sequences seems to be similarly affect sensitive, as we see in the next section.

Affect and Behavior Regulation in Complex Encounters

As the above experiments suggest, even mild, temporary mood states can have a significant influence on the way people select and activate goals, the way they formulate action plans, and the way they execute and monitor complex social behaviors. In another series of experiments, we investigated affective influences on the regulation of complex behavior sequences such as negotiating encounters (Forgas, in press-b). Positive, control, or negative mood was induced by giving participants positive, negative, or neutral feedback about their performance on a demand-ing verbal task ($N = 72$). Next, they engaged in an informal, interper-sonal, and a formal, intergroup negotiating task with another team in what they believed was a separate experiment. We were interested in how temporary moods might influence people's goal-setting strategies and behavior-regulation techniques. Results showed that participants

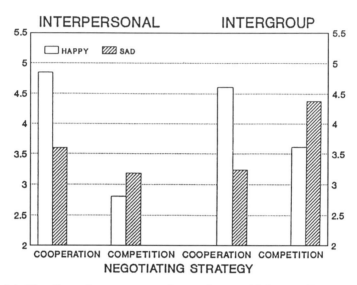

FIG. 3.4. The effects of temporary mood on goal-oriented behaviors: Positive mood increases and negative mood decreases cooperation in both interpersonal and intergroup bargaining encounters; the opposite mood effects were observed for competitive bargaining strategies. *Note:* From "Feeling Good and Getting Your Way: Mood Effects on Negotiation, Cognition, and Bargaining Outcomes," by J. P. Forgas. *Journal of Personality and Social Psychology,* in press-b, Adapted with permission.

who were in an induced positive mood set themselves higher and more ambitious goals, formed higher expectations about the forthcoming encounter, and also formulated specific action plans that were more cooperative and integrative than did control or negative mood participants. Furthermore, individuals who formulated cooperative goals as a result of feeling good actually behaved more cooperatively and were more willing to make and reciprocate deals than were those in a negative mood (Fig. 3.4). Perhaps the most interesting finding is that these mood-induced differences in goal setting and behavior regulation actually resulted in more successful performances; people who felt good did significantly better in this bargaining task than did those who felt bad. These results provide relatively clearcut evidence that even slight changes in mood due to an unrelated prior event can significantly bias the kind of goals that people set for themselves, the action plans they formulate, and the way they execute and regulate their subsequent interpersonal behaviors.

In terms of the AIM, these mood effects on behavior regulation can be explained as due to the operation of affect-priming mechanisms. Thinking about and planning a bargaining encounter is by definition a complex, indeterminate, and personally involving cognitive task where substantive processing should be the dominant strategy adopted in terms of the AIM. Positive mood should selectively prime more positive thoughts and associations when people construct their goals and plans and should ultimately lead to the formulation of more optimistic expectations and the adoption of more cooperative expected and actual bargaining strategies. In contrast, negative mood should result in more pessimistic, negative thoughts and associations, leading to less ambitious goals and less cooperative and successful bargaining strategies.

The second experiment in this series showed that these mood effects are much less marked for individuals who scored high on individual differences measures, such as machiavellism and need for approval ($N = 132$). In terms of the AIM, these individuals should have approached the bargaining task from a more predetermined, motivated perspective that limited the degree of open, constructive processing they employed and thus reduced the effects of affect infusion on their behaviors. These results suggest that Carver and Scheier's model of behavior regulation could be extended to give explicit consideration to when and how affective states might influence goal formation and performance, rather than just motivation intensity. Further, individual differences in a person's tendency to use open and constructive or guided and motivated processing strategies may significantly influence the extent to which affective states are likely to infuse their goal setting and their strategic behaviors (Rusting, 1998a, 1998b).

Affective Influences on Behavior Monitoring and Feedback

We agree with Carver and Scheier that the accurate monitoring and interpretation of strategic social behaviors is a critical aspect of effective goal-directed performance. However, as we argued previously, within Carver and Scheier's model, affect is primarily thought of as a by-product, a consequence of the feedback-comparison processes that accompany the cognitive monitoring of goal-directed behavior. In contrast, we would like to suggest that affect should also be thought of as a critical antecedent and a significant biasing influence on how people process and evaluate strategic information about their own and other people's behaviors. In addition to affective influences on the activation of goals and the planning and execution of strategic behaviors demonstrated earlier, there is also evidence that moods can influence the way people monitor and interpret their own and others' interpersonal behaviors.

Empirical evidence supporting this proposition was collected in an experiment by Forgas, Bower, and Krantz (1984). This study included a particularly challenging test of mood effects on behavior monitoring. Rather than just looking at implicit behavior monitoring and evaluation, we provided participants with objective, videotaped evidence about their actual social behaviors. This study was carried out over two consecutive days. On the first day, pairs of participants were videotaped while engaging in four kinds of complex interactions of varying formality and intimacy with female confederates. The next day, the same people returned for a "social perception experiment." They were hypnotized, induced to feel happy or sad, and were then asked to monitor the videotapes of the interaction episodes from the previous day in order to identify and score instances of positive and skilled or negative and unskilled behaviors both for themselves and for their partners as they saw it on the videotape. There was a significant affective bias on this behavior monitoring task, despite the availability of objective, videotaped information. In a good mood, people saw more positive, skilled and fewer negative, unskilled behaviors both in themselves and in their partners than did sad subjects. Negative mood in turn resulted in more negative behavior interpretations for the self, but not necessarily others—a pattern also commonly found in depression. Observers who received no mood manipulation showed no such monitoring biases. These results confirm the existence of a significant mood-induced bias on how behavior is monitored and interpreted, even when objective, videotaped information is readily available. Mood effects are likely to be even greater on the kind of subtle, implicit behavior evaluation judgments described in Carver and Scheier's model.

In several subsequent experiments, we also demonstrated the impact of temporary moods on more complex, elaborate inferential judgments about the causes of various behavioral episodes. Results show that people in a negative mood tend to make more critical, self-deprecatory interpretations of their own behaviors, whereas those in a positive mood selectively look for and find lenient explanations for identical outcomes (Forgas, Bower, & Moylan, 1990). Remarkably, such mood-induced distortions on behavior interpretation can also influence evaluations of highly familiar, intimate interaction episodes, such as real-life conflicts experienced in people's long-term relationships (Forgas, 1994). In these experiments, partners involved in long-term intimate relationships were asked to monitor and interpret their behaviors in more or less serious interpersonal conflict episodes. Results again show a significant mood-congruent bias, with people in a positive mood selectively finding lenient, self-serving explanations. Further, in a counterintuitive pattern, these mood effects on behavior monitoring were greater for more complex and serious conflicts that required more extensive and constructive processing strategies to be adequately explained.

Studies such as these strongly suggest that the online monitoring and feedback about goal-oriented behaviors that plays such a critical role in Carver and Scheier's model of behavior regulation may not be thought of as an entirely rational and logical process. Rather, temporary mood states can have a major impact on how complex behaviors are interpreted and how this information may be subsequently used in behavior regulation.

Affect Control and Behavior Control

The theoretical framework proposed by Carver and Scheier is relatively silent on one critical aspect of behavior regulation: How do people go about controlling and managing their own affective states? Arguably one of the most common and important goals people seek to implement in their everyday lives has to do with maintaining a reasonably positive, optimistic affective balance despite the manifold challenges they face. The goals of mood maintenance and mood regulation (Clark & Isen, 1982) do not feature prominently in Carver and Scheier's analysis, yet these goals probably occupy a disproportionately important role in regulating our everyday behavioral strategies and take up a great deal of our mental resources.

People may use a number of motivated strategies to control their affective states, such as selective exposure to mood-incongruent information (Forgas, 1992a), recalling mood-incongruent memories (Erber & Erber, 1994), engaging in mood-incongruent behaviors (Cialdini & Kenrick, 1976), interacting with rewarding partners (Forgas, 1991), or distracting themselves from the source of their mood (Rusting, 1998b). Within the AIM framework, the ongoing task of affect management and control can be understood in terms of people routinely and automatically switching between two complementary information-processing strategies: substantive processing that results in affect infusion and the accentuation of the existing affective state, and motivated processing that results in conscious affect control outcomes. Such an affect management model was proposed (Forgas, Johnson & Ciarrochi, in press) in what is a refinement and development of relevant aspects of the earlier and more general Affect Infusion Model (Forgas, 1995a).

A schematic summary of the affect management hypothesis is presented in Fig. 3.5. As this figure shows, the choice of either a substantive (affect infusion) or motivated (affect control) processing strategy is determined by a combination of personal, situational, and task-related input variables and the extremity of the prevailing affective state. So far, research suggests that motivated rather than substantive processing is more likely when (a) the task is of direct personal relevance (Forgas,

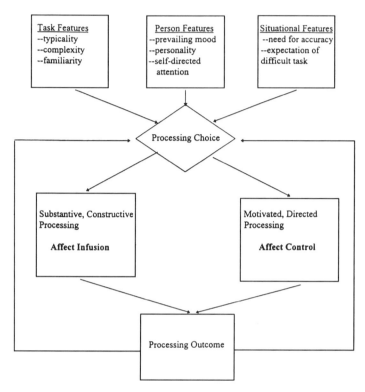

FIG. 3.5. A processing theory of spontaneous mood management: Substantive processing accentuates, and motivated processing attenuates the valence of the existing affective state, and automatic switching due to a feedback loop between these two processing modes produces a homeostatic mood management system. *Note:* From "Affect Control and Affect Infusion: a Multiprocess Account of Mood Management and Personal Control," in M. Kofta, G. Weary, and G. Sedak (Eds.), *Personal Control in Action: Cognitive and Motivational Mechanisms,* (p.), New York: Plenum. Copyright (1998) by Adapted with permission.

1991), (b) people are aware of the cause or consequence of their mood (Berkowitz & Troccoli, 1990; Clore et al., 1994), (c) people score high on individual differences measures that indicate motivated-processing tendencies (Forgas, in press-b) and (d) people experience an extreme or aversive affective state (Forgas & Fiedler, 1996). Situational variables may also influence processing and behavioral choices (Forgas, 1995a; Wegner & Erber, 1993). For example, persons who expect to engage in a demanding interaction with a stranger may prefer to tone down their mood by reading articles that are the opposite in affective tone to their own mood (Wegner & Erber, 1993).

A critical feature of the affect management model is that it incorporates a feedback loop between the valenced outcome of the existing behavior and processing strategy and subsequent processing choices. As a consequence, the model provides for the possibility of continuous changes in behavior and processing as a function of the prevailing mood state, a suggestion that is supported by empirical evidence (Clark & Isen, 1982; Forgas, 1995a; Sedikides, 1994). In practical terms, this means that if, as a result of an existing substantive processing strategy and ongoing affect infusion, the level of negativity in a person's thinking and behavior reaches a threshold level, an automatic correction should take place that consists of a switch to motivated processing.

The mood management model predicts that negative mood initially leads to affect infusion and mood-congruent thoughts until a threshold level of negativity is reached, at which point people should switch to motivated mood control and mood-incongruent associations. Sedikides (1994) found some initial support for such a hypothesis. We (Forgas & Ciarrochi, 1998) conducted three additional studies to test the hypothesis that affect leads first to affect infusion, followed by a motivated affect-control strategy. In experiment 1, participants who were feeling good or bad after recalling sad or happy events from their past generated a series of trait adjectives. Negative mood initially produced mood-congruent adjectives, but over time, subjects spontaneously switched to generating mood-incongruent (positive) adjectives consistent with the adoption of a motivated affect-control strategy. In study 2, a different word completion task was used to measure mood effects on associations. A time-series regression analysis revealed that sad subjects rapidly changed from affect-congruent to affect-incongruent recall. It appears that once a threshold level of negativity was reached due to affect-infusion processes, sad people switched to motivated, incongruent recall as if seeking to control and eliminate their aversive mood (Fig. 3.6).

Study 3 also explored the role of individual difference variables such as self-esteem in such affect management strategies. Previous work suggests that people low in self-esteem are less likely than others to engage in conscious affect control (Smith & Petty, 1995). To induce mood, participants received positive or negative feedback about their performance on a spatial abilities task. Next, they completed a series of sentences asking for self-descriptive adjectives. Results again indicated a clear "first congruent, then incongruent pattern," and this result was particularly marked for high self-esteem people. Those scoring high on self-esteem were able to rapidly eliminate a mood-congruent bias in their associations by producing mood-incongruent, positive words after initially negative responses. Low self-esteem people persevered with mood-congruent

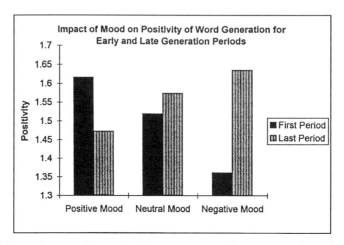

FIG. 3.6. Evidence consistent with the automatic mood management hypothesis: Initially mood-congruent associations are spontaneously reversed, and these effects are greater in a negative than in a positive mood. *Note.* After Forgas & Ciarrochi, 1998.

responses throughout the entire task. This finding suggest that traits such as self-esteem may moderate people's ability to adopt motivated behavioral strategies to control their affective states. These studies (Forgas & Ciarrochi, 1998; Sedikides, 1994) support the notion of a homeostatic feedback-loop model of affect control, suggesting that fluctuating affective states can play an important role in goal setting and execution. Other research also suggests that simply making people aware of their mood can trigger motivated affect-control strategies (Berkowitz & Troccoli, 1990). Goals related to the management and control of affective states could be readily incorporated in Carver and Scheier's theory, and features of the kind of homeostatic affect management system described here could provide a useful addition to an overall theory of behavior regulation.

SUMMARY AND CONCLUSIONS

The theory of behavior regulation presented by Carver and Scheier is impressive in its scope and represents a highly significant contribution to theoretical integration in our discipline. Our aim in this chapter was to highlight potential areas of weakness in the theory that could be rectified by the incorporation of additional principles and mechanisms. Our main concern was with the relatively inadequate treatment accorded to affective phenomena in the model. Carver and Scheier correctly recognize that affective reactions can arise as a consequence of feedback mechanisms in behavior regulation, and they are also correct in pointing to the functions of such affective reactions in regulating the intensity of motivational states. Our main point here is that affect does much more than that. Extensive research has documented the highly significant influence that emotions and moods can play in the way people perceive and interpret social situations, the kinds of goals and plans they formulate, and the way they execute and regulate strategic social behaviors. The role of affect as a source of such purposive behaviors does not at present receive sufficient recognition in Carver and Scheier's model.

One recurring problem with incorporating affective phenomena in explanations of behavior is that their effects are neither simple nor uniform. There is ample evidence for both mood congruity and incongruity in people's thoughts and behaviors, and these effects appear to be highly context sensitive. We suggested here that theories such as the Affect Infusion Model (AIM; Forgas, 1992a, 1995b) can offer a simple and parsimonious explanation of when and how affective states infuse purposive behaviors. We also reviewed a range of empirical studies illustrating how such principles can be translated into behavioral research and how affective states can be shown to influence strategic social behaviors. Mood effects were demonstrated on the formulation of and responses to requests (Forgas, 1998a, 1998b, in press-a), the planning and execution of strategic negotiations (Forgas, in press-a), and the monitoring and interpretation of complex interactive behaviors (Forgas, 1994; Forgas, Bower, & Krantz, 1984; Forgas, Bowers, and Moylan, 1990).

Further, we proposed that the need to control and manage affective states is itself one of the more important and recurring goals of everyday behavior regulation. We described a preliminary affect management model, which predicts that people may switch between two complementary processing strategies, that is, substantive processing (producing affect infusion) and motivated processing (producing affect control), in an automatic, homeostatic system of mood management. Several experiments illustrating the spontaneous recovery from aversive moods by people engaging in targeted, mood-incongruent behaviors were also described (Forgas & Ciarrochi, 1998). It seems to us that a comprehensive theory of behavior regulation such as the one proposed by Carver and Scheier could easily be expanded to take explicit account of the critical role affect plays in the planning and execution of purposive behaviors.

We started this discussion by suggesting several extensions and modifications to Carver and Scheier's conceptualization of goals. We pointed to important similarities between dispositional concepts in behavior regulation such as traits, attitudes, and goals and suggested that some of the metaphors and operationalizations developed in trait research and attitude research could be readily applied to goal theories as well. We may conclude by observing that one critical difference between concepts such as traits and attitudes on the one hand and goals on the other is that both traits and attitudes contain an explicit affective dimension. Enduring differences in affectivity between people, or *temperament* are an essential aspect of trait formulations (Mayer & Salovey, 1988; Rusting, 1998a, 1998b; Salovey & Mayer, 1990), and attitudes have always been understood to contain an strong affective, evaluative component. A comprehensive goal-based theory of behavior regulation such as the one developed by Carver and Scheier would clearly also benefit from a more differentiated treatment of affective phenomena. We hope that these comments will be of some use as Carver and Scheier proceed to elaborate and develop what will surely be regarded as a landmark contribution to social psychological theorizing.

ACKNOWLEDGMENTS

This research was supported by a Special Investigator award from the Australian Research Council, and the Research Prize by the Alexander von Humboldt Foundation to Joseph P. Forgas. The contribution of Stephanie Moylan to this project is gratefully acknowledged.

REFERENCES

Aizen, I. (1991). The theory of planned behavior. *Organizational Behavior and Human Decision Processes, 50,* 179–211.

Anderson, J. R. (1982). Acquisition of cognitive skill. *Psychological Review, 89,* 369–406.

Berkowitz, L. (1993). Towards a general theory of anger and emotional aggression. In T. K. Srull & R. S. Wyer, Jr. (Eds.) *Advances in social cognition* (Vol. 6, pp. 1–46). Hillsdale, NJ: Lawrence Erlbaum Associates.

Berkowitz, L., & Troccoli, B. T. (1990). Feelings, direction of attention, and expressed evaluations of others. *Cognition and Emotion, 4,* 305–325.

Blascovich, J., & Tomaka, J. (1996). The biopsychosocial model of arousal regulation. *Advances in Experimental Social Psychology, 28,* 1–51.

Bower, G. H. (1981). Mood and memory. *American Psychologist, 36,* 129–148.

Bower, G. H. (1991). Mood congruity of social judgments. In J. P. Forgas (Ed.), *Emotion and social judgments* (pp. 31–53). New York: Pergamon.

Cialdini, R. B., & Kenrick, D. T. (1976). Altruism as hedonism: A social development perspective on the relationship of negative mood state and helping. *Journal of Personality and Social Psychology, 34,* 907–914.

Clark, M. S., & Isen, A. M. (1982). Towards understanding the relationship between feeling states and social behavior. In A. H. Hastorf & A. M. Isen (Eds.), *Cognitive social psychology* (pp. 73–108). Amsterdam: Elsevier/North-Holland.

Clore, G. L., Schwarz, N., & Conway, M. (1994). Affective causes and consequences of social information processing. In R. S. Wyer, Jr. & T. K. Srull (Eds.), *Handbook of social cognition*, (2nd ed., Vol. 1, pp. 323–419). Hillsdale, NJ: Lawrence Erlbaum Associates.

Damasio, A. R. (1994). *Descartes' error*. New York: Grosste/Putnam.

De Sousa, R. D. (1987). *The rationality of emotion*. Cambridge, MA: MIT Press.

Erber, R., & Erber, M. (1994). Beyond mood and social judgment: Mood incongruent recall and mood regulation. *European Journal of Social Psychology, 24*, 79–88.

Fazio, R. H. (1987). Self-perception theory: A current perspective. In M. P. Zanna, J. M. Olson, & C. P. Herman (Eds.), *Social influence: The Ontario symposium* (Vol. 5, pp. 129–150). Hillsdale, NJ: Lawrence Erlbaum Associates.

Festinger, L. (1957). *A theory of cognitive dissonance*. Evanston, IL: Row, Peterson.

Fiedler, K. (1990). Mood-dependent selectivity in social cognition. In W. Stroebe & M. Hewstone (Eds.), *European review of social psychology* (Vol. 1, pp. 1–32). New York: Wiley.

Fiedler, K. (1991). On the task, the measures and the mood in research on affect and social cognition. In J. P. Forgas (Ed.), *Emotion and social judgments* (pp. 83–104). Elmsford, NY: Pergamon.

Fiedler, K., & Forgas, J. P. (Eds.). (1988). *Affect, cognition, and social behavior: New evidence and integrative attempts* (pp. 44–62). Toronto, Canada: Hogrefe.

Fishbein, M., & Aizen, I. (1975). *Belief, attitude, intention, and behavior: An introduction to theory and research*. Reading, MA: Addison-Wesley.

Forgas, J. P. (1991). Mood effects on partner choice: Role of affect in social decisions. *Journal of Personality and Social Psychology, 61*, 708–720.

Forgas, J. P. (1992a). Affect in social judgments and decisions: A multi-process model. In M. Zanna (Ed.), *Advances in experimental social psychology* (Vol. 25, pp. 227–275). San Diego, CA: Academic Press.

Forgas, J. P. (1992b). On bad mood and peculiar people: Affect and person typicality in impression formation. *Journal of Personality and Social Psychology, 62*, 863–875.

Forgas, J. P. (1994). Sad and guilty? Affective influences on the explanation of conflict episodes. *Journal of Personality and Social Psychology, 66*, 56–68.

Forgas, J. P. (1995a). Mood and judgment: The affect infusion model (AIM). *Psychological Bulletin, 117*(1), 39–66.

Forgas, J. P. (1995b). Strange couples: Mood effects on judgments and memory about prototypical and atypical targets. *Personality and Social Psychology Bulletin, 21*, 747–765.

Forgas, J. P. (1998a). Affective influences on language use: The effects of mood on request formulations. Unpublished manuscript, University of New South Wales, Australia.

Forgas, J. P. (1998b). On being sad and polite: Mood effects on the use of more or less polite requests. Unpublished manuscript, University of New South Wales, Australia.

Forgas, J. P. (in press-a). Asking nicely? Mood effects on responding to more or less polite requests. *Personality and Social Psychology Bulletin*.

Forgas, J. P. (in press-b). On feeling good and getting your way: Mood effects on negotiation strategies and outcomes. *Journal of Personality and Social Psychology*.

Forgas, J. P., & Bower, G. H. (1987). Mood effects on person-perception judgments. *Journal of Personality and Social Psychology, 53*(1), 53–60.

Forgas, J. P., Bower, G. H., & Krantz, S. (1984). The influence of mood on perceptions of social interactions. *Journal of Experimental Social Psychology, 20*, 497–413.

Forgas, J. P., Bower, G. H., & Moylan, S. J. (1990). Praise or blame? Affective influences in attributions for achievement. *Journal of Personality and Social Psychology, 59*, 809–818.

Forgas, J. P. & Ciarrochi, J. (1998). *Mood congruent and incongruent thoughts over time: The role of self-esteem in mood management efficacy*. Manuscript submitted for publication.

Forgas, J. P., & Fiedler, K. (1996). Us and them: Mood effects on intergroup discrimination. *Journal of Personality and Social Psychology, 70*, 36–52.

Forgas, J. P. Johnson, R., & Ciarrochi, J. (in press). Affect control and affect infusion: A multiprocess account of mood management and personal control. In M. Kofta, G. Weary, & G. Sedek (Eds.), *Personal control in action. Cognitive and motivational mechanisms*. New York: Plenum.

Higgins, E. T. (1996). Ideals, oughts, and regulatory focus: Affect and motivation from distinct pains and pleasures. In J. S. Uleman & J. A. Bargh (Eds.), *Unintended thought: The limits of awareness, intention, and control* (pp. 75–123). New York: Guilford.

Hilgard, E. R. (1980). The trilogy of mind: Cognition, affection and conation. *Journal of the History of the Behavioral Sciences, 16*, 107–117.

Kruglanski, A. W. (1989). *Lay epistemics and human knowledge: Cognitive and motivational bases.* New York: Plenum.

Mayer, J. D. (1986). How mood influences cognition. In N. E. Sharkey (Ed.), *Advances in cognitive science* (Vol. 1, pp. 290–314). Chichester, England: Ellis Horwood.

Mayer, J. D., Gaschke, Y. N., Braverman, D. L., & Evans, T. W. (1992). Mood congruent judgment is a general effect. *Journal of Personality and Social Psychology, 63*, 119–132.

Mayer, J., McCormick, L., & Strong, S. (1995). Mood-congruent memory and natural mood: New evidence. *Personality and Social Psychology Bulletin, 21*, 736–746.

Mayer, J. D., & Salovey, P. (1988). Personality moderates the interaction of mood and cognition. In K. Fiedler & J. P. Forgas (Eds.), *Affect, cognition, and social behavior* (pp. 87–99). Göttingen, Germany: Hogrefe.

Nisbett, R. E., & Wilson, T. D. (1977). Telling more than we can know: Verbal reports on mental process. *Psychological Review, 84*, 231–259.

Petty, R. E., & Krosnick, J. A. (Eds.), (1995). *Attitude strength: Antecedents and consequences.* Hillsdale, NJ: Lawrence Erlbaum Associates.

Rusting, C. L. (1998a). *Interactive effects of personality and mood on judgment and recall.* Manuscript submitted for publication.

Rusting, C. L. (1998b). *Personality, mood and cognitive processing of emotional information: Three alternative models.* Manuscript submitted for publication.

Salovey, P., & Mayer, J. D. (1990). Emotional intelligence. *Imagination, Cognition, and Personality, 9*, 185–211.

Sedikides, C. (1992). Mood as a determinant of attentional focus. *Cognition and Emotion, 6*, 129–148.

Sedikides, C. (1994). Incongruent effects of sad mood on self-conception valence: It's a matter of time. *European Journal of Social Psychology, 24*, 161–172.

Sedikides, C. (1995). Central and peripheral self-conceptions are differentially influenced by mood: Tests of the differential sensitivity hypothesis. *Journal of Personality and Social Psychology, 69*(4), 759–777.

Smith, S. M. & Petty, R. E. (1995). Personality moderators of mood congruence effects on cognition: The role of self-esteem and negative mood regulation. *Journal of Personality and Social Psychology, 68*, 1092–1107.

Skinner, B. F. (1953). *Science and human behavior.* New York: MacMillan.

Thurstone, L. L. (1928). Attitudes can be measured. *American Journal of Psychology, 38*, 368–389.

Wegener, D. T., Downing, J. D., Krosnick, J. A., & Petty, R. E. (1995). Measures and manipulations of strength-related properties of attitudes: Current practice and future directions. In R. E. Petty & J. A. Krosnick (Eds.), *Attitude strength: Antecedents and consequences* (pp. 455–487). Hillsdale, NJ: Lawrence Erlbaum Associates.

Wegner, D. M., & Bargh, J. A. (1997). Control and automaticity in social life. In D. A. Gilbert, S. T. Fiske, & G. Lindzey (Eds.), *Handbook of social psychology.* Boston: McGraw-Hill.

Wegner, D. M. & Erber, R. (1993). Social foundations of mental control. In D. M. Wegner & J. W. Pennebaker (Eds.), *Handbook of mental control* (pp. 36–56). Englewood Cliffs, NJ: Prentice-Hall.

Zajonc, R. B. (1980). Feeling and thinking: Preferences need no inferences. *American Psychologist, 35*, 151–175.

4

The Speed of Goal Pursuit

Peter M. Gollwitzer
Uwe B. Rohloff
University of Konstanz

In the early 1990s, Heckhausen and Gollwitzer (1987; Gollwitzer, 1990; Heckhausen, 1991) suggested a model of action phases that describes people's attempts to realize their wishes and desires. The model assumes that on the long way from wishes to goal attainment, various different tasks have to be solved, and it associates a different action phase with each of these tasks. The first task to be solved in the so-called *predecisional phase* is selecting between one's various wishes and desires by turning some of them into binding goals. This transition to goal commitment is described as a decision that commits the person to actually performing goal-directed actions. The next task to be solved is the promotion of action initiation, which is done in the *preactional phase*. This is commonly achieved by planning when, where, and how one wants to get started with goal implementation. In the subsequent third phase (called *actional phase*), the task is to bring the started goal pursuit to a successful ending, even if barriers, hindrances, difficulties, slow downs, and so forth are encountered. Finally, after relevant outcomes have been achieved, the individual's task is to evaluate whether the actually achieved outcomes match the originally desired outcomes. On the basis of this evaluation, it will be decided whether further goal pursuit is necessary and worthwhile. This *postactional phase* comprises the last of the four action phases.

In the past, we have focused on the question of whether these different action phases are associated with a typical kind of information processing (e.g., Gollwitzer, Heckhausen, & Steller, 1990; Gollwitzer & Kinney, 1989; Taylor & Gollwitzer, 1996). More specifically, we postulated that deliberating one's wishes and desires leads to a deliberative mind-set, whereas planning the implementation of a chosen goal leads to an implemental mind-set. As it turned out, people's information processing in a deliberative mind-set differs drastically from their information processing in an implemental mind-set (Gollwitzer, 1991). In general, people process information in ways that are functional to solving the task at hand, which is making the best choice between desires and getting started with goal-directed actions, respectively.

We also analyzed what kind of planning is most conducive to solving the task of the preactional phase (i.e., initiating goal-directed actions without delay). We observed that very simple plans that link suitable anticipated situations (good opportunities) to appropriate goal-directed actions are powerful self-regulatory tools when it comes to getting started (Gollwitzer, 1993, 1996). Such plans, called *implementation intentions*, automatize action initiation and thus guarantee that goal-directed actions will be elicited even when the individual is distracted by performing other tasks, is caught up in ruminative thoughts, or is simply tired.

Only very recently we have been concerned also with the task of the actional phase: bringing started goal pursuit to a successful ending. It is assumed (Gollwitzer & Rohloff, 1997) that any falling back on this task leads to a spontaneous effort increase and potentially to performance improvement. The commitment resting on one's decision to achieve the set goal pushes the individual toward goal attainment. A threat to this goal commitment should stimulate a reactive effort increase in an attempt to stick to one's commitment. Accordingly, it is not just explicit failure experiences that should trigger this spontaneous response. Any threat to this goal commitment, even if it is only caused by a temporal slowdown in the speed of goal pursuit, should suffice. In order to test this assumption, we developed a new experimental paradigm in which participants can be given false feedback on their changes in speed (velocity) with which they approach the goal. Before we report the collected data, we would like to discuss Carver and Scheier's view of the speed of goal pursuit.

SPEED OF GOAL PURSUIT AS PERCEPTUAL INPUT TO THE METAMONITORING FEEDBACK LOOP

The speed of reducing a discrepancy to a set standard is, according to Carver and Scheier, regulated by a system that serves a metamonitoring function. This process operates simultaneously and in parallel with the behavior-guiding function served by the action loop feedback system. The metamonitoring system is thus checking on how well the action loop is doing at reducing its discrepancies. In more technical terms, "the perceptual input for the metamonitoring loop is a representation of the rate of discrepancy reduction in the action system over time." To make this easier to grasp, Carver and Scheier state that the action loop deals with distance, whereas the metamonitoring loop deals with velocity (speed).

The reference value for the perceptual input of the metamonitoring loop is an acceptable or desirable rate of discrepancy reduction. The primary output of the metamonitoring loop is, according to Carver and Scheier, affect in the sense of feeling positively or negatively. If the metamonitoring system detects a high speed of discrepancy reduction, there should be positive affect; if it senses a low speed, there should be negative affect. In support of these ideas, Carver and Scheier refer to the work by Hsee and Abelson (1991) who observed that people link velocity to satisfaction. For instance, students report that they would feel more satisfied if an improvement in class standing from the 30th percentile to the 70th percentile occurs during a short period of time (3 weeks) as compared to a long period of time (6 weeks). And when asked which change in value of a stock would be more satisfying (different charts are presented), subjects prefer fast velocities when the outcome was improving and slow velocities when the outcome was declining. Lawrence, Carver, and Scheier (1997) conducted an experiment where participants personally experienced different velocities of change. Manipulated performance feedback was given over time on an ambiguous task. Various speed patterns were established, whereby all participants finally ended up with a medium performance on the task. However, some subjects experienced a positive change of performance over time (starting poor and gradually improving), whereas others experienced a negative change (starting well and gradually worsening). With improving performances, high speeds led to better moods than low speeds, and with declining performances, low speeds led to less bad moods than high speeds.

Carver and Scheier also speculate about people's affective responses to accelerations and decelerations. Moving from a low-speed level to a high-speed level with a high velocity (fast acceleration) is not assumed to produce positive affect, but surprise. And the same is assumed for fast reductions from a high-speed level to a low-speed level (fast deceleration). Carver and Scheier admit that there is no direct evidence for this assumption, but they point to suggestive support for this position in the literature on emotion.

Most important, Carver and Scheier argue that the affect produced by the metamonitoring loop influences action. Based on a line of thought called the cruise control model, it is suggested that people respond to the negative affect produced by low velocities of discrepancy reduction with an effort increase, as things are not moving forward fast enough. Positive feelings associated with a high speed of moving toward the goal lead to coasting (an effort decrease) as things are going better than they need to. As "a discrepancy is still a discrepancy, and discrepancies are to be reduced," either quality of affect or deviation from the standard speed represents an error and should lead to changes in output focused at discrepancy reduction. Carver and Scheier argue that it makes sense to assume that people reduce positive discrepancies in speed because, as they are typically working on several goals simultaneously, continuing to serve one goal effectively has the cost of ignoring other pressing goals. In addition, it is pointed out that the effort increase postulated for negative speed discrepancies does not have to be understood solely in terms of invigorating a given course of goal-directed action. Rather, switching to other, more effective behaviors to meet the goal is also implied.

REDUCTION IN SPEED OF GOAL PURSUIT AS A THREAT TO GOAL COMMITMENT

According to our theorizing (Gollwitzer & Rohloff, 1997), slowdowns in the speed of moving toward a goal (in comparison to a desired speed) contradict a person's commitment to goal attainment. As a consequence, reactive efforts to hold on to the goal should be triggered. We do not assume that a person needs to experience negative affect for such reactive effort increases to occur. In line with theorizing by Bargh and Gollwitzer (1994; Bargh, Gollwitzer, Chai, & Barndollar, 1997), we assume that much of people's goal pursuit should run off implicitly and does not need explicit thoughts or feelings as a triggering condition. Therefore, people should respond to slowdowns in speed of progress toward the goal by a spontaneous effort increase that is not based on negative affect.

Moreover, our theorizing implies that positive speed discrepancies do not contradict a person's commitment to goal attainment. Accordingly, such positive discrepancies should not lead to a reduction in effort; rather, people should continue to strive with a high velocity. Only when other important goals have to be served at the same time might one observe a decrease in effort, as solely promoting the goal at hand could imply a threat to these competing goal commitments. But when these competing goals can be served one by one, a high-speed approach to the goal at hand seems highly functional, as this would allow the person to readily complete the goal at hand and move on to competing goals in time.

It becomes apparent that our theorizing on changes in speed in goal pursuit does not assign a functional role to positive and negative affect. Still, we assume that changes in affect can be associated with changes in speed of goal pursuit. In our view, this depends on the quality of the standard to which a person compares his or her speed of progress. In the case of social standards (i.e., the speed of progress is compared to another person), negative or positive affect should be experienced as one feels like a loser or winner. This negative affect, however, should not further the person's effort increase, but instead hamper it. In the case of an ipsative standard (i.e., the person compares the present speed of progress with the speed of progress he or she had achieved before), we do not expect intensive affective responses to an increase or decrease in speed and no effect of affect on effort increase or decrease, respectively.

A NEW EXPERIMENTAL PARADIGM FOR STUDYING THE EFFECTS OF SPEED DISCREPANCIES

To give participants false feedback on their changes in the speed with which they approach a task goal, we asked two participants at a time to take part in the following experiment. Participants are told that they would take part in an experiment in which they have to perform arithmetic tasks that are commonly used in social cognition experiments on cognitive load. The problem, however, is that these tasks probably create not only cognitive load but also changes in mood. To test for this, participants would have to report on their mood repeatedly while performing the tasks. Moreover, to create a realistic dual-task situation, participants were also asked to attend carefully to the information provided on their speed of progress toward goal attainment. Participants would have to report on their speed later on.

The arithmetic tasks are then presented at the computer screen, and the participants solve one task after the other in a self-paced manner. The tasks consist of one to three numbers presented in an upper line, and one to three numbers presented in a lower line. Participants are asked to compute the sum of each line and then subtract the smaller sum from the larger sum. The participants' goal is to make 350 points, and participants are told that each correct task is awarded with 1 to 10 points depending on its difficulty. Proximity to the goal is indicated on the screen by a column that rises in steps of 50 points. Irrespective of their performance, participants receive the same false feedback about their proximity to the goal (i.e., whenever 15 tasks are completed the column rises one step).

What is varied, however, is the perception of the velocity in moving toward the goal.

RESULTS OF AN EXPERIMENT

In a study by Gollwitzer and Rohloff (1997) using this paradigm, two different groups of participants were created. In the social comparison group, participants received false feedback about their changes in speed with respect to the partner participant. In the ipsative comparison group, participants received false feedback on changes in speed with respect to their own prior baseline speed. In both comparison groups, participants' false feedback on their velocity changed after each fifth task. In the social comparison group, this feedback was said to be related to the momentary speed of their partner participant. In the ipsative comparison group, this feedback was said to be related to the 10 tasks performed at the beginning of the experiment (i.e., the so-called baseline phase).

Within each of the two comparison groups, four different velocity patterns of moving toward the goal were implemented. The patterns differed from each other in the following way: At the beginning and the end of task performance, the velocities of all different patterns were the same and described a zero discrepancy. In between, the patterns differed drastically. Pattern B showed a zero discrepancy throughout the full course of goal pursuit. In Pattern A, participants learned that they slowed down after the beginning but recovered toward the end. In Patterns C and D, participants found that they increased in speed after the beginning, but slowed down towards the end—this was more pronounced in Pattern D than in Pattern C.

At eight different points in time, separated by about 5 minutes each (depending on the participants' performance), participants were asked to fill out a questionnaire that assessed various aspects of mood, such as hedonic tonus (bad mood–good mood), tension arousal (calm–nervous, relaxed–anxious), energetic arousal (not energized–energized, passive–active) and anger (not angered–angered, well-balanced–irritated). Moreover, participants reported on their being surprised and on being satisfied/dissatisfied with the momentary situation. For the seven time periods cut out by these eight assessments, we later computed participants' effort expenditure by determining the amount of time they needed for completing one arithmetic task. We actually took the mean of the last 15 tasks. In addition, we computed quality of performance by dividing the achieved number of correct tasks through the time participants took to solve these tasks.

Based on our theorizing, we postulated that the negative discrepancy in speed of goal pursuit indicated in Pattern A implies a threat to participants' goal commitment. It is therefore responded to with effort and performance increases. People should spontaneously try to hold on to the desired velocity and thus increase effort and performance. This should be true no matter whether goal pursuit is solitary or social. We established two different positive speed discrepancy groups, because our theorizing differs from Carver and Scheier's metamonitoring loop notion with respect to the effect of positive discrepancies on effort expenditure. Contrary to Carver and Scheier, we do not assume that an above-standard speed leads to reduction in effort and performance; moving faster than standard neither threatens a person's goal commitment nor renders it obsolete. To Carver and Scheier, however, an above-standard speed is as much a deviation from the standard as a below-standard speed, and both types of discrepancies are responded to by adjustments toward the standard speed.

Speed Discrepancy Effects on Effort and Performance

Negative speed discrepancies led to an increase in effort and performance as compared to zero discrepancies, and this was true for both the social comparison group and the ipsative comparison group. This observation is in line with Carver and Scheier's theorizing as well as our own perspective. Positive speed discrepancies, on the other hand, no matter whether these were minor or major, did not induce any reduction in effort and performance for both the social comparison group and the ipsative comparison group. This contradicts Carver and Scheier's metamonitoring loop notion and supports our commitment notion of goal pursuit.

Speed Discrepancy Effects on Affect and Satisfaction

Negative speed discrepancies produced a lower hedonic tonus (bad mood–good mood) than positive discrepancies, but only in the social comparison condition and not in the ipsative comparison condition. This questions Carver and Scheier's postulate that affect is the error signal of the metamonitoring loop that triggers the output function of that loop (i.e., an adjustment in the rate of progress). As negative speed discrepancies had produced an effort and performance increase in the ipsative comparison group, it appears that this adjustment runs off without assigning a functional role to affect. The observation that positive/negative affect is triggered by positive and negative speed discrepancies only in the social comparison group is interesting in its own right. One might want to argue that the social comparison feedback produced a heightened self-focus and thus a more emotional self-evaluation. However, at the end of the experiment, participants of both feedback comparison groups did not differ either in terms of private or public self-consciousness or in the perceived importance of the feedback they received for self-evaluation. It seems possible then that the social comparison feedback simply stimulated competitive urges, which in turn emotionalized the participants.

Moreover, other aspects of affect were also affected by speed discrepancies in the social comparison feedback group. Participants' anger showed the same pattern as hedonic tonus. No reliable differences in tension arousal were observed. Moreover, the energetic arousal of the high-speed discrepancy group differed from the remaining groups, which were all the same. Finally, when we analyzed participants' experienced satisfaction with the situation at hand, we discovered that negative speed discrepancies led to more dissatisfaction than positive discrepancies, and this was true for social and ipsative comparison feedback. This observation seems to suggest that satisfaction is of a more reflective quality and thus originates no matter whether one falls short with respect to another person's speed of progress toward a goal or with respect to one's own prior progress.

Lack of Mediation of Effort/Performance Increases Through Negative Affect and Dissatisfaction

We computed regression analyses (following Baron & Kenny, 1986) to explore the question of whether negative affect and dissatisfaction mediated the observed effort and performance increases after negative speed discrepancies as compared to zero speed discrepancies. As it turned out, neither the various measured aspects of affect (hedonic tonus, tension arousal, energetic arousal, or anger) nor dissatisfaction qualified as an effective mediator. These findings suggest again that affect does not serve the signaling function ascribed to it in Carver and Scheier's metamonitoring loop theorizing. It is interesting, that we even observed within participants who had received negative speed discrepancy feedback (social comparison group) that negative affect hampered performance and reduced effort. This also suggests that negative affect does not signal negative speed discrepancies and thus lead to effort and performance increases.

There seems to be good reason, however, why negative affect fails to serve the signaling function ascribed to it by Carver and Scheier. How could a vague psychological quality such as negative or positive affect be a reliable indicator of a present negative or positive speed discrepancy?

Negative affect may originate from many different sources, such as a sick, tired, or exhausted body or a negative environmental stimulus (e.g., noise). This implies that negative affect would mostly mislead people in assuming that an ongoing goal pursuit is associated with a negative speed discrepancy and thus lead to an unnecessary invigoration of goal pursuit. Similar arguments can be advanced with respect to the assumption that positive affect signals to the comparator of the metamonitoring loop that a reduction in effort is called for. People would frequently coast their goal pursuits simply because pleasant internal and external stimuli are present. Moreover, as Carver and Scheier point out, people commonly pursue more than one goal at a time. Assuming that a person's responding to speed discrepancies is regulated via general positive/negative affect, it would seem impossible for the individual to detect which of the ongoing goal pursuits needs intensification. The person should not be able to distinguish the various positive/negative affects stemming from the different goal pursuits, because these do not carry distinct features. Our commitment notion of goal pursuit gets around this problem. We assume that a negative speed discrepancy with respect to a certain goal pursuit leads to spontaneous effort and performance increases in this goal pursuit alone. Each threat to one of the person's goal commitments is specific in the sense that only this goal is affected. There is no need to interpret vague signals.

Our observation that dissatisfaction did not play a mediating role between negative speed discrepancy and effort/performance increase also speaks to the model of Hsee and Abelson (1991). Hsee and Abelson postulated that people's striving for satisfaction is pervasive and, therefore, concluded that people prefer high speeds because of the associated feelings of satisfaction. According to this hypothesis, the effects of negative speed discrepancies on effort and performance should be mediated by feelings of dissatisfaction. Our data do not support this hypothesis. Therefore, we wonder whether it is indeed satisfaction that people go for when trying to move fast toward a goal.

Acceleration

Carver and Scheier suggest that intense accelerations (moving quickly from a low-speed level to a high-speed level) and decelerations (moving quickly from a high-speed level to a low-speed level) produce surprise. Even though we explicitly asked participants for surprise experiences, our participants did not report more surprise after accelerations or decelerations (as compared to zero accelerations or zero decelerations). What we observed instead was a difference in tension arousal between participants who experienced acceleration and participants who experienced deceleration. Apparently, decelerations made our participants anxious and tense, whereas accelerations reduced such feelings. One could argue that the accelerations and decelerations implemented in our experimental study were not intense enough to produce surprise. On the other hand, even intense accelerations and decelerations may not guarantee surprise experiences, as other variables (e.g., expectations, control beliefs, level of prior and subsequent speed) should also play an important role.

Hsee, Salovey, and Abelson (1994) observed an effect of acceleration on satisfaction. Participants had looked at two different hypothetical developments of stock. Both stock developments ultimately reached the same rate of progress (velocity), but one of them arrived at this level of progress after a period of intense acceleration and the other after a period of weak acceleration. Participants preferred the stock with strong acceleration. Hsee, Salovey, and Abelson do not offer an explanation of this finding. However, if one assumes that participants consider the velocity of stock development at the beginning as a standard to which they compare the velocity of stock development at the end, it follows that participants perceive a strong positive speed discrepancy in the first case of stock development and a weak positive speed discrepancy in the second case. In other words, we are not dealing here with an acceleration effect on satisfaction but with a speed discrepancy effect on satisfaction—an effect that was also observed in our experiment.

Goal Distance and Goal Attainment

We observed that the hedonic tonus of participants' affect tended to become more positive at the end of goal pursuit. Apparently, a small distance to goal attainment leads to more positive affect than a large distance. Certainly, such distance effects should depend on the joy or pain associated with making progress toward the goal (people should feel bad when they come to the end of a pleasant activity, and they should feel good if the activity is unpleasant) and the anticipated positive consequences of goal attainment. It is difficult to accept the postulate of Carver and Scheier, however, that goal distance should have no effect at all on a person's positive/negative affect.

Carver and Scheier also postulate that goal attainment per se should fail to affect a person's positive/negative feelings. In our study, goal attainment led to positive affect and satisfaction, and it reduced tension arousal and anger. We had measured these variables shortly before and shortly after goal attainment. Even though goal attainment per se may not have affective consequences, one must keep in mind that goal attainment gives people access to the consequences of goal attainment. If these are positive (e.g., a positive self-evaluation, a positive evaluation by significant others, progress toward some important life goal), goal attainment should be associated with positive affect.

Goal Commitment and Speed Discrepancy Effects on Effort/Performance

Our commitment theory of goal pursuit states that negative speed discrepancies produce increases in effort and performance because negative speed discrepancies are a threat to goal commitment. If this notion is correct, it follows that negative speed discrepancies should produce stronger effort and performance increases in people who feel a strong commitment to the goal as compared to people with a weak commitment to the goal. Accordingly, we inquired about participants' commitment to the task at hand (i.e., making 350 points by computing simple arithmetic tasks) by asking them repeatedly during task performance whether they would prefer to perform a different task. When we split participants into low versus high commitment groups on the basis of these assessments, the high commitment group showed a stronger effort/performance increasing effect of negative speed discrepancies than the low commitment group. It is interesting, that not only high levels but also low levels of commitment evidenced the negative speed discrepancy effect on effort and performance for the social comparison feedback group.

SUMMARY

We have focused on Carver and Scheier's ideas about the metamonitoring feedback loop, which is said to monitor the speed of reducing discrepancies toward a set goal. Carver and Scheier make explicit predictions of how perceived speed discrepancies affect positive/negative feelings and subsequent efforts. We have contrasted these predictions with our own view, which we labeled the commitment theory of goal pursuit. By reporting on findings obtained by use of a new paradigm that allows us to manipulate perceived speed discrepancies, we discussed the differences between these two perspectives. The two perspectives overlap in predicting effort and performance increases as a result of negative speed discrepancies. Differences in perspectives are related to Carver and Scheier's expectation that (a) positive speed discrepancies lead to reduced effort and performance, and (b) performance increases and decreases are mediated by negative and positive affect, respectively. We predicted and observed instead that positive speed discrepancies leave effort and performance unaffected and that effort and performance increases as spontaneous responses to negative speed discrepancies are not mediated by negative affect.

In the present analyses of the differences between Carver and Scheier's and our perspective, we ignored the content of the goal. Some goal theories (for a review see Gollwitzer & Moskowitz, 1996), however, argue that the type of goal content greatly affects how goal pursuit is regulated. In Dweck's (1996) theory, for instance, learning goals put the person in a better position to cope with failure than performance goals. What type of goal content is relevant to the observed speed discrepancy effects on effort and performance? The relation between speed discrepancies and effort/performance should be different with avoidance goals as compared to approach goals. In the experiment reported above, positive speed discrepancies in approaching the goal did not lead to a decrease in effort; instead, participants kept performing on a high level. It seems possible, however, that positive speed discrepancies lead to drastic decreases in effort with avoidance goals. This is because having moved effectively away from a negative event makes further avoidance less necessary, whereas having effectively approached a goal makes further approach still necessary until one has attained one's goal.

Finally, the goal we set in our experiment was not associated with a deadline. Participants could take as much time as they wanted to reach the 350 points. But, although people find it painful, most goals in our everyday life do have deadlines. Such time-sensitive goals should make people respond even more readily to fallbacks in speed of goal pursuit than observed in this study. Future research might also want to explore the question of how speed discrepancies are noticed or detected by the individual. In this study, we gave our participants explicit feedback. But in our everyday lives, such changes will have to be detected by the person involved. Questions arise with respect to when and how often people compare with others' or their prior velocity to receive feedback on changes in speed.

It is most intriguing, that results of the presented study suggest that speed discrepancies based on social comparisons as compared to ipsative comparisons differentially influence effort and performance as well as people's affective experiences. Apparently, speed discrepancies based on social comparisons do have strong affective consequences, whereas those based on ipsative comparisons fail to do so. And negative speed discrepancies based on social comparison feedback increase effort and performance even when there is low commitment to the goal, whereas negative speed discrepancies based on ipsative comparisons necessitate a high commitment for effort and performance increases to occur. We take these findings to mean that the human being is a social animal and, when people are placed into competitive situations, their goal pursuit becomes additionally energized and emotionalized, the latter being a potential hindrance for effective goal pursuit.

REFERENCES

Bargh, J. A., & Gollwitzer, P. M. (1994). Environmental control of goal-directed action. In W. Spaulding (Ed.), *Nebraska symposium on motivation: Integrative views of motivation, cognition, and emotion* (Vol. 41, pp. 71–124). Lincoln: University of Nebraska Press.

Bargh, J. A., Gollwitzer, P. M., Chai, A. L., & Barndollar, K. (1997). *Bypassing the will: Nonconscious self-regulation through automatic goal pursuit.* Manuscript submitted for publication.

Baron, R. M., & Kenny, D. A. (1986). The moderator-mediator variable distinction in social psychology research: Conceptual, strategic, and statistical considerations. *Journal of Personality and Social Psychology, 51,* 1173–1182.

Dweck, C. S. (1996). Implicit theories as organizers of goals and behavior. In P. M. Gollwitzer & J. A. Bargh (Eds.), *The psychology of action: Linking cognition and motivation to behavior* (pp. 69–90). New York: Guilford.

Gollwitzer, P. M. (1990). Action phases and mind-sets. In E. T. Higgins & R. M. Sorrentino (Eds.), *Handbook of motivation and cognition* (Vol. 2, pp. 53–92). New York: Guilford.

Gollwitzer, P. M. (1991). *Abwaegen und Planen* [Deliberation and planning]. Goettingen, Germany: Hogrefe.

Gollwitzer, P. M. (1993). Goal achievement: The role of intentions. In W. Stroebe & M. Hewstone (Eds.), *European review of social psychology* (Vol. 4, pp. 141–185). Chichester, England: Wiley.

Gollwitzer, P. M. (1996). The volitional benefits of planning. In P. M. Gollwitzer & J. A. Bargh (Eds.), *The psychology of action: Linking cognition and motivation to behavior* (pp. 287–312). New York: Guilford.

Gollwitzer, P. M., Heckhausen, H., & Steller, B. (1990). Deliberative versus implemental mind-sets: Cognitive tuning toward congruous thoughts and information. *Journal of Personality and Social Psychology, 59,* 1119–1127.

Gollwitzer, P. M., & Kinney, R. F. (1989). Effects of deliberative and implemental mind-sets on illusion of control. *Journal of Personality and Social Psychology, 56,* 531–542.

Gollwitzer, P. M., & Moskowitz, G. B. (1996). Goal effects on thought and behavior. In E. T. Higgins & A. W. Kruglanski (Eds.), *Social psychology: Handbook of basic principles* (pp. 361–399). New York: Guilford.

Gollwitzer, P. M., & Rohloff, U. B. (1997, October). *Competitive versus solitary goal pursuit.* Paper presented at the annual meeting of the Society of Experimental Social Psychology in Toronto, Canada.

Heckhausen, H. (1991). *Motivation and action.* New York: Springer-Verlag.

Heckhausen, H., & Gollwitzer, P. M. (1987). Thought contents and cognitive functioning in motivational versus volitional states of mind. *Motivation and Emotion, 11,* 101–120.

Hsee, C. K., & Abelson, R. P. (1991). Velocity relation: Satisfaction as a function of the first derivate of outcome over time. *Journal of Personality and Social Psychology, 60,* 341–347.

Hsee, C. K., Salovey, P., & Abelson, R. P. (1994). The quasi-acceleration relation: Satisfaction as a function of the change of velocity of outcome over time. *Journal of Experimental Social Psychology, 30,* 96–111.

Lawrence, J. W., Carver, C. S., & Scheier, M. F. (1997). *Velocity and affect in immediate personal experience.* Manuscript submitted for publication.

Taylor, S. E., & Gollwitzer, P. M. (1995). Effects of mindset on positive illusions. *Journal of Personality and Social Psychology, 69,* 213–226.

5

Content Versus Structure in Motivation and Self-Regulation

Heidi Grant
Carol S. Dweck
Columbia University

There have been two distinct approaches to the study of motivation and self-regulation. One approach, often called a "content" approach, identifies particular types of goals or particular forms of self-regulation and studies them in detail. The other approach, often called a "structural" approach, empties motivation and self-regulation of content and attempts to formulate general principles that cut across all goals or all self-regulatory processes.

The advantage of the content approach is that, at its best, it can yield deep insights into important phenomena, such as aggression, depression, achievement, or resistance to temptation. It can specify the processes involved in a way that illuminates the character of the phenomenon and that allows one to chart its causes, follow its consequences, and design effective interventions. The potential limitation of this approach is that what one learns may be limited to that phenomenon or domain alone.

The advantages of the structural approach, at its best, are clear. It can generate principles that apply widely and can shed light on human behavior across domains. For example, principles about goal setting, goal implementation, and goal conflict can be informative independent of particular goal content. The potential limitation is that the structural approach may not tell us enough about any one phenomenon for us to really understand it and its origins, trajectories, and malleability.

The work of Carver and Scheier is a tour de force in the structural tradition. The authors present a general model, grounded in cybernetic theory, of the nature of human behavior. Their guiding insight—that behavior is fundamentally self-regulatory in nature and is organized around the attainment of important goals—is sweeping in its scope while providing a parsimonious model through which we can understand both the production of behavior and the experience of affect. Carver and Scheier have provided compelling accounts of phenomena as important and diverse as emotion, social comparison, self-focused attention, and the experience of "flow." Their feedback loop model is consistent with and informed by biological models of approach and avoidance, a noteworthy asset in theories at the social–personality level of analysis. Theirs is a model that is both elegant in its simplicity and intuitively appealing of how goals, all goals, energize, direct, and control behavior.

To their credit, the authors have also made a critically important content distinction in their description of the workings of discrepancy-reducing (approach) and discrepancy-enlarging (avoidance) feedback loops. This is a clearly a goal content distinction—they are distinguishing two classes of goals based on whether the individual seeks to approach something positive or avoid something negative. As they show, this distinction has many implications for goal structure and process (e.g., each kind of loop involves a different affective dimension and behavioral tendencies with different energy mobilization needs, etc.).

However, they have left other potentially important and illuminating differences in goal content unattended. There are many readily justifiable reasons for this, not the least of which is the authors' intention, as stated in the first line of their text, to discuss "the structure of behavior." Also, as we will argue, content distinctions have typically been conceptualized in a way that renders them less useful and largely unappealing to goal theorists of personality and behavior who are seeking general laws or principles.

In this chapter, we embrace the aims of both the content and structural approaches and argue the necessity of an approach that combines structure and content. Indeed, we propose that structure is often inherent in content and that a search for structure must take account of differences in content. Thus, we focus on goals and argue that (1) when one identifies classes of goals at the right level of analysis, structural properties fall out and (2) without identifying different classes of goals one cannot arrive at meaningful general principles, because different classes of goals, we propose, are characterized by qualitatively different patterns of goal pursuit.

A GOAL IS A GOAL IS A GOAL?

Several theorists have drawn the distinction between content and structural models of goal-driven behavior (see Austin & Vancouver, 1996; Gollwitzer & Moskowitz, 1996; Kruglanski & Shah, 1997). However, as asked earlier, is it really possible to have a content-free structural model or does one require some content distinctions in order to have a complete model of goal structure? To answer this question, we believe that the field must acquire an understanding of different kinds of content.

We propose that content theorists and structural theorists have both confused "content" with "domain-specificity." In other words, content distinctions are often taken to mean differences in goal domain. For example, a researcher who examines differences in the behavior produced by achievement goals as opposed to social goals is considered to be examining a difference in goal content. Although this is undeniably true, it is a limited and often misleading way to think about content distinctions. The result of such a conceptualization has been that content is rendered less meaningful, and without meaningful content distinctions, one must use structural distinctions (e.g., goal importance, conflict, commitment) in order to make predictions about behavior and to tap into general principles.

Beyond differences in goal domain, however, there is another sense in which goals can be qualitatively different from one another. We have argued (Grant & Dweck, in press) that there are qualitative differences that are explicitly domain general among types of goals. Specifically, we proposed that there are *basic classes* of goals that differ from one another in the way in which they satisfy higher order values and needs such as self-esteem and security and that predict unique and meaningful patterns of behavior across domains. After elaborating the basic-class goal concept, we turn to the question of whether structural principles may apply differently to different basic classes of goals.

BASIC CLASSES OF GOALS

Our search for the basic class distinction began with the observation that goal analysis is an underutilized tool in many theories of personality and social interaction (Grant & Dweck, in press). One reason may be that in the field of social–personality psychology as a whole, there has been little in terms of principled distinctions between types of goals beyond their domain, and there have been few principled arguments for the appropriateness of using one level of goal abstraction over another. This has resulted in an infinite profusion of possible goals and little agreement on the usefulness of particular types of goals. Even among goal theorists of personality, we found that each focuses on people's self-articulated, thematic-laden goals and that these goals typically vary across different levels of abstraction. Thus, these approaches, although they have in some ways demonstrated the usefulness of the goal construct for understanding the dynamics of personality, have not offered needed parsimony to the field. Knowing people's favored goal domain tells us little about their patterns of striving, that is, their strategies, their cognitions, their affective responses, their persistence in the face of obstacles, and so on.

We, therefore, asked whether there might be ways of identifying goals where knowing the goal can tell us important things about the cognitions, affects, and behaviors that will characterize goal pursuit: Is there a way to classify goals into meaningful categories that cut across domains? Can these categories of goals help us make clear, precise predictions about how people think, feel, and act? Evidence from our own research suggested a different way of classifying goals. In past work, we identified two distinct patterns of behavior in both achievement and social interaction settings produced by two qualitatively different classes of goals. These patterns differed in their structure—in the nature and timing of affect, cognitions, and behavior.

These two different classes of goals have been termed performance goals and learning goals. When individuals have *performance* goals, their purpose is to attain favorable judgments and to avoid unfavorable judgments of their own competence (i.e., to display and validate their competence). *Learning* goals refer to those goals where the individual's purpose is to acquire new knowledge or skills (i.e., to increase his or her competence; Dweck & Elliott, 1983; Elliott & Dweck, 1988; Mueller & Dweck, 1998; see also Diener & Dweck, 1978, 1980).

PERFORMANCE AND LEARNING GOALS PRODUCE UNIQUE PATTERNS

The pattern of behavior produced by a performance goal is marked by a focus on ability, performance, and evaluation. In achievement settings, students pursuing performance goals are more likely to produce cognitions, affect, and behavior organized around ability and validation of ability, being more outcome focused than those students with learning goals (Diener & Dweck, 1978, 1980; Elliott & Dweck, 1988; Mueller & Dweck, 1998). These students tend to perceive highly challenging tasks or obstacles as threatening (Dweck & Elliott, 1983) and prefer easier tasks that allow them to take pride in performing well or outperforming others (Bandura & Dweck, 1985). For example, it has been found that those with performance goals will knowingly sacrifice an opportunity to learn if offered an alternative task on which they are likely to perform better (Elliott & Dweck, 1988). These students also report that they feel smart when tasks are easy for them, when they finish quickly, when they do not make any mistakes, and when they do better than their peers (see Dweck & Bempechat, 1983). Mueller and Dweck (1998) further showed that persons entering an achievement situation with a performance goal are likely to pay particular attention to aspects of the situation (e.g., performance of peers) that will enable them to gauge or evaluate their ability. In a series of studies, students who had either a performance or learning goal orientation were given an opportunity to look at one of two folders. One folder contained information about the past performance of other students on the experimental task; the other contained information about strategies for performing better on the task. Students with a performance goal were far more likely than students with a learning goal to select the folder containing information about peer performance, so that they might gauge their own ability, even when it deprived them of information that might be important for their own subsequent performance.

In stark contrast, the pattern of behavior produced by a learning goal is marked by a focus on effort and challenge. In achievement situations, students with learning goals tend to produce cognitions, affect, and behavior organized around effort and effort expenditure, being more process and progress focused (Elliott & Dweck,1988; Mueller & Dweck, 1998; see also Ames, Ames, & Felker, 1977; cf. Bruner 1961, 1965). These students perceive challenging tasks as opportunities for skill acquisition and growth, often expressing enthusiasm (along with renewed effort) in the face of increasing difficulty, and disappointment when a task appears too easy or familiar (Bandura & Dweck, 1981; Elliott & Dweck, 1988; see also Diener & Dweck, 1980). They also report that they feel smart when tasks are hard for them and they make progress and when they do not understand something and then through their own effort or persistence, they do (Dweck & Bempechat, 1983). Upon entering an achievement situation, these students are likely to pay attention to aspects of the situation that will allow them to improve their skills. For example, as noted in the study by Mueller and Dweck (1998), these students were much more likely to select the folder containing information about strategy improvement than students with a performance goal.

These two classes of goals have also been linked to different patterns of responding to a setback or failure. Diener and Dweck (1978, 1980) identified these unique, coherent patterns of responding as mastery-oriented and helpless patterns, and these patterns have been documented by other researchers as well (Ames & Archer, 1988; Boggiano, Shields, Barrett, Kellam, Thompson, Simons, & Katz, 1992; Elliot & Church, 1997; Nichols, 1984; Seligman, 1975; Weiner, 1985).

Elliott and Dweck (1988) reasoned that approaching a situation with the goal of displaying and validating your ability would lead you to use your performance as a measure of the level of your ability. Thus, a failure could readily be interpreted as meaning that you have low ability, and a helpless reaction might result. Several studies have shown that students with performance goals in achievement situations are in fact more vulnerable to the helpless pattern of responding, tending to read their own ability from failure, generate negative prognoses for future performance, display significant negative affect, and show deterioration of problem-solving strategies (Elliott & Dweck, 1988; Hong, Chiu, & Dweck, 1995; Mueller & Dweck, 1998; Smiley & Dweck, 1994).

In contrast, if you approach a situation with the goal of learning or developing a skill, a failure is more likely to be seen as information about your learning strategy and an opportunity for improvement in the future. Evidence from several studies have supported this hypothesis, indicating that students with learning goals do in fact tend to produce mastery-oriented responses to setbacks, using them as a way to evaluate their effort or strategies and as a signal for improvement. These students are likely to increase their strategy generation and use, make positive prognoses about their own future performance, and spontaneously express constructive cognitions (see Dweck & Elliott, 1983; Dweck & Leggett, 1988; Elliott & Dweck, 1988; Smiley & Dweck, 1994).

Performance and learning goals each belong to a broader class of goals that we have termed *judgment* goals and *development* goals, respectively (see Dweck & Leggett, 1988; Grant & Dweck, 1998). The performance versus learning distinction might be seen as most appropriate in understanding achievement, whereas these broader classes of goals are true basic classes of goals, in that they allow us to link patterns of behavior across domains.

Judgment refers to the goal of seeking to judge or validate an attribute. The attribute can be an attribute of oneself (e.g., one's intelligence, personality, moral character, physical attractiveness) or it can be an attribute of other people or groups of people (see Chiu, Hong, & Dweck, 1997;

Erdley & Dweck, 1993; Grant & Dweck, in press; Levy, Stroessner, & Dweck, 1998). When the attribute that is being judged is one's own, this goal will often take the form of seeking positive judgment and seeking to avoid negative judgment, as with the performance goals described earlier.

Development refers to the goal of seeking to develop an attribute. When the attribute that is being developed is one's own, this goal will often take the form of seeking to acquire new skills or knowledge, as with the learning goals described earlier.

Everyone pursues both classes of goals—both are natural and important in our everyday lives. But which goal one pursues in a given situation or which goal one tends to pursue in a given domain will give the goal striving a unique, predictable, and coherent character. Moreover, as we show, these two types of goals are each linked to meaningful patterns of behavior that are similar or analogous across domains.

Several researchers, including those in our own laboratory, have documented behavior patterns produced by what we would classify as judgment and development goals in the domains of social interaction (Erdley, Cain, Loomis, Dumas-Hines, & Dweck, 1997; Goetz & Dweck, 1980), aggression (Erdley & Asher, 1996; La Greca, Dandes, Wick, Shaw, & Stone, 1988; Taylor & Asher, 1989), and intimate relationships (Brundage, Derlega, & Cash, 1977; Kamins, Morris, & Dweck, 1997; McAdams, 1989), analogous to those found in the achievement domain. Specifically, evidence suggests that having a judgment goal during social interaction produces a seeking out of interaction partners who will validate the self and increase prestige, as well as a vulnerability to negative affect, negative evaluation of self or others, and withdrawal or aggression after a perceived rejection. In contrast, having a development goal produces a seeking out of interaction partners that will help to develop and improve the self (even through criticism), persistence, and new strategy generation after a perceived rejection (Erdley et al., 1997; Kamins, Morris, & Dweck, 1997).

We are also exploring the nature of one's goals toward others, rather than for the self, in areas such as social judgment and stereotyping. Here we find evidence suggesting that the judgment class of basic goals may be relevant to stereotyping behavior. For example, work by Levy, Stroessner, and Dweck (1998) suggested that persons with the goal of judging, labeling, and categorizing others (a judgment goal toward others) may be particularly prone to endorsing existing stereotypes and forming new ones.

Judgment goals may play a part not only in the perception of other persons or social groups, but also in one's behavior toward these persons or groups. For example, Sorich and Dweck (1997) found evidence suggesting that persons with the goal of judging, labeling, and categorizing others are more likely to endorse the punishment of wrongdoers and less likely to advocate education and rehabilitation for criminals (see also Chiu, Dweck, Tong, & Fu, 1997). Thus, basic classes of goals appear to predict meaningful patterns of cognition, affect, and behavior not only with respect to goals for the self, but also when another person or group is the target.

LEVELS OF ABSTRACTION—WHERE DO BASIC CLASSES OF GOALS FIT IN?

Returning to the work of Elliott and Dweck (1988), which linked the helpless and mastery-oriented patterns to goals, we can examine the goals of the students in the experimental situation at three salient levels of analysis. At the highest level of abstraction, there is the general need or value that one seeks to fulfill or attain (see Carver & Scheier, 1982; Gollwitzer & Moskowitz, 1996). In this example, both groups of students could be described as striving toward the same value—competence ("I want to possess competence.") This is a goal at a level of abstraction of such goals as self-esteem, relatedness, or security. Clearly, this level is too abstract to predict specific behaviors because it does not differentiate between the two groups, and one could easily imagine any number of behaviors arising from a desire to possess competence or self-esteem.

At a lower level of abstraction, both groups want to solve the problems given to them by the experimenter. Again, this level of abstraction will not provide us with predictions about specific patterns of responding, but because it is too concrete rather than too abstract.

Between these two levels lies the level of goal abstraction at which the superordinate goal takes a more specific form, and the two groups can be seen to diverge. At this level, the superordinate goal of possessing competence takes on a particular nature and determines the particular way in which the individual will self-regulate to achieve the competence goal. In the Elliott and Dweck achievement study, one group's goal was to demonstrate competence (judgment goal), whereas the other's was to gain competence (development goal). After the method of fulfilling the superordinate need is delineated, corresponding behavioral responses to failure can be expected. For example, as noted, at this level Elliott and Dweck found that seeking to demonstrate competence can result in a vulnerability to helplessness in the face of failure, whereas seeking to gain competence results in a tendency to display a mastery orientation.

We propose that this is the level of goal abstraction that is conceptually the most useful in predicting specific behaviors. It is the goal that is both the purpose of the lower, nominal level goal (solving the problems correctly), and the means through which the higher level goal (competence, self-esteem) is achieved.

Our analysis of levels of goal abstraction is analogous to Powers' (1973) model of the hierarchical organization of control systems, following the lead of Carver and Scheier (1982). Most germane to our ideas are the highest levels of the 9-level hierarchy. The system concept level is the highest level of abstraction, corresponding to goals like self-esteem, relatedness, and identity. The directly subordinate level is the principle control level, which specifies the way in which the system concept goal or need can be satisfied. In the case of the system concept *self-esteem*, for example, the principle control level goal could be "look good in front of my friends," or "develop a new skill."

In other words, the principle level specifies how people self-regulate with respect to the system level. We suggest that goals at the principle level of abstraction are generally the most useful in predicting an individual's behavior in a particular situation.

By identifying the appropriate level of abstraction for goal analysis, that is, basic classes, goals can provide a greater degree of parsimony in the study of personality and self-regulation. Often goals have been grouped together according to the need they satisfy (e.g., affiliation goals, moral goals, power goals). However, we are suggesting that basic classes of goals should instead be based in the ways in which higher order needs are satisfied, because here we find unique, meaningful patterns of behavior that are similar or analogous across domains.

Our selection of the term *basic classes* was largely influenced by Rosch's use of the word *basic* in her description of levels of categorization (Rosch & Mervis, 1975). Rosch described a *basic level category* (e.g., car) as one whose level of abstraction minimizes within-category differences (e.g., cars, in many respects, are essentially similar to one another) and maximizes between-category differences (e.g., cars are very different from boats).

Similarly, basic classes of goals minimize within-goal-type differences, in that a particular class of goal is expected to produce similar or analogous patterns of behavior across situations and domains. Basic classes of goals also maximize between-goal-type differences, in that each basic class of goal predicts unique patterns of cognition, affect, and behavior.

Goal typologies based on domain-specific categories (e.g., achievement goals, social goals, etc.) cannot be said to exist at the basic level of analysis. For example, a group of persons can have a wide variety of goals in social situations, including being popular, making new relationships, understanding others, having fun, being admired, and avoiding rejection. Each of these goals might result in different behaviors in a particular social setting, but each could be described as a social goal. Therefore, domain-specific goal categories do not minimize within-category differences in behavior.

In addition, a person may have the goals of looking smart and being praised in school and looking "cool" and being admired among friends. Whereas the former goal might be considered an achievement goal, and the latter a social goal, one might expect a rejection or failure in either domain to produce a similar pattern of behavior (e.g., negative affect, lowered confidence, helplessness and withdrawal, etc.). Therefore, domain-specific goal categories do not maximize between-category differences in behavior.

The judgment versus development goal distinction seems to satisfy the requirements of basic classes, and with such a class of basic goals, we can refer to seeking to judge versus develop in any domain (vis-à-vis the self or others), and we can examine the similarities in behavior patterns across domains.

In their insightful and elegant model of goal hierarchies, Carver and Scheier largely refrain from drawing distinctions within levels of the hierarchy. In other words, they rarely describe lateral movement within a level or differences in content at a particular level of abstraction (the exception being their discussion of approach and avoidance feedback loops). Carver and Scheier acknowledge that "a given goal can be obtained via multiple pathways," but do not say anything about which path a person will take and why. We suggest that if the model contained more in the way of content distinctions, the authors could say even more about the qualitative differences in the structure and patterning of behavior.

CONTENT DIFFERENCES IMPLY STRUCTURAL DIFFERENCES

To illustrate better how understanding goal content can be critical to understanding goal structure in a meaningful, predictive sense, we discuss several points made by the authors regarding their theorizing about affect and confidence and suggest how they might be illuminated by a consideration of goal content.

The authors propose that affect is produced as a form of feedback from the self-regulatory system. Specifically, they argue that affect is feedback about the rate of progress toward a goal (or away from an antigoal). They go on to make the explicit claim that affect is not feedback about goal attainment or nonattainment per se, but solely the rate of goal attainment. How well does this model capture what we know about the affective reactions produced by judgment and development goals?

Implicit in the nature of development goals is the notion of progress over time. Students with development goals in achievement settings have been characterized as seeking to learn and master new materials, showing persistence despite initial setbacks, and revealing less concern with the outcome of a particular task episode. For these students, affect may well be the product of a sense of rate of development and, hence, adequately captured by Carver and Scheier's model.

But what of judgment goals? Do notions of progress and discrepancy reduction tell the whole story for students with performance goals in achievement settings? The essence of a performance (or judgment) goal is not simply that one is making progress toward a valued state, but that one is certain of reaching it or has already reached it and, thus, demonstrated ability. Take the example of a competitive sporting event. An athlete may regulate in terms of progress during the training and practicing interval before a game, but surely it is typically the athlete's performance as reflected in the outcome of the game that is the primary determinant of his or her affect after a game. The experience of pride or shame in this example is usually based on a definitive outcome, rather than a perception of progress. Clearly, we would expect and have in fact found that judgment goal-oriented students are strongly outcome focused and that their affective reactions are best predicted by the attributions made after goal attainment or nonattainment (Dweck & Bempechat, 1983; Elliott & Dweck, 1988; Weiner, 1985). The outcomes have clear meanings about ability for these individuals, illustrating one way in which understanding content is critical to understanding structure.

Carver and Scheier also explore the structural dimension of *goal efficacy*, or the confidence with which a person approaches a goal. The authors make the widely accepted claim that low confidence results in disengagement from the goal or, if not complete disengagement, then rather relegation of the goal to a less accessible state. Does this claim about the effects of goal efficacy apply equally to different basic classes of goals? Several studies show that whereas low confidence casts serious doubt on an outcome when approaching a judgment (i.e., performance) goal, low confidence does not appear to exert the same degree of influence when the subject is approaching a development (i.e., learning) goal, because having somewhat low confidence does not rule out the possibility of progress, which is in itself valuable (Elliott & Dweck, 1988; Henderson & Dweck, 1990; cf. Mueller & Dweck, 1998). In other words, although high confidence is necessary for the vigorous pursuit of a judgment goal, it is not a prerequisite for the vigorous pursuit of a development goal. Low-confidence, development-goal subjects continue to show persistence and mastery-oriented behavior after a setback and seem to actually relish challenge. Thus, principles relevant to variables, such as affect and when it is experienced or confidence and its impact in goal pursuit, may depend on the class of goals one is dealing with. Development and judgment goals may also differ in such things as the level of intrinsic motivation that typically accompanies their pursuit (Heyman & Dweck, 1992). Moreover, because of differences in the patterns of affect (including intrinsic motivation), cognition, and behavior that may typically characterize the pursuit of judgment and development goals, it is likely that different self-regulatory strategies are necessary or optimal for the two classes of goals.

CONCLUSION

Carver and Scheier have presented a conceptualization of the structure of behavior that is perhaps without parallel in its scope and depth. In responding to this insightful and provocative work, we have drawn on our own expertise to argue that goal-based models of behavior and goal theorists of behavior should reexamine their assumptions about the roles of content and structure in our understanding of goal striving. Specifically, we have suggested that goal content distinctions can be rendered more meaningful if we identify basic classes of goals that are few in number but cut across domains to capture the diversity of human behavior. We propose that judgment and development goals are examples of this useful and parsimonious kind of goal classification.

We have also argued that models of goal structure must take into account important content distinctions in order to more fully identify and understand the workings of particular structural dimensions of goal striving. For example, we have argued that in order to predict goal-related affect and the influence of confidence on goal engagement, we must understand the type of goal one is striving toward. Carver and Scheier demonstrate the richness of a discussion of goal structure that is informed by goal content in their description of the workings of approach and avoidance feedback loops. We applaud this kind of integrative approach to self-regulation and issue a call to future researchers to work in the spirit of a reunion of content and structure.

REFERENCES

Ames, C., Ames, R., & Felker, D. W. (1977). Effects of competitive reward structure and valence of outcome on children's achievement attributions. *Journal of Educational Psychology, 69,* 1–8.

Ames, C. & Archer, J. (1988). Achievement goals in the classroom: Students' learning strategies and motivation processes. *Journal of Educational Psychology, 80*, 260–267.

Austin, J. T., & Vancouver, J. B. (1996). Goal constructs in psychology: Structure, process, and content. *Psychological Bulletin, 120*(3), 338–375.

Bandura, M., & Dweck, C. S. (1985). *The relationship of conceptions of intelligence and achievement goals to achievement-related cognition, affect, and behavior.* Unpublished manuscript, Harvard University at Cambridge, MA.

Boggiano, A. K., Shields, A., Barrett, M., Kellam, T., Thompson, E., Simons, J., & Katz, P. (1992). Helplessness deficits in students: The role of motivation orientation. *Motivation and Emotion, 16*(3), 271–296.

Brundage, L. G., Derlega, V. J., & Cash, T. F. (1977). The effects of physical attractiveness and need for approval on self-disclosure. *Personality and Social Psychology Bulletin, 3*, 63–66.

Bruner, J. S. (1961). The act of discovery. *Harvard Educational Review, 31*, 21–32.

Bruner, J. S. (1965). The growth of mind. *American Psychologist, 20*, 1007–1017.

Carver, C. S., & Scheier, M. F. (1982). Control theory: A useful conceptual framework in personality-social, clinical, and health psychology. *Psychological Bulletin, 92*, 111–135.

Chiu, C. Y., Dweck, C. S., Tong, J. Y., & Fu, J. H. (1997). Implicit theories and conceptions of morality. *Journal of Personality and Social Psychology, 73*, 923–940.

Chiu, C. Y., Hong, Y. Y., & Dweck, C. S. (1997). Lay dispositionism and implicit theories of personality. *Journal of Personality and Social Psychology, 73*, 19–30.

Diener, C. I., & Dweck, C. S. (1978). An analysis of learned helplessness: Continuous change in performance and strategy and achievement cognitions following failure. *Journal of Personality and Social Psychology, 36*, 451–462.

Diener, C. I., & Dweck, C. S. (1980). An analysis of learned helplessness II: The processing of success. *Journal of Personality and Social Psychology, 39*, 940–952.

Dweck, C. S., & Elliott, E. S. (1983). Achievement motivation. In P. Mussen & E. M. Hetherington (Eds.), *Handbook of child psychology* (pp. 643–691). New York: Wiley.

Dweck, C. S., & Bempechat, J. (1983). Children's theories of intelligence: Implications for learning. In S. Paris, G. Olsen, & H. Stevenson (Eds.), *Learning and motivation in children*. Hillsdale, NJ: Lawrence Erlbaum Associates.

Dweck, C. S., & Leggett, E. L. (1988). A social-cognitive approach to motivation and personality. *Psychological Review, 95*, 256–273.

Elliot, A. J., & Church, M. A. (1997). A hierarchical model of approach and avoidance achievement motivation. *Journal of Personality and Social Psychology, 72*, 218–232.

Elliott, E. S., & Dweck, C. S. (1988). Goals: An approach to motivation and achievement. *Journal of Personality and Social Psychology, 54*, 5–12.

Erdley, C. A., & Asher, S. R. (1996). Children's social goals and self-efficacy perceptions as predictors of their responses to ambiguous provocation. *Child Development, 67*, 1329–1344.

Erdley, C. A., Cain, K. M., Loomis, C. C., Dumas-Hines, F., & Dweck, C. S. (1997). The relations among children's social goals, implicit personality theories, and responses to social failure. *Developmental Psychology, 33*, 263–272.

Erdley, C. A., & Dweck, C. S. (1993). Children's implicit theories as predictors of their social judgments. *Child Development, 64*, 863–878.

Goetz, T. S., & Dweck, C. S. (1980). Learned helplessness in social situations. *Journal of Personality and Social Psychology, 39*, 246–255.

Gollwizter, P. M., & Moskowitz, G. B. (1996). Goal effects on action and cognition. In E. T. Higgins & A. W. Kruglanski (Eds.), *Social psychology: Handbook of basic principles* (pp. 361–399). New York: Guilford.

Grant, H., & Dweck, C. S. (in press). A goal analysis of personality and personality coherence. In D. Cervone & Y. Shoda (Eds.), *Social-cognitive approaches to personality coherence*. New York: Guilford.

Henderson, V., & Dweck, C. S. (1990). Achievement and motivation in adolescence: A new model and data. In S. Feldman & G. Elliott (Eds.), *At the threshold: The developing adolescent*. Cambridge, MA: Harvard University Press.

Heyman, G. D., & Dweck, C. S. (1992). Achievement goals and intrinsic motivation: Their relation and their role in adaptive motivation. *Motivation and Emotion, 16*(3), 231–247.

Hong, Y. Y., Chiu, C. Y., & Dweck, C. S. (1995). Implicit theories of intelligence: Reconsidering the role of confidence in achievement motivation. In M. Kernis (Ed.), *Efficacy, agency, and self-esteem* (pp. 197–216). New York: Plenum.

Kamins, M. L., Morris, S. M., & Dweck, C. S. (1997, May). *Implicit theories as predictors of goals in dating relationships.* Poster session presented at the annual meeting of the Eastern Psychological Association, Washington, DC.

Kruglanski, A. W., & Shah, J. Y. (1997, October). *Intrinsic and extrinsic motivation: A little structure, a little substance.* Paper presented at the meeting of the Society for Experimental Social Psychology, Toronto, Canada.

La Greca, A. M., Dandes, S. K., Wick, P., Shaw, K., & Stone, W. (1988). Development of social anxiety scale for children: Reliability and concurrent validity. *Journal of Consulting Clinical Psychology, 17,* 84–91.

Levy, S. R., Stroessner, S. J., & Dweck, C. S. (1998). Stereotype formation and endorsement: The role of implicit theories. *Journal of Personality and Social Psychology, 74*(6), 1421–1436.

McAdams, D. P. (1989). *Intimacy: The need to be close.* New York: Doubleday.

Mueller, C. M., & Dweck, C. S. (1998). Praise for intelligence can undermine children's motivation and performance. *Journal of Personality and Social Psychology, 75*(1), 33–52.

Murray, H. A. (1938). *Explorations in personality.* New York: Oxford University Press.

Nichols, J. G. (1984). Achievement motivation: Conceptions of ability, subjective experience, task choice, and performance. *Psychological Review, 91,* 328–346.

Powers, W. T. (1973). *Behavior: The control of perception.* Chicago: Aldine.

Rosch, E., & Mervis, C. B. (1975). Family resemblances: Studies in the internal structure of categories. *Cognitive Psychology, 7,* 573–605.

Seligman, M. E. P. (1975). *Helplessness: On depression, development, and death.* San Francisco: W. H. Freeman.

Smiley, P. A., & Dweck, C. S. (1994). Individual differences in achievement goals among young children. *Child Development, 65,* 1723–1743.

Sorich, L., & Dweck, C. S. (1997). *Implicit theories and endorsement of punishment and rehabilitation.* Unpublished manuscript, Columbia University, New York.

Taylor, A. R., & Asher, S. R. (1989). *Children's goals in game playing situations.* Paper presented at the annual meeting of the American Psychological Association, New York.

Weiner, B. (1985). An attributional theory of achievement motivation and emotion. *Psychological Review, 92,* 548–573.

6

Considering the Role of Development in Self-Regulation

Eva M. Pomerantz
Ellen Rydell Altermatt
University of Illinois, Urbana-Champaign

Carver and Scheier consider a variety of important issues regarding self-regulation in their target chapter. They elaborate on many of their prior proposals (e.g., Carver & Scheier, 1981), providing a rich account of the processes involved in their model. Perhaps it is most significant that Carver and Scheier afford the opportunity for insight into the complexity of these processes by viewing self-regulation through a dynamic systems framework. Despite the comprehensiveness of the issues regarding self-regulation that these authors explore in their chapter, Carver and Scheier do not explore the *development* of self-regulation. How do the processes proposed by Carver and Scheier develop? Do they change with age? If so, how do they change? Moreover, what underlies the development of these processes? If they do change with age, what mechanisms cause the change? If they do not change, what mechanisms cause the stability? The answers to such questions are important in fully understanding self-regulation. Thus, the purpose of our commentary is to explore the role of development in the processes Carver and Scheier suggest are involved in self-regulation.

Since the 1980s, there has been a good deal of theory and research directed toward understanding the development of the processes involved in self-regulation prior to the preschool years (e.g., Bullock & Lutkenhaus, 1988; Kopp, 1982, 1991; Kopp & Wyer, 1994). Although this is an important first step, fully elucidating the development of self-regulation requires examining development in the preschool years and onward as well. Unfortunately, however, almost no theory or research has done so (see Higgins, 1989, 1991; Higgins, Loeb, & Moretti, 1995; Zimmerman & Martinez-Pons, 1990, for exceptions). This is particularly striking given that there is a wealth of research indicating that there are important social developmental changes during the preschool years and into adolescence that influence self-evaluation (see Dweck & Elliott, 1983; Eccles, Wigfield, & Scheifele, 1998; Higgins, 1989, 1991; Rholes, Newman, & Ruble, 1990; Stipek & Mac Iver, 1989, for recent reviews). Given the key role of self-evaluation in self-regulation, the social developmental changes influencing self-evaluation may also influence self-regulation.

Here, we highlight a variety of social developmental changes occurring during the preschool years and into adolescence that may lead to developmental changes in self-regulation during this time. We view these changes as influencing every process Carver and Scheier suggest to be involved in self-regulation. Moreover, we propose that such changes may be quite relevant to Carver and Scheier's application of a dynamic systems framework to self-regulation. We end our commentary by highlighting how a consideration of the development of self-regulation may provide insight into self-regulation in general.

SOCIAL DEVELOPMENT

A wealth of theory and research suggests that a variety of social developmental changes during the preschool years and into adolescence significantly influence self-evaluation. In this section, we highlight five of these changes and speculate on their implications for self-regulation. Specifically, we suggest that developmental changes in children's conceptions of ability, conceptions of feedback, goals, knowledge about how to delay gratification, and school environment influence self-regulation at every stage of the model proposed by Carver and Scheier.[1] Prior to these changes, self-regulation among children is expected to differ substantially from self-regulation among adults.

---

[1]Other social developmental changes during the preschool years and into adolescence may also influence self-regulation. Given space limitations, however, we cannot provide a full review of all such changes. Thus, we focus on those that we view as most important and that have not received attention in prior work (see Higgins, 1989, 1991; Higgins et al., 1995).

Conceptions of Ability

A substantial body of research indicates that during the elementary school years striking developmental changes occur in the extent to which children view ability as a stable entity (e.g., Beneson & Dweck, 1986; Droege & Stipek, 1993; Nicholls, 1978; Nicholls & Miller, 1984; Pomerantz & Ruble, 1997; Ruble & Flett, 1988; see Rholes et al., 1990; Stipek & Mac Iver, 1989, for reviews).[2] Whereas younger elementary school children view ability as unstable and easily influenced by effort, older elementary school children, similar to adults, view it as stable and inversely related to effort. This developmental change appears to have implications for the significance children assign to performance-related information. For younger children, performance-related information is seen as relatively unimportant because current performance is not viewed as predictive of future performance. Older children, in contrast, assign relatively high importance to performance-related information as they view such information as having significant implications for later achievement. Because younger children view performance-related information as less significant than older children, they may be less concerned with assessing their performance and may be less likely to seek out performance-related information, particularly in terms of social comparison (e.g., Rholes et al., 1990; Ruble, 1994; Ruble & Flett, 1988).

These consequences of conceiving of ability as unstable may alter self-regulation considerably. Because of their relative lack of concern with self-assessment, younger children may be less likely than older children to compare their actual and desired performance. In Carver and Scheier's terms, younger children's comparator may be relatively inactive. Moreover, younger children may notice discrepancies between their actual and desired performance less often than older children because they lack the information to do so. That is, their comparator may be relatively impaired because their input function may provide relatively sparse information. Consequently, younger children may be less likely than older children to adjust their goals, standards, and reference values in accord with reality (i.e., their secondary output function may be relatively inactive) and to engage in discrepancy-reducing behavior (i.e., their primary output function may be relatively inactive). In

---

[2]These findings come from two lines of research focusing on children's conceptions of ability. One has focused on conceptions of ability as constant, whereas the other has focused on conceptions of ability as capacity. Although these two conceptions are similar on a variety of dimensions, they also differ (see Pomerantz & Ruble, 1997). However, these differences are not relevant to the present discussion, and thus, we treat the two as representing conceptions of ability as stable.

addition, because younger children do not view performance as having significant long-term implications, they may experience fewer positive emotions as a consequence of attaining a goal and fewer negative emotions upon failing to do so. Finally, when younger children do engage in discrepancy-reducing behavior, they may be more persistent than older children because they do not view ability as inversely related to effort and, thus, may be less likely to be interrupted by anxiety. That is, younger children's primary output function may be relatively effective.

A number of findings are consistent with the proposals we have presented here. A wealth of evidence indicates that younger elementary school children have less accurate self-perceptions of competence than older elementary school children (e.g., Eccles, Midgely, & Adler, 1984; Eshel & Klein, 1981; Morris & Nemcek, 1982; Nicholls, 1978; see Eccles et al., 1998; Stipek & Mac Iver, 1989, for reviews). This inaccuracy has been linked to conceiving of ability as unstable (e.g., Nicholls & Miller, 1984; Pomerantz & Ruble, 1997). Younger children are also less likely to give up in the face of failure than older children (Rholes, Blackwell, Jordan & Walters, 1980), and this too has been linked to conceiving of ability as unstable (Miller, 1985; Rholes, Jones, & Wade, 1988).

Conceptions of Feedback

Developmental changes in how children view feedback from others during the elementary school years may also influence self-regulation at this time. A good deal of research finds that younger children are less likely than older children to detect information about incompetence in teachers' feedback (e.g., Barker & Graham, 1987; Graham & Barker, 1990; Pomerantz & Ruble, 1997; see Graham, 1990, for a review). For example, Lord, Umezaki, and Darley (1990) presented children with a scenario in which a teacher responded differently to the same performance of two children. Following one child's performance, the teacher gave the child a hug, but following the other child's performance, the teacher suggested that the child needed to try harder in the future. Younger children viewed the hugged child as more competent, whereas older children viewed the hugged child as less competent. Research yields similar findings for elementary school children's conceptions of parental behavior (Pomerantz & Eaton, 1999). Specifically, younger children are less likely than older children to view parents' attempt to help children with homework, monitor children's progress on homework, and make decisions for children as indicating that children are incompetent.

The changes in children's conceptions of others' feedback are particular striking when taken in the context of another change during the elementary school years. Although younger children are generally less concerned than older children with assessing their performance (see prior section), research suggests that younger children may be more likely than older children to rely on feedback from external rather than internal sources when they do assess their performance (Harter, 1981). Thus, feedback from others may play a relatively important role in younger children's assessments of their performance, and their lack of awareness of incompetence cues in such feedback may lead them to possess relatively positively biased information regarding their performance.

Given these consequences, the developmental changes in elementary school children's conceptions of feedback may lead to significant changes in their self-regulation. Because younger children are unlikely to detect cues about incompetence in feedback from others, they may possess, relative to older children and adults, positively biased information regarding their performance. In Carver and Scheier's terms, their input function may be relatively positively biased. This may cause younger children to overestimate the extent to which they have met their goals (i.e., their comparator may be relatively positively biased). Consequently, younger children may engage in fewer discrepancy-reducing behaviors than older children. In other words, their primary output function may be relatively inactive. Moreover, younger children may be less likely than older children to adjust their goals, standards, and reference values so that they are in line with reality. That is, their secondary output function may be relatively inactive.

Consistent with these proposals, research indicates that younger elementary school children's self-perceptions are not only less accurate than those of older children (see prior section), but also more favorable (e.g., Eccles, Midgely, & Adler, 1984; Eshel & Klein, 1981; Frey & Ruble, 1987; Morris & Nemcek, 1982; Nicholls, 1978; see Eccles et al., 1998; Stipek & Mac Iver, 1989, for reviews). Moreover, research indicates that younger children set higher standards for their performance than older children (Pomerantz & Saxon, 1999). The link between children's conceptions of feedback and their self-perceptions of competence and standards still needs to be established empirically. However, this connection is suggested by evidence that children's conceptions of significant others' feedback are associated with their conceptions of ability. Specifically, children who do not detect cues about competence in others' feedback tend to view ability as unstable and as easily influenced by effort (e.g., Graham & Barker, 1990; Pomerantz & Eaton, 1999; Pomerantz & Ruble, 1997).

Goals

Since the mid-1980s, investigators have increasingly argued that individuals' self-evaluative processes are governed by their goals (e.g., Butler, 1993; Dweck & Leggett, 1988; Gollwitzer, 1990; Nicholls, 1984; Ruble & Frey, 1991; Taylor & Lobel, 1989; Tesser, 1986; Trope, 1986; Wood, 1989). Children's goals appear to change as they progress through elementary school, with younger children possessing mastery goals and older children possessing performance goals (e.g., Butler, 1989a, 1989b, 1990; Pomerantz, Ruble, Frey, & Greulich, 1995). Younger children are primarily concerned with learning how to do the tasks with which they are confronted, whereas older children are concerned with assessing their performance on these tasks. Although the changes in children's goals may be due to changes in their conceptions of ability (Rholes et al., 1990), they may also be due to a variety of other factors including children's phase of knowledge acquisition (Ruble & Frey, 1991), their classroom environment (Stipek & Mac Iver, 1989), and the emphasis that their parents place on performance versus learning goals.

The changes in children's goals are significant because they may lead to changes in their information seeking. Children with mastery goals seek out information that will help them to learn (e.g., Butler, 1989a, 1989b, 1992; Ruble & Frey, 1991). Children with performance goals, in contrast, seek out information that will aid them in assessing their performance (e.g., Butler, 1989a, 1989b, 1992; Ruble & Frey, 1991). In addition, mastery goals have been linked to intrinsic motivation and persistence in the face of failure, whereas performance goals have been linked to extrinsic motivation and helplessness in the face of failure (e.g., Butler, 1989a, 1992; Elliott & Dweck, 1988; see Dweck & Leggett, 1988; Nicholls, 1984, for reviews). Moreover, mastery goals often lead to better achievement than performance goals (e.g., Butler, 1989a, 1992).

Developmental changes in children's goals during the elementary school years may lead to significant changes in their self-regulation during these years. Many of these are similar to those that may result from changes in conceptions of ability and feedback. First, because younger children tend to be less concerned with performance than older children, they may also be less concerned with evaluating whether they have performed up to standards—that is, their comparator may be relatively inactive. Even when younger children do assess the extent to which they have performed up to standards, they may have less information to draw upon than older children. Their input function may be relatively sparse in Carver and Scheier's terms. The emotional consequences of failing to meet goals may also vary developmentally. Specifically, younger children may find discrepancies between their performance and standards less threatening than older children because their primary concern is with learning and not with performance.[3] Finally, younger children's mastery goals may lead to persistence in the face of failure, whereas older children's performance goals may lead to helplessness. Thus, younger children may be more effective than older children at reducing discrepancies. In other words, their primary output function may be relatively effective. Although research directly examining these proposals is needed, the empirical evidence presented in the prior two sections is suggestive of their validity.

Delay of Gratification Knowledge

According to Carver and Scheier, a key element of self-regulation is the ability to engage in behavior that reduces discrepancies between current performance and desired performance (i.e., output function). Such behavior depends, in part, on knowledge about how to reduce discrepancies. For many discrepancies, knowledge about how to delay gratification may be essential. For example, attaining high grades in school may depend on refraining from stimulating social interactions in order to spend time studying.

There appear to be developmental changes in children's ability to delay gratification in terms of concrete entities, such as food, during the preschool and elementary school years (e.g., Toner & Smith, 1977; Yates, Lippett, & Yates, 1981). This research indicates that younger children are less adept than older children at delaying small but immediate forms of gratification (e.g., one marshmallow right away) for large but delayed forms (e.g., three marshmallows in 15 minutes). This appears to be due to younger children's lack of knowledge about strategies that are helpful in delaying gratification (e.g., H. N. Mischel & Mischel, 1983). Indeed, even younger children are able to delay gratification if they have been given knowledge about how to do so (e.g., W. Mischel & Baker, 1975; W. Mischel & Patterson, 1976). The developmental changes during the preschool and elementary school years in children's knowledge about how to delay gratification in terms of concrete entities may lead to developmental changes during this time in the effectiveness of discrepancy-reducing behaviors (i.e., primary output function) for goals that involve delaying gratification in terms of such objects.

---

[3]Success may foster positive emotions in children regardless of whether they adopt learning or performance goals. Children may be pleased with either having learned how to do the task or having performed well (see Dweck & Leggett, 1988).

There may also be important developmental changes in the preschool and elementary school years in delay of gratification in terms of abstract entities. To the extent that accurate information about oneself is negative, such information may have short-term costs as it is threatening at the moment, but long-term benefits as it allows for improvement in the future (e.g., Banaji & Prentice, 1994; Taylor, Wayment, & Carrillo, 1996). Thus, accurate self-assessment of progress toward goals may require delaying immediate gratification (i.e., feeling good about oneself) in return for long-term gratification (i.e., performing well; Trope, 1986; Trope & Neter, 1994; Trope & Pomerantz, 1998). Adults have knowledge about how to manage the short-term negative consequences of receiving negative but accurate information about themselves. Specifically, research conducted by Trope and Neter (1994) indicates that adults are likely to seek out positive information about themselves prior to receiving negative information about themselves.

Although younger elementary school children are not often concerned with assessing their performance (see prior sections), when they are concerned with doing so, they may not possess the appropriate knowledge. Specifically, they may not know how to delay gratification in terms of abstract entities. No research to date has examined this issue directly. However, there are several empirical findings that are consistent with our proposal that younger elementary school children do not possess such knowledge. First, as described earlier, younger children possess more positive self-perceptions of competence than older children. Second, observations of children's behavior in the classroom indicate that younger children are more likely than older children to engage in behavior that makes them feel good (e.g., exclaiming that they are the best in the class) rather than behavior that provides information about their performance (e.g., comparing their progress to peers; Frey & Ruble, 1985; Pomerantz et al., 1995). Third, despite the fact that older elementary school children understand that they should not publicly announce that they have performed better than others because it might hurt others' feelings, they may continue to do so (Pomerantz et al., 1995). Thus, even older elementary school children may not be capable of delaying gratification in terms of abstract entities. We must stress that this research is highly conjectural concerning the issue of whether younger elementary school children possess the knowledge necessary to delay gratification in terms of abstract entities. This research only examines developmental patterns that may be reflective of developmental changes in such knowledge. Further research will be essential to determine if there are developmental changes in children's knowledge about delaying gratification in terms of abstract entities during the elementary school years.

Such research is particularly important given the impact that developmental changes in children's knowledge about delaying gratification in terms of abstract entities may have for self-regulation. Developmental changes in such knowledge may have many of the same consequences for self-regulation as the developmental changes identified in the prior sections. In particular, younger children's possible lack of knowledge about how to delay gratification in terms of abstract entities may inhibit them from obtaining accurate, but negative, information regarding whether they have met goals. In Carver and Scheier's terms, younger children's input function may be relatively positively biased. Consequently, compared to older children, younger children may underestimate the discrepancy between their actual performance and their desired performance. That is, their comparator may be relatively positively biased. This, in turn, may cause younger children to engage in less discrepancy-reducing behavior than older children (i.e., their output function may be relatively inactive). Moreover, younger children may be less likely than older children to adjust their goals, standards, and reference values so that they are in line with reality. Their secondary output function may be relatively inactive in Carver and Scheier's terms.

School Transitions

Until now, we have focused on developmental changes that occur within the child. However, developmental changes in the child's environment may also lead to developmental changes in self-regulation. One of the most salient of these is that of the school transition. Of particular importance may be the transition from elementary to junior high school and from junior high to high school. These transitions may have several consequences that influence self-regulation. First, it may often be more difficult for children to meet performance standards following school transitions as more stringent criteria are set for success and fewer high grades are given by teachers (Eccles & Midgley, 1989; Eccles et al., 1993; Simmons & Blyth, 1987). Second, the new criteria for success that typically accompany school transitions may cause children to feel uncertain about how to meet performance standards and about whether they have actually met these standards (Higgins, Loeb, & Ruble, 1995; Ruble, 1994; Ruble & Seidman, 1996). Finally, children are often confronted with a new group of peers following the transition (Ruble & Seidman, 1996; Simmons & Blyth, 1987). Their lack of knowledge regarding the competence of these peers may make informative social comparisons difficult.

Given these consequences, what role might school transitions play in self-regulation? First, school transitions may disrupt the adequacy of children's discrepancy-reducing behaviors (i.e., impair their primary output function). Specifically, to the extent that it is difficult to meet performance standards and it is unclear how to go about doing so, children may be incapable of fully reducing discrepancies between their actual and desired performance. Moreover, children may find that the strategies they used in elementary school to reduce discrepancies are no longer effective. Second, following school transitions, children may not have adequate information to assess the extent to which they have met their goals. In other words, their input function may be relatively sparse. Their lack of knowledge about the new criteria for success may cause them to feel uncertain about whether they have met standards. Moreover, children may be unable to make informative social comparisons because they lack knowledge about the ability level of their new peers. Third, any information children do possess may be negatively biased because of the difficulty of meeting standards. Thus, children may have a difficult time assessing whether they have met standards and may underestimate the extent to which they have done so. In Carver and Scheier's terms, their comparator may be relatively impaired and negatively biased. Finally, school transitions may cause children to change their goals, standards, and reference values (i.e., their secondary output function may be relatively active). Upon realizing that the criteria for success in junior high school are more difficult to meet than in elementary school, children may lower their goals, standards, and reference values. After children adjust to the transition, their self-regulatory processes may return to their prior state and be quite similar to those of adults not confronted by a transition.

Research to date has not examined these proposals directly. However, much of the research that has been conducted is consistent with this perspective. Wigfield and colleagues (Wigfield, Eccles, Mac Iver, Reuman, & Midgley, 1991) have found that children's self-perceptions of competence and self-esteem decrease following the transition from elementary school to junior high school. Girls are particularly likely to experience a decrease in self-esteem following school transitions (e.g., Abramowitz, Petersen, & Schulenberg, 1984; Simmons & Blyth, 1987; Lord, Eccles, & McCarthy, 1994). Girls may be more vulnerable than boys to such transitions for a variety of reasons (see Eccles et al., 1993, 1998; Nolen-Hoeksema & Girgus, 1994; Ruble, Greulich, Pomerantz, & Gochberg, 1993). Most relevant to the current proposals is that girls may ruminate over their lack of ability to meet the new criteria for success that accompany the transition to junior high (e.g., Nolen-Hoeksema & Girgus, 1994). Moreover, girls may feel more compelled than boys to meet performance standards and thus failure to do so may be more upsetting to them (Higgins, 1991; Pomerantz & Ruble, 1998; Pomerantz & Saxon, in press; Ruble et al., 1993).

Summary

A review of the social developmental changes during the preschool through adolescent years suggests that there may be significant developmental changes in self-regulation at these times. Both younger elementary school children's conceptions of ability as unstable and their mastery goals may lead them to be less likely than older elementary school children and adults to assess the extent to which they have met performance standards. Younger elementary school children's conceptions of ability as unstable, lack of awareness of incompetence cues in others' feedback, mastery goals, and lack of knowledge about delay of gratification may all lead them, compared to older elementary school children and adults, to possess less accurate information as to whether they have successfully met their standards. It is significant that younger children's information may be relatively positively biased, and thus they may be less likely to identify discrepancies between their actual performance and their desired performance than older children and adults. This may decrease the likelihood that younger children will adjust their goals, standards, and reference values in accord with reality and may correspondingly decrease their discrepancy-reducing behavior. However, when younger children do engage in such behaviors, their conceptions of ability as unstable and as easily influenced by effort as well as their mastery goals may cause them to be more persistent than older children and adults. Another decrease in the accuracy with which children assess whether they have met their goals may occur during adolescence, following the transition from elementary to junior high school. However, at this time, children's assessments may be relatively negatively, rather than positively, biased. Following the transition, children's discrepancy-reducing strategies may also not be very effective. Finally, children's conceptions of ability as unstable and their mastery goals may decrease the emotional consequences they experience as a result of meeting or failing to meet their goals.

SOCIAL DEVELOPMENT AND DYNAMIC SYSTEMS

Perhaps the most innovative aspect of Carver and Scheier's target chapter is their application of a dynamic systems framework to their model of self-regulation. The social developmental changes we have outlined here may be quite relevant to the themes that Carver and Scheier present as part of this framework. The first theme Carver and Scheier highlight is that of nonlinearity. Such a theme has also been of significance to investigators concerned with social developmental changes, such as those we have outlined (e.g., Emmerich, Goldman, Kirsh, & Sharabany, 1977; Ruble & Goodnow, 1998). For example, Ruble (1994) suggests that when children first acquire a conception of ability as stable, their concern with assessing their competence increases significantly, but that once they have come to a conclusion about their competence, such a concern decreases. Thus, there may be a curvilinear relation between conceptions of ability and concern with assessing competence that leads to a curvilinear relation between conceptions of ability and the processes involved in self-regulation. Many of the other developmental changes we have highlighted may show a similar pattern of influence on self-regulation. It is also quite possible that developmental changes may lead to changes in self-regulation in terms of step or threshold functions. For example, developmental changes in children's goals may only influence the processes involved in self-regulation after the primacy of a particular goal has reached a certain level.

A second theme highlighted by Carver and Scheier in their discussion of a dynamic systems framework is that of phase space. The phase space represents an array of states that the individual occupies over time. The phase space is characterized by attractors to which individuals are drawn. Carver and Scheier suggest that attractors represent goals. Individuals move from one attractor to another when the phase space is disturbed. The social developmental changes we have outlined may disturb the phase space leading to changes in attractors. That is, the social developmental changes may lead to goal shifts. For example, as children's conceptions of others' feedback change, children may readjust their goals to bring them more in line with reality. This may require changing not only the level of their goals but also the goals themselves. Consequently, a new conception of others' feedback may lead activity to be directed toward a new goal that was previously not of primary importance.

Third, Carver and Scheier address the theme of variability from a dynamic systems framework. They highlight the idea that variability may foster phase changes. This concept may be important in understanding the onset of developmental changes and their impact on self-regulation. When children first make a developmental change, variability may be high for several reasons. Children may often revert back to their prior state. For example, when children first come to view ability as stable, they may not do so under all circumstances. In addition, even when children are in their new state, they may not always be capable of optimizing this state. For example, when children first acquire the knowledge to delay gratification, they may not be capable of applying it under all circumstances because they do not know when it is relevant. Finally, when children have just entered a new state, they may implement the new state with a variety of methods differing in effectiveness. For example, children who have just acquired a conception of ability as stable may seek out information about performance using a variety of strategies differing in the accuracy of information they provide. The heightened variability children experience as they initially make a developmental change may lead to variability in self-regulation. For example, when children make the transition from elementary to junior high school, they may engage in a variety of strategies to meet their goals, and these strategies may differ in their effectiveness. Consequently, their goals may be quite variable as they attempt to adjust them to the effectiveness with which they are capable of reaching them.

A final theme of a dynamic systems framework highlighted by Carver and Scheier is that of sensitive dependence on initial conditions. Specifically, they suggest that a small difference in starting points can foster large differences at a later point. Until now, we have focused on normative developmental changes and have assumed not only that all children experience such changes but that they also do so at approximately the same time. However, substantial variability within age groups in some of the constructs we have highlighted suggests that children may experience changes at different times. Small differences in the timing of these changes may lead to large individual differences in self-regulation because such differences may have implications for whether these changes intersect with other changes. For example, if children develop a conception of ability as stable prior to or at the same time that they are confronted with a new teacher with new standards for performance, children may be at risk for experiencing negative affect. Increased difficulty in trying to met their goals may lead children with stable conceptions of ability toward a declining trajectory of mental health. In contrast, children who continue to conceive of ability as unstable may not be negatively influenced by a new teacher.

SOCIAL DEVELOPMENT AND SELF-REGULATION IN GENERAL

Although understanding the development of self-regulation is important in its own right, it has a number of important implications for understanding self-regulation in general. Investigators have highlighted how insight into the development of a phenomenon may provide insight into the phenomenon in general (Higgins & Wells, 1986; Ruble & Goodnow, 1998). First, understanding the development of self-regulation can lead to the identification of factors that moderate self-regulation. The same factors that cause developmental differences in self-regulation among children may also produce situational and individual differences in self-regulation among adults. For example, differences in the extent to which situations make mastery versus performance goals salient may lead to differences in self-regulation among adults that mirror developmental differences in self-regulation among children. Second, insight into development can pinpoint the mechanisms that underlie self-regulation. Specifically, if younger children's self-regulation is impaired because they lack a particular mechanism, it is quite likely that that mechanism underlies self-regulation. For example, finding that younger children's lack of knowledge about delaying gratification impairs their self-regulation would suggest that such knowledge is essential to self-regulation among adults. Third, identifying the social developmental changes that affect children's self-regulation will help to identify changes that affect adults' self-regulation. For example, if school transitions influence children's self-regulation because they lead to uncertainty about how to meet performance standards, then any transition leading to uncertainty at any age may influence self-regulation similarly.

CONCLUSIONS

It is our hope that our commentary emphasizes the significance of considering the role of development in self-regulation. We have highlighted five social developmental changes occurring during the pre-school years and into adolescence that may lead to significant developmental changes in self-regulation. Consideration of these social developmental changes is a first step toward answering some of the questions we posed at the beginning of our commentary. There is substantial evidence to suggest that the processes involved in self-regulation according to the model proposed by Carver and Scheier change as children progress from preschool into elementary school and then into adolescence. Moreover, it appears that social developmental changes both internal and external to children underlie such changes. It is quite probable that developmental changes in self-regulation are not always linear, are sensitive to variability, and react to small changes in initial conditions. It is our view that considering development expands the understanding of self-regulation among both children and adults.

ACKNOWLEDGMENTS

Preparation of this commentary was facilitated by NSF grant 9708981 and a University of Illinois Research Board grant to the first author. We are grateful to Bob Wyer for his constructive comments.

REFERENCES

Abramowitz, R. H., Petersen, A. C., & Schulenberg, J. E. (1984). Changes in self-image during early adolescence. In D. Offer, E. Ostrov, & K. Howard (Eds.), *Patterns of adolescent self-image* (pp. 19–28). San Francisco: Jossey-Bass.

Banaji, M. R., & Prentice, D. A. (1994). The self in social contexts. *Annual Review of Psychology, 45,* 297–332.

Barker, G. P., & Graham, S. (1987). Developmental study of praise and blame as attributional cues. *Journal of Educational Psychology, 79,* 62–66.

Beneson, J. F., & Dweck, C. S. (1986). The development of trait explanations and self-evaluations in the academic and social domains. *Child Development, 57,* 1179–1187.

Bullock, M., & Lutkenhaus, P. (1988). The development of volitional behaviors in the toddler years. *Child Development, 59,* 664–674.

Butler, R. (1989a). Interest in the task and interest in peers' work in competitive and noncompetitive conditions: A developmental study. *Child Development, 60,* 562–570.

Butler, R. (1989b). Mastery versus ability appraisal: A developmental study of children's observations of peers' work. *Child Development, 60,* 1350–1361.

Butler, R. (1990). The effects of mastery and competitive conditions on self-assessment at different ages. *Child Development, 61,* 201–210.

Butler, R. (1992). What young people want to know when: Effects of mastery and ability goals on interest in different kinds of social comparisons. *Journal of Personality and Social Psychology, 62,* 934–943.

Butler, R. (1993). Effects of task- and ego-achievement goals on information seeking during task engagement, *Journal of Personality and Social Psychology, 65,* 18–31.

Carver, C. S., & Scheier, M. F. (1981). *Attention and self-regulation: A control-theory approach to human behavior.* New York: Spring-Verlag.

Droege, K. L., & Stipek, D. J. (1993). Children's use of dispositions to predict classmates behavior. *Developmental Psychology, 29,* 646–654.

Dweck, C. S., & Elliott, E. S. (1983). Achievement motivation. In P. H. Mussen (Series Ed.) & E. M. Hetherington (Vol. Ed.), *Handbook of child psychology: Vol. 4. Socialization, personality, and social development* (4th ed., pp. 387–467). New York: Wiley.

Dweck, C. S., & Leggett, E. (1988). A social-cognitive approach to motivation and personality. *Psychological Review, 95,* 256–273.

Eccles, J. S., & Midgley, C. (1989). Stage/environment fit: Developmentally appropriate classrooms for adolescents. In R. E. Ames & C. Ames (Eds.), *Research on motivation in education* (Vol. 3, pp. 139–186). San Diego, CA: Academic Press.

Eccles, J. S., Midgely, C., & Adler, T. (1984). Age-related changes in the school environment: Effects on achievement motivation. In J. G. Nicholls (Ed.), *The development of achievement motivation* (pp. 283–331). Greenwich, CT: JAI.

Eccles, J. S., Midgley, C., Wigfield, A, Buchanan, C. M., Reuman, D., Flanagan, C., & Mac Iver, D. (1993). Development during adolescence: The impact of stage-environment fit on young adolescents' experiences in schools and in families. *American Psychologist, 48,* 90–101.

Eccles, J. S., Wigfield, A., & Schiefele, U. (1998). Motivation to succeed. In W. Damon (Series Ed.) & N. Eisenberg (Vol. Ed.), *Handbook of child psychology: Vol. 3. Social, emotional, and personality development* (5th ed., pp. 1017–1095). New York: Wiley.

Elliott, E. S., & Dweck, C. S. (1988). Goals: An approach to motivation and achievement. *Journal of Personality and Social Psychology, 54,* 5–12.

Emmerich, W., Goldman, K. S., Kirsh, B., & Sharabany, R. (1977). Evidence for a transitional phase in the development of gender constancy. *Child Development, 48,* 930–936.

Eshel, Y., & Klein, Z. (1981). Development of academic self-concept of lower-class and middle-class primary school children. *Journal of Educational Psychology, 73,* 287–293.

Frey, K. S., & Ruble, D. N. (1985). What children say when the teacher is not around: Conflicting goals in social comparison and performance assessment in the classroom. *Journal of Personality and Social Psychology, 48,* 18–30.

Frey, K. S., & Ruble, D. N. (1987). What children say about classroom performance: Sex and grade differences in perceived competence. *Child Development, 58*, 1066–1078.

Graham, S. (1990). Communicating low ability in the classroom: Bad things good teachers sometimes do. In S. Graham & V. S. Folkes (Eds.), *Attribution theory: Applications to achievement, mental health, and interpersonal conflict* (pp. 17–36). Hillsdale, NJ: Lawrence Erlbaum Associates.

Graham, S., & Barker, G. P. (1990). The down side of help: An attributional-developmental analysis of helping behavior as a low-ability cue. *Journal of Educational Psychology, 82*, 7–14.

Harter, S. (1981). A new self-report scale of intrinsic versus extrinsic orientation in the classroom: Motivational and informational components. *Developmental Psychology, 17*, 300–312.

Higgins, E. T. (1989). Continuities and discontinuities in self-regulatory and self-evaluative processes: A developmental theory relating self and affect. *Journal of Personality, 57*, 407–444.

Higgins, E. T. (1991). Development of self-regulatory and self-evaluative processes: Costs, benefits, and tradeoffs. In M. R. Gunnar & L. A. Sroufe (Eds.), *Self processes and development: The Minnesota symposium on child psychology* (Vol. 23, pp. 125–166). Hillsdale, NJ: Lawrence Erlbaum Associates.

Higgins, E. T., Loeb, I., & Moretti, M. (1995). Self-discrepancies and developmental shifts in vulnerability: Life transitions in the regulatory significance of others. In D. Cicchetti & S. L. Toth (Eds.), *Emotion, cognition, and representation. Rochester symposium on developmental psychopathology* (Vol. 6, pp. 191–230). Rochester, NY: University of Rochester Press.

Higgins, E. T, Loeb, I., & Ruble, D. N. (1995). The four A's of life transition effects: Attention, accessibility, adaptation, and adjustment. *Social Cognition, 13*, 215–242.

Higgins, E. T., & Wells, R. (1986). Social construct availability and accessibility as a function of social life phase: Emphasizing the "how" versus the "can" of social cognition. *Social Cognition, 4*, 201–226.

Kopp, C. (1982). Antecedents of self-regulation: A developmental perspective. *Developmental Psychology, 18*, 199–214.

Kopp, C. (1991). Young children's progression to self-regulation. In M. Bullock (Ed.), *The development of intentional action: Cognitive motivational, and interactive processes. Contributions to human development* (Vol. 22, pp. 38–54). Basel, Switzerland.

Kopp, C., & Wyer, N. (1994). Self-regulation in normal and atypical development. In D. Cicchetti & S. L. Toth (Eds.), *Disorders and dysfunctions of the self: Rochester symposium on psychopathology* (Vol. 5, pp. 31–56). Rochester, NY: University of Rochester Press.

Lord, C. G., Umezaki, K., & Darley, J. M. (1990). Developmental differences in decoding the meanings of the appraisal actions of teachers. *Child Development, 61*, 191–200.

Lord, S., Eccles, J. S., & McCarthy, K. A. (1994). Surviving the junior high school transition: Family processes and self-perceptions as protective and risk factors. *Journal of Early Adolescence, 14*, 162–199.

Miller, A. T. (1985). A developmental study of the cognitive basis of performance and improvement after failure. *Journal of Personality and Social Psychology, 49*, 529–538.

Mischel, H. N., & Mischel, W. (1983). The development of children's knowledge of self-control strategies. *Child Development, 53*, 603–619.

Mischel, W., & Baker, N. (1975). Cognitive appraisals and transformations in delay behavior. *Journal of Personality and Social Psychology, 31*, 254–261.

Mischel, W., & Patterson, C. J. (1976). Substantive and structural elements of effective plans for self-control. *Journal of Personality and Social Psychology, 34*, 942–950.

Morris, W. N., & Nemcek, D. (1982). The development of social comparison motivation among preschoolers: Evidence of step-wise progression. *Merrill-Palmer Quarterly, 28*, 413–425.

Nicholls, J. G. (1978). The development of concepts of effort and ability, perceptions of academic attainment, and the understanding that difficult tasks require more ability. *Child Development, 49*, 800–814.

Nicholls, J. G. (1984). Achievement motivation: Conceptions of ability, subjective experience, task choice, and performance. *Psychological Review, 91*, 328–346.

Nicholls, J. G., & Miller, A. G. (1984). Reasoning about the ability of self and others: A developmental study. *Child Development, 55*, 1990–1999.

Nolen-Hoeksema, S., & Girgus, J. S. (1994). The emergence of gender differences in depression during adolescence. *Psychological Bulletin, 115*, 424–443.

Pomerantz, E. M., & Eaton, M. M. (1999). *Developmental differences in children's conceptions of parental control.* Manuscript submitted for publication.

Pomerantz, E. M., & Ruble, D. N. (1997). Distinguishing multiple dimensions of conceptions of ability: Implications for the development of self-evaluation. *Child Development, 68*, 1165–1180.

Pomerantz, E. M., & Ruble, D. N. (1998). The role of maternal control in the development of child self-evaluative factors. *Child Development, 69*, 458–478.

Pomerantz, E. M., Ruble, D. N., Frey, K. S., & Greulich, F. (1995). Meeting goals and confronting conflicts: Children's changing perceptions of social comparison. *Child Development, 66*, 723–738.

Pomerantz, E. M., & Saxon, J. L. (1999). [Self-evaluative development]. Unpublished data set.

Pomerantz, E. M., & Saxon, J. L. (in press). Sex differences in self-evaluation: A developmental perspective. In G. B. Moskowitz (Ed.), Future directions in social cognition.

Rholes, W. S., Blackwell, J., Jordan, C., & Walters, C. (1980). A developmental study of learned helplessness. *Developmental Psychology, 16*, 616–624.

Rholes, W. S., Jones, M., & Wade, C. (1988). Children's understanding of personal dispositions and its relationship to behavior. *Journal of Experimental Child Psychology, 45*, 1–17.

Rholes, W. S., Newman, L. S., & Ruble, D. N. (1990). Understanding self and other: Developmental and motivational aspects of perceiving persons in terms of invariant dispositions. In E. T. Higgins & R. M. Sorrentino (Eds.), *Handbook of motivation and cognition: Foundations of social behavior* (Vol. 2, pp. 369–407). New York: Guilford.

Ruble, D. N. (1994). A phase model of transitions: Cognitive and motivational consequences. In M. Zanna (Ed.), *Advances in experimental social psychology* (Vol. 26, pp. 163–214). New York: Academic Press.

Ruble, D. N., & Flett, G. L. (1988). Conflicting goals in self-evaluative information seeking: Developmental and ability level analysis. *Child Development, 59*, 97–106.

Ruble, D. N., & Frey, K. S. (1991). Changing patterns of comparative behavior as skills are acquired: A functional model of self-evaluation. In J. Suls & T. A. Wills (Eds.), *Social comparison: Contemporary theory and research* (pp. 79–113). Hillsdale, NJ: Lawrence Erlbaum Associates.

Ruble, D. N., & Goodnow, J. J. (1998). Social development in childhood and adulthood. In D. Gilbert, S. Fiske, & G. Lindzey (Eds.), *Handbook of social psychology* (4th ed., pp. 741–787). New York: McGraw-Hill.

Ruble, D. N., Greulich, F., Pomerantz, E. M., & Gochberg, B. (1993). The role of gender-related processes in the development of sex differences in self-evaluation and depression. *Journal of Affective Disorders, 29*, 97–128.

Ruble, D. N., & Seidman, E. (1996). Social transitions: Windows into social psychological processes. In E. T. Higgins & A. W. Kruglanski, *Social psychology: Handbook of basic principles* (pp. 830–856). New York: Guilford.

Simmons, R. G., & Blyth, D. A. (1987). *Moving into adolescence: The impact of pubertal change and school context.* New York: Aldine.

Stipek, D., & Mac Iver, D. (1989). Developmental change in children's assessment of intellectual competence. *Child Development, 60*, 521–538.

Taylor, S. E., & Lobel, M. (1989). Social comparison activity under threat: Downward evaluation and upward contacts. *Psychological Review, 96*, 569–575.

Taylor, S. E., Wayment, H. A., & Carrillo, M. (1996). Social comparison, self-regulation, and motivation. In R. M. Sorrentino & E. T. Higgins (Eds.), *Handbook of motivation and cognition* (Vol. 3, pp. 3–37). New York: Guilford.

Tesser, A. (1986). Some effects of self-evaluation maintenance on cognition and affect. In R. M. Sorrentino & E. T. Higgins (Eds.), *Handbook of motivation and cognition: Foundations of social behavior* (Vol. 1, pp. 435–464). New York: Guilford.

Toner, I. J., & Smith, R. A. (1977). Age and overt verbalization in delay maintenance behavior in children. *Journal of Experimental Child Psychology, 24*, 123–128.

Trope, Y. (1986). Self-assessment and self-enhancement in achievement motivation. In R. M. Sorrentino & E. T. Higgins (Eds.), *Handbook of motivation and cognition: Foundations of social behavior* (Vol 1, pp. 350–378). New York: Guilford.

Trope, Y., & Neter, E. (1994). Reconciling competing motives in self-evaluation: The role of self-control in feedback seeking. *Journal of Personality and Social Psychology, 66*, 646–657.

Trope, Y., & Pomerantz, E. M. (1998). Resolving conflicts among self-evaluative motives: Positive experiences as a resource for overcoming defensiveness. *Emotion and Motivation, 22*, 53–72.

Wigfield, A., Eccles, J., Mac Iver, D., Reuman, D., & Midgley, C. (1991). Transitions at early adolescence: Changes in children's domain-specific self-perceptions and general self-esteem across the transition to junior high school. *Developmental Psychology, 27*, 552–565.

Wood, J. V. (1989). Theory and research concerning social comparisons of personal attributes. *Psychological Bulletin, 106*, 231–248.

Yates, G. C. R., Lippett, R. M. K., & Yates, S. M. (1981). The effects of age, positive affect induction, and instructions on children's delay of gratification. *Journal of Experimental Child Psychology, 32*, 169–180.

Zimmerman, B. J., & Martinez-Pons, M. (1990). Student differences in self-regulated learning: Relating grade, sex, and giftedness to self-efficacy and strategy use. *Journal of Educational Psychology, 82*, 51–59.

7

Approaching and Avoiding Self-Determination: Comparing Cybernetic and Organismic Paradigms of Motivation

Richard M. Ryan
Edward L. Deci
University of Rochester

A comparison of different theoretical and empirical approaches to self-regulation can illuminate much about the nature of current psychological science. The field of self-regulation (or, more broadly, the field of human motivation) contains within it several classically distinct paradigms that are founded upon different metaphors and employ widely varied constructs, focal questions, and empirical strategies. These paradigms yield substantially different kinds of knowledge about human motivation and suggest different interventions for behavior change and social design.

Carver and Scheier's target chapter, which presents their approach to self-regulation and highlights differences between it and other current theoretical approaches, including our own self-determination theory (Deci & Ryan, 1985; 1991; Ryan, Deci, & Grolnick, 1995), is thus an important and welcomed endeavor. It raises clear questions concerning the differences in the problems posed by different theories, including the issues addressed by each that are avoided or downplayed in the others.

In this commentary, we present our view of the differences between the cybernetic approach of Carver and Scheier's control theory and the organismic-dialectical approach of self-determination theory. The contrast is stark indeed. Their theory is built upon the metaphor of an auto-correcting machine, whereas ours begins with the metaphor of a living entity. Accordingly, theirs has no theoretical place for human needs, whereas ours considers human needs to be at the core of regulatory strivings. Their analysis begins with goals, whereas our analysis views goals as an interactive product of basic needs, the strivings they engender, and the affordances of the social context. Their model conceptualizes variation in regulatory styles in terms of approach versus avoidance dynamics, whereas our model views different types of regulation as a reflection of different processes of internalization and different degrees of integration of one's goals with respect to the self. As such, we see the phenomena of choice, will, and volition as among the most interesting and central aspects of human experience and behavior, whereas they suggest that these phenomena might even be illusory products of introspection.

Because of these dramatic differences, it is particularly interesting to compare the two models, noting that indeed our comparison itself differs rather dramatically from Carver and Scheier's comparison of the two theoretical approaches. We begin with a very brief statement of some central tenets of self-determination theory to provide a basis for making the contrast.

SELF-DETERMINATION THEORY IN BRIEF

Three concepts that are central to self-determination theory are necessary for comparing it with Carver and Scheier's control theory of motivation: self, regulatory styles, and human needs.

The concept of *self* within self-determination theory is both phenomenological and structural. In our theorizing, the self refers to a sense of agency, initiative, and congruence that begins with innate elements and evolves, in part, through internalization and integration. For our present purposes we focus on those aspects of self that underlie the regulation of behavior, suggesting that regulatory processes differ in the extent to which they have been integrated into the self and thus are the basis for subsequent behaviors' being more versus less self-determined. Through acting volitionally to achieve goals and satisfy needs, the self maintains a sense of effectance and integrity that is the hallmark of healthy development. The self is thus the basis for self-determined action, which is experienced as volitional and emanating from the self. However, the self can also fall victim to controlling or antagonistic forces within the social environment that can diminish its capacity for self-regulation.

Implicit in this view of self is the proposition that some processes involved in the regulation of action are *self*-organized and some are not. This stands in sharp contrast to the way self is used in most other current empirical theories, where self is considered equivalent to person. Thus, not only Carver and Scheier's theory of self-regulation, but also self-efficacy theory (Bandura, 1977) and numerous other theories, have placed the word *self*, with a hyphen, in front of some other word, yet no meaning is added by the term *self*. In the Carver and Scheier chapter, self is synonymous with person, such that all of one's psychic makeup is considered self. Thus, being regulated and being self-regulated mean the same thing. Similarly, what is the difference between one's efficacy and one's self-efficacy? Our point is that if one does not distinguish the concepts of *self* and *person*, recognizing that some aspects of the person do not constitute self, then there is no basis for differentiating between regulation and self-regulation, between alienation and authenticity, between conformity and commitment, between introjection and integration, or between efficacious actions that are volitional and efficacious actions that are coerced.

For concepts such as self-regulation and self-efficacy to have real meaning, there must also be aspects of the person's psyche that are external to the self—that is, discrepancies from standards that are not part of the self and efficacy with respect to standards that are self-alien rather than self-endorsed. Although unaddressed in most social-cognitive theories, this issue has great phenomenological salience to individuals who experience in everyday life the difference between authentic and inauthentic behaviors in themselves and others (Sheldon, Ryan, Rawsthorne, & Ilardi, 1997). And this issue also has important consequences regarding performance, persistence, and mental health. It is an issue that is directly considered in self-determination theory using the concept of regulatory styles that vary with respect to an underlying dimension of autonomy.

Self-Regulation, Non-Self-Regulation, and Nonregulation

From our perspective, understanding the meaning of *self*-regulation requires that one distinguish between those adopted goals that are truly accepted as one's own and those that are imposed from outside the self. A goal that forms the basis for self-regulation is one that is phenomenologically and structurally consistent with and valued by one's integrated sense of who one really is—by one's true sense of self (Deci & Ryan, 1991, 1995). In attributional terms, such a goal would have an internal perceived locus of causality (deCharms, 1968; Ryan & Connell, 1989). By contrast, a non-self-regulated goal is experienced as being imposed by forces exogenous to self—by controls that are either external to the person or have been taken in by the person but not resolved with respect to the self. Such goals would have an attributional status referred to as an external perceived locus of causality and would either be compartmentalized or would be in open conflict with other important goals or needs of the self (e.g., Deci & Ryan, 1991; Ryan et al., 1995). Finally, nonregulation refers to the state of amotivation in which there is lack of intentionality and thus lack of goal-directed behavior. In attributional terms, nonregulation has an impersonal perceived locus of causality (Heider, 1958). Although the idea of nonregulation is contained within Carver and Scheier's theory, as well as most other motivational theories, it is the distinction between self-regulation and non-self-regulation that is absent from those theories.

Figure 7.1 provides a schematic of the variation in styles of behavioral regulation, herein arrayed along a dimension representing perceived locus of causality. On the far left side is the state of amotivation. Here, the person does not engage in a goal-directed behavior because the goal lacks relevance, because of a perceived noncontingency of outcomes, or because of a perceived incompetence to perform the requisite behaviors. As we move to the right, beyond the first dotted line, we enter the realm of intentional or goal-directed behavior. Indeed, all of the types of regulation to the right of amotivation represent distinctions within the general category of intentional action, distinctions that are critical for predicting the quality of behavior and experience.

Within intentional regulation, we differentiate among behaviors that are purely *externally regulated* (i.e., compelled by reward and punishment contingencies that are external to the person); those that are *introjected* (i.e., pressured by internal controls such as the avoidance of guilt or the opportunity for egoistic pride); those that are products of *identification* (i.e., that are self-valued or central to one's identity); and those that are characterized by *integration* (i.e., that result from a full assimilation and reflective self-prioritization). These four regulatory styles thus reflect the degree to which an extrinsic goal or regulatory process has been taken in by the person and integrated with his or her sense of self.

Finally, at the far right side of the schematic, beyond the second dotted line, stands the category of *intrinsic motivation* in which a goal is pursued because the person finds the activity interesting and inherently satisfying. This type of motivated regulation is simply unrecognized in many contemporary theories, as many do not appreciate the inherent experiential rewards that often energize behaviors—particularly exploratory, playful, and growth-related behaviors.

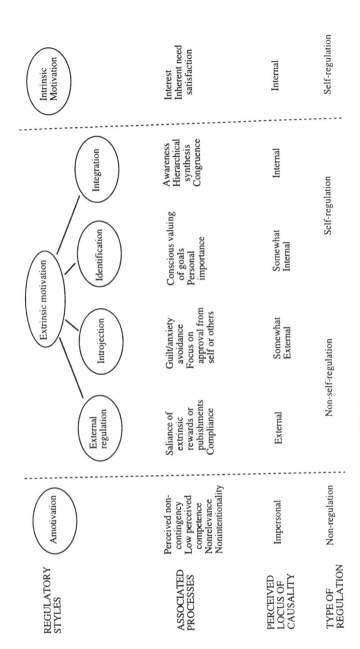

FIG. 7.1. A taxonomy of regulatory styles.

REGULATORY STYLES	Amotivation	External regulation	Introjection	Identification	Integration	Intrinsic Motivation
ASSOCIATED PROCESSES	Perceived non-contingency Low perceived competence Nonrelevance Nonintentionality	Saliance of extrinsic rewards or pubishments Compliance	Guilt/anxiety avoidance Focus on approval from self or others	Conscious valuing of goals Personal importance	Awareness Hierarchical synthesis Congruence	Interest Inherent need satisfaction
PERCEIVED LOCUS OF CAUSALITY	Impersonal	External	Somewhat External	Somewhat Internal	Internal	Internal
TYPE OF REGULATION	Non-regulation	Non-self-regulation		Self-regulation		Self-regulation

197

These different regulatory styles have been shown empirically to fit within a continuum or quasi-simplex model (e.g., Ryan & Connell, 1989; Vallerand, 1997), and the dimension underlying this continuum is theorized to be that of autonomy. The further one moves from left to right along this continuum with respect to a behavior, a class of behaviors, or a general orientation, the more one has moved from nonregulation through non-self-regulation toward self-regulation.

When one pursues a goal for reasons that represent identification, integration, or intrinsic motivation, one has the phenomenological experience of the behaviors emanating from one's self, and thus there is self-regulation. In contrast, goals pursued for external or introjected reasons are experienced as compelled by forces external to the self, as being self-alien, and thus there is non-self-regulation. These latter types of goal-directed behaviors are, in a sense, the most interesting, because they are intentional actions that do not, properly speaking, represent self-regulation.

Within Carver and Scheier's cybernetic model, the concept of *self-alien goals* has no meaning because the theory does not differentiate between goals that one has adopted as "have tos" (for example, out of social conformity) and those that are wholly endorsed as worthwhile and meaningful. It is for this reason, we argue, that their model does not differentiate self-regulation from mere regulation. By contrast, our distinction between intentional behaviors that are self-regulated (i.e., that are autonomous) and those that are regulated by introjected or external controls (i.e., that are controlled) acknowledges that some goal-directed actions are self-congruent and others are self-incongruent—an issue of perennial relevance among psychotherapists and social critics. Indeed, our model specifies differences in both the antecedents and functional consequences of autonomous versus controlled actions, as we discuss throughout. Further, this distinction has important experiential relevance because people are ongoingly concerned with the perceived causes of their own and others' actions (Heider, 1958) and have personal knowledge (deCharms, 1968; Ryan & Connell, 1989) that typically allows them to differentiate between actions stemming from an authentic personal goal endorsement and those that are based in conformity, incongruity, or conflict.

Human Needs

Finally, self-determination theory posits that there are three fundamental psychological needs—the needs for *autonomy* or self-determination (deCharms, 1968), *competence* or effectance (White, 1959), and *relatedness* or affiliation (Harlow, 1958; Baumeister & Leary, 1995). People are assumed to be inherently in need of feeling connected to others within their social milieu, of experiencing effectance, and of feeling a sense of volition and congruence in their activity. The scientific justification for positing basic needs goes beyond the scope of this chapter, but has been discussed elsewhere (e.g., Ryan, 1995; Ryan et al., 1995).

The concept of fundamental psychological needs is important in two ways for our comparison of self-determination theory and control theory. First, human needs represent the linking pin in the dialectic between the person and the social world, such that interpersonal environments that allow satisfaction of the psychological needs are theorized to promote healthier, more effective functioning and, in particular, to promote the internalization and integration of goals and regulatory processes. Thus, when individuals adopt goals in social contexts that support their autonomy, competence, and relatedness, the goals will more likely be integrated and thus provide the basis for self-regulation of the ensuing goal-directed behavior.

Second, we are concerned not only with the regulatory processes for goal-directed action, but also with the nature or content of the goals themselves. Specifically, we suggest that the attainment of some goals is more consistent with the satisfaction of one's fundamental needs than is the attainment of other goals. As such, some goal attainment is hypothesized to be associated with well-being whereas other goal attainment is hypothesized to be associated with ill-being. As we see it, "all goals are not created equal" (Ryan, Sheldon, Kasser, & Deci, 1996), and the relation of goals to basic needs is a critical issue regarding the meaning of optimal self-regulation.

We elaborate each of these points as we address several fundamental issues raised by Carver and Scheier. First, we discuss the difference between an analysis of regulation that "begins with a goal" and one that begins with the question of why people are pursuing a goal. Second, we address Carver and Scheier's skepticism concerning whether autonomy is a true functional property of behavior or merely an illusory figment of our introspective imaginations. Third, we dispute the attempt by Carver and Scheier to reduce the problem of autonomy versus control to approach versus avoidance dynamics by showing that approach goals can be either controlled or autonomous, as can avoidance goals. Finally, we argue that when the issue of self-regulation is considered from an organismic perspective, the concern is not only with how well a person adheres to a goal but also with how well a goal serves basic human needs. This latter question, we argue, takes one beyond the current fixation on efficacy to a larger set of concerns with the relation of goals to psychological development and well-being and also allows for an analysis of goals from a more socially relevant and culturally critical perspective.

GOALS AND SELF-REGULATION

All current theories of self-regulation involve goals, standards, or aims as central constructs. However, there are two quite different issues regarding goals and self-regulation that are addressed to differing degrees by various theories of self-regulation. The first concerns how people stay on track, making progress toward their goals or aims. The second concerns the nature of the goals that people adopt in the first place—specifically, why they adopt them and how the goals relate to underlying needs or motives.

Although, in our view, a cybernetic approach can be usefully applied to the first of these questions (i.e., staying on course), it is quite ill-suited to the second. The cybernetic approach begs the questions of goal selection and the needs of living entities that give rise to goal selection and goal-related activities (Ryan, Kuhl, & Deci, 1997). In contrast, the organismic approach, whose basic metaphor is a living system rather than a programmable machine, views goals as servants of a more basic phenomenon—namely, a struggle to fulfill the physical and psychological needs of the organism.

By way of explication, consider the cruise control mechanism used in many of the examples of regulation presented in the Carver and Scheier chapter. A cruise control mechanism operates to keep a car moving at a constant speed. The mechanism has neither goals nor needs of its own, so it is never called upon to reevaluate or change its standards or to examine their congruence with the needs of the overall system—a system that includes both car and driver. An analysis of the regulatory dynamics of such a mechanism has to begin with goals because goals are exogenously provided. Accordingly, the goal flexibility of a cruise control mechanism is totally constrained. It is stuck on the goal given it, in much the same way that an individual might be stuck compulsively on an introjected goal.

Suppose for illustrative purposes that the cruise control mechanism is set at 70 miles per hour as the car heads toward Chicago on a road that safely affords a speed of only 50 miles per hour. The mechanism might be effective in regulating a constant speed, but it might also result in a fatal crash. In the same way, a person who is slavishly stuck on maintaining a very low weight might be effective in remaining extremely thin but may in the process do damage to the system. What is missing in these cases is a reevaluation of the goal by a self. As such, a cruise control metaphor of regulation is more fitting for what, in self-determination theory, is referred to as controlled regulatory processes and orientations than for autonomous ones. In other words, the metaphor is more fitting for models of non-self-regulation than for models of self-regulation.

Carver and Scheier do have a caveat in their model to address goal revaluations. They appeal here to the idea that goals are hierarchicalized. But this only further begs the question of where such goal hierarchies and their prioritizations come from. Even when one recognizes that goals are hierarchical, one needs to know something about human nature and human needs in order to understand how goals can be optimally ranked and what it means to have one goal be more central than another.

The self-determination analysis does not take the goal as a given but rather asks the prior question of "Why this goal?" And to address that question, we focus on the driver instead of his or her cruise control device. We want to know why a driver might set such a high speed (e.g., social pressure?, a desire for stimulation?) and why a person might be so focused on being thin (e.g., a prerequisite for a modeling career?, a compensatory motive to be in control of something?). It is a consideration of such issues that we use as a basis for making predictions about the likely outcomes of pursuing various goals for various reasons.

As already mentioned, there are process differences that follow from differences in the origin or impetus behind a goal. Of particular note is the difference between goals that have been imposed upon the self (i.e., that are experienced as being regulated by external or introjected processes) and those that are initiated or endorsed by the self. Thus, whereas self-determination theory focuses on the motives of the driver—on their determinants, experiential qualities, and functional consequences—control theory focuses primarily on the car's cruise control device and how it autocorrects to keep moving toward the given goal. Both analyses are relevant to the problem of the car's speed after the goal is set, but they are not equally relevant to an analysis of types of goals. Self-determination theory suggests that not all goal attainment is good for the person, but control theory, because it begins uncritically with the goal, leaves unaddressed the issue of whether successful goal pursuit will result in positive consequences for the individual.

One of the particularly important aspects of goal regulation considered by the Carver and Scheier approach concerns the relation of feedback loops to motivation. Their model suggests a continuous process of discrepancy evaluation in which discrepancies are both an impetus for action and the basis of ongoing regulatory feedback. Because discrepancies and feedback loops are central to the cruise control metaphor, Carver and Scheier raised the question of whether a feedback process can be thought of as autonomous. That, however, is the wrong question. We would not say that a feedback loop is itself autonomous (or controlled) but rather that a feedback loop can operate in the service of either autonomous or controlled actions.

After one considers the degree to which a goal has been integrated and thus the relative autonomy of a goal-directed action, then one can also find instances where the same feedback can result in dramatically different outcomes. For example, we have found that positive feedback following behavior that is performed out of introjected regulation (e.g., experimentally induced ego-involvement) leads to decreased free-choice persistence, because in such regulation one's goal is to prove one's self-worth and positive feedback satisfies that extrinsic goal, leading to a quick exit (Ryan, 1982; Ryan, Koestner, & Deci, 1991). Furthermore, although positive feedback for controlled activities may produce satisfaction, it typically does not enhance vitality (Nix, Ryan, Manly, & Deci, in press). In contrast, positive feedback following the more autonomous regulatory style of intrinsic motivation (e.g., task involvement) leads to further persistence, greater task interest, and enhanced vitality. Conversely, when a person is intrinsically motivated, negative feedback tends to diminish persistence, whereas, when ego-involved, negative feedback can even enhance persistence (Ryan et al., 1991). Our point is that one would not predict such functional differences in the effects of feedback unless one made the distinctions among the types of regulatory processes.

AUTONOMY: A MERE ILLUSION?

Carver and Scheier are refreshingly clear about their suspicions regarding the autonomy that we argue is true self-regulation, suggesting that the construct of autonomy may even be an illusory property of introspection.

Some of their skepticism regarding the concept of autonomy might be warranted if the methods used to study variations in autonomous versus controlled regulation were based entirely on introspection. But such a critique fails to deal with the fact that the effects of autonomous versus controlled motivations have been established not only through self-report methods, but also through careful experimental inductions and observer rating procedures. For example, experiments in which conditions intended to control behavior were compared to conditions that afford autonomy consistently yield important differences in behavior, affect, and motivation (e.g., Ryan, Mims, & Koestner, 1983; Zuckerman,

Porac, Lathin, Smith, & Deci, 1978). Introjected regulation, which would seem more difficult to instantiate, has also been induced experimentally with ego-involving or other nonreactive manipulations (e.g., Deci, Eghrari, Patrick, & Leone, 1994; Kuhl & Kazen, 1994; Ryan, 1982), establishing differential effects.

Indeed, we have even used constructs drawn from control theory to instantiate controlled regulation experimentally. We reasoned that regulating oneself through the eyes of the other, what Carver and Scheier (1981) called public self-consciousness, is typically a heteronomous state. The concern with the other's evaluation that is often the basis of public self-consciousness represents for us an external perceived locus of causality for action. Accordingly, we showed that public self-consciousness can diminish intrinsic motivation (Plant & Ryan, 1985) and is associated with an increased susceptibility to social conformity (Ryan & Kuczkowski, 1994).

Studies of autonomous versus controlled regulation have also used self-reports (e.g., Ryan, Rigby, & King, 1993; Williams, Grow, Freedman, Ryan, & Deci, 1996), observations (Deci, Driver, Hotchkiss, Robbins, & Wilson, 1993), and projective methods (e.g., Avery & Ryan, 1988; Ryan & Grolnick, 1986) and reveal comparable results showing substantially different outcomes for these different regulatory processes. The use of questionnaires has been particularly valuable in field research where large samples allow ideographic distortions to become error variance and the important consequences associated with autonomous versus controlled processes can still be detected. Thus, although we also think that introspection alone would be a poor foundation for a science of regulation, the current body of work on autonomy versus control hardly rests on such a single undergirding. Rather, it rests on an entire nomological network of findings yielded by multiple methods in multiple settings.

Carver and Scheier further suggested that the concept of *autonomy* is closely related to that of *will* and that "maybe what people recognize from introspection as effortful decision making and planning—the sort of things that make it obvious to you that you have your own will—is actually self-delusional" (p. 8). But there are two problems with that analysis. First, there is ample evidence that when people believe they have their own will (i.e., greater autonomy), there are empirically specifiable consequences. For example, when people feel more autonomous, they tend to be more intrinsically motivated (Swann & Pittman, 1977), learn and perform better (Grolnick & Ryan, 1987; Utman, 1997), and are healthier and happier (V. Kasser & Ryan, in press; Schulz, 1976; Sheldon, Reis, & Ryan, 1996). Thus, although one might wish to argue for the self-delusional nature of will on philosophical grounds, the empirical evidence argues against such a position.

Second, our theory does not equate effortful decision making with autonomy. Indeed, many of one's most autonomous acts feel effortless, as when one spontaneously engages in intrinsically motivated play or, without hesitation, throws oneself into working toward a valued outcome. And many of one's most heteronomously motivated activities entail effortful decisions, precisely because one may be deciding to let a part of oneself dominate over other parts (as in introjection). Deliberateness, in short, can support either control or autonomy.

Even the philosophical critique of autonomy misses the point of our functional approach to this phenomenon. For us, autonomy concerns a regulatory process involving holistic self-representations (Kuhl & Fuhrmann, 1998) and an integrated systems-level endorsement of one's behavior. Autonomous behavior is contrasted with controlled action because the latter process can occur with very little access to self-representations and, indeed, typically involves either a compartmentalized motivational push or a conflicted one. Thus, both autonomous and controlled regulations are real processes, each of which has its own determinants, process characteristics, and functional consequences. These differences are undoubtedly manifest at all levels of analysis, from biological to phenomenological (Ryan et al., 1997), although our focus has been primarily at the levels of social determinants and experiential concomitants. Any philosophical critique that views autonomy as merely a mental illusion misses the central definition of autonomy—it is not a freedom from determinants but instead is a functional process by which the self more fully resonates to some determinants and influences than to others.

Referring to the work of Pervin (1992), Carver and Scheier emphasized "the trouble people have in exercising will" as if that, in some way, diminished the importance of the concept. However, the fact that some people are more able to act with autonomy than others and that all people are more autonomous in some settings than in others simply highlights a fascinating set of issues for empirical exploration. Indeed, much of our research is related to exactly this set of issues and is focused on social contextual factors—both in the current situation and in one's developmental history—that contribute to this variability across individuals and across situations.

Furthermore, as already noted, we consider many forms of effortful behaving to be examples not of autonomy but of controlled motivation. As anyone who has ever worked with a restrictive anorexic knows, willpower can be as much a form of totalitarian self-control as a form of self-regulated discipline. There is no clear isomorphism between the colloquial use of the terms *will* or *willpower* and true self-regulation as we conceptualize it.

We find repeatedly that social contexts that thwart satisfaction of one's basis psychological needs lead to less autonomous (or self-willed) action regulation, both situationally and as an individual difference (Deci & Ryan, 1987; 1991). Forces in the world that can cause "trouble ... in exercising will" are indeed daunting, and self-determination theory provides a basis for understanding such forces and their akratic impact.

AUTONOMY/CONTROL AND APPROACH/AVOIDANCE

Moving beyond their skepticism about whether human autonomy versus heteronomy is a meaningful concept, Carver and Scheier further claimed that autonomy (true self-regulation) versus control (regulation by forces external to self) may be reducible to approach versus avoidance processes. Specifically, they questioned whether what we call autonomy is simply approach motivation and what we call controlled regulation is simply an ill-formed notion of avoidance. This is an important claim because there is a burgeoning interest in the relations between the approach versus avoidance and autonomous versus controlled concepts (Elliot, 1997; Kuhl & Fuhrmann, 1998; Ryan, 1998). Let us, therefore, examine this issue closely.

Approach Goals and Autonomy

Consider first the issue of approach goals, which are theorized by Carver and Scheier to have relatively positive consequences and to account for various phenomena we have found to be associated with autonomy. Are all approach goals autonomous?

The answer is clearly no. Take, for example, the seeking of a reward—clearly something that, in most instances, is unarguably an approach goal. According to self-determination theory, the seeking of rewards can be either autonomous or controlled, but data show quite clearly that rewards often prompt controlled regulation (Deci, Koestner, & Ryan, 1997). Indeed, the pursuit of rewards represents a kind of archetype of what we would label controlled regulation, and, more specifically, the external regulation that is depicted toward the left end of Fig. 7.1.

Numerous studies have shown that approaching monetary rewards, especially task-contingent rewards, can yield a variety of negative effects that would not be predicted by an approach/avoidance conceptualization in which approach goals would be expected to yield more positive consequences. For example, rewards have typically been found to undermine intrinsically motivated persistence, subjective task interest, and the desire for challenge (e.g., Danner & Lonky, 1981; Deci et al., 1997; Ryan et al., 1983). The pursuit of rewards has also been shown to negatively affect conceptual learning, complex task performance, and creativity (Amabile, 1983; Utman, 1997) under specifiable circumstances. We have specifically shown that this is due not to their impact on perceived competence but rather to their effects on task-related autonomy. Thus, we have documented instances of approach goals undermining autonomy and leading to negative outcomes, something that makes clear how the approach concept can not explain autonomy.

An even more complex example is the approach behavior of "trying to win" a competitive outcome. According to self-determination theory, this approach goal, like pursuing rewards, can have either positive or negative effects on experience and performance depending on its relation to the individual's autonomy. For example, it has been shown that trying to win a competition in order to prove oneself to be better than others (an example of introjected regulation) has a variety of negative consequences compared to the same goal when one is focused more on task mastery or "doing one's best" (e.g., Reeve & Deci, 1996). This difference between introjected versus more autonomous types of regulation is reflected as well in the literature contrasting ego-involved versus task-involved competitors (e.g., Duda, 1989; Frederick & Ryan, 1995).

The point, quite simply, is that classically clear approach behaviors such as reward strivings or trying to win a game can, in our model, sometimes be instances of external or introjected regulation rather than self-regulation and, when that is the case, they have a variety of negative consequences that would not be predicted from an approach/avoidance perspective.

Considering now the converse, Carver and Scheier argued that "it is apparent that self-determined behavior is approach behavior" (p. 10) and that they know of no instances in which an avoidance goal would be self-determined (p. 18). We offer a few examples. A person who is attempting to break an alcohol addiction may decide to avoid situations of temptation such as gatherings in bars, and thus volitionally head straight home from work when his office mates are headed for their favorite hangout. A basketball player suffering from a sprained knee may resolve to avoid risky moves in subsequent games and thus, with a full sense of autonomy and volition, attempt to inhibit actions such as diving for the ball. And a person who has had an isolated malignant tumor removed might enter chemotherapy quite autonomously in order to avoid a recurrence of the disease. In each of these cases, an antigoal is the clear motivator of behavior and yet it is quite possible for the regulation to be autonomous. From such examples it seems clear that there is no logical exclusion of avoidance goals from the realm of autonomy nor would such an exclusion fit with the theoretical tenets of self-determination theory.

Although we dispute their attempt to reduce autonomy to approach motivation, we agree with Carver and Scheier that autonomous behaviors are more likely to involve approach than avoidance goals. This would be the case because most self-determined strivings consist of the positive, proactive visions of an actor with respect to attaining future outcomes.

To summarize, some approach goals involve heteronomous regulation of action, because the goals have been either introjected or imposed by external contingencies. Further, self-determined behavior can involve avoidance as well as approach goals. Thus, not all approach behavior is autonomous and not all autonomous behavior involves approach goals.

Avoidance Goals and Controlled Regulation

Carver and Scheier further suggested that controlled regulation is explicable in terms of avoidance goals. Indeed, they stated, "the essence of a controlling force on behavior is that it involves the engagement of an avoidance loop" (p. 17). As an example, they cited a person acting to avoid guilt, which is an instance of an avoidance goal that we would also categorize as a controlled regulation. Behaving out of a fear of punishment or social disapproval would be other instances. These are cases wherein the goal entails both avoidance and controlled motivation.

But what about a student who religiously does homework to get gold stars from the teacher; the adolescent who wants clothes with a particular logo so other kids will think he or she is cool; or the entrepreneur who feels he or she must make billions more in order to advance several ranks on the list of the world's wealthiest individuals? Here, we have instances of controlled behaviors that are more approach than avoidance oriented. Indeed, we have already argued that much of our controlled activity, such as reward and approval seeking, is clearly based in approach rather than avoidance goals. One can be controlled by carrots as well as by sticks, as any good behavior modifier knows. Indeed, seduction rather than coercion underlies the most pervasive and effective forms of social control in our modern world, and it is socially acquired approach goals that most frequently compel people into self-alien and/or conformist actions that in turn are associated with many forms of ill-being. So it is clear that at least some significant proportion of controlled behaviors involve approach goals.

Furthermore, we have argued that avoidance goals can be self-determined, as well as controlled, and we used the alcoholic avoiding tempting situations and the injured basketball player avoiding risky moves as illustrations. We have also empirically investigated functional differences that can result from avoidance goals that are pursued in an autonomous versus controlled fashion. For example, Williams, Grow, Freedman, Ryan, & Deci, (1996) examined morbidly obese patients facing serious medical risks who entered a weight-loss program. The goal of reducing their weight and risks surely involved both multiple avoidance (e.g., avoiding high fat foods) and approach processes (e.g., doing more exercise). Yet we found substantial differences in maintained weight loss as a function of the degree to which the participants were self-determined (versus controlled) with respect to these goals. Those whose weight loss was more autonomous displayed significantly greater maintained weight loss and exercise at 2-year follow-up.

A more direct test of this thinking was recently accomplished by Elliot and Sheldon (in press) who made use of constructs from both the approach/avoidance and the self-determination traditions. These researchers found that the pursuit of avoidance goals was positively linked to greater physical illness, as manifested in symptom reports, even controlling for factors such as the "big five" trait of neuroticism. However, they further found that this relation was mediated by perceptions of being controlled and/or incompetent. That is, it was only insofar as the avoidance goals were associated with a sense of being a "pawn" (deCharms, 1968) or being ineffective that they yielded their negative health effects.

To summarize, we argue that avoidance goals can be associated with either autonomous or controlled regulation and that there will be differential consequences of the one versus the other type of regulation. In fact, we speculate that the negative consequences often found to be associated with avoidance goals accrue primarily in situations where the avoidance goals are controlled rather than self-determined—situations that are no doubt plentiful in life.

Approach and Avoidance

In discussing introjection as a form of controlled regulation, Carver and Scheier suggested that "it seems to involve the functioning of both approach and avoidance processes" (p. 10). On this point we agree. Controlled behaviors that are driven by desires for approval clearly have an approach aspect, but the fear of disapproval is also likely to be inexorably involved. Indeed, we think the desire for approval and the fear of rejection are two sides of the same dynamic coin we refer to as introjected regulation. Similarly, both approach and avoidance goals can be servants of either external or identified regulations as well, as we specified in previous examples. This quite simply underscores how the regulatory processes we study are not reducible to approach and avoidance; indeed, they more typically make use of both systems.

To us, the mere fact that there are semi-independent, biologically based approach and avoidance systems in the brain (the Behavioral Activation System, BAS, and the Behavioral Inhibition System, BIS; Gray, 1987) does not, therefore, provide an adequate explanation of self-regulation, although it does clarify some of the process dynamics of regulated actions. Knowing that people's dispositional sensitivities can lead them to be "lead footed" or alternatively to vigilantly "ride the brakes" is interesting and important, and it does provide information about how people pursue their goals. But these facts do not tell us much about why and how people choose a destination or about how worthwhile and beneficial the trip may be. Psychological needs and social processes activate both goals and the different systems energizing their pursuit, and these too must be considered for a full explanation of self-regulation.

It also seems worth noting that the neurological basis of the BAS/BIS model seems to inspire a greater tendency toward bottom-up or reductionistic explanations of behavior. Although some bottom-up models may be tenable in specific contexts, a bottom-up view ignores people's potential to alter or supervise regulatory processes, as for instance in actively down-regulating certain systems through self-modulation of moods or in changing one's attitudes through reflection and value re-examination (Kuhl & Fuhrmann, in press). We know very little about the brain mechanisms of such supervisory activity and self-regulated change (see Ryan et al., 1997 for some speculations), but one cannot doubt that there are higher order cortical controls that can mediate BAS/BIS dynamics. Our point is that one should not jump from the discovery of specific mechanisms to the organization of a whole system of regulation, especially one that might involve very complex vertical coactions (Gottlieb, 1992) or emergent phenomena (Sperry, 1977). Thus, although the study of mechanisms is important, we believe such knowledge must be understood within an organismic framework to provide an understanding of living systems.

IN SEARCH OF NEED FULFILLMENT: GOAL CONTENT MATTERS

In our organismic model, goals, whether they be approach or avoidance, are viewed as direct or indirect attempts by the person to fulfill basic needs. Not all goals are equally useful in need fulfillment, however, and understanding why requires specifying needs and addressing the way they operate—issues that are not illuminated by the sharp yet narrowly focused beam of cybernetic thought.

We have proposed three fundamental psychological needs: autonomy, competence, and relatedness. By referring to these as needs we have stated explicitly that they should, when fulfilled, promote integrity, health, and well-being and, when thwarted, lead to various negative consequences. For instance, using diary methodologies, we have been able to show how day-to-day fluctuations in fulfillment of each of our specified needs is associated with fluctuations in well-being (e.g., Reis, Sheldon, Gable, Roscoe, & Ryan, 1997; Sheldon, Reis, & Ryan, 1996).

We have further suggested that some goals are more consistent with the fulfillment of these basic needs and thus should have differential relations to well-being. Studies by T. Kasser and Ryan (1993, 1996), which were organized with this in mind, identified two categories of life goals. One category, which includes goals for wealth, image, and fame, is referred to as *extrinsic* because these goals are considered instrumental and do not seem closely related to basic psychological need satisfaction. The other category, which includes self-acceptance, affiliation, and community contribution goals, is labelled *intrinsic* because these goals are typically rewarding in their own right and seem to be more closely related to the satisfaction of basic psychological needs. Results indicate that individuals who place a strong emphasis on the extrinsic aspirations for wealth, fame, and image are more likely to evidence greater anxiety, depression, and physical symptoms and less vitality, positive affect, and self-actualization (T. Kasser & Ryan, 1993, 1996). In contrast, placing stronger emphasis on self-acceptance, affiliation, and community is associated with greater well-being. Our interpretation of these findings is that goal content affects well-being because it relates differentially to basic need satisfaction. The so-called intrinsic goals are more closely linked to basic need satisfaction and thus yield enhanced well-being, whereas extrinsic goals are less linked to basic need satisfaction and thus yield less well-being benefits.

Other studies show that even perceived success at extrinsic goals is not associated with enhanced well-being, whereas success at intrinsic goals is (e.g., T. Kasser & Ryan, 1997; Ryan et al., 1998; Sheldon & Kasser, 1998). In other words, not only holding, but actually achieving, some approach goals can lead to neutral or negative outcomes. We interpret this, of course, in terms of the relation of the goals to underlying satisfaction of the needs for competence, autonomy, and relatedness.

In cybernetic models, there is no direct consideration of human needs. Implicitly, however, competence is considered highly important because it leads to goal efficacy. For us, on the other hand, competence, like autonomy and relatedness, represents a basic need. This means that the experience of competence is itself satisfying and growth promoting, independent of any effects that might accrue from the actual outcomes to which the competence leads. Carver and Scheier's model does not consider competence to be a need in this sense of the term nor does it give any consideration to other needs. Indeed, although they, like us, argue that goals are hierarchically organized, they provide no basis for explaining how such hierarchies are established nor how different hierarchical orderings might affect one's functioning and well-being.

ONCE AGAIN, THE SELF

Before concluding, we return briefly to the concept of *self*, not only because it is so central in our theory but also because the self of self-determination theory is so different from the self of most current social-cognitive theories, including Carver and Scheier's. Both implicitly and explicitly throughout the Carver and Scheier chapter, one finds the self portrayed as a *me* that is known and acted on rather than an *I* that knows and acts (James, 1890). Their self is a system that operates with a Test-Operate-Test-Exit-like mechanism (Miller, Galanter, & Pribram, 1960) to keep on target, whereas ours is an agent that sets goals and uses feedback to keep on target toward those goals. Missing from control theory is a self that develops, makes choices, keeps in touch with its innate needs, and tries to ensure their satisfaction; or, alternatively, that balks at challenge and/or becomes alienated in the face of excessive control, social isolation, or negative feedback.

Carver and Scheier pointed out that "in self-determination theory, the term *self* is limited to the identified and integrated values that represent the true self" and they added that "Deci and Ryan probably would not agree that the ought self [Higgins, 1987] is part of the true self" (p. 17). They went on to say that they "can think of no case in which a value of the true self as [Deci and Ryan] discuss it incorporates an avoidance tendency." They were correct in their portrayal of our view of self and in their interpretation that the ought self is not part of the true self as we define it. To us, what Higgins calls the ought self results from introjection—it is a set of motives or standards that have been internalized but poorly integrated with respect to the true self. Thus, regulation by the ought self is for us relatively nonautonomous.

Nonetheless, Carver and Scheier were wrong in suggesting that there are no instances of avoidance tendencies within the true self. The true self is a set of integrated standards, affects, and regulations that are the basis of self-determined activity (Ryan, 1993). Acting from the self, people pursue both approach and avoidance goals and in doing so are informed by both positive and negative feedback loops. The false self also acts to reduce discrepancies with standards, but the standards are not owned or assimilated by the self. Thus, the standards are pursued either because of reward contingencies being attached to them or because of fears about failures of attainment, rather than because of their experienced worth or meaning or because of the inherent task interest. It matters from whence the standard for behavior is engendered and whether it is anchored within the self of the person who is pursuing it.

DIFFERENT PARADIGMS, DIFFERENT CONCERNS

We began this chapter with the statement that different paradigms in the field of human motivation address different issues with different degrees of clarity. The preponderance of Carver and Scheier's work, founded upon a cybernetic metaphor, focuses on how people stay on track toward a goal after they have adopted one. This focus has been a generative one, as their review indicates. But our comments concern their attempt to extend this cybernetic model to consideration of questions we consider to be more fully treated within an organismic view. In this respect, we found that their cybernetic framework leaves unaddressed issues such as the inherent growth tendencies, the phenomenology and functional impact of autonomy and relative integration, and the optimal satisfaction of human needs. We showed that approach and avoidance categorizations do not subsume or explain autonomy versus control nor do they explain the relations of goal contents to well-being outcomes. Put differently, we found their approach/avoidance explanation of behavior to be more informative with respect to how persons enact goals than it is with respect to what they strive for, or, more deeply, why they seek what they do. Ultimately, we suggest that the more we learn about the activation of BIS/BAS systems and the general tendency of humans to attempt to reduce discrepancies between internalized standards and current states, the more we will need to consider the whole process of self-regulation and the basic psychological needs and social forces whose interplay sets these processes in motion.

REFERENCES

Amabile, T. M. (1983). *The social psychology of creativity*. New York: Springer-Verlag. Avery, R. R., & Ryan, R. M. (1988). Object relations and ego development: Comparison and correlates in middle childhood. *Journal of Personality, 56,* 547–569.

Bandura, A. (1977). Self-efficacy: Toward a unifying theory of behavioral change. *Psychological Review, 84,* 191–215.

Baumeister, R., & Leary, M. R. (1995). The need to belong: Desire for interpersonal attachments as a fundamental human motivation. *Psychological Bulletin, 117,* 497–529.

Carver, C. S., & Schier, M. F. (1981). *Attention and self-regulation: A control theory approach to human behavior.* New York: Springer-Verlag.

Danner, F. W., & Lonky, E. (1981). A cognitive-developmental approach to the effects of rewards on intrinsic motivation. *Child Development, 52,* 1043–1052.

deCharms, R. (1968). *Personal causation: The internal affective determinants of behavior.* New York: Academic Press.

Deci, E. L., Driver, R. E., Hotchkiss, L., Robbins, R. J., & Wilson, I. M. (1993). The relation of mothers' controlling vocalizations to children's intrinsic motivation. *Journal of Experimental Child Psychology, 55,* 151–162.

Deci, E. L., Eghrari, H., Patrick, B. C., & Leone, D. R. (1994). Facilitating internalization: The self-determination theory perspective. *Journal of Personality, 62,* 119–142.

Deci, E. L., Koestner, R., & Ryan, R. M. (1998). *Extrinsic rewards and intrinsic motivation: A clear and consistent picture.* Unpublished manuscript, University of Rochester, Rochester, New York.

Deci, E. L., & Ryan, R. M. (1985). *Intrinsic motivation and self-determination in human behavior.* New York: Plenum.

Deci, E. L., & Ryan, R. M. (1987). The support of autonomy and the control of behavior. *Journal of Personality and Social Psychology, 53,* 1024–1037.

Deci, E. L., & Ryan, R. M. (1991). A motivational approach to self: Integration in personality. In R. Dienstbier (Ed.), *Nebraska symposium on motivation: Vol. 38. Perspectives on motivation* (pp. 237–288). Lincoln: University of Nebraska Press.

Deci, E. L., & Ryan, R. M. (1995). Human autonomy: The basis for true self-esteem. In M. Kernis (Ed.), *Efficacy, agency, and self-esteem* (pp. 31–49). New York: Plenum.

Duda, J. L. (1989). Relationship between task and ego orientation and the perceived purpose of sport among high school athletes. *Journal of Sport and Exercise Psychology, 11,* 318–335.

Elliot, A. J. (1997). Integrating the "classic" and "contemporary" approaches to achievement motivation: A hierarchical model of approach and avoidance achievement motivation. In M. Maehr & P. Pintrich (Eds.), *Advances in motivation and achievement* (Vol. 10, pp. 143–179). Greenwich, CT: JAI.

Elliot, A. J., & Sheldon, K. M. (in press). Avoidance personal goals and the personality–illness relationship. *Journal of Personality and Social Psychology.*

Frederick, C. M., & Ryan, R. M. (1995). Self-determination in sport: A review using cognitive evaluation theory. *International Journal of Sport Psychology, 26,* 5–23.

Gottlieb, G. (1992). *Individual development and evolution: The genesis of novel behavior.* New York: Oxford University Press.

Gray, J. S. (1987). *The psychology of fear and stress.* Cambridge, England: Cambridge University Press.

Grolnick, W. S., & Ryan, R. M. (1987). Autonomy in children's learning: An experimental and individual difference investigation. *Journal of Personality and Social Psychology, 52,* 890–898.

Harlow, H. F. (1958). The nature of love. *American Psychologist, 13,* 673–685.

Heider, F. (1958). *The psychology of interpersonal relations.* New York: Wiley.

Higgins, E. T. (1987). Self-discrepancy theory: A theory relating self and affect. *Psychological Review, 94,* 319–340.

James, W. (1890). *The principles of psychology.* New York: Holt.

Kasser, T., & Ryan, R. M. (1993). A dark side of the American dream: Correlates of financial success as a central life aspiration. *Journal of Personality and Social Psychology, 65,* 410–422.

Kasser, T., & Ryan, R. M. (1996). Further examining the American dream: Differential correlates of intrinsic and extrinsic goals. *Personality and Social Psychology Bulletin, 22,* 80–87.

Kasser, T., & Ryan, R. M. (1997). *Be careful what you wish for: Optimal functioning and the relative attainment of intrinsic and extrinsic goals.* Unpublished manuscript, Knox College, Galesburg, IL.

Kasser, V. M., & Ryan, R. M. (in press). The relation of psychological needs for autonomy and relatedness to vitality, well-being, and mortality in a nursing home. *Journal of Applied Social Psychology.*

Kuhl, J., & Fuhrmann, A. (1998). Decomposing self-regulation and self-control: The Volitional Components Inventory. In J. Heckhausen & C. S. Dweck (Eds.), *Motivation and self-regulation across the life span,* (pp. 15–49). New York: Cambridge University Press.

Kuhl, J., & Kazen, M. (1994). Self-discrimination and memory: State orientation and false self-ascription of assigned activities. *Journal of Personality and Social Psychology, 66,* 1103–1115.

Miller, G. A., Galanter, E., & Pribram, K. H. (1960). *Plans and the structure of behavior.* New York: Holt.

Nix, G., Ryan, R. M., Manly, J. B., & Deci, E. L. (in press). Revitalization through self-regulation: The effects of autonomous and controlled motivation on happiness and vitality. *Journal of Experimental Social Psychology.*

Pervin, L. A. (1992). The rational mind and the problem of volition. *Psychological Science, 3,* 162–164.

Plant, R., & Ryan, R. M. (1985). Intrinsic motivation and the effects of self-consciousness, self-awareness, and ego-involvement: An investigation of internally controlling styles. *Journal of Personality, 53,* 435–449.

Reeve, J., & Deci, E. L. (1996). Elements within the competitive situation that affect intrinsic motivation. *Personality and Social Psychology Bulletin, 22,* 24–33.

Reis, H. T., Sheldon, K. M., Gable, S. L., Roscoe, J., & Ryan, R. M. (1997). *Daily well-being: The role of autonomy, competence, and relatedness.* Unpublished manuscript, University of Rochester.

Ryan, R. M. (1982). Control and information in the intrapersonal sphere: An extension of cognitive evaluation theory. *Journal of Personality and Social Psychology, 43,* 450–461.

Ryan, R. M. (1993). Agency and organization: Intrinsic motivation, autonomy and the self in psychological development. In J. Jacobs (Ed.), *Nebraska symposium on motivation: Developmental perspectives on motivation* (Vol. 40, pp. 1–56). Lincoln: University of Nebraska Press.

Ryan, R. M. (1995). Psychological needs and the facilitation of integrative processes. *Journal of Personality, 63,* 397–427.

Ryan, R. M. (1998). Human psychological needs and the issues of volition, control and outcome focus: A commentary on the initial conference proceedings. In J. Heckhausen, C. S. Dweck (Eds.), *Motivation and self-regulation across the life span,* (pp. 114–133). New York: Cambridge University Press.

Ryan, R. M., Chirkov, V. I., Little, T. D., Sheldon, K. M., Timoshina, E., & Deci, E. L. (in press). *The American dream in Russia: Extrinsic aspirations and well-being in two cultures. Personality and Social Psychology Bulletin.*

Ryan, R. M., & Connell, J. P. (1989). Perceived locus of causality and internalization: Examining reasons for acting in two domains. *Journal of Personality and Social Psychology, 57,* 749–761.

Ryan, R. M., Deci, E. L., & Grolnick, W. S. (1995). Autonomy, relatedness, and the self: Their relation to development and psychopathology. In D. Cicchetti & D. J. Cohen (Eds.), *Developmental psychopathology: Vol. 1. Theory and methods* (pp. 618–655). New York: Wiley.

Ryan, R. M., & Grolnick, W. S. (1986). Origins and pawns in the classroom: Self-report and projective assessments of individual differences in children's perceptions. *Journal of Personality and Social Psychology, 50,* 550–558.

Ryan, R. M., & Kuczkowski, R. (1994). The imaginary audience, self-consciousness, and public individuation in adolescence. *Journal of Personality, 62,* 219–238.

Ryan, R. M., Koestner, R., & Deci, E. L. (1991). Ego-involved persistence: When free-choice behavior is not intrinsically motivated. *Motivation and Emotion, 15,* 185–205.

Ryan, R. M., Kuhl, J., & Deci, E. L. (1997). Nature and autonomy: Organizational view of social and neurobiological aspects of self-regulation in behavior and development. *Development and Psychopathology, 9,* 701–728.

Ryan, R. M., Mims, V., & Koestner, R. (1983). Relation of reward contingency and interpersonal context to intrinsic motivation: A review and test using cognitive evaluation theory. *Journal of Personality and Social Psychology, 45,* 736–750.

Ryan, R. M., Rigby, S., & King, K. (1993). Two types of religious internalization and their relations to religious orientations and mental health. *Journal of Personality and Social Psychology, 65*, 586–596.

Ryan, R. M., Sheldon, K. M., Kasser, T., & Deci, E. L. (1996). All goals are not created equal: An organismic perspective on the nature of goals and their regulation. In P. M. Gollwitzer & J. A. Bargh (Eds.), *The psychology of action: Linking cognition and motivation to behavior* (pp. 7–26). New York: Guilford.

Schulz, R. (1976). Effects of control and predictability on the physical and psychological well-being of the institutionalized aged. *Journal of Personality and Social Psychology, 33*, 563–573.

Sheldon, K. M., & Kasser, T. (1998). Pursuing personal goals: Skills enable progress but not all progress is beneficial. *Personality and Social Psychology Bulletin, 24*, 1319–1331.

Sheldon, K. M., Ryan, R. M., Rawsthorne, L., & Ilardi, B. (1997). Trait self and true self: Cross-role variation in the Big Five traits and its relations with authenticity and subjective well-being. *Journal of Personality and Social Psychology, 73*, 1380–1393.

Sheldon, K. M., Reis, H. T., & Ryan, R. M. (1996). What makes for a good day? Competence and autonomy in the day and in the person. *Personality and Social Psychology Bulletin, 22*, 1270–1279.

Sperry, R. W. (1977). Bridging science and values: A unifying view of mind and brain. *American Psychologist, 32*, 237–245.

Swann, W. B., & Pittman, T. S. (1977). Initiating play activity of children: The moderating influence of verbal cues on intrinsic motivation. *Child Development, 48*, 1128–1132.

Utman, C. H. (1997). Performance effects of motivational state: A meta-analysis. *Personality and Social Psychology Review, 1*, 170–182.

Vallerand, R. J. (1997). Toward a hierarchical model of intrinsic and extrinsic motivation. In M. P. Zanna (Ed.), *Advances in experimental social psychology* (Vol. 29, pp. 271–360). San Diego, CA: Academic Press.

White, R. W. (1959). Motivation reconsidered: The concept of competence. *Psychological Review, 66*, 297–333.

Williams, G. C., Grow, V. M., Freedman, Z., Ryan, R. M., & Deci, E. L. (1996). Motivational predictors of weight loss and weight-loss maintenance. *Journal of Personality and Social Psychology, 70*, 115–126.

Zuckerman, M., Porac, J., Lathin, D., Smith, R., & Deci, E. L. (1978). On the importance of self-determination for intrinsically motivated behavior. *Personality and Social Psychology Bulletin, 4*, 443–446.

8

Issues in Self-Control Theory and Research: Confidence, Doubt, Expectancy Bias, and Opposing Forces

Janet A. Sniezek
University of Illinois, Urbana–Champaign

Self-regulation refers to a narrow but critical slice of behavior that permeates most human activities. Without self-regulation, I cannot be, do, or get what I want. None of my actions follow from consciousness. With it, I can make ideas reality. I have power over myself, and my thoughts influence my actions.

The theory presented in the chapter by Carver and Sheier—which I shall refer to interchangeably as self-regulation or control theory—provides an exceedingly thoughtful, detailed explanation of self-regulation. My goal here is to identify important questions arising from their work, and where appropriate, offer some answers.

From Carver and Scheier's perspective, a self-regulatory event can be construed as the process by which one initiates or maintains action given awareness of a desire or intention. Their theory provides creative and well-developed answers to numerous important questions about this process. Yet, some truly important problems concerning self-control are outside the domain addressed by their theory: How do we decide what to do? Where do desires originate? Is there a meaningful distinction between a desire and something we decide to do? How do unconscious desires influence behavior? Either we expand their definition of self-regulation to address these issues or we must look to other theories for answers.

But in this commentary it is more fruitful to attend to those issues relevant to an understanding of self-regulatory behavior that have not been addressed by the theory as Carver and Scheier have defined it or have been addressed in a preliminary manner. These issues are organized around two conceptual themes: expectancy and opposing forces. The first section is a treatment of expectancy and includes discussion of the roles of effort, confidence, and doubt. The second section raises a very real problem for self-regulation: bias in the expectancies. The final section on opposing forces concerns a variety of goal conflicts that are recurring issues in self-control.

EXPECTANCY

Expectancy is a great conceptual breakthrough in the application of control theory to humans. After all, actions follow from judgments, not reality. And humans make judgments about future events—such as the likelihood that their actions will eventually lead to success. The expectancy concept allows for uniquely human/animal characteristics in a model that is mechanistic in origins. This aspect of control theory allows for an internal, cognitive influence on behavior in addition to the external influence of environmental feedback that is the hallmark of control theory.

Effort

Examination of other theoretical approaches to expectancy suggests alternative views of the role of expectancies in self-regulation. Crucial in choice theories of motivation (e.g., Naylor, Pritchard, & Ilgen, 1980), expectancy refers to a future-oriented belief about the connection between one's expenditure of effort and the products of that effort. Note that in control theory, expectancy is a judgment of a single event—goal attainment. It does not require an explicit specification of the level of effort that will be allocated in pursuit of the goal. In contrast, expectancy in cognitive motivation theories is a judgment about a relationship between the event and a given level of effort. One's sense of personal control is reflected in one's expectancy; to the extent that the likelihood of success varies with amount of effort to be put forth, one believes one has personal control. Thus, there is an important distinction between the use of expectancy in control theory and in cognitive motivation theory. In the former, the expectancy of success is a function of the comparison between feedback and referent signals. But in the latter, it is a joint function of anticipated level of effort and belief about personal control. The conceptualization offered by Naylor et al. recognizes that effort level can vary and that expectancy depends on effort level. Whereas effort level varies in response to a feedback loop in control theory, in the Naylor et al. theory, effort level results from a choice made in order to maximize affect.

Another critical feature of the expectancy concept is that it does not represent a continuous variable, such as the degree of belief in success. Instead, expectancy captures two qualitatively different beliefs—confidence and doubt—that have distinct consequences for behavior. As we shall see, this has implications for a definition of expectancy bias in control theory.

The origin of confidence and doubt is defined clearly in Carver and Scheier's chapter: They are a by-product of the comparison process in the feedback loop. The description of confidence (or doubt) is brief—"... a hazy and nonverbal sense of expectancy"—but rich in meaning. The expectancy construct is a particular type of belief, one that entails both belief and uncertainty, and is future oriented. But, as argued in the next section, confidence and doubt themselves are more elusive.

Confidence, Doubt, and Affect

Assorted forms of confusion result because confidence is not conceptually distinct from the other by-product of comparison, affect. The authors imply that positive affect accompanies confidence whereas negative affect accompanies doubt. This seems to say that the concept of interest is one, a belief-affect pairing akin to an attitude. It is true that numerous studies show a correlation between expectancy and affect. Indeed, this is similar to the problem that has nagged at expectancy-value theories of motivation as well as subjective expected-utility theories of decision making. Although independence between the constructs is assumed, increasing attractiveness of an outcome is sometimes shown to increase its subjective likelihood. But this is not to say that the two factors have the same origins or must necessarily coexist. Other ways of thinking about confidence seem equally valid. For example, might not affect follow from belief, rather than directly from the comparator itself? That is, if I believe success is likely, I perceive a progress rate sufficiently high for producing positive affect.

A related matter concerns formation of new expectations. This can happen if obstacles to progress arise. Then there are interruptions in the midst of behaving for the purpose of generating an expectancy. What is the trigger for deliberate evaluation of ongoing behavior? Carver and Scheier point to the affect feedback loop. They propose that when feelings become more negative due to deceleration, one consciously judges the likelihood of success. But now we see that affect would have to precede expectancy. This is opposite to the conclusion drawn in the earlier paragraph.

Trouble With Confidence

Assuming confidence and affect as well as doubt and affect are separable constructs, it is possible to speak of confidence and doubt as causes of action. The authors imply that doubt is more troublesome than its counterpart, confidence. At one point, they state "Many of people's problems have their roots in doubts." The point is that doubt leads to reducing effort and that giving up effort without giving up commitment to the goal produces depressed affect. In other words, quitting is incomplete, and depressed affect results from the perpetual discrepancy from the comparator. But should such a troubling state of affairs be attributed to doubt? Not if the goal was unattainable. Then the problem is not that one has given up effort, but rather that one has not given up the goal.

Of course, doubt can lead to trouble but it is not the only source. It can be argued that many of people's problems have their roots in confidence. As the authors do make clear, giving up is essential to functioning because it allows a redirection of effort from unattainable to attainable goals. But there are two potential timing problems with giving up a goal: doing it too soon and doing it too late. If doubt is the culprit in the former, confidence is to blame in the latter. Which error is worse? Generally neither; it depends on the consequences in a given situation. There is a cost to each; giving up too soon means the opportunity for success is foregone whereas giving up too late means that effort that could have been directed toward another equally important goal is wasted. Either way, effort is spent without success.

I might even argue that the problem produced by confidence is usually more severe. If it is appropriate to disengage because the goal is unattainable, but confidence makes one keep on going and going and going, the amount of effort wasted due to perseverance must exceed that lost to giving up too soon due to doubt. It is only by assuming that confidence and doubt are linked to positive and negative affect, respectively, that we can justify more scorn for doubt than confidence. But recall the conceptual problem of requiring the pairing.

Although it surely has its utility, confidence is not always necessary. The catastrophe theory application shows how not just confidence but extreme confidence can be necessary for effort at important tasks. But it is interesting that it can be better to mobilize effort by manipulating task importance than by trying to boost confidence. Even though very high confidence would help, it is not necessary.

There is also a problem stemming from the proposition that affect follows from an assessment of the experienced rate of progress. Two brief scenarios illustrate the problem. One, I rapidly progress toward the goal, thereby experiencing positive affect. But suddenly, I receive new information and my judgment of my chances for goal attainment is that they are too low to continue, so I quit. I quit before obtaining any feedback that the rate has slowed so there is doubt but no chance for affect to switch from positive to negative. In the second scenario, my rate of progress toward the goal is pitiful, and I have substantial negative affect. Despite this, I persist with the confidence that eventually I will succeed. I can push on the asymptote eternally with confidence and negative affect.

Time

The treatment of time in the theory has some intriguing and curious implications. The assumption is that affect results from rate of progress toward the goal, not goal attainment per se. It seems difficult to make predictions about affect without a time deadline for goal attainment. Consider three single individuals, each of whom has the goal of marriage but is currently not in a relationship. Persons A and B both want to be married before age 35 whereas Person C wants to get married "when the right mate comes along." Is A less happy being uncommitted at age 29 than at age 24? If A expects signs of incremental progress the answer is yes. But if B's mental model of courting represents the route to marriage as a step function, B is equally happy at all ages (up to the age at which the minimum duration of the step exceeds the time remaining until 35.) So two persons with the same goal, both of whom approach it at the same rate and achieve it at the same time, have different levels of happiness en route due to different notions about rate of progress. A's affect rises slowly with feedback of progress whereas B has stable affect followed by an enormous leap upward. And, if neither marries, they both have negative affect, albeit at different ages. And what about Person C at ages 24 and 29? Without having a temporal deadline, the notion of rate of progress is meaningless. The conclusion must be that C will have a static level of affect throughout life—even if remaining single. A somewhat different index of progress can serve the same function and retain the beauty of the role of rate. For example, C may assess progress in terms of the percentage of all dates with two or more necessary qualities. In summary, a temporal deadline is necessary if progress is evaluated by rate of movement toward the goal. But if other indicators of eventual goal attainment are allowable, deadlines are not necessary.

As self-control theory stands, explaining the origins of positive and negative affect is not necessary. Carver and Scheier's discussion of emotion allows for a richer story that will become even more interesting with a better developed understanding of the consequences of emotion and changes in emotion for self-regulatory behaviors. In control theory language, affect is the error signal from a second feedback system. There is a need to integrate the output function of the feedback loop monitoring acceleration, or the second derivative of distance over time, with the feedback loop for action with respect to the primary goal. We actually know a great deal about the effect of emotions on behavior. As the authors note, mood can influence decisions as well as behavior. It seems that affect would influence not only action, but also expectations and comparison processes.

This discussion of expectancies suggests several critical problems. First, assumptions about effort must be explicit. Naylor et al.'s theory (1980) provided a more thorough explanation of the role of effort in motivation in general and expectancy in particular. Another problem is clarifying the conceptual distinction between expectancy and affect. It must be possible to have one without the other, even if data show a correlation. If they are distinct concepts, all possible pairings of positive and negative affect and confidence and doubt are possible. (They may not be equally frequent due to mutual influence of affect and expectancy on one another.) We need a more developed theory about the origins of confidence, doubt, and affect. And we need more data on the consequences of each possible pairing. When this is clear, we are in a better position to make value judgments about the relative merits of confidence compared to doubt.

EXPECTANCY BIAS

From my point of view, the most prominent neglected issue is the veridicality of expectations. We expect all sorts of things that just do not happen and things we do expect to happen do not. The problem is not simply that surprises occur. It is a much larger problem for theory and practice. Expectations are biased in ways that influence actions, for better or worse. This is particularly important in a control theory that allows but two discrete and opposing types of expectancy, confidence or doubt. Here, expectancy errors are big. To get some idea of the significance of bias in expectations, let us turn to the abundant research defining expectancy as a continuous variable. Here, we can see the consequence of relatively small expectancy errors.

The Perils of Optimism

A variety of judgments about the outcomes of one's future or current actions have been shown to be optimistic. That is, they are too high relative to some objective standard. Specifically, predictions about one's future success have been shown to be inflated. For example, Radhakrishnan, Arrow, and Sniezek (1996) reported a positive bias in forecasts of exam scores for the majority of students. In this study, the extent of the bias worsened with increasing temporal distance between the prediction and performance. But why should expectancies be positively biased at all?

Many reasons have been offered (cf. Radhakrishnan et al., 1996; Sniezek, Paese, & Switzer, 1990). Let us consider the effect of expectancy bias from the perspective of the theory of self-regulation. What function might it serve? It could exist to discourage disengagement when it is better to achieve the goal at a higher cost of more effort than to miss it. Of course, reducing the chance of one kind of error increases the chance of another. The expectancy bias would have to increase the incidence of delayed disengagement where disengagement is appropriate.

But this assumes that an optimistically biased expectancy, that is, confidence, leads to a greater amplitude or persistence in effort or maintains attention and focus on the target goal. Simply stated, confidence must enhance goal-directed actions. But there is a real possibility of insufficient effort given an expectancy bias. If the current rate of progress is deemed sufficient when it in fact is not, there is no reason to take actions to increase the rate. Instead one coasts. And if one is confident about goal A, one may shift attention to goal B, thereby missing error signals from the feedback loop. Each of these routes ends with failure to achieve the goal.

And then there are the consequences for affect. Because affect results from rate of progress toward goal, positively biased expectations must necessarily lead to negative affect resulting from a disappointing feedback about the rate of progress. Positive affect must necessarily be rare. And negative affect must be everywhere there is an optimistic bias in expectancy.

The potentially negative consequences of expectancy bias seem to outweigh the positives except under rather peculiar circumstances. The bottom line is that it is difficult to see how control theory could treat expectancy bias as anything other than a source of error that is not in the person's best interest. As such, it is hardly outside the boundary of the theory and deserves further theoretical and empirical attention.

There are numerous other challenges for control theory in data from studies of people's assessments of their own performance. One is the observation that assessments made during ongoing performance are more positively biased than those made after performance, but before feedback (Sniezek & Buckley, 1991). Even more curious is the observation that the assessments following performance but preceding feedback can be negatively biased despite a strong positive bias in the pretask expectations (Radhakrishnan et al., 1996; Sniezek et al., 1990).

Judgmental Control

We turn now to a different matter concerning bias in expectancies. Suppose expectancy bias is useful. Then why not try to achieve it? The ability to control the direction and degree of bias in expectancies could prevent some undesirable outcomes. Of course, as Carver and Scheier point out, manipulating outcomes is not the same as effecting personal control. This form of personal control, which I will call judgmental control, is present if one can choose the most likely direction and degree of expectancy error. I may choose to be optimistic, recognizing fully that what I am expecting is not as likely as some alternative. By definition, most of the time my actions will not be matched ideally to the true state of the environment. Consequently, my outcomes will be more negative or less positive than they would have been without expectation error. But sometimes, they are superior. Regardless of the valence, the actual outcome itself is irrelevant to my sense of judgmental control. Because I chose the most likely form of error, I had personal control. Absent judgmental control, unknown influences dictate the bias in my expectations, and I am their victim.

There is reason to believe that people exercise their judgmental control to produce biased expectations. In any environment with uncertainty, setting an expectation is a gamble. Rather than gambling according to probability laws, people follow an array of gambling strategies. A well-established principle is probability matching, by which the rate of betting on an alternative is matched to its observed relative frequency. This is widely observed despite the fact that outcomes are maximized by consistently betting on the most likely alternative.

The issue of personal control raises larger questions about one's control over the control system. The authors imply that personal control concerns the relationship between one's actions and the environment. With control, the environment can be manipulated in predictable and desirable ways.

Without it, environmental change is disconnected from any exercise of effort. As I see it, the matter of personal control has more extensive relevance in the self-regulation of behavior. People are not passive receivers of feedback, but active seekers—and distorters—of it. Following Carver and Scheier's medical example, we can see many ways in which personal control can be important to the individual other than the obvious ability to take actions to control health outcomes. Personal control over the input function would mean an ability to obtain information from the environment. Can I detect an adverse drug reaction? Will I be able to persuade the health care provider to tell me the whole truth? Similarly, we can expect the self-regulation process to change with personal control over the comparator. Being able to set the sensitivity of comparator enables one to ignore trivial discrepancies that would otherwise intrude. Alternatively, it allows one to learn to detect minute discrepancies. Put another way, the patient can choose to keep indicators of erratic fluctuations in distance between desired and current bodily state out of mind and tune into the slightest evidence of progress. Finally, personal control over the referent itself makes a significant difference in self-regulatory behavior. Some goals one can change all by oneself. Others are subject to the influence of others. Even if the goal concerns one's own and only one's own, behavior, it may be negotiated with or set by someone else. The extent of one's personal control over the referent determines goal level and direction. Personal control over each of the components of a control system improves self-regulation, unless, of course, the perception of personal control is an illusion.

In summary, this section demonstrates the agony and ecstasy that expectation bias can produce. It lays out the assumptions necessary for expectation bias to be an asset in self-regulation. The considerable challenges to control theory are noted. A lot has to give to explain some reliable phenomena. But if expectation bias can be valuable, it may be possible to let preferences dominate beliefs. That is, one can control expectations by deciding to believe something other that what one believes is most likely. Personal control—or more accurately, the judgment of personal control—appears to be instrumental in achieving three ends: feel better, do better, and be better off. Control theory allows for several ways for personal control to do each, beyond the given way of effecting action.

OPPOSING FORCES

Of course, real human behavior is inevitably more complex than even the best of theories can convey. Carver and Scheier have succeeded in capturing a great deal of complexity: the existence of both approach and avoidance in ought goals but not ideal goals, the shifting importance of alternative goals, the hierarchical structure of goal systems, and differences between attaining rewards and avoiding punishment.

Another form of complexity in self-control is the existence of opposing forces. In the spirit of the chapter's physical metaphors, consider the natural opposition between order and entropy, electrons and protons, fire and water. It is not sufficient to describe the motion of rising warm air because it is necessarily accompanied by the opposing force of sinking cold air. Control is necessary precisely because there are opposing forces. In riding a bicycle, pedaling force is required to counter the combined force of friction and gravity. Controlling the bicycle is managing the opposing forces.

To understand the self-regulation of behavior, the opposing forces view demands that we study the opposing forces that act on behavior in the pursuit of goals. One place to start is to look at the inevitable consequence of multiple goals: goal conflict. The problem of competing, mutually exclusive goals is common: intimacy versus independence, recognition versus conformity, or career versus family. It is not clear how control theory can explain the experience of pursuing disparate ends. If an individual embraces conflicting goals at different points in time, it is presumably the case that one or the other receives attention. As in the hot soup analogy, the goals alternate turns as the object of conscious thought and action.[1] There is no provision for a change in the sequence of attention to multiple goals due to conflict between them. But it is interesting that the hot soup analogy allows explicitly for concurrent activity in service of the goal that is temporarily out of mind. This activity has no effect on regulatory action regarding the goal on top of awareness. However, with two opposing goals, there is no escaping the simultaneous direction of action toward each of them. With multiple, competing, and contradictory goals, one simultaneously moves forward and backward with respect to the goal on top. Granted the forward motion exceeds the backward one, but the net effect is a slower rate of progress toward the more important or salient goal due to the existence of the conflicting goal. The process becomes even more complicated if there is a shift in attention between conflicting goals. As time passes, this becomes more likely.

A similar process takes place as one attends to goals that exist in different points in time. Varying temporal perspective can bring some of the most intense, fascinating, and disturbing goal conflict. Simply stated,

---

[1] Will I ever again be able to make hot soup without their metaphor bubbling to the surface of my consciousness?

long-term and immediate goals are incompatible. We can think of two control systems in opposition. One involves intentions resulting from a decision-making process and requires sustained efforts and repeated goal attainment over long periods of time. It regulates behaviors directed at satisfying intentions to improve physical fitness, be ethical, or spread peace and love. Achieving such ends requires dodging the grip of desires to relax, yield to temptation, or express rage in the here and now. The second control system directs behavior in fulfillment of these immediate, unchosen, and often unexpected desires. The future-oriented intentions can be thought of as the product of what the authors call "will." The opposing force is a desire for immediate gratification. Lowenstein (1996) explained much irrationality as the triumph of "visceral influences" over self-interest.

Thaler and Sheffrin (1981) made a similar distinction between the short- and long-term perspectives in self-control. They postulate two selves with opposing preferences and choices: the "Planner" and the "Doer." But rather than merely oppose actions directed at the goals of the other self, there is a coordination of effort between them. A function of the Planner is to control the Doer because the Doer is incapable of satisfactory self-regulation alone. Without a Planner, the myopic Doer sinks into the joys/perils of hedonism.

In discussing lapses in self-control, Carver and Scheier tell how alcohol can leave one susceptible to the cues of the moment and lead one to do things that conflict with one's principles. In short, alcohol can ruin the control system. But it takes a priori damage to the control system in order for such alcohol consumption to occur. How can this happen?

The foregoing variations on the basic idea of dual control systems offer an explanation. In both of these theories, it is considered possible to be aware of both opposing forces at the same time. Thaler and Sheffrin's Planner takes into account the opposing force of the Doer. Lowenstein's examples of addicts succumbing to temptation make it clear that people can be fully aware of how their actions are increasing the discrepancy between their current and desired states. This is not a relatively simple matter of shifting attention from one goal to another. It is more the case that there is a decision to respond to the opposing force, that is, the feedback loop of the other system.

This discussion raises many issues about self-regulation. Can intertemporal goal conflict exist with self-determined behavior? Or are these opposing forces restricted to controlled behavior? If the latter, the long-term goal must have an element of ought or fear, with avoidance of an antigoal that is powerfully attractive as well as repellent. And what is the role of choice? Can one choose a goal and choose behavior incompatible with that goal—as in choosing to quit smoking and also choosing to smoke a cigarette? Or perhaps, sometimes we choose and sometimes we choose to not choose. If so, where does choice end?

ACKNOWLEDGMENT

The author is grateful to Clayton Buerkle and Lyn Van Swol for comments on an earlier draft.

REFERENCES

Lowenstein, G. (1996). Out of control: Visceral influences on behavior. *Organizational Behavior and Human Decision Processes, 63*(3), 272–292.

Naylor, J. C., Pritchard, R., & Ilgen, D. (1980). *A theory of behavior in organizations.* New York: Academic Press.

Radhakrishnan, P., Arrow, H. A., & Sniezek, J. A. (1996). Hoping, performing, learning, and predicting: Changes in the accuracy of self-evaluations of performance. *Human Performance, 9*(1), 23–49.

Sniezek, J. A., & Buckley, T. (1991). Confidence depends on level of aggregation. *Journal of Behavioral Decision Making, 4*, 263–272.

Sniezek, J. A., Paese, P. W., & Switzer, F. S., III. (1990). The effect of choosing on confidence in choice. *Organizational Behavior and Human Decision Processes, 46*(2), 264–282.

Thaler, R. H., & Sheffrin, H. M. (1981). An economic theory of self-control. *Journal of Political Economy, 89*, 392–406.

9

Responding to Attempts at Control: Autonomy, Instrumentality, and Action Identification

Abraham Tesser
University of Georgia

Carver and Scheier have given us a tour de force on self-regulation. Their contribution contains a thorough review of self-regulation themes and issues. Not only is it comprehensive with regard to substance but also it takes us from current approaches to these issues to cutting-edge approaches concerned with nonlinearity, parallel processing, and catastrophes. Because of its comprehensiveness it is difficult to know where to jump in. What makes it even more difficult is that I agree with most of their conclusions. Therefore, instead of developing what is likely to turn out to be a laundry list of points that I think are particularly valuable or quibbles I might have with this conclusion or that conclusion, I decided to present a related model and then try to see where and how well it fits with Carver and Scheier's perspective. The model described here is called the e-control model because it deals with self's responses to external attempts at being controlled.

Some of the fundamental issues dealt with by Carver and Scheier concern feelings of personal control, goal hierarchies, and approach/avoidance issues in the framing of action, affect, and behavioral persistence. Although most of the e-control model resonates quite well with the Carver and Scheier perspective, some of the assumptions on which the e-control model is based are quite different from the implications of those articulated in the Carver and Scheier chapter. The e-control model is new and highly speculative. Perhaps the reader will find something interesting in the present applications of some of Carver and Scheier's ideas. The reader may even find the assumptions that differ from those made by Carver and Scheier plausible enough to warrant further study.

Carver and Scheier observe that "Many people believe that the sense of control is an important element in successful adjustment to stressful events." (p. 45) They show some skepticism for this belief and point to Burger's (1989) work showing circumstances under which feelings of control are undesirable and may even be detrimental. Indeed, the literature on authoritarianism suggests that for some persons (Adorno, Frenkel-Brunswik, Levinson, & Sanford, 1950) and under some circumstances (Doty, Peterson, & Winter, 1991) there is a desire for a strong leader, or someone to control what self does. Given these divergent literatures, I share Carver and Scheier's skepticism but I resolve the apparent contradiction differently.

According to Carver and Scheier, a focus on control may be beside the point. The issue is positive outcomes. If one is confident in his or her own abilities, then control will be desired; if one is confident that others will provide more beneficial outcomes, then one will desire control by other. This elegant resolution is consistent with the data that they cite and is parsimonious. By contrast, my resolution incorporates the spirit of Carver and Scheier's emphasis on control hierarchies and positive outcomes, and it also preserves the focus on control.

As pointed out by Carver and Scheier, the word *control* has many meanings. Here, control refers to perceived attempts by external agents to gain compliance, that is, the kind of attempts we see in television advertising, a doctor prescribing a regimen for a patient, religious proselytizing, social influence, and so forth. For clarity, such external control is referred to as e-control. By reaction to e-control, I have in mind the three classes of variables delineated by Burger (1989). These include affective responses, task performance, and acceptance or rejection of the control attempt.

In the spirit of Carver and Scheier, the notion of goal hierarchy, in particular action identification (ActID; Vallacher & Wegner 1985, 1987), is essential. ActID suggests that the identification of any action can vary from low to high. For example, writing this chapter can be thought of as moving a pencil on the page, generating sentences, creating a chapter, or acting like a psychologist. In general, the question of how drives identification to lower levels. For example, how does one write a chapter? By creating sentences. How does one create sentences? By generating words and so forth. The question of why tends to drive identification to higher levels. Why does one write a chapter? To promulgate a research idea. Why does one want a research idea promulgated? To advance our knowledge of psychology and so forth.

Carver and Scheier are relatively neutral on issues of will and maintaining a sense of self-integrity. An *autonomy mediator* is part of the e-control model, and it is intended to capture the idea that individuals wish to maintain a positive view of self and their own effectiveness. Accepting e-control can threaten that view. On the other hand, the notion of felt competence, confidence, or what we call *instrumentality* also has implications for acceptance of e-control. (There is a striking resemblance between instrumentality and Carver and Scheier's emphasis on positive outcomes in the control domain.) Acceptance of e-control is a threat to self-autonomy. So, the greater the concerns with self-autonomy, the greater the avoidance of e-control. Instrumentality issues make one open to e-control; the greater the concerns with instrumentality, the more open to e-control. So far, all is consistent with the Carver and Scheier spirit. It is in the putting together of the variables that the e-control model diverges from Carver and Scheier.

SKETCHING THE E-CONTROL MODEL

High levels of ActID engage our most cherished aspects of self more clearly than do low levels of identification. So, higher levels of ActID should be associated with greater avoidance of e-control via the self-autonomy mediator. On the other hand, higher levels of ActID tend to be associated with greater perceived task difficulty and ambiguity. External agents often provide clear and unambiguous solutions to ambiguous and difficult problems. Accepting e-control can reduce uncertainty in a way that minimizes the necessity to accept personal responsibility. So higher levels of ActID should be associated with greater acceptance of e-control via the instrumentality mediator.

Combining the Autonomy and Instrumentality Mediators

The mediating responses to e-control as a function of ActID are complex. Higher levels of ActID should be associated with greater avoidance of e-control, via the autonomy mediator, and, at the same time, greater acceptance of e-control, via the instrumentality mediator. If these two response tendencies are combined additively, the net result would be a flat function indicating that ActID has little net effect on response to e-control, which is not very interesting (see Carver and Scheier's discussion of nonlinearity, pp. 58–59). But, assuming a multiplicative combination has some interesting implications.

When the response tendencies are combined multiplicatively (i.e., interactively), a bit of the complexity noted earlier is captured. The resulting responses to e-control attempts are an inverted-U function of ActID. As ActID increases from low levels, attempts at e-control are more favorably received. Beyond some intermediate point, however, increasing levels of ActID result in less favorable responses to attempts at e-control. So, responses to e-control are not uniformly negative (or positive). The multiplicative combination has additional intuitive appeal. For example, at very high levels of threat to self-autonomy, e-control attempts are rejected regardless of the amount of ambiguity they may reduce. It also suggests that when there is very little utility in accepting an e-control attempt, for example, reduction of ambiguity, that attempt is also resisted, even if it may carry very little threat to self-autonomy.

The curvilinear function clearly shows when responses to e-control may be more or less positive and negative. However, it is a single parameter model, response to e-control is a function only of ActID, and thus it fails to capture the richness of our intuitions concerning responses to e-control. Further, testing for an inverted U is very difficult.[1] The model becomes more realistic if we allow the self-autonomy and instrumental mediators to vary. With this addition, the formulation becomes richer and more easily tested even with fallible manipulations and measures. Next, I indicate that the autonomy and instrumental mediators may be varied. In each case, an interaction hypothesis is derived and an initial study is reported.

The Autonomy Mediator

One can imagine many things that raise or lower the autonomy mediator. For example, anything that makes the self salient (e.g., individuating clothing, mirrors) or raises self-esteem will tend to make responses to

---

[1]It is often difficult to map empirical operations to the relevant theoretical dimensions in any clear one-to-one fashion. For example, suppose we manipulate action identification across two levels. Although we may know that the levels differ, we often do not know how high or low or how far apart or close together they are on the absolute theoretical scale. Thus, if participants are more positive in their response to control attempts at the higher level of action identification, we could simply assume that the manipulated levels of action identification were to the left of the inflection point. If the curve is flat, it might mean that we are straddling the inflection point. If participants are less positive to the higher level, it could mean that we are at the right of the inflection point. In short, any possible outcome (except an upright U over many points) is consistent with the present formulation. This state of affairs makes such tests unconvincing.

e-control attempts less positive because of autonomy concerns. On the other hand, circumstances that make the self less salient or lower self-esteem should make responses to e-control attempts less negative as a result of autonomy concerns.

When combined multiplicatively with the instrumental mediator, changes in the autonomy mediator generate a family of curves with a number of implications. First, there is no net main effect on responses to e-control across the range of ActID. This may be surprising because increasing the autonomy mediator is associated with more negative responses to attempts at e-control and decreasing the autonomy mediator with more positive responses to e-control. Although surprising, this implication of the model may help explain why the evidence for the obvious relationship between self-autonomy variables (e.g., self-esteem, self-awareness, deindividuation) and acceptance of social influence has been mixed or relatively weak.

More interesting is that the effects of varying self-autonomy depend on the level of ActID. In agreement with our intuitions, the model predicts that increases in self-autonomy should make persons more negatively disposed to e-control than decreases in autonomy. But this is only when ActID is high. It also predicts that increases in autonomy will make persons more positively disposed to e-control than decreases in self-autonomy (when ActID is low).

A Study of Self-Autonomy, Action Identification, and the Acceptance of E-Control[2]

Hypothesis 1. Hypothesis 1 predicts an interaction between autonomy and ActID such that the effect of autonomy on responses to e-control will be relatively more negative[3] the higher the ActID. Or, put another way, the effect of ActID on responses to e-control will be relatively more negative the higher the self-autonomy.

To test Hypothesis 1, female undergraduates were recruited for a study on "interpersonal predictability." The purpose of the experiment was explained as being concerned with interpersonal predictability, " ... the ability to form impressions of others based on few facts, for instance, upon meeting someone being able to tell right away whether he was a good friend, parent, or worker ... people who are high in interpersonal

---

[2]The data for Pilot Studies 1 and 2 were collected by Kim Moore. Her help is gratefully acknowledged.

[3]"Relatively more negative" implies that the first relationship is negative and the second positive or, that both are negative but the first is more negative, or that both are positive but the first is less positive.

predictability have good social skills and get along well with others." The present study focused on interpersonal predictability and "verbal and analytical skills."

The Self-Autonomy Manipulation. The participant and confederate (in a separate room) took a computer administered "test," consisting of 6 answerable and 19 impossible analogies. To increase self-autonomy, participants were led to believe that they had done well on the test; to decrease self-autonomy, participants were led to believe they had done poorly on the test.

The Task. The participant and confederate were brought back together and reminded of the meaning of interpersonal predictability. They were told that to measure their interpersonal predictability they would be provided with biographical information about several life insurance salespeople whose success at their jobs is known. The participant's task was to look over the biographies, form an impression of each, and then rank order them with respect to how successful they were. The participant and then the confederate were asked to comment on how they might approach the task.

The ActID Manipulation and Attempt at E-Control. At this point, the confederate indicated that physical attractiveness was very important in sales. He looked right at the participant and indicated that if "we" want to complete the task (quickly for Low ActID and accurately for High ActID), "we" should rank the people in terms of attractiveness. At this point, the experimenter took the confederate to another room so each could work privately on the rank-order task. Each biography consisted of a photograph and a number of biographical facts.

Measuring Acceptance of E-Control. The confederate "demanded" that the participant use physical attractiveness in rank ordering the candidates. A separate sample from the same population provided normative attractiveness rankings of the photographs. Acceptance of e-control was indexed by the rank order correlation between a participant's ranking of the biographies with the normative attractiveness rankings. This index clearly reflects acceptance of the e-control attempt, but it does not rely on self-report nor does it rely on awareness.

Results. The rank order correlation between each participant's salesperson ranks and the normative physical attractiveness ranks was computed to serve as an index of acceptance of the confederate's attempt at e-control. On the average, there was marginally more acceptance of influence in the low ActID condition than in the high ActID condition. More important, the predicted interaction was in the right direction and significant. The effect of ActID on acceptance of control was more negative when autonomy was high (the success condition) than when autonomy was low (the failure condition).

Similar interactions on measures of affect and task persistence should be observed. That is, if an individual is subjected to e-control, then self-autonomy should decrease the effect of ActID on task persistence, task effort, and affect. Carver and Scheier (pp. 30–36) make a compelling case for the idea that approach, or discrepancy-reducing goals, are associated with qualitatively different affective responses than are avoidance, or discrepancy-enlarging goals. If the autonomy mediator is construed as being concerned with the avoidance of e-control, then, following Carver and Scheier, we would expect greater changes in affect on an anxiety/relief dimension than on an elation/depression dimension.

The Instrumentality Mediator

Like the autonomy mediator, variations in the instrumentality mediator can also be studied. For example, there may be chronic individual differences in concern with the reduction of ambiguity, task completion, and so on. And, there are also a number of circumstantial differences that may affect the instrumental mediator, such as variations in task ambiguity or difficulty, the importance of task completion, time pressures, and the need to be correct.

Raising or lowering the instrumentality mediator and combining it multiplicatively with self-autonomy also generates a family of curves with a number of implications. The implication on which I focus concerns the interaction between ActID and variations in the instrumentality mediator. At low levels of ActID, increasing the instrumentality mediator leads to more positive responses to attempts at e-control. It is surprising that at high levels of ActID, increased concern with instrumentality is predicted to lead to less positive responses to attempts at e-control.

A Study of Task Ambiguity, Action Identification, and the Acceptance of E-Control

Hypothesis 2. Hypothesis 2 predicts that the effect of concern with instrumentality on responses to e-control will be relatively more positive when ActID is low than when it is high. Or, put another way, ActID will have a more positive influence on responses to e-control when the concern with instrumentality is relatively low.

To test hypothesis 2, female undergraduates were again recruited for a study on "interpersonal predictability." In this study, there was no ability test. In explaining the task to the participants, the experimenter manipulated task ambiguity/difficulty. The ActID manipulation was set up in a way that was, perhaps, more theoretically satisfactory than in the earlier study.

The Task.   The meaning of interpersonal predictability was explained as before. Again, the participant and confederate were told that they would be provided with biographical information about several life insurance salespeople whose success at their jobs is known. The participants' task was to look over the biographies, form an impression of each, and then rank order them with respect to how successful they thought they were.

Manipulating the Instrumental Mediator.   Under low ambiguity conditions, the experimenter added: "People seem to find this task relatively easy. They seem to home in on the relevant information without much trouble . . . . "Under high ambiguity conditions, the experimenter added: " . . . this is a difficult task. Even we can't figure out how people are forming these rank orders . . . ."

Manipulating ActID and the E-Control Attempt.   As noted earlier, ActID level can be raised by asking the question "Why?" The experimenter summarized the participant's task in a way that provided answers to an implicit series of why questions. "So, a careful examination of the biographical information will allow you to pick out the relevant information to form a judgment of how good a salesperson this is in order to show your interpersonal predictability." By providing this specific hierarchy, that is, pick information, form judgment, then show interpersonal predictability, we do not have to guess at what the subject may be thinking and the confederate can identify the behavior at a higher or lower level.
The confederate manipulated the level of ActID and the attempt to control the participant by saying: "it is important that we focus on relevant information" (low-level ActID) or "try to demonstrate our interpersonal predictability level" (high-level ActID). "Physical attractiveness is important . . . So, if we [looks directly at participant] want to [use the most relevant information/demonstrate our level of interpersonal predictability] . . . we should rank the people in order of attractiveness." The participant then worked privately on the rank ordering.
As before, acceptance of e-control was indexed by the rank order correlation between a participant's ranking of the biographies with the

normative rankings. The predicted interaction was marginally significant; the effect of ActID on responses to e-control was relatively more positive the lower the concern with instrumentality.

Here too similar interactions on measures of affect and task persistence should be observed. If an individual is subject to e-control, then, the greater the concern with instrumentality, the more negative the effect of ActID on task persistence, task effort, and affect. Borrowing from Carver and Scheier, something more can be said about the kind of affective changes to expect if the instrumentality mediator could be classified as an approach or an avoidance tendency. What is focal is the e-control attempt. Because greater concerns with instrumentality make one more open or accepting of e-control, the instrumentality mediator appears to be an approach tendency. If this is so, then, again following Carver and Scheier (pp. 30–36), we would expect greater changes in affect on an elation/depression dimension than on an anxiety/relief dimension.

SOME E-CONTROL ISSUES FOR THE CARVER AND SCHEIER APPROACH

Is There Something Special About Feelings of Control?

For Carver and Scheier, there is nothing special about control. The issue is positive and negative outcomes, and control is important only insofar as it has implications for positive and negative outcomes. Some of that thinking is captured here in what is labelled the instrumentality mediator. The notion of the instrumentality mediator implies that persons will accept e-control to the extent that the situation is ambiguous, they feel overwhelmed, they feel incapable of success, and so forth. Beyond positive and negative outcomes per se, however, the e-control model implies that taking responsibility, a control-related concept, may also be painful under these conditions.

Carver and Scheier have no problem with the notion of maintaining one's self-concept. The idea underlying the autonomy mediator is that control issues have a special status because they have clear implications for one's self. Failure to maintain feelings of control with respect to a central aspect of self diminishes that aspect of self.

On the Use of ActID

At the heart of Carver and Scheier's theorizing is the notion of goal hierarchies. Vallacher and Wegner's (1987) notion of ActID resonates with

Carver and Scheier's thinking as well as any other formulation available in the late 1990s. Moreover, Carver and Scheier suggest that "The higher you go into the organization, the more fundamental to the overriding sense of self are the qualities encountered" (p. 15). Thus, they appear to agree that issues of self-autonomy ought to become more important with increasing levels of ActID.

Carver and Scheier's discussion (p. 13) is also consistent with Vallacher and Wegner's (1987) hypothesis that task accomplishment seems easier at lower levels of ActID. This hypothesis, that issues of instrumentality tend to become more important with increasing levels of ActID, is another fundamental assumption of the e-control model.

On Putting It All Together

Carver and Scheier are sympathetic to using nonlinear (interactive) approaches to understanding behavior. However, there is little in their theorizing that implies that the focal level of a goal hierarchy should interact with concerns about autonomy; nor is there much to suggest that the focal level of goal hierarchy should interact with instrumentality concerns; and, although Carver and Scheier sympathetically deal with notions of self-concept maintenance and instrumental concerns, there is little in their discussion to imply that these concerns might interact.

In sum, each of the concepts used in the e-control model are more or less consistent with Carver and Scheier's parsing of the behavior domain. Moreover, Carver and Scheier are philosophically sympathetic to the nonlinear nature of the e-control model. On the other hand, the specific ways in which the e-control model suggests that the variables operate together are not implied by Carver and Scheier. Nevertheless, they seem promising and perhaps worthy of additional research.

ACKNOWLEDGMENT

The support of NIMH Grant number K05 MH01233 is gratefully acknowledged.

REFERENCES

Adorno, T. W., Frenkel-Brunswik, E., Levinson, D. J., & Sanford, R. N. (1950). *The authoritarian personality*. New York: Harper & Row.

Burger, J. M. (1989). Negative reactions to increase in precieved personal control. *Journal of Personality and Social Psychology, 56*, 246–256.

Doty, R. M., Peterson, B. E., & Winter, D. G. (1991). Threat and authoritarianism in the United States, 1978–1987. *Journal of Personality and Social Psychology, 61*, 629–640.

Vallacher, R. R., & Wegner, D. M. (1985). *A theory of action identification.* Hillsdale, NJ: Lawrence Erlbaum Associates.

Vallacher, R. R., & Wegner, D. M. (1987). What do people think they're doing? Action identification and human behavior. *Psychological Review, 94*, 3–15.

10

The Dynamics
of Self-Regulation

Robin R. Vallacher
Florida Atlantic University

Andrzej Nowak
Warsaw University

Throughout their careers, Carver and Scheier have demonstrated a remarkable and enviable knack for theoretical synthesis, and the present target chapter is no exception. When one considers the enormous range of topics and issues they explore, their ambition in attempting to achieve conceptual integration is truly impressive. Yet, they have managed to lay out a broad framework within which a century's worth of theories and empirical phenomena can at least be discussed in similar language and related to a common set of issues. This framework represents a mix of two rather different orientations, each of which has been forwarded as an integrative vehicle for otherwise disparate ideas and data but that differ in fundamental respects. On the one hand, they offer a broadly cybernetic interpretation (cf. Powers, 1973) of such diverse phenomena as emotion, self-awareness, motivation, consciousness, mental representation, adaptation, personal consistency, and autonomy. Since the early 1980s, this framework has proven remarkably effective for dealing with issues in control and self-regulation, especially those centering on goals, as evident in the work of the authors themselves (cf. Carver & Scheier, 1981). On the other hand, they invoke certain ideas associated with dynamical systems theory (cf. Schuster, 1984) and related developments such as catastrophe theory (Thom, 1975). Only in recent years has the dynamical perspective emerged as a potential integrative vehicle for many of these same issues (cf. Vallacher & Nowak, 1994), so Carver and Scheier are understandably tentative in using it to reframe self-regulatory phenomena. Our aim in this comment is to sketch how the issues raised by Carver and Scheier might be addressed somewhat more comprehensively from a purely dynamical systems perspective. In so doing, we consider how cybernetic assumptions can be integrated into an explicit dynamical framework.

THE BEHAVIOR OF DYNAMICAL SYSTEMS

Broadly defined, a *dynamical system* is a set of interconnected elements that undergo change (cf. Schuster, 1984). In fact, the ability to evolve in time is the most basic property of a dynamical system. The state of each element at a given instant may be described by values of one or more variables. Because these values change in time depending on the state of the system and in response to external influences, the variables describing elements are referred to as *dynamical variables.* The primary task of dynamical systems theory is to characterize the relations among the dynamical variables and, hence, the mutual influences among elements and the macrolevel properties of the system to which these relations give rise.

In social psychology, systems and their associated elements can be defined on different levels. The coordination of motor movements produces a system of action, for example, whereas the interplay of cognitive and affective elements forms a system of attitudes and judgments and the influence among people creates a system at the level of social groups. In each case, the interactions among elements (i.e., among limbs, thoughts, or individuals) generate macrolevel properties that characterize the system as a whole. Thus, systems of judgment, action, and group behavior are each associated with phenomena that can be discussed independently of the elements comprising the system. Action, for example, may ultimately derive from the coordination of limb movements, but it can be characterized in terms of such dimensions as goal-directedness and appropriateness that are not inherent in specific movements.

Dynamical variables can change in time by adjusting their values to one another, so that the system as a whole can evolve in time in the absence of external influences. When a system's evolution is internally generated in this manner, the system is said to display *intrinsic dynamics* in its behavior (Vallacher & Nowak, 1997). Social judgment, for instance, may display a sustained pattern of change under some conditions because of the interaction of cognitive and affective elements in the judgment system

(Vallacher, Nowak, & Kaufman, 1994). At a higher level of social reality, group behavior and norms may change as a result of mutual influences among the individuals comprising the group (Nowak, Szamrej, & Latané, 1990). Dynamical systems tend to demonstrate especially interesting and complex intrinsic dynamics when the mutual influences among elements are nonlinear in nature. By *nonlinear*, we simply mean that a change in one element does not produce a proportional change in other elements. Sometimes even a slight influence from an element may lead to a big change in the state of another element, whereas at other times, even a strong influence from an element may lead to negligible effects. It is also conceivable that up to some value, increases in the value of one element produce corresponding increases in another element, but that beyond this value, further increases in the first element produce decreases in the other element.

Over time, a system's intrinsic dynamics tend to cohere into reliable patterns, referred to as *attractors*. The attractor for a system may involve a specific state, representing a stable equilibrium, in which case it is referred to as a *fixed-point attractor*. A person's simultaneous concerns with safety versus novelty seeking, for instance, may result in a stable preference representing an optimal level of stimulation. But, a system may also evolve toward a sustained pattern of changes in its global behavior. Depending on the regularity of this pattern, the attractor is referred to as either periodic, quasi-periodic, or chaotic (Nowak & Lewenstein, 1994; Schuster, 1984). The person concerned with both safety and novelty, for instance, may alternate regularly between boring activities and thrill-seeking or perhaps display a more complex pattern of choice between these alternatives. The emergence of complex attractors is especially likely in systems characterized by nonlinearity in the relations among elements. If the relation between safety and novelty concerns is best described in terms of a threshold function, for example, the person trying to satisfy both concerns may display seemingly random and unpredictable changes in his or her behavior orientation.

The fact that dynamical systems display sustained patterns of intrinsic dynamics does not mean that systems do not react to external influences. Environmental obstacles obviously affect action, new information influences judgments, and external threats can transform group behavior. The influence of some factors tend to be short-lived, so that the system quickly returns to its attractor. Bumping someone who is walking, for example, will impact on the pattern of walking, initiating perhaps a sequence of rapid movements aimed at restoring the walking pattern.[1] Other external

---

[1]Of course, a sufficiently strong external influence may move the system to a different attractor if the system has more than one attractor. A particularly intense bump, for example, may knock the person to the ground.

factors may influence a system in a much more fundamental way, however, by changing the internal workings of the system. Factors that have this potential are termed *control parameters*. Some changes in a control parameter may have only a quantitative effect on a system's dynamics. Telling a person to speak up, for example, may induce him or her to talk somewhat louder. Other changes in control parameters, however, lead to qualitative changes in a system's dynamics. Intense pressure to speak up, for example, may promote a transition from talking to yelling or, alternatively, may make the person stop talking altogether. Qualitative changes in the structure of a system's attractors (i.e., the number or type of attractors) are referred to as *bifurcations* (cf. Nowak & Lewenstein, 1994; Schuster, 1984). Because control parameters can promote bifurcations, they dictate (i.e., control) the internal workings of the system. From a dynamical perspective, then, control over a process is equivalent to adjusting a system's control parameters. Hence, any factor that provides for such adjustment controls the system in question.

SELF-CONTROL

The potential for self-control is an important feature of dynamical systems. In essence, *self-control* means that a system is capable of controlling its own dynamics. This occurs when a feedback loop is established between the settings of control parameters and the current state or dynamics of the system. In other words, the settings of control parameters not only dictate a system's dynamics but also depend on the system's current operation. The familiar furnace thermostat metaphor in cybernetics provides a simple example of feedback-based self-control. The control parameter in this example is the rate of fuel supplied to the furnace, and the state of the system is described by the temperature. The feedback loop is established by a thermostat, which adjusts a valve controlling the rate of fuel supplied, depending on the temperature inside the furnace. In fact, this is actually a dynamical system with a fixed-point attractor representing a single equilibrium for the system.[2]

A more elaborate and psychologically relevant example of self-control is provided by Lewenstein and Nowak (1989a, 1989b), who introduced self-control mechanisms in attractor neural networks (Hopfield, 1982).

---

[2]Closer examination might reveal that the system's attractor is periodic rather than fixed-point. This is because the system is likely to systematically overshoot its target value due to inertia in both the thermostat and the furnace, resulting in a time delay in the feedback loop. Thus, rather than settling on a fixed value, the temperature will oscillate around the equilibrium in a relatively regular manner.

Attractor neural networks, which are programmable dynamical systems, are often used to model cognitive processes such as recognition and learning (cf. McClelland & Rumelhart, 1986). In this approach, memories are encoded as attractors of the network. Lewenstein and Nowak (1989a, 1989b) observed that when a pattern is presented, the network can determine whether it is familiar or novel in the first moments of processing, long before it recognizes the pattern. This is accomplished in one of two ways, both of which provide an immediate measure of the proximity of the network's state to its closest attractor. The system can prerecognize the novelty of a pattern, first of all, by monitoring the volatility of its own dynamics. When the incoming pattern approximates a well-known pattern in the network, corresponding to an attractor, the network is characterized by relatively slow dynamics (i.e., a small proportion of neurons changing their state). When the incoming pattern is novel and thus does not approximate one of the network's attractors, however, the network is characterized by relatively fast and random dynamics. The second means of prerecognition involves checking the coherence of the signals traveling in the network. In the vicinity of an attractor, the signals arriving at a given neuron from other neurons are consistent in dictating the state of the neuron. When the network is far from an attractor, however, the system is characterized by incoherence, in that the signals arriving at a given neuron from other neurons dictate conflicting states of the neuron.

Either of these properties (rate of neuronal change and network incoherence) may be used to construct a self-control feedback loop (Lewenstein & Nowak, 1989a, 1989b). The control parameter in this feedback loop is the level of noise in the network, representing the random firing of neurons. Self-control consists of making the noise level dependent on either the rate of neuronal change or the degree of network incoherence. With increasing levels of incoherence, for instance, the network increases its noise level, which has the effect of making progressively stronger attractors inaccessible, thereby erasing progressively stronger memories. Because familiar patterns are coherent and hence produce only low levels of noise, the feedback loop results in their correct recognition. By the same token, the network avoids false recognition of novel patterns by raising the noise to a level where no attractor can capture a system's dynamics. In essence, the network tentatively forgets progressively stronger memories, until at some level of noise the network is unable to recognize any incoming pattern. The dynamics of the network in effect become governed by noise (i.e., the dynamics become random) and may be interpreted as a "don't know" response. By means of this feedback loop, in sum, the network is able to regulate its own recognition process. The recognition process is maintained when the network is characterized by coherence (produced by familiar patterns), but is interrupted by strong noise when the network detects its own incoherence (produced by novel patterns).

We should note that this relatively simple self-control mechanism may be used as an element in a larger system capable of more complex self-regulatory functions. In a system composed of several networks in which each network encodes separate memories, for example, the presentation of a stimulus will block the recognition process in all the networks that have not encoded the stimulus, so that recognition will take place only in the network that actually remembers the stimulus (Zochowski, Lewenstein, & Nowak, 1993). It is also possible for a neural network to switch dynamically between a recognition mode and a learning mode (Zochowski, Lewenstein, & Nowak, 1995). In this model, the network engages in a recognition process when presented with familiar stimuli. But upon detection of its own incoherence during recognition, the network will stop its own recognition process and initiate instead a process of learning. In this way, the network acquires memories for unknown patterns, which can be subsequently used in recognition. In short, the introduction of self-control mechanisms into attractor neural networks provides for richer dynamics and allows such networks to perform much more complex functions.

HIERARCHIES OF SELF-CONTROL

Building on the work of Powers (1973), Carver and Scheier argue that human self-regulation is organized in a hierarchical fashion, with different representations of the action in question displaying a superordinate–subordinate relationship. In their view, the hierarchy of action reflects a recursive structure of reference values, usually defined in terms of goals and subgoals. This feature of self-regulation can be captured in dynamical terms. Carver and Scheier themselves suggest that goals can be understood in terms of attractors for a system. From a strict cybernetic perspective, however, goals correspond to fixed-point attractors. In the furnace thermostat system, for example, the goal is to keep the temperature at a prespecified value. As Carver and Scheier point out, the dynamical perspective extends the goal construct to include patterns of dynamics, such as periodic, quasi-periodic, and chaotic evolution (cf. Vallacher & Nowak, 1997). A person's goal, for example, may be to alternate between intense stimulation and periods of rest, rather than experiencing only one state or the other. The hierarchy of goals, from this perspective, implies a hierarchy of attractors.[3]

A hierarchical structure of attractors is established when the attractors of higher order systems dictate the nature and values of attractors in lower level systems. This occurs when the control parameters dictating the attractors in one system become dynamical variables in another system. Because the factors that control dynamics in the first system are responsive to changes in the dynamics of the second system, a hierarchical relation is established such that the second system is superordinate to the first. The temporal evolution of the higher order system will thus dictate the changes in the attractors of the lower order system. Usually after a relatively short time, the higher order system will evolve (or stabilize) on one of its attractors. Its evolution on the attractor will be reflected in the systematic pattern of changes in the attractors of the lower level system. As a special case, if the higher level system converges on a fixed-point attractor, the value of this attractor will determine the value of the attractor of the lower level system. The control parameters of the higher order system, in turn, may become dynamical variables in a yet higher order system, and so on, resulting in a multilevel hierarchically organized dynamical system.

We should note that, as pointed out by Carver and Scheier, a hierarchy of feedback loops can be used to establish a hierarchy of regulation based on goals in cybernetic systems (cf. Powers, 1973). In such a hierarchy, each higher level system attempting to minimize differences between its state and its standard of regulation—the goal—imposes specific standards of regulation on lower level systems. Alternatively, the system may attempt to maximize the discrepancy between its state and its standard of regulation. In either case, the behavioral output of the higher level system provides goals for the systems beneath it in the hierarchy. In

---

[3]Carver and Scheier suggest that standards of self-regulation may involve repellers as well as attractors. Thus, action is sometimes oriented to avoidance of negatively valenced states as well as approach toward positively valenced states. The states and patterns to be avoided may be defined as repellers in a dynamical system. Because repellers correspond to unstable equilibria, a system in the vicinity of a repeller tends to move away rapidly. Repeller dynamics have been modeled in the context of repeller neural networks (Nowak, Lewenstein, & Tarkowski, 1994). In this model, repellers are established by a learning algorithm. Repellers do not affect a system's dynamics until the system achieves a state close to one of them, at which point the system dynamics change to escape the repeller. A specific control parameter regulates how close a system can approach a repeller before being affected by it. It is also possible to establish a system containing both specific repellers and specific attractors. Such a system will seek some specified states and avoid others.

dynamical systems, the feedback loop between control parameters and the system's dynamics may be much more complex than the feedback loop commonly portrayed in cybernetics. The settings of control parameters, first of all, may depend on properties of dynamics in the system rather than only on the state of the system. It is also the case that the control parameters may regulate a pattern of dynamics rather than movement toward a prespecified state (i.e., a goal). Finally, the nature of coupling between system properties and control parameters can take various forms (including, of course, discrepancy reduction and maximization, as discussed by Carver and Scheier). Examples of such forms are illustrated in the Lewenstein and Nowak (1989a, 1989b) model, described earlier. Nonetheless, when self-regulatory feedback loops are aimed at discrepancy reduction between a current state and a specified equilibrium (i.e., a goal), the cybernetic and dynamical systems accounts are largely compatible. To be fair, Carver and Scheier argue that goals may represent a sequence of activities rather than a particular state of homeostasis. It is not clear, however, how such a system of self-regulation would function. The model we have described may provide the missing mechanism.

The principles by which hierarchies of attractors are formed also apply when separate systems become integrated to form a higher order system. Each system in effect becomes an element in the resultant higher order system. The acts of swinging a baseball bat and running to first base, for instance, are each associated with a distinct pattern of movements and an associated feedback loop promoting self-control. Because of their co-occurrence, these separate systems of action may become integrated into a higher order action system associated with hitting a baseball. Each state of an emergent higher order system imposes patterns of dynamics in the component systems by setting their respective control parameters.[4] In playing baseball, for example, a high degree of motivation or enthusiasm may establish a specific dynamic pattern for batting (e.g., rapid movement of arms with little leg motion) and running (e.g., rapid leg motion). The temporal evolution of the higher order system, then, will result in a pattern of systematic changes in the dynamics of the lower order systems. As enthusiasm waxes and wanes during the course of a baseball game, for instance, there will be corresponding changes in the dynamics of batting and running.

---

[4]A similar idea has been formally developed in the approach of synergetics (cf. Haken, 1978), where the evolution of so-called master equations, describing the evolution of a higher order system, changes the control parameters of so-called slave equations, describing the evolution of the system's components.

Dynamical systems with self-control may be organized in a similar fashion. This is possible because the properties of systems with self-control often depend on the values of some control parameters beyond the control parameters in the self-control feedback loop. Consider the earlier furnace thermostat example. The nature of this system's feedback loop, and hence the equilibrium (i.e., the attractor) for the system, can be controlled by adjusting the settings of the thermostat. The thermostat can be set by factors outside the system (e.g., by a person), of course, but it can also depend on other feedback loops in the system. The thermostat can be made to reset to a lower temperature, for example, if the fuel valve stays maximally open for more than 80% of the time, and to reset to a higher temperature if the valve stays maximally open less than 10% of the time. In this example, the higher level self-control feedback loop in effect sets the goal for the lower level system. The higher order dynamical system has its own control parameters which, like those in the original system, may be controlled from outside or by means of a self-control loop involving dynamics of the system itself.[5]

The higher order control parameters often dictate the nature of the self-control feedback loop between control parameters and dynamics in the lower level system. A simple example of this basis for hierarchical control in human systems is provided by locomotion. Specific settings of self-control loops may sustain a pattern of walking, whereas other settings may sustain a pattern of running. The higher order feedback loop can switch between these settings, providing for walking when there are signals of fatigue and for running when there are signals of energy recovery. The goals of the lower level systems will change in an alternating fashion as a result of the higher order self-control feedback loop.

In hierarchically organized systems, self-control feedback loops may be defined at different levels and may be implemented between levels. Thus, the setting of control parameters in a higher level system may depend on the state or dynamics of a lower level system. The existence of such a feedback loop upsets the clear distinction between higher and lower levels in a hierarchy, because feedback loops necessarily involve bidirectional causality. The distinction between higher and lower levels can be established according to different criteria, however. The work on synergetics (cf. Haken, 1978), for example, suggests that control parameters usually change on a longer timescale (i.e., at a slower rate) than

---

[5]The principle at work here recasts in dynamical terms Carver and Scheier's notion of readjustment in standards of regulation by a metacontrol loop and provides a mechanism for its occurrence.

do other dynamical variables. The timescale underlying change thus may serve as a criterion for distinguishing levels in a self-regulatory system (cf. Powers, 1973), a point made by Carver and Scheier as well. It is also the case that control parameters of a higher level system often react to the entire configuration of dynamics in the lower level system. Incoherence among lower level elements, for example, may result in readjustment of control parameters aimed at restoring coherence. This provides the basis for self-organization in dynamical systems, such that the system can reconfigure itself to meet changing demands without the intervention of higher order entities.

Because of the interdependence among levels, the image of firmly entrenched hierarchies of self-regulatory systems may be somewhat misleading, especially with respect to psychological systems. Such systems rarely maintain a fixed organization, but rather evolve and otherwise change in response to changing conditions. First of all, the relations among system elements change in response to changes in the system's control parameters. Second, systems may be assembled and disassembled, with new elements added or old elements eliminated, and with new self-control feedback loops supplanting existing feedback loops. Finally, two or more systems, each associated with different or conflicting goals, may try to organize overlapping lower level elements. Playing a good tennis match and trying to impress a romantic partner observing the match may be associated with conflicting action patterns and thereby impose incoherent standards of regulation. In short, the nature of self-control feedback loops in human self-regulation may get very complex, linking several levels and not be readily organized in a well-defined hierarchical arrangement. A more appropriate image of human self-regulation is one of constantly evolving systems punctuated by periods of disorder and the emergence of new patterns, in a manner reminiscent of Gestalt notions of pattern formation and reorganization (cf. Vallacher, Nowak, Markus, & Strauss, 1998).

CONSCIOUSNESS

Issues centering on the notion of consciousness are notoriously tricky. Because the basic principles of dynamical systems were developed in mathematics and physics, areas of science for which such issues are largely moot, the role of consciousness in our account of self-regulation is necessarily speculative (as it is in cybernetic accounts, and for the same reason). To this point, we have provided a depiction of how systems can function and become self-regulating in a fairly automatic manner.

But as Carver and Scheier point out, consciousness plays an important role in human self-regulation, especially in the context of controlled as opposed to automatic processing. If the dynamical perspective is to provide an adequate account of self-regulation, then, it must allow for this self-evident feature of human systems.

One likely role for consciousness is in the assembly of systems. Although some systems may be hardwired by genetic and other biological mechanisms, as Carver and Scheier note, others may require active assembly on the person's part. Quite often, it is far from trivial how to assemble elements and establish self-control feedback loops into a system that will produce desired patterns. In such instances, consciousness may be required to select elements and establish basic connections among them and thus establish a dynamical system. In such systems, consciousness may play the role of an outside agent that adjusts the control parameters online, thereby exercising direct control over the system's dynamics. This is especially likely when there is little direct experience with putting together elements for an unfamiliar or difficult task. Imagine, for example, the conscious effort required by someone from Eastern Europe trying to learn the movement configurations associated with some aspect of playing baseball (e.g., swinging a bat). The suggestion that conscious attention is necessary to establish a workable dynamical system corresponds to the notion of controlled processing (cf. Bargh, 1997; Schneider & Shiffrin, 1977).[6]

With repeated activation of the system, control parameters may become more directly linked to the system's dynamics, so that the system becomes increasingly capable of self-regulation and, therefore, relatively autonomous in its operation. The progressive automaticity in patterns of thought and behavior is consistent in broad form with the literature on both automaticity (cf. Wegner & Bargh, 1998) and skill acquisition (Anderson, 1990). As noted by Carver and Scheier, overlearned acts become very rigid and follow the same pattern each time they are performed. In our account, when a dynamical system becomes firmly established with feedback loops controlling its evolution, its dynamics closely follow a well-defined attractor. The transition to automatic

---

[6]The conscious regulation of action is interesting to consider in light of Carver and Scheier's discussion of the role of intention. They cite work by Kelso (1995) on the switching between phase and antiphase coordination in motor control. Usually at some value of a control parameter (e.g., the rate of movement), a transition naturally occurs between these two forms of coordination. Kelso observed, however, that subjects were able, by virtue of intention, to delay the onset of the transition. In terms of the present analysis, intention served as the means by which consciousness adjusted the functioning of the natural feedback loop in this system of self-regulation.

self-regulation in a system through the establishment of self-control feedback loops obviates the need for consciousness to micromanage the dynamics of the system. When consciousness is relieved of the task of adjusting control parameters, it becomes available to assemble the system with other autonomous systems to create a higher order system. After achieving relative expertise at both catching and throwing a baseball, for example, a person's conscious concern is likely to center on the integration of these two acts in playing catch. In principle, there is no limit to the tendency toward progressive integration of separate systems and the concomitant upward mobility of consciousness. In the absence of constraining factors, then, the content of conscious thought could become increasingly devoid of the details of self-regulation, defined instead in terms of increasingly comprehensive plans, goals, and the like (cf. Vallacher & Wegner, 1987; Vallacher et al., 1998).

Reality, of course, is not so accommodating. A number of factors provide constraints on the progressive integration of systems and thus keep consciousness firmly tethered to lower levels of personal regulation. For one thing, systems with overlapping elements but incompatible dynamics may be difficult to assemble into a higher order system. It is easy to integrate walking and talking, for instance, but talking and singing make conflicting demands on the same vocal elements and thus are poor candidates for integration. The progressive integration of systems is also constrained by the difficulty of the component systems. Some acts involve highly complex patterns of temporal coordination among basic movements and never achieve complete automaticity. No matter how experienced one is with golf, writing essays, or raising a child, a considerable degree of conscious attention is required to maintain a desired pattern of thought and behavior for these action domains. Research on optimality in action identification has established a linear relation between the personal difficulty of action and the degree of conscious attention to the action's basic elements (cf. Vallacher, 1993). A related constraint on progressive integration concerns environmental instability. Even simple, overlearned action patterns require adjustment to accommodate novelty in the action context from one occasion to another. No matter how routine the trip from work to home has become, for example, it is possible for situations to arise (e.g., an airplane landing in the road) that the autonomous driving system is not prepared to handle. In short, the conscious regulation of action systems diminishes greatly with automatization but does not evaporate entirely.

Consciousness is also critical in the resetting and repair of systems of human self-regulation that have become dysfunctional. If the existing elements in a system do not cohere into a pattern that is instrumental in achieving a goal, it is necessary to change the relations among elements or the dynamics of any specific set of elements in order to establish the desired pattern. Carver and Scheier suggest that a system monitors its functionality by directly comparing its current state with a goal. This is clearly the case in many instances of self-regulation. The Lewenstein and Nowak (1989a, 1989b) model, however, suggests a different mechanism that does not require direct comparison between a system's current state and a goal. Recall that in their model, a system may detect its own dysfunction by observing its own dynamics. The degree of coherence in such dynamics is an important indicator of the system's functionality. If functionality cannot be restored by the system's self-control feedback loops, consciousness is directed to the system's elements in an attempt to reassemble them so as to achieve and maintain a desired pattern. This is true whether the system's dysfunctionality is due to a discrepancy between the system's dynamics and a goal or instead is due to internal incoherence of the system. A person may reconsider the appropriateness of his or her action, for example, by observing poor progress toward a goal or, alternatively, he or she may reconsider his or her action because of distress due to inability to coordinate different elements in the action, regardless of his or her representation of the action's goal.

In this view, consciousness is not simply awareness of ongoing processes of self-regulation, but rather constitutes a vital element of the regulatory process itself. Systems incapable of automatic self-regulation cannot function effectively in the absence of conscious attention. On the other hand, if conscious attention is focused on a well-functioning self-regulating system, it is likely to switch the system's operation from automatic to manual control, disrupting the flow and slowing the system down by substituting serial for parallel processing (cf. Schneider & Shiffrin, 1977). It follows that for every process, there is an optimal level in the hierarchy of self-regulation to which consciousness should be directed. Action identification theory describes how the optimal level of conscious attention depends on the characteristics of the system and task demands (cf. Vallacher, 1993; Vallacher & Wegner, 1987). The results of research on action identification provide support for this line of reasoning (e.g., Vallacher, Wegner, & Somoza, 1989). Tasks that are novel and difficult tend to focus attention on lower levels of the action system, whereas tasks that are overlearned and easy tend instead to focus consciousness on higher levels of the action system. In this view, the level at which an action is identified is indicative of the level at which consciousness assembles the self-regulation system for human action or intervenes in its operation. Research on this issue also establishes, however, that attention can be drawn to nonoptimal levels of identification, thereby undermining action effectiveness. When important consequences are associated with a difficult action, for example, attention is likely to be focused on the higher level identities for the action, even though the lower level systems require direct monitoring.

Considered together, the progressive assembly of lower order systems into higher order systems and the repair of disrupted systems impart a dynamic pattern to conscious experience. Each time one's attention is diverted from a higher order system to lower level elements and systems, there is a tendency for consciousness to reassemble the elements into a higher order system and reestablish consciousness in more comprehensive and abstract terms. This sequence of disassembly and self-organization is consistent with the emergence process specified in action identification theory (Vallacher & Wegner, 1987). Research on action emergence has shown that whenever consciousness is redirected to lower level identities for an action, there is readiness to embrace higher level identities that provide coordination for the lower level ones (e.g., Wegner, Vallacher, Macomber, Wood, & Arps, 1984). To the extent that the resultant coordination differs from the earlier pattern of inter-element connections, the emergent high-level identities may be qualitatively different from the antecedent high-level identities as well. With each enactment of the disruption-repair pattern, then, there is potential for the creation of a new higher order system of self-regulation. From this perspective, the content of consciousness is open ended and ever changing, representing a constructive process that fosters adaptation to changing task demands.

EMOTION

Emotion is every bit as tricky as consciousness, and judging from the vast and conflicting literature on this topic reviewed by Carver and Scheier, there are as many solutions to the trick as there are interested theorists. The dynamical systems approach was developed in the context of decidedly nonemotional domains, so it cannot hope to account at this point for all the subtleties and empirical generalizations associated with emotion-related phenomena. This perspective, however, can shed some light on the role of emotion in the dynamics of self-regulation. Carver and Scheier tie emotion to the effectiveness of self-regulation systems, suggesting that it signals the rate of progress toward whatever goal is salient at the time. Our account is consistent with this general emphasis but it assigns an even more pronounced role to emotion in self-regulation.

Emotions can be viewed as control parameters in self-regulatory systems. As such, they enter into the self-control feedback loops that define self-regulation. Emotions can make the relationships between certain elements more pronounced, for example, while weakening the relationships among other elements. In doing so, they qualitatively change the functioning of the self-regulatory system and establish new attractors for the system's dynamics. A feeling of happiness, for example, can promote strong connections among cognitive elements with a positive valence, creating a pattern of subsequent thought in which the person remembers primarily positive events and encodes new events in optimistic terms. This account is consistent with the perspective on emotion forwarded by Oatley and Johnson-Laird (1987). They suggest that emotions set the system into one of few relatively different modes, turning some processes on and other processes off. Because of their global and encompassing nature, emotions can reset all elements of a self-regulatory system into a congruent mode, in which specific systems of self-regulation can be activated. We should note, of course, that although emotions are likely to enter many systems of self-regulation, they are clearly not the only control parameters defining system dynamics.

Negative emotions are also capable of changing control parameters in such a way that they can disrupt the dynamics of a system and thus stop ongoing action (cf. Mandler, 1964; Simon, 1967). Negative emotions are likely to be aroused by dysfunction in a system, reflecting either insufficient progress toward a goal or incoherence in system dynamics. They can stop action and bring consciousness to repair an existing action system or to assemble a new system capable of goal attainment. A special role in this regard may be assigned to self-conscious emotions (cf. Tangney & Fischer, 1995). Such emotions not only are likely to inhibit an ongoing pattern of action, but also tend to promote the salience of standards of regulation contained in the self system, in a manner that follows the rationale developed by Carver and Scheier. Consciousness is then brought to bear in order to reassemble the system, in line with our earlier discussion. In sum, negative emotions are associated with dysfunctionality and disassembly of existing self-regulatory systems.

Positive emotions, in contrast, are evoked by coherence in the system and satisfactory progression toward a goal. Because they can be treated as signals of effective self-regulation at a given level, they free up consciousness and allow it to move upward to assemble higher level systems. In this view, positive emotions are associated not only with efficient functioning, but also with progression to higher levels of integration. In the context of the right task demands, when a system has been assembled that functions autonomously and has the potential for continuing self-organization, it may produce action that has flow-like properties (Csikzentmihalyi, 1990; Wicklund, 1986). Progressive integration generates positive emotions, yet consciousness is free from monitoring the functioning of the self-regulatory system underlying the action. This perspective bears on the asymmetry between positive and negative emotions noted by Carver and Scheier (cf. Cacioppo & Bernston, 1994; Peeters & Czapinski, 1990). Positive and negative emotions not only serve different functions, they are also asymmetrically reflected in consciousness. When negative emotions are salient, they serve to focus consciousness on the factors that produced them. Positive emotions, on the other hand, direct consciousness to higher levels, including those centering on plans, goals, and meanings. This reasoning also suggests that negative emotions have a more enduring quality than positive emotions (cf. Kahneman, Fredrickson, Schreiber, & Redelmeier, 1993). Ongoing integration usually has its temporal limits and the same is true of progression toward a goal. There are no limits, however, on how long a system can remain in an incoherent state or continue to fail in making progress toward a goal.

SELF-REGULATION DYNAMICS IN PERSPECTIVE

Carver and Scheier's account of self-regulation goes beyond traditional models of cybernetics by incorporating many principles and insights from the work on nonlinear dynamical systems. As such, it provides a very broad framework within which a wide variety of important personal and interpersonal phenomena can be considered. Our aim in this comment was to provide additional ideas regarding integration of the cybernetic and dynamical systems account. For the most part, their insights into self-regulation are easily incorporated into an explicitly dynamical framework. Thus, goals may be viewed as attractors in a dynamical system, the hierarchical arrangement of goals represents in more general terms a hierarchy of attractors, changing standards of regulation can be related to changes in the settings of control parameters, and self-regulation generally can be understood in terms of self-control feedback loops between control parameters and system dynamics.

The dynamical systems perspective, however, does more than simply mirror the cybernetic view of self-regulation. Our point instead is that the classic ideas of cybernetics—and of related approaches such as general systems theory (von Bertalanffy, 1968)—can be recast in broader terms in light of developments in the understanding of nonlinear dynamical systems. This allows one to frame self-regulation in terms of the dynamic properties associated with the functioning of any complex system. Thus, self-regulatory phenomena can be understood in terms of such properties as intrinsic dynamics (e.g., periodicity and chaotic evolution), pattern formation and change (e.g., bifurcations), self-organization (e.g., emergent properties), and stability (e.g., attractors and repellers). The dynamical approach is very general, providing basic heuristics for rethinking a host of otherwise diverse phenomena. Indeed, the integrative potential of this perspective has led many to view dynamical systems theory as an integrative vehicle for vastly different realms of scientific understanding, ranging from hydrodynamics and optical physics to ecology, chemistry, and economics. At the same time, this framework provides precise understanding of dynamics and is associated with very sophisticated tools and methods. This combination of breadth and precision means that one can gain highly specific and detailed insight into the invariant properties characterizing complex phenomena across nature.

Carver and Scheier are to be commended for their impressive track record in establishing the heuristic and integrative potential of their model of self-regulation. By adapting the basic principles of cybernetics, they have not only advanced our understanding of many diverse and central topics in psychology over the years, but also they have shown how such topics can be understood within the broader framework of self-regulatory systems. In their target chapter, Carver and Scheier have demonstrated an appreciation for the potential relevance of nonlinear dynamical systems to the themes and issues associated with self-regulation. Although the dynamical perspective is fairly new to social psychology, we believe that this perspective holds potential for reframing self-regulatory processes and, perhaps more important, integrating such processes with other domains of personal and interpersonal experience (cf. Nowak & Vallacher, 1998). With continued theoretical and empirical work on the part of talented scholars like Carver and Scheier, there is reason to be optimistic that this potential will become increasingly manifest in the years to come.

ACKNOWLEDGMENTS

Preparation of this article was supported in part by Grant SBR-11657 from the National Science Foundation, and Grant 1H01F07310 from the Polish Committee for Scientific Research.

REFERENCES

Anderson, J. R. (1990). *Cognitive psychology and its implications* (3rd ed.). New York: W. H. Freeman.

Bargh, J. A. (1997). The automaticity of everyday life. In R. S. Wyer, Jr. (Ed.), *Advances in social cognition* (Vol. 10, pp. 1–61). Mahwah, NJ: Lawrence Erlbaum Associates.

Cacioppo, J. T., & Berntson, G. G. (1994). Relationship between attitudes and evaluative space: A critical review, with emphasis on the separability of positive and negative emotions. *Psychological Bulletin, 115,* 401–423.

Carver, C. S., & Scheier, M. F. (1981). *Attention and self-regulation: A control-theory approach to human behavior.* New York: Springer-Verlag.

Csikszentmihalyi, M. (1990). *Flow: The psychology of optimal experience.* New York: Harper & Row.

Haken, H. (1978). *Synergetics.* Berlin, Germany: Springer.

Hopfield, J. J. (1982). Neural networks and physical systems with emergent collective computational abilities. *Proceedings of the National Academy of Sciences, 79,* 2554–2558.

Kahneman, D., Fredrickson, B. L., Schreiber, C. A., & Redelmeier, D. A. (1993). When more pain is preferred to less: Adding a better end. *Psychological Science, 4,* 401–405.

Kelso, J. A. S. (1995). *Dynamic patterns: The self-organization of brain and behavior.* Cambridge, MA: MIT Press.

Lewenstein, M., & Nowak, A. (1989a). Fully connected neural networks with self-control of noise levels. *Physical Review Letters, 62,* 225–229.

Lewenstein, M., & Nowak, A. (1989b). Recognition with self-control in neural networks. *Physical Review A, 40,* 4652–4664.

Mandler, G. (1964). The interruption of behavior. In D. Levine (Ed.), *Nebraska symposium on motivation* (Vol. 12, pp. 163–219). Lincoln: University of Nebraska Press.

McClelland, J. L., & Rumelhart, D. E. (Eds.). (1986). *Parallel distributed processing: Explorations in the microstructure of cognition* (Vol. 2). Cambridge, MA: MIT Press.

Nowak, A., & Lewenstein, M. (1994). Dynamical systems: A tool for social psychology? In R. R. Vallacher & A. Nowak (Eds.), *Dynamical systems in social psychology* (pp. 17–53). San Diego, CA: Academic Press.

Nowak, A., Lewenstein, M., & Tarkowski, W. (1994). Repellor neural networks. *Physical Review E, 48,* 1491–1498.

Nowak, A., Szamrej, J., & Latané, B. (1990). From private attitude to public opinion: A dynamic theory of social impact. *Psychological Review, 97,* 362–376.

Nowak, A., & Vallacher, R. R. (1998). *Dynamical social psychology.* New York: Guilford.

Oatley, K., & Johnson-Laird, P. N. (1987). Towards a cognitive theory of emotions. *Cognition and Emotion, 1,* 29–50.

Peeters, G., & Czapinski, J. (1990). Positive-negative asymmetry in evaluations: The distinction between affective and informational negativity effects. In W. Stroebe & M. Hewstone (Eds.), *European review of social psychology* (Vol. 1, pp. 33–60). London: Wiley.

Powers, W. T. (1973). *Behavior: The control of perception.* Chicago: Aldine.

Schneider, W., & Shiffrin, R. M. (1977). Controlled versus automatic human information processing: I. Detection, search, and attention. *Psychological Review, 84,* 1–66.

Schuster, H. G. (1984). *Deterministic chaos.* Vienna: Physik Verlag.

Simon, H. A. (1967). Motivational and emotional controls of cognition. *Psychological Review, 74,* 29–39.

Tangney, J. P., & Fischer, K. W. (Eds.). (1995). *Self-conscious emotions: The psychology of shame, guilt, embarrassment, and pride.* New York: Guilford.

Thom, R. (1975). *Structural stability and morphogenesis.* New York: Addison-Wesley.

Vallacher, R. R. (1993). Mental calibration: Forging a working relationship between mind and action. In D. M. Wegner & J. W. Pennebaker (Eds.), *The handbook of mental control* (pp. 443–472). New York: Prentice-Hall.

Vallacher, R. R., & Nowak, A. (Eds.). (1994). *Dynamical systems in social psychology.* San Diego, CA: Academic Press.

Vallacher, R. R., & Nowak, A. (1997). The emergence of dynamical social psychology. *Psychological Inquiry, 8*, 73–99.

Vallacher, R. R., Nowak, A., & Kaufman, J. (1994). Intrinsic dynamics of social judgment. *Journal of Personality and Social Psychology, 67*, 20–34.

Vallacher, R. R., Nowak, A., Markus, J., & Strauss, J. (1998). Dynamics in the coordination of mind and action. In M. Kofta, G. Weary, & G. Sedek (Eds.), *Personal control in action: Cognitive and motivational mechanisms* (pp. 27–59). New York: Plenum.

Vallacher, R. R., & Wegner, D. M. (1987). What do people think they're doing? Action identification and human behavior. *Psychological Review, 94*, 1–15.

Vallacher, R. R., Wegner, D. M., & Somoza, M. P. (1989). That's easy for you to say: Action identification and speech fluency. *Journal of Personality and Social Psychology, 56*, 199–208.

von Bertalanffy, L. (1968). *General system theory.* New York: Braziller.

Wegner, D. M., & Bargh, J. A. (1998). Control and automaticity in social life. In D. Gilbert, S. T. Fiske, & G. Lindzey (Eds.), *Handbook of social psychology* (4th ed., pp. 446–496). Boston: McGraw-Hill.

Wegner, D. M., Vallacher, R. R., Macomber, G., Wood, R., & Arps, K. (1984). The emergence of action. *Journal of Personality and Social Psychology, 46*, 269–279.

Wicklund, R. A. (1986). Orientation to the environment versus preoccupation with human potential. In R. M. Sorrentino & E. T. Higgins (Eds.), *Handbook of motivation and cognition* (Vol. 1, pp. 64–95). New York: Guilford.

Zochowski, M., Lewenstein, M., & Nowak, A. (1993). Memory that tentatively forgets. *Journal of Physics A, 26*, 2453–2460.

Zochowski, M., Lewenstein, M., & Nowak, A. (1995). SMARTNET: A neural network with self-controlled learning. *Network, 6*, 93–101.

11

A Few More Themes, a Lot More Issues: Commentary on the Commentaries

Charles S. Carver
University of Miami

Michael F. Scheier
Carnegie Mellon University

The preceding chapters have raised a number of thought-provoking issues for our consideration. We thank the authors of those chapters for extending the arguments we made, pointing out places where we omitted discussion of processes that are important in their own right, and sometimes gently suggesting that the ideas we presented might not be quite as useful as we seem to think they are. In this reply, we attend mostly to points of disagreement expressed in those chapters. We take this opportunity to clarify some misimpressions we left in the initial chapter (and one outright error), as well as to point to a few conceptual themes that go beyond those we presented earlier.

As several of the commentators noted, the approach we sketched in the target chapter was a structural analysis of behavior rather than a content analysis. It was a depiction of relations among some of the processes we think are always in motion as people live their lives. We think these principles are informative both about adaptive functioning and about problems in functioning. We must acknowledge, however, that there are aspects of the human experience we didn't intend to address with those principles. We also ignored some aspects of human experience that *can* be addressed with the principles, but which require more stretching, or perhaps just greater precision and detail, than we provided earlier. In what follows, another of our goals is to stretch a little further and provide some of that additional detail.

ISSUES REGARDING GOALS AND THEIR USE IN BEHAVIOR

Several points of clarification and elaboration concern the nature of the goal construct. These points range from its causal status, to its breadth of applicability, to several ways in which this construct can be differentiated into subcategories.

Are Goals Actually Involved in Behavior?

A fundamental question, raised by Forgas and Vargas (chap. 3) is whether goals actually have causal status. Perhaps goals are epiphenomena, with no impact on behavior. Vallacher and Nowak (chap. 10) also raised this issue by implication, but from a very different direction. They seemed to suggest that the goal construct may be unnecessary, that self-organizing processes yield behavior that attains particular ends, despite there having been no preexisting goal to make that end come to pass.

We recognize certain merits in the view asserted by Vallacher and Nowak. Certain kinds of actions do seem to emerge without the prior formation of an intention. Certain patterns do seem to be self-organizing. However, we're not ready to recant our commitment to the utility of the goal construct. We don't think *all* activity is self-organizing. We see an interplay in action between self-organizing tendencies and goal-driven tendencies, which we address in more depth later on.[1]

---

[1]Somewhat tangential to this point, though not entirely unrelated to it, is Vallacher and Nowak's suggestion that dynamics per se can account for self-controlling systems (p. 10) in a way that does not require a comparison between the system's current state and a goal. In the model they allude to, a neural network detects its own functionality versus dysfunctionality by observing its dynamics, in the form of an index of the volatility of changes taking place in the network (or the coherence among signals). If the system simply assesses volatility (indicating dysfunction), no explicit comparison is needed. This system will always perceive dysfunction, ranging from zero upward. In contrast, if the system has a threshold for shifting from perceiving functionality to perceiving dysfunction, it would seem to need a comparison of some form to test whether the threshold had been passed. This would return the process to one of goal-related dynamics.

We are less favorably disposed to other criticisms of the goal construct. We don't believe that control over behavior rests in a pattern of reinforcements (Skinner, 1953), except insofar as these reinforcements provided information in the past about the utility of attempts to attain desired ends. Nor are we swayed by McFarland and Bösser (1993), who argued that the notion of goal-directedness is incompatible with what they call the "trade-off principle"—the idea that there is a continual trade-off among the costs and benefits of various possible activities, and the trade-offs are continuously being sorted out as behavior is being conducted. We do not see a problem there. In a system with multiple competing goals in place, all can be monitored (at some level) and managed, with the most demanding or urgent at any given moment being accorded the highest priority. As priorities change, overt behavior shifts its character. Maes (1990) showed how the behavior of such a multiple-goal-seeking system will vary as a function of certain parameters in its prioritizing system. But we see nothing that would make this kind of system inherently unable to deal with the issue on which McFarland and Bösser (1993) focused.

In some measure, however, we would acknowledge that our commitment to the goal construct can be seen as a metatheoretical preference, adopted as something of an article of faith. There is evidence consistent with its plausibility, and the construct fits well with ideas we think have a great deal of predictive utility. As we've said about the feedback construct more generally (Carver & Scheier, 1998), even if it's wrong, it certainly resembles the phenomena of interest well enough to render it useful.

Though most of the authors were comfortable with the goal concept as a central theoretical element, several points of disagreement in the commentaries appear to have arisen from confusions about how we were using it.

Goals Vary Enormously

One point of confusion concerned the breadth of the construct. As we said in the target chapter, our use of the term *goal* is very broad in scope. As we used it there, a goal is isomorphic to a reference value in a feedback loop. Thus, wherever there's a feedback process, there's a goal. The position we argued for is that feedback processes are involved in creation of motor movements (implying a reference value for the intended movement) and that structurally similar processes are involved in attempts to create more abstract actions, including the carrying out of intentions to engage in programs of activity and the attempt to match oneself to one's idealized self-image.

Thus, when Csikszentmihalyi and Nakamura (chap. 2) said that we would presumably agree with them that early in life goals are not the primary reference point against which feedback is evaluated (p. 2-2), they were quite wrong. The goals in place during that period of life are primitive and restricted, but an infant's behavior is certainly an attempt to attain desired states. Indeed, just after saying that goals are not the primary reference point early in life, Csikszentmihalyi and Nakamura said that early in life behavior is regulated by the "intent" to optimize experiential states. Whether that particular intent is what motivates the infant or not (which can be debated), an intent means a goal.

Our broader point here is this: There seems to us to be a continuity of form or structure that spans the cases of primitive or concrete goals (the goal of grasping an object), more abstract ones (continue to engage in activities you enjoy), and even more abstract ones (try to be the kind of person you want to be). This continuity of structure suggests a common conceptual core.

The examples that Csikszentmihalyi and Nakamura (chap. 2) invoke to try to show either that goals are not necessary or that they emerge from experience show principally that goals can be synthesized (or stumbled across) from experience with other goals. The quotation they offered from Pauling says that he never sat down and asked himself what he was going to do in life; he just went ahead doing things he liked to do. The latter (the things he liked to do) were clearly programmatic goals. They were smaller in scale and less ambitious than the goal of winning a Nobel prize (a goal which he may never have adopted), but they were goals nonetheless.

This particular illustration raises interesting questions about the level of abstraction at which goal pursuits are managed most efficiently (e.g., is it more effective to "do things you like to do" or to "plan a career"?). It also raises an interesting point about self-organization and emergence of a quality of behavior—Nobel-prize-worthiness—from an ongoing stream of lower level activity. But it certainly doesn't argue against the utility of the goal construct.

Ryan and Deci (chap. 7), emphasizing core aspects of self-regulation, argued that goals are servants of a more basic phenomenon—the physical and psychological needs of the organism. Our position is that those needs themselves constitute goals. If you want to create in your life an approximation to the condition of relatedness or autonomy, then that condition (relatedness or autonomy) is serving as a reference value. It's helping you guide your efforts at attaining it.

The idea that all goals are the same in some structural respects does *not* imply that they are the same in *all* important respects. Means and ends are both goals, but goals of different types. Goals can concern the overall sense of self, they can concern what to do next while following a recipe. A goal can be to demonstrate a skill, it can be to expand or stretch a skill. These various qualities all are goals, but they are all different from one another in important ways. Although we touched on some of these differences in the earlier chapter, we didn't dwell on them, partly because they haven't been the focus of our thinking and partly because we already were trying to include more than one chapter would hold. The differences, however, are important. Let us briefly consider some of the differences noted by the other authors and how (and whether) they fit with our thinking.

Demonstration of Skill Versus Extension of Skill

Grant and Dweck (chap. 5) presented a very straightforward description of an important difference between two types of goals, both of which seem to exist at more or less the same level of abstraction in the kind of goal hierarchy we discussed. Grant and Dweck were careful to make it clear that the distinction they were pointing to differs from the notion of domain specificity (e.g., achievement versus social goals). Rather, it's a content difference that cuts across domains. In previous work these have been termed *learning* goals and *performance* goals (a pair of labels we prefer to the terms *development* goals and *judgment* goals, which are broader but to us seem less evocative and more ambiguous). The learning goal is to acquire skill in some domain, whereas the performance goal is to demonstrate the existence of the skill.

It's clear that these types of goals predict different patterns of behavior, both in terms of information sought out about a potential task and in terms of emotional and behavioral responses to the task. These latter differences are particularly pronounced when the person's task-directed efforts are leading to failure. We agree that these differences are important. However, we would also argue that these differences among goal orientations do not fundamentally alter the structure of behavior. Rather, we think they involve variations in the parameters that surround the behavior.

That is, both kinds of goal orientations lead to positive feelings and continued effort when the relevant goal is being attained. Although there is less evidence on this point, we are also certain that both goal orientations will lead to negative feelings and reduction in effort when the relevant goal is *not* being attained. It will usually take longer to realize that no progress is being made toward a learning goal than it takes to realize that no progress is being made toward a performance goal. Thus, the two kinds of situations will typically have different time courses. Nonetheless, a continued failure to make progress toward learning must eventually yield the sense of a failure to learn. Thus, although a disengagement response to failure is likely to take longer to develop for learning goals, we believe the structure of the processes remains the same.

Probably our greatest disagreement with Grant and Dweck (chap. 5) in this regard concerns affect that arises during goal pursuit. Again, despite a difference in pacing, we see no difference in structure regarding the generation of affect. In either case, positive affect comes from doing well at what you are trying to do. In the process of displaying a skill you want to have, you experience positive feelings. In the process of moving forward in the acquisition of a desired skill, you experience positive feelings.

In arguing for a structural difference, Grant and Dweck used the example of a competitive sports event, a situation that's infused with the character of a performance goal (i.e., it's an attempt to demonstrate that you have desired skills). They focused there on the outcome of the event—winning or losing. But it's important to recognize that the event isn't just its end point. It takes place over a period of time and activity. Do athletes experience no affect until the final gun sounds?

As two former athletes who were at one time invested in demonstrating skills in sports, we can state unequivocally that that's not the case. Affective responses occur throughout the contest. Joy (and pride) come with each dominating play in, for example, a football game. Frustration, anxiety, and even shame arise when one is losing ground. All of those way stations in the ebb and flow of the contest have implications for evaluation of one's ability, and they can all be viewed as markers of progress or regress. Structurally, they are no different (in this respect, at least) from progress and regress with respect to skill acquisition.

Extension and Validation as a Developmental Sequence

Pomerantz and Altermatt (chap. 6) also addressed the two classes of learning and performance goals, noting that they seem to display a developmental sequence. That is, they said that younger children tend to be more likely to have learning goals, with a developmental shift toward performance goals later on (although certainly there are great individual differences at any age). We find this apparent developmental progression quite interesting.

Pomerantz and Altermatt suggested a number of possible bases for the shift, but one thing they didn't point out is that there is an actual developmental shift in the fluidity and malleability of skills (at least, many types of skills). The rate of change in children's skills of virtually all types is very rapid early in life; farther along in life the changes become more gradual.

There apparently are also certain opportunities for skill acquisition that are very accessible early in life and become less so later on (e.g., learning of a second language). Although change does continue to occur, with most adults continuing to learn new skills throughout life, much of the skill base of adulthood does have more of an entity character than does the skill base of early childhood. Perhaps this is what causes many older children and adults to lose track of the fact that skills *can* be acquired.

Goal Importance

Another goal-related issue that came up in the commentaries concerns the determinants of relative goal importance. Forgas and Vargas (chap. 3) took issue with the general assumption that "be" goals tend to be more important than "do" goals. This assumption on our part was a rule of thumb. Strongly implied in our discussion was that the real issue behind importance is the strength or directness of the link between the behavioral goal and the core of the self (for a broader treatment see Carver & Scheier, 1998).

This view is illustrated graphically in Fig. 11.1. We assume that a very important concrete behavioral goal is important because it links strongly to the core of the self. We also assume, however, that the link between an important concrete goal and the core of the self typically travels through

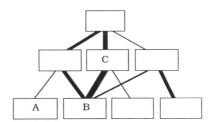

FIG. 11.1. Importance accrues to a given concrete action goal in either of two ways. The action can contribute in a major way to the attainment of a higher order goal (indicated here by a thicker line), or the action can contribute to several higher order goals at once (indicated here by a larger number of upward projections). On both of these criteria, concrete action goal A is relatively unimportant, whereas B is more important. Ultimately, the importance of these action goals concerns their relation to the core ideal self, at the top of the hierarchy. Thus, the importance of a concrete goal is also reflected in the importance of the more abstract values (e.g., C) between it and the ideal self. *Note*: Adapted from *On the Self-Regulation of Behavior* (p. 90), by C. S. Carver and M. F. Scheier, 1998, New York: Cambridge University Press. Adapted with permission.

an intermediate "be" value, which is also important—indeed, more important than the corresponding "do" goal, because its link to the core self is more direct.

Forgas and Vargas went on to make the suggestion that the frequency with which a goal is reflected in behavior should be a criterion for whether the goal is included in the self. In certain respects this idea makes intuitive sense: If you play softball often and go bowling twice a year, the chances are your softball-player role is more a part of your self than your bowler role. The problem with this suggestion concerns the confluence of importance and abstractness. A person who has a habitual tic, or a habitual gesture, makes that movement with great frequency. Actions directed toward goals at a higher level of abstraction (e.g., being honest) are probably less frequent and may be more consciously regulated. Does the frequency of the tic mean that the tic is more a part of the self than the honesty? Do Forgas and Vargas mean to suggest that habitual goals are part of the self and goals whose attainment must be consciously regulated are not? (p. 3-3).

Goals Can Be Dynamic

Our statement in the target chapter about goals as a psychological construct was abbreviated in several ways. One of the more important abbreviations was our light treatment of the idea that goals are not just static end points, but often are dynamic in nature, consisting of complex activities played out across an extended period of time. This point deserves re-emphasis, in light of remarks in the commentaries. For example, although one goal of mountain climbing might well be to be standing at the top of the mountain, that's often not the main goal of the activity. The main goal is to create the experiences of doing the climbing. In this case, it is the "going" that is the goal of the activity rather than the "arriving."

The same is true of many human activities, which are conducted because the activity itself is desirable. The goal of a vacation trip is not to be at its endpoint, but to undergo the experiences that the trip incorporates. The goal of playing a concerto is to create the multiple experiences that playing of music can create. Indeed, many human goals are continuous and never ending, for example, the goal of acting honorably when dealing with other people or the goal of having a good relationship with your spouse. These are goals toward which people are always trying to move, and which they never have the experience of reaching once and for all. The fact that these goals are dynamic makes it harder to create a mental image of certain structural aspects of the broader model. For example, it's harder to get a feel for what it means to have a high velocity toward the goal of having a good relationship than toward the goal of finishing a report. But this is a challenge that we must confront, because the dynamic quality of certain goals is beyond question.

Development of Self-Regulatory Skills

We turn next to two points raised by Pomerantz and Altermatt (chap. 6) about issues in development. As personality psychologists with virtually no training in developmental psychology, we've avoided thinking very hard about developmental issues. Clearly, they are important, but we don't have much confidence that we would have any idea where to start in thinking about them. It was heartening, then, to see ideas in the thinking of these developmental psychologists that mesh well with some of the themes we raised in the target chapter.

Pomerantz and Altermatt discussed several kinds of skill acquisition in development, suggesting that they moderate the flow of self-regulatory processes. We concur. We have a slightly different interpretation of the phenomena that Pomerantz and Altermatt described than the interpretation they presented, but our view is not fundamentally at odds with their suggestions.

We don't think that younger children are less likely than older children to compare their actual and intended actions (or at least not so unlikely as to indicate an inactive comparator). We suspect that the difference is largely in the nature of the representations of both actual and reference values, and in the error sensitivity of the comparator. Younger children are probably making sloppier comparisons, using perceptions of their current actions that are more positively biased, and comparing them to less well-developed intentions than are older children. Younger children have difficulties decoding social feedback and thus rely on different cues than do older children. Rather than an inactive comparator, however, we would guess that the comparisons are simply more lax and less precise. The regulatory process is loose, flexible, and not as closely tied to objective reality.

Dynamic Systems and Changes in Interdependent Domains

Something we found to be of particular interest in the Pomerantz and Altermatt chapter (chap. 6) concerns the dynamic notion of sensitive dependence on initial conditions. They suggest that individual differences in the timing of various changes (discontinuous jumps forward) can lead to substantial differences in overall self-regulatory implications. This is because changes of several types—all of which ultimately are needed—are not necessarily mutually entrained. That is, they don't come as a package. Thus, a child who experiences one change early (developmentally) and another change late may have very different experiences (and wind up with a different orientation to some important aspect of life) than a child who experienced the two changes at more or less the same time, or in the opposite order. This view on the patterning of changes raises very interesting possibilities for thinking about social and emotional development more generally.

Goals and Feedback Processes

Finally, a point about how goals are used in behavior. A basic construct in the view we outlined in the target chapter is the feedback loop. Most of the commentaries addressed issues in such a way as to indicate understanding of the nature of this construct, but this did not appear to be entirely true of the Csikszentmihalyi and Nakamura (chap. 2) commentary. They said that in their view "past experience" should replace "goal, standard, reference value" in the schematic of the feedback loop. The loop then would operate to try to make present experience conform to past experience (p. 2-3).

It is not at all clear to us why they would want to say that. Such a transformation would have the effect of transforming all of human behavior into an effort to recreate prior experiences. Those authors surely wouldn't want to suggest that human behavior is an effort to recapture infantile experience. We would agree that sometimes people's actions are undertaken to create an experience that's similar to one from the past, but certainly not always.

Csikszentmihalyi and Nakamura said later in the same section that if the comparison between present and past experiences is "in favor of" the present experience, the goal becomes maintaining that state. In a feedback loop, however, the result of the comparison is not to "favor" one value or the other, but to determine whether they are the same or not. This characterization thus suggests a misunderstanding of the basic nature of the feedback process.

WHERE DO NEW GOALS COME FROM?

As several of the commentators pointed out, our target chapter left relatively untouched the question of where goals come from, particularly new goals. The creation of new goals (indeed, the evolution of the hierarchical organization) is not a subject about which we have written much. It is a question that clearly demands more attention than we gave it there.

New Goals Transformed From Old Ones

There's one respect in which our target chapter did address creation of new goals, by discussing the shifting of old ones. That is, we talked about how goals that aren't being attained are sometimes scaled back to be less demanding. Similarly, goals that are being attained too easily are sometimes raised to be more demanding. Making these changes allows the person to continue in the same general domain of activity, at a level that's both challenging and attainable. The goal isn't the same as it was, although it bears on the same domain or content as it did before.

This doesn't take us very far into the creation of new goals, but it's a start. Another small step in the direction of new goals comes from thinking about the case where the person engages in an activity (e.g., going to a gym to work out) for one purpose (to lose weight) and finds that it also satisfies a second purpose (making new friends). The activity thereby acquires a second kind of usefulness and becomes connected to a different higher goal than it was connected to before.[2] It has evolved a new link upward in the goal hierarchy. The behavioral goal (going to the gym and exercising) already was a goal, and thus isn't new itself. But its broader implications are now different—perhaps quite different—than they were. It has a different psychological "feel" now. This change in its connectedness is a small step into newness, but not a trivial one.

New Goals When New Acts Turn Out to Satisfy Higher Needs

Usually, however, when people raise the question of how new goals are acquired, they have in mind new goals that differ qualitatively from those a person has pursued thus far. Unquestionably, people do take up altogether new goals from time to time. How does this happen? Although

---

[2]Sometimes an activity that's done for one purpose continues to be conducted even when that purpose no longer exists (or no longer is served by that activity). The activity is then said to have acquired *functional autonomy*. Something about the activity itself has become desirable enough to continue it for its own sake. An interesting question is whether in such cases the activity continues simply because nothing has countermanded it or whether something about its execution remains pleasurable, either by virtue of its prior association with its earlier purpose, or because this activity has become enmeshed with goals other than the one that originally sustained it.

other processes are also sometimes at work, we think these cases also depend partly on hierarchicality.

In many cases, the new activity is undertaken precisely because it has been preidentified in some way as potentially relevant to a higher order goal in the person's life. For example, a person who likes exploration and learning about different ways of life may decide to undertake a vacation tour of Europe or Asia, or try scuba diving, or experiment with bicycle racing. In each case, the new activity is approached because it's been identified as a possible means to satisfy the desire (the goal) of exploration. Someone who doesn't like exploration is far less likely to undertake a tour of Europe voluntarily, and indeed may have to be dragged there kicking and screaming.

Exploration provides an easy illustration, but it's certainly not the only higher level desire that can lead to new activities. Any time someone says "You ought to try this—I think you might enjoy it," an inference is being made that the activity will satisfy a broader desire the person has. Any time people contemplate undertaking a new activity, they are considering how that activity might fit into their current patterns of preferences.

Self-Organization and New Goals

The examples in the previous section were cases in which a link was somehow prespecified between the "new" goal and an existing one. Sometimes, though, an activity seems to come together without forethought or planning and (upon its occurrence) is found to be enjoyable. In such a case, the person may seek to identify the activity's essence, so as to make the positive experience repeatable. Thus, it becomes a new goal. Such a process seems to have been at least alluded to in several commentaries, in discussing where new goals come from (Csikszentmihalyi and Nakamura, chap. 2) and in discussing how people sometimes infer their goals from their behavior (Forgas and Vargas, chap. 3). This process has a flavor of self-assembly and emergence that is also very consonant with Vallacher and Nowak's (chap. 10) discussion of dynamics in behavior.

We would agree that there seem to be elements of bottom-up self-organization of the new experience in such a case. We would also point out explicitly that the bottom-up quality is not the end of the line when a new goal is being acquired in this way. Rather, the person comes to encode the nature of the experience in memory in a manner that renders it accessible to top-down use later on. Thus, the effort to repeat the broad outlines of the experience (which seems to be the operational definition of having acquired a new goal for behavior) has the characteristics of feedback control.

Furthermore, we would suggest that even in this bottom-up self-organizing experience there's an absolutely crucial element that the other authors all disregarded. In particular, there's a need to account for why the new experience is "enjoyable." It's easy to allude to "enjoyable new experiences," but there must be a mechanism *behind* the enjoyment, to explain *why* it's enjoyable. Most new experiences aren't wired directly to the pleasure centers of the brain. Given a particular experience, some will find it enjoyable, others won't. As we noted earlier, a tour of Europe will be enjoyable to a person with a desire to explore, but not to a person who likes things to stay the same.

Finding an experience enjoyable, we suggest, means that engaging in the experience serves to move the person toward another goal that's already in place as part of the self. The person may have had no idea beforehand that the new activity was going to connect to that already incorporated goal. But because it does connect, the experience of the new activity creates positive affect. Thus, a new action, as well as an old one, can fairly quickly acquire an upward link to a higher order goal. A given principle (for example) can be fulfilled in myriad activities, even activities that might at first not have seemed relevant to the principle.

Csikszentmihalyi and Nakamura's (chap. 2) example of the social activist is a good illustration of how a single principle can be manifested in multiple programs of action. The principle didn't change as the person's patterns of actions took on a new focus. She simply learned that one pattern of activity was ineffective at maintaining conformity to the principle and subsequently shifted to a new activity that seemed to be better at creating that desired conformity. Different programs are often used to manifest the same principle, depending on the situation the person encounters.

How did that new pattern of activity come to be organized and represented in this person's repertoire of potential activities? We suspect that part of the answer is that there was a self-organizing tendency from lower levels (or a sideways inducement from friends) and that part of the answer is that the beginnings of the activity (when first begun) created a discernable discrepancy reduction with respect to this principle.

Two Modes of Functioning

It has not been part of our thinking until quite recently, but we suspect that the evolution of a person's goals involves both top-down self-regulation with regard to principles and programs and bottom-up synthesis of new patterns of organization of action. Our experience of creating this chapter was, in fact, an interesting exercise in how the two tendencies can converge in behavior. Our work on the chapter was guided by several abstract principles (e.g., to be as clear as possible; to spend most effort on countering the strongest critiques; to frame replying arguments in a conciliatory manner; to write with style), not all of which were perfectly compatible. We also engaged fairly often in a top-down application of theoretical principles in framing the arguments. These influences all suggest an upper level executive control process behind the behavior.

But the writing was also guided by the bottom-up emergence of ideas to implement and tacks to take. We had the experience of sitting, thinking about the ideas raised in the commentaries we had been provided, waiting for a response to surface and take over our thinking. It was *not* the case that the responses we ended up writing were always obvious to us at first. And even when the general form of the response was clear, there often were multiple potential pathways to take in creating the reply. The subjective experience we had while crafting this chapter was often very much that of settling into a kind of mutual satisfaction of multiple constraints (cf. Read, Vanman, & Miller, 1997; Thagard, 1989).[3]

The idea that two rather different modes of functioning coexist in every person (discussed in greater detail in chap. 17 of Carver & Scheier, 1998) is not ours. As we pointed out in the target chapter, there are several two-mode models of behavior in personality–social psychology and others in cognitive psychology. Despite their presence, the impact of these theories has not yet been felt as widely as perhaps it should. This is a theme that we suspect is going to command considerably more attention in the coming years.

Comparisons to Other Views

Our account of where new goals come from is different in form from the accounts that were suggested by others in their commentaries, but we are not sure the principles are so very different. Ryan and Deci (chap. 7) said that the self begins with innate elements (presumably needs for autonomy, relatedness, and congruence) and evolves through processes of "internalization" and "integration." But what are these processes, and under what conditions do they occur?

---

[3]Which mode of control dominated the activity varied from phase to phase, but rarely was the activity all one mode or the other. In some periods, the activity was largely principle-driven, with brief intrusions of novel organizational ideas, examples, or the occasional stray impulse to go for someone's throat (which generally then was overridden by the principle of conciliation). There were also periods, however, in which bottom-up self-organization was the more dominant mode.

We would argue that goals and values become internalized and integrated to the extent that engaging in the activities to which they pertain fosters a reduction of discrepancies with regard to core values of the self, yielding a greater degree of coherence within the self. This is similar to saying that activities (and their goal representations) are added to the person's behavioral repertoire to the extent they turn out to facilitate attainment of higher order goals, as suggested earlier.

Ryan and Deci wrote, "interpersonal environments that allow satisfaction of the [core] psychological needs are theorized to promote healthier, more effective functioning, and in particular to promote the internalization and integration of goals and regulatory processes." (p. 7-6) This passage makes the process sound to us too passive and unconnected—too much like "put the person in the right environment and the things he's doing (whatever they are) will become absorbed into the self." It may be that they meant to imply that the goals and regulatory processes mentioned are moving the person toward congruence regarding core needs. If so, it would be consistent with the point made just earlier. It seems important, however, to be quite explicit about that underlying assumption: that the goals in question must be enhancing congruence within the self. Without this principle, we see no obvious basis for the absorption of the goals into the self.

Csikszentmihalyi and Nakamura (chap. 2) asked what conditions might foster the emergence of new goals, such as transition points in the life course. However, they provided little indication of how the process of goal emergence occurs. Later in their comment, they said that action leads to affect, which leads to goals. They wrote that new goals arise because "they provide experiences that, in comparison to the person's baseline, are emotionally more positive," (p. 2-4) but without indicating what makes the experiences more positive. They wrote that people who are doing things they enjoy are enjoying those activities because these are "experiential goals." (p. 2-9) With all due respect, this would seem to be a clear case of deus ex machina. It certainly does not provide an understanding of *why* enjoyment should derive selectively from experiential goals.

Nor does it even seem fully accurate. Do people really develop goals only if they initially experience positive affect in actions pertinent to the goal? How would Csikszentmihalyi and Nakamura account for the child whose first experience with football was filled with misery and tears, but who eventually acquired the goal of playing the game at the highest level? Although we haven't collected accounts of diverse people the way Csikszentmihalyi (1996) has, this example comes from the life of a National Football League player whom we happen to know slightly.

We would, in fact, suggest that many goals are acquired through a path of initial frustration and negative feelings, leading to efforts to acquire greater competence and only later to emergence of positive affect. A key question here—unaddressed by Csikszentmihalyi and Nakamura—is *under what conditions is the person in this situation willing to keep exerting effort, over what may be an extended period of time, in order for the positive feelings eventually to arise?* Our view is that this will happen when the activity has a clear connection to a higher order goal. In the case of the football player in our example, an important factor appears to have been the desire to make his father proud. (The activity thus may have been undertaken at first for controlled reasons. Once in place, however, it proved to satisfy more intrinsic desires as well.)

ISSUES PERTAINING TO AFFECT

The previous section began to raise some questions about affect. In fact, many of the issues that were raised in the commentaries pertain, directly or indirectly, to the affect model presented in our target chapter. Some of these points, which are addressed in the following sections, involve clarifications; others require us to extend our reasoning beyond the earlier presentation.

What Causes Positive Affect?

What makes positive feelings arise? We made our best guess about the answer to this question in the target chapter. Not everyone agreed with us. However, neither was there a great outpouring of suggested alternative mechanisms. Csikszentmihalyi and Nakamura wrote a good deal in their chapter (chap. 2) about positive feelings and optimizing of experience. They said "it is important to agree on what constitutes positive affect," (p. 2-7) but they provided very little information on what they think it is, or on the further question of where they think it comes from. What they did say appears to raise more questions than it answers.

They said that mountain climbers experience joy not because they are making good progress toward the peak, but because "they are meeting the challenges of the climb" (p. 2-7). But what does "meeting the challenges of the climb" *mean*? Climbing experiences are not identical. There's no single universal challenge that's either met or not met. If you are going more slowly than you had planned, aren't you failing to meet the challenge of the climb as well as you had expected? If you are climbing with no errors, making good time (compared to your expectations), wouldn't you be meeting the challenge of the climb quite well? Freedom from errors, smoothness of execution, doing things you weren't sure you could do, making good time—all these qualities would seem to be involved in the emergent sense of "meeting the challenges of the climb." Meeting the challenge well (as an aggregate of all these qualities)—at a rapid enough pace—results in a good feeling.

Csikszentmihalyi and Nakamura (chap. 2) also wrote that people feel best when they fulfill their potentialities. That seems wrong. We think people feel their best when they *exceed* what they had thought were their potentialities (overshoot the reference value). Surely exceeding your previously perceived potential feels better than simply matching it.

Responses to Positive Affect

Another misunderstanding of the affect portion of the model (its cruise control aspect) concerns the response to positive feelings it incorporates. We said in the target chapter that we think positive feeling leads to coasting. Several readers inferred that we meant by this a conscious decision to ease back and coast. Although there are probably cases in which such a conscious decision process occurs, that was not our point. We were arguing that the human organism is organized in such a way as to induce this tendency to coast. We would suggest that the attempt to keep going at a rapid pace gets harder and harder to maintain as it continues. The result is a kind of enforced coasting.

Do people coast? There isn't a lot of hard evidence on the question, but at least a little support exists for our assertion (Melton, 1995; Mizruchi, 1991). The question is obviously one that deserves further scrutiny.

Velocity and Affect: Faster Is Not Always Better

The notion of velocity control also raised some problems. Our discussion of a velocity loop somehow led Csikszentmihalyi and Nakamura (chap. 2) to misinfer that the model incorporates the principle that faster is better. Sometimes faster is better, but the goal of this loop isn't usually to make things happen as fast as possible. Rather, the velocity goal is a rate value that's appropriate to the activity. This setting manages the flow of activity with respect to external demands, or with respect to the person's habitual flow of that sort of activity, or with respect to whatever other issues are relevant to the activity.

Csikszentmihalyi and Nakamura asked in this context whether the pi-ano player is trying to play the piece as fast as possible. Of course not. Nor is she trying to play it as slowly as possible. In the case of the concerto, too fast is bad, too slow is bad. But why? Why is any particular pace prefer-able to any other pace? Why do musical scores include information about recommended pace? Because the writer of the music believed that a par-ticular pace represents an optimal speed for that set of musical passages.

The pianist typically tries to play at a pace that approximates the ideal. If she tries to play at a pace different from the one specified by the com-poser, why does she do so? Because she perceives that the alternate pace sounds better. Whatever value is identified as most pleasing (whether by composer or performer) becomes the reference point for the pacing loop. Too fast (compared to that criterion) is bad, too slow (compared to that criterion) is bad.

To even raise this question in the first place is to ignore a critical element of the affect model, which we thought was clearly spelled out in the target chapter. The model doesn't hold that faster is better. It holds that there is an implicit (or explicit) reference point for velocity. Slower than the reference point is worse; faster than the reference point is, in a sense, also worse.

Affect From Dynamic Goals and Time-Dependent Goals

The case of piano playing does, however, raise another set of issues. They stem in part from the fact that, in this particular behavior, pace is an element of the *behavioral* goal—to play the concerto as written. That is, pacing of notes is part of the action goal, without even considering the existence of a meta-level goal. This action goal is intrinsically time related. When an activity is intrinsically paced in time, doing it either too fast or too slow deviates from the behavioral intention. Such a deviation does have an impact at the meta level as well. If the pianist goes either too slow or too fast, she's thereby losing ground in her effort to execute her intention. Thus, either of these behavioral deviations also yields a negative discrepancy at the meta level (and negative affect).

What permits the person engaged in this kind of activity to ever feel *good*? Our tentative answer to that question shows how tricky the veloc-ity concept can be. Sometimes velocity is obviously literal. Sometimes—when the behavioral goals are dynamic rather than static—it seems al-most metaphysical—or at least a lot harder to pin down. Our intuition suggests to us two things about how good feelings can arise during the playing of a concerto. First, if the pianist realizes she is playing too slowly and speeds up to the intended pace, the speedup should feel good. In the same way, if she realizes she's going too fast and slows down, the slowdown should feel good. The "shifting-back-on-track" experience (in its many potential aspects) should yield good feelings.

Our second intuition is that the velocities that will be of greatest issue for the fairly skilled pianist bear on dynamic goal qualities the activity incorporates. The pianist will be intending to create qualities that are emergent from a confluence of many sources—qualities such as the languid sense of legato, the drawn out sense of suspense, or the exhilaration of a stirring climax. The quality she is striving for will, of course, depend partly on the piece being played. But we think the positive feeling that comes from the playing of the piece (as opposed, for example, to positive feelings that come from knowing you have an appreciative audience) comes largely from velocity toward those harder-to-pin-down goals.[4]

We are aware that this answer will not be completely satisfying to everyone. This is one of the places where working with this model is admittedly difficult.

Action and Affect; Perception and Affect

In our target chapter, we emphasized that affect arises with respect to progress in self-regulation regarding behavioral discrepancies. Although none of the commentaries raised this issue, we'd like to point out that other kinds of discrepancies besides behavioral exist. For example, a person may have difficulty assimilating a traumatic experience (or even just a very unusual experience) to his or her understanding of reality. This inability to assimilate would leave a discrepancy between what the person believes about life and what the person has experienced (cf. Martin & Tesser, 1996).

It may be that resolution of these kinds of discrepancies also contributes to affect. While the experience remains unassimilated, negative affect is being created, because there's no progress toward bringing the two together. When the experience finally fits to a schema—is suddenly interpretable—there is immediate (high velocity) closing of the gap and a positive feeling. A similar process can be seen in the reorganization of perceptual field so that a perception comes into focus (e.g., the popular pictures that are printed in such a way as to permit viewers to resolve

---

[4]We are addressing this issue more or less as it was raised by Csikszentmihalyi and Nakamura: in the context of what is presumably a fairly skilled pianist playing a piece she knows well. In some cases, however, other dynamic goals may be more salient than the ones we are discussing here. For example, happiness for the child who has a learning goal may derive from how quickly progress is made in learning to play this concerto.

them into three-dimensional images), the sudden realization of "who-dunnit" in a mystery story or movie, and the realistic assimilation of a person's experiences while reading a novel.

A similar mechanism may underlie the positive feelings that arise from humor. A common approach to understanding humor is an arousal-release model (Wyer & Collins, 1992). That is, an instance of experienced humor entails a sudden shift of some sort, which is sometimes viewed as a release of tension. We wonder whether this shift is better construed as a brief acceleration. The shift has to be abrupt in order for the event to be experienced as humor. And it seems to be the shift of the mental reorganization that constitutes the sense of amusement.

In some respects, this shift is like the reorganization of a reversing figure. Something else apparently is required beyond reorganization per se, however, or people would laugh at reversing figures. It's not entirely clear what the further requirement is, but at least a couple of possibilities have been suggested.

Suls (1972) likened humor appreciation to problem solving: When you "get" the joke, there's a sudden lurch to solution. The harder the "problem" (i.e., the less obvious is the punch line), the greater is the lurch and the greater the humor. This model suggests that the experience of humor comes from a sudden resolution to a construal that makes more sense of the situation than existed before.

Apter (1982) argued that the newly reached construal must somehow be less important than the previously apparent one. This "diminishment" criterion means that the end point must be more mundane than what existed before, or perhaps more favorable to the self. Diminishing someone else is good, because it creates a relative rise for oneself. A loss of importance for someone else eliminates a potential challenge to oneself. In either of these events, there would be a basis for suggesting creation of positive affect.

Simultaneity of Action Control and Affect Creation

Another point of clarification we must make concerns the simultaneous nature of goal pursuit and affect generation. In our view, the two kinds of loops are intrinsically linked—not requiring shifting of attention from one to the other, as Csikszentmihalyi and Nakamura (chap. 2) seemed to assume. Furthermore, we don't believe the affect-generating loop entails the kind of abstract cognitive synthesis that Forgas and Vargas (chap. 3) and Gollwitzer and Rohloff (chap. 4) seemed to assume. We don't regard the affect creation system as a "high level inferential [process]" (chap. 3, p. 3-6). We regard it as an automatic process that occurs right along with action. The evaluation of goal-related performance is continuous and implicit, rather than consciously pondered only on specific occasions.[5]

We devoted our discussion of affect in the target chapter to trying to create an accurate image of the micro-level processes that we think underlie the creation of the feeling quality itself. We wanted to deal there as well as we could with a number of issues and questions that we know are commonly raised about the model. However, the detailed, micro-level depiction fails to do justice to the immediacy of the experience that we are assuming these processes create.

We believe that as a person falls behind with regard to something that's in mind to do (get the oil changed in the car), the person begins to feel a slight, nagging displeasure. The person puts more effort into fulfilling that intention (takes a half-hour off work to get that chore attended to), and the displeasure is replaced by a positive feeling of satisfaction. Turning to another intention for the day—this one work related—the person spends two hours on a report and is surprised to see it's in better shape than expected. The person carries the positive feeling that comes from the sense of moving forward on that task into the next topic that comes to mind: his relationship with his kids, which has been a little rocky lately. The happy sense of progress from the report may spill over into a sense of confidence that he can make amends, and he thinks about how a day of family fun at the lake may be a good way to start. This person's experience through the day is a continuing flow of shifting action and shifting affect, as one goal after another comes to mind and is addressed either well or poorly. The flow of action and the flow of affect are simultaneous and continuous.

This merging of affect and action appears to have important functional properties (see also Carver & Scheier, 1998, chap. 8). The mutual operation of a position loop and a velocity loop has been studied in detail by control engineers. In the engineering context, this arrangement is often used to produce quick-yet-stable responses in mechanical and electronic devices. A velocity loop can have divergent consequences for a position loop (Clark, 1996, chaps. 7 & 10), however, depending on the degree of "damping" the velocity system creates for the response of the position system. Damping varies with the velocity system's sensitivity.

---

[5]This is not to say that more deliberative processing never occurs. As we noted in the target chapter, people sometimes interrupt the ongoing flow of behavior and consider more carefully their chances of being able to succeed at the task they are pursuing. Such a deliberative process may well have an influence on subsequent affect. Our discussion here, however, focuses on the online creation of affect during action.

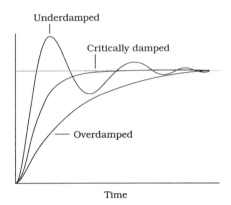

FIG. 11.2. Deviations of a position-regulating system from its reference value as a function of three sensitivities of a velocity-regulating system. In the *overdamped* case, the system responds slowly, but eventually settles in on the reference value (the gray line). In the *underdamped* case, the system responds quickly, but it overshoots, then oscillates, before eventually settling in on the reference value. In the *critically damped* case, the system responds moderately quickly and reaches the reference value without overshooting or oscillating. In all three cases, the system eventually reaches the reference value but after different patterns of behavior. *Note*: From On the Self-Regulation of Behavior (p. 144), by C. S. Carver and M. F. Scheier, 1998, New York: Cambridge University Press. Reprinted with permission.

In what's called an *overdamped* case, the position system responds sluggishly, moving to its goal value slowly (see Fig. 11.2). In an *underdamped* case, the position system responds very quickly but overcompensates, overshoots its goal, then oscillates around it, gradually closing in on it. The ideal case, called *critically damped*, is a compromise between these two. It creates a relatively rapid response (though not as rapid as the underdamped case) with little or no overshoot. Thus, when the velocity loop is properly "tuned," responses are comparatively quick but also stable (i.e., without oscillations).

What does any of this have to do with feelings and behavior? These cases appear to parallel the influence of differences in emotional reactivity. The overdamped case corresponds to a person who is emotionally very unreactive. It takes this person's behavior a long time to return to its reference point. The underdamped case corresponds to a person who is highly reactive emotionally. The strong emotional response in this person leads to overcompensation. If this person is "behind" (sad or anxious), he speeds up sharply; if he's "ahead" (happy or relieved), he may stop trying altogether. Each of these responses then leads to deviations in the opposite direction (provoking the opposite emotional and behavioral response).

The ideal case, critical damping, corresponds to a person who is emotionally reactive but not *too* reactive. This person responds fairly quickly to the perturbation (the emotional responsiveness promotes quick responses), but he doesn't overrespond in such a way as to throw himself into behavioral oscillation (the moderate damping keeps his responses fairly stable). This person responds quickly but appropriately to an emotion-inducing event.

What Is Flow and What Circumstances Elicit It?

This discussion of issues surrounding affect may be an appropriate place to mention the construct of *flow*. The flow experience is an engagement and total absorption in some activity. Our inference from descriptions of flow is that the person is fully focused on the activity and that the activity is not being interrupted either by intrusions of unrelated thoughts or by stepping aside to engaged in deliberative expectancy assessment. Rather, the action continues unimpeded.

Csikszentmihalyi and Nakamura (chap. 2) said that flow occurs when the person is simultaneously experiencing high environmental challenge and perception of high skills. Their statement was framed in terms of absolute skills or abilities. It seems to us, however, that what's really relevant is not absolute skill, but rather the fit of the skill level to the challenge. A match between the two creates full engagement. If the skill is not up to the challenge (whatever level the challenge is), the person cannot keep up, and flow will be disrupted. If the skill level greatly exceeds the challenge (again, whatever level the challenge is), the mind is less likely to be fully engaged in the activity.

Given this "matching" assumption, a person with low skill can be fully engaged in the pursuit of a relatively low-level challenge and thereby experience flow. Similarly, a person with moderate skills facing a moderate challenge would have to be fully engaged to carry out that behavior and may experience flow. Without the matching assumption, though, the flow experience would be impossible for many people.

Why does flow require your skill to be equal to the task? We would say that lower skills create slower movement toward attainment of the goal represented by the challenge. If you aren't doing well, there's an intrusion—the stepping out of the stream to ask yourself whether you can do this. Thus, the failure of flow in this circumstance seems quite compatible with our model of behavior.

It's of interest that flow also seems to be hard to sustain if things are going *too* well—if skills are high and challenge is not. Overshooting and exceeding one's previously perceived potential may raise questions about the accuracy of your previous perceptions. It suggests a reason to step outside the action and think over the nature of things. Alternatively, if your mind isn't completely occupied by the task (because it isn't challenging enough), your mind may simply drift to other things to occupy it. Either of these possibilities would disrupt flow. Again, these ideas are fully compatible with our model of action and affect.

Csikszentmihalyi and Nakamura (chap. 2) asserted that the flow experience incorporates growth. Why? Why isn't absorption in an activity (to the exclusion of other concerns) all that's involved in a flow experience? Without a conceptual mechanism, the assumption of growth would be another deus ex machina. We would suggest that if there is growth in a flow experience, the model we presented in the target chapter has a mechanism to account for it. Specifically, we noted how the criterion for affect can shift over time, such that a person performing well will have to perform gradually better to have the same affect (whether neutral or positive). This is a kind of growth—becoming better at the activity by virtue of performing close to one's current ability.

Affect Has Further Effects on Processing

We turn now to some of the further consequences of affect. Most of Forgas and Vargas's commentary (chap. 3) concerned the question of how affect can influence cognition and action after the affect has come to exist. They also raised definitional issues, however. We reply to their queries in that regard as follows: We chose the word *affect* in our discussion because we were focusing on feelings that arise through specific experiences (which we understand the word *affect* to imply). We tried to avoid the term *emotion*, because that word is often assumed to imply reference to the physiological changes that accompany feeling states, and that aspect of the experience was not the object of our analysis. We concur with Forgas and Vargas that the term *mood* refers to affective experiences that are generally low intensity, diffuse, and relatively enduring.

Moods were not the focus of our analysis. Their effects are very much the focus of Forgas's work and of the Forgas and Vargas commentary. Their commentary (chap. 3) introduced many issues that embellished upon the model we presented, in ways that would not necessarily have occurred to us. The work discussed there is certainly important in its own right. Unfortunately, however, their presentation was marred by several errors, as we shall see in the following paragraphs.

Forgas and Vargas implied throughout their writing that we are unaware of the fact that affect (mood, but also affect pertinent to the ongoing flow of action) conveys information that can be absorbed into other sorts of cognitive activities. We are in fact very much aware of it. Indeed, the idea that a positive feeling is isomorphic to a state of confidence (the basis for effects Forgas and Vargas described in which positive mood yields optimistic expectations) was explicitly discussed in the target chapter (see also Carver & Scheier, 1998, chap. 6).

A more minor error is the assertion that our model pays little attention to the possibility that feelings such as anger or fear motivate specific goal-oriented thinking and behavior (p. 3-11). This is incorrect, although the point was not emphasized in the target chapter. Our first theoretical statement on affect (Carver & Scheier, 1990) discussed the idea that affect from discrepancies regarding a goal monitored out of focal awareness could intrude on consciousness and force a reprioritization of goals (as suggested earlier by Simon, 1967). An example we used was anxiety arising while attempting to approach a feared stimulus. This example is certainly one in which fear caused adjustments both in thinking about what to do and in overt action (Carver, Blaney, & Scheier, 1979; Carver & Scheier, 1998, chap. 10).

Forgas and Vargas also said that we are silent on how people manage and control their affective states (this discussion bears largely on negative affect). This also is wrong. The most straightforward strategy of affect management is to do something that makes the situation better. Another affect management strategy is to demand less of oneself. Another is to reduce one's psychological investment in the situation. Students who are disheartened about low test scores can study more, can scale back their aspirations, or can downgrade their psychological investment in the course. All of these possibilities were addressed in the target chapter.

Is Affect an Epiphenomenon?

Earlier in this chapter, we addressed the question of whether goals have causal status or were epiphenomenal. Gollwitzer and Rohloff raised the question of whether *affect* is epiphenomenal. Their chapter (chap. 4) was based on a contrast between our affect model and ideas derived from the Heckhausen and Gollwitzer (1987) model of deliberative and implemental mind-sets. Gollwitzer and Rohloff said that a slowdown in moving toward a goal contradicts the person's commitment to goal attainment and thus is countered automatically. No affect is involved. Because positive discrepancies don't threaten commitment to goal attainment, they lead to continuation of efforts to maintain the high velocity.

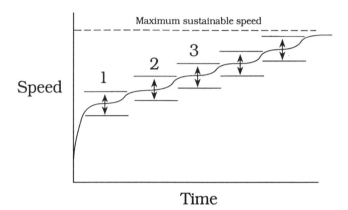

FIG. 11.3. Gollwitzer and Rohloff suggested that slow speeds are adjusted upward automatically, but overshoots in speed are not adjusted downward. This seems to suggest an inevitable continued drift upward, if any random variability in performance exists. In any given segment of performance (marked by parallel lines and two-headed arrows), random variability will occasionally produce both undershoots and overshoots. Because undershoots are countered but not overshoots, the occurrence of an overshoot (block 1) establishes a new base speed with random variability around *it* (block 2). Again, only undershoots are countered, and the sequence will continue until performance reaches an asymptote at the maximum speed the person can sustain (because no random deviations upward can occur).

Several things about this line of reasoning are curious. First, it is not apparent why the result of a goal commitment should not, in every case, be a gradual acceleration to the highest level of speed the person is capable of maintaining at the activity, which is then sustained throughout the activity (Fig. 11.3). That is, undershoots are countered automatically, overshoots are never countered. If the person is capable of overshooting the reference speed, it should happen occasionally through random variability. Because this overshoot won't be readjusted downward, the new speed becomes the base speed; this new base speed should also be overshot occasionally (again, due to random variability); with no downward adjustment, the person should continue to drift faster, asymptoting at his or her maximum ability to perform. This, we suggest, is not a very accurate depiction of reality.

Second, this view appears to contain no basis for the experience of positive affect. It does seem to have a basis for negative affect, which is said to arise strictly from adverse comparison with another person's performance speed. In any case, however, affect is irrelevant to subsequent performance. It appears, then, that feelings (which the authors rather disparagingly characterized as "vague signals," chap. 4, p. 11) have no meaning in this model. We have occasionally felt some trepidation over the extent to which our thinking about affect was dry and informational (it has been muttered that only Carver could create a model of feelings in which the feelings don't matter, only the information they convey), but we clearly have been outdone by this theory.[6]

Gollwitzer and Rohloff defended their theoretical position with data from a study in which subjects presumably experienced variations in speed of performance discrepancy reduction. The key finding, from Gollwitzer and Rohloff's viewpoint, was that changes in feelings (which did occur, at least in some groups, although the pattern was specified only for certain groups) did not mediate performance. We are unable to comment further on these results, because Gollwitzer and Rohloff's description of both the procedures and the results was quite sketchy, omitting critical details. Let us simply say that the issue remains little tested thus far, and leave it at that.

We do have further reactions to what Gollwitzer and Rohloff said, however. They correctly noted that affect may originate from many sources and that people can have difficulty in telling exactly what goal a feeling relates to. One potential consequence of this is that people may respond inappropriately to a feeling—coasting because they are feeling good, even if that feeling doesn't pertain to the goal they are working toward. Gollwitzer and Rohloff seem to think this potential for confusion somehow makes it implausible that people do respond to affect. We would argue instead that people *do* sometimes respond inappropriately to a feeling and do sometimes get confused about the sources of their feelings. Indeed, we think the difficulty in being clear on the origin of feelings is one reason why feelings have seemed so mysterious over the years. However, the fact that people use feelings to make further decisions about their actions seems beyond question (Forgas and Vargas, chap. 3; Martin, Ward, Achee, & Wyer, 1993).

We should not leave this point without making brief note of a related issue: the issue of primacy among affect, the hazy sense of expectancies, and the information conveyed by the error signal of the meta loop. Gollwitzer and Rohloff would favor a view in which the error signal has primacy. Vallacher and Nowak (chap. 10) would seem to favor a view in which affect has primacy. Earlier in our careers, we favored a view in which confidence versus doubt had primacy, as Sniezek appears to do in

---

[6]The irony is further compounded by the fact that Vallacher and Nowak, whose theoretical position can only be regarded as even more abstract and informational than is ours, asserted that emotions have a very pronounced role in self-regulation.

her commentary (chap. 8). At present, our best guess is that affect and relative confidence are subjective readouts of the system that controls rate, which can mutually influence and entrain one another. But we know of no evidence that conclusively indicates primacy of one over the other.

ISSUES ABOUT AUTONOMY

Two points of discussion arose in the commentaries concerning the concept of autonomy and will. We consider these points in this section, then turn more explicitly to a further consideration of other themes of experiential-organismic models.

Is Autonomy Illusory?

Ryan and Deci devoted part of their chapter (chap. 7) to the question of whether autonomy is illusory. We raised this question in the target chapter, asking whether something that is a feedback loop can be seen as autonomous. Ryan and Deci said (p. 7-9) this is the wrong question, that carrying out an action may embody a feedback process, but that feedback process can operate in the service of either a controlled or autonomous intent.

There are two ways to read this statement, and we don't know which one was meant. One possibility could be paraphrased as follows: "Both autonomous and controlled behavior embody the properties of feedback control, but knowing this fact about them doesn't help address the really important questions about them." For example, the feedback model would not intrinsically lead to a distinction between autonomous and controlled actions. Thus, you need something more than just the feedback structure in order to talk about the diversity of human behavior. The loops involved in these kinds of actions do two different kinds of things, which should be distinguished from each other.

If this is the message they meant to convey, we are in general agreement with it. The feedback hierarchy would not intrinsically lead one to make the distinction that Ryan and Deci have made, and the distinction is indeed important.

The other interpretation of what they wrote might be paraphrased as "Behaviors may be managed by feedback loops, but these behaviors are put into motion by something else, and that something else is not a feedback loop." This we would not agree with. We believe that actions—even at the level of abstraction that Ryan and Deci characterize as autonomous—embody the principle of feedback control, because the purpose behind the action is to create congruence within the self. Creating congruence (reducing discrepancies) is what a feedback loop does. Our question might then be reframed as whether the feedback loops that initiate actions that Ryan and Deci label as autonomous really are autonomous.

If the "true self" were exerting an internal pressure to have its core values expressed in behavior, it would represent a kind of control over behavior. Clearly, this control would differ from that exerted by guilt and external social pressure. After all, this is the authentic self that's exerting the influence, not some self-irrelevant or self-alien goal. Yet, would such an influence be compatible with the notion of autonomy?

What *is* autonomy? Ryan and Deci wrote that autonomy "is not freedom from determinants but instead is a functional process by which the self more fully resonates to some determinants and influences than to others" (p. 7-12). This phrasing seems to suggest that autonomy is entirely a matter of whether an influence has the effect of enhancing congruence within the self. If it does enhance congruence, the self resonates to it, and movement in that direction is by definition autonomous. It is of considerable interest to us how automatic—indeed, cybernetic—this description of the nature of autonomy makes it sound.[7]

Ryan and Deci's defense of the existence of autonomy rested heavily on the fact that differences of several kinds have been shown to emerge between conditions in which behavior is rendered more autonomous versus conditions in which behavior is rendered more controlled. Unfortunately, this evidence doesn't really resolve the problem, unless autonomy is nothing more than the absence of controlling forces.

The difficulty here can be framed in terms of whether the dimension in question is bipolar, ranging from autonomous to controlled behavior, or unipolar, ranging from highly controlling conditions to absence of controlling conditions. The research may all examine variations in extent of controlling forces. The absence of coercive control does not intrinsically imply the presence of something else, however. (The issue is analogous to variations in how much dynamite you explode under a cliff face—

---

[7]Ryan and Deci wrote that the basic metaphor of the organismic approach is a living system, whereas that of the cybernetic approach is an autocorrecting machine. We would remind them that cybernetic concepts had their origins partly in the concept of homeostasis (a process that takes place in living systems) and that systems theorists from Wiener onward have placed great emphasis on the functioning of living organisms (see, e.g., DeAngelis, Post, & Travis, 1986; Ford, 1987; Miller, 1978; Miller & Miller, 1992; Wiener, 1948). As Powers (1978) put it, "the servomechanism has always been only an imitation of the real thing, a living organism, ... The analogy developed from man to machine—not the other way." In short, we believe the contrast is not as stark as they said it is.

different amounts of dynamite have different impacts on the cliff, but the absence of dynamite doesn't imply the presence of something else).

Coercion, Autonomy, and Self-Determination

A theme of the Ryan and Deci comment (as is true of most of their work) is that autonomous behavior differs from controlled behavior (see also Tesser, chap. 9). Controlled behavior is done for reasons other than an intrinsic or identified valuing of the activity. It is behavior done because you "have to" do it, because you feel social pressure to do it, because you "ought to" do it, because you are forcing yourself to do it to avoid a feeling of guilt (or to gain a feeling of "egoistic pride").[8] Ryan and Deci said that we don't distinguish this sort of controlled behavior from other behavior.

We are surprised at this assertion, because one of the issues we took up in the target chapter was the ought self, as formulated by Higgins (1987, 1996). We suggested that behavior regulated with respect to the ought self has its origin in an effort to avoid some punishing anti-goal. Thus, the attempt to conform to an ought is secondary to an attempt to stay away from an undesired state. As such, conformity to an ought is responsive to a kind of coercion (or self-coercion). Indeed, it was the case of oughts—and what we take to be the resemblance between oughts and introjected values—that led us to suggest that an avoidance tendency may constitute a common basis for regulation that fails to connect to the authentic self. Thus, it's hard for us to understand why Ryan and Deci would say we don't distinguish between controlled behavior and other behavior.

Although we think the model we presented does address this distinction, we would have to say we did a poor job of accounting for the distinction in the target chapter. There are at least two reasons for our failure. First, an error in our wording created a critical misimpression about the crux of our argument. Second, upon further reflection, we don't think the case we were trying to describe covers all controlled regulation (as we suggested there). Rather, it covers only one subclass of such regulation (albeit an important subclass).

The error in wording is this: The essence of one class of regulatory events that represent controlled behavior is that they have an avoidance

---

[8]Although we think we understand the point underlying the phrase "egoistic pride," it does beg the question of whether pride is always "egoistic," or whether people can experience a different variety of pride, and if so, what would differentiate the two experiences from each other.

tendency as their *prime* motivation. We're not speaking here of an avoidance tendency that occurs in service to an approach tendency. That arrangement is not a problem (Carver & Scheier, 1998, chap. 6). Rather, we meant to highlight activities in which avoidance is the starting point, the first and fundamental motive, and in which approach—if it occurs at all—*occurs in service to that avoidance.* Approaching an ought or an introjected value seems to occur in the service of avoidance of disapproval or self-disapproval. That, we think, renders the behavior controlled. The final sentence of that section of the target chapter should more properly have said "We can think of no case in which a value of the true self as they discuss it has an avoidance tendency as its core motivational basis."

We retain that belief, despite Ryan and Deci's examples to the contrary (and despite having no actual evidence to supply in support of it). We think, at the motivational core, the alcoholic they described is trying to move toward being a healthier and more intact person (using the avoidance of alcohol to serve that approach motive); the injured basketball player is trying to retain the ability to play and continue competing (using restraint as a tactic to move toward that affirmative goal); and the patient undergoing adjuvant treatment is trying to affirmatively extend life. In each case, if the behavior in question is really autonomous rather than reactive to a controlling influence, we believe that the avoidance of the anti-goal (alcohol, risky plays, and recurrence) is occurring in service to the affirmative approach goal.

Simultaneous Approach and Avoidance

While we are discussing the issue of approach in service to avoidance and vice versa, let us also speak to that issue as it emerged in Csikszentmihalyi and Nakamura's chapter (chap. 2). In discussing our treatment of simultaneous approach and avoidance goals, they provided an example of a writer who became absorbed in music and thereby avoided an unpleasant home situation. This example appears to us to make a very different case than they think it does. In our view, that is a person who has an intrinsic interest in music and who is simply being drawn into pursuit of the interest. The fact that music also served as an escape from other undesired circumstances was a secondary gain for this person, not the primary purpose of the activity. Thus that action was autonomous.

A useful point of contrast here is the behavior of the obsessive-compulsive person. The obsessive-compulsive person, who ritually does an activity over and over again, gets little pleasure from the activity (though certain obsessive-compulsive tendencies can have positive side effects, such as a house that's clean and neat). At its core, this activity is an act of avoidance, a means to fend off anxiety. This is certainly not the case in the example presented by Csikszentmihalyi and Nakamura.

We regard these as very different situations structurally: The music-lover is engaged fundamentally in approach, with the secondary benefit of avoiding family difficulties; the obsessive-compulsive person is engaged fundamentally in avoidance, with the (potential) secondary benefit of approaching neatness.

AUTHENTICITY AND THE TRUE SELF

The preceding discussions have led us inexorably deeper into the question of what constitutes the self. In this section, we consider several angles on this question.

Ryan and Deci (chap. 7) said we failed to distinguish between two broad categories of goals, which differ in the "why" of behavior rather than in the "how" of behavior. As we acknowledged earlier, our primary concern throughout our work has been with the how rather than the why. This is true relatively, however, rather than absolutely. We are certainly able to address the why question, and (as Ryan and Deci anticipated) we do so by appealing to the notion of hierachicality.

Ryan and Deci did not seem favorably impressed by the possibility that the principle of hierachicality might enable us to deal effectively with this issue. We think it does a better job than they realize. Indeed, as they noted in passing, hierarchicality is part of their own thinking. Without this structural principle, they would have the same conceptual problem as they ascribed to us. The structural principle turns out to work just as well for us as it does for them.

Hierarchicality, Goal Pursuit, and Self-Alien Goals

Ryan and Deci distinguished between standards they called "self-alien" (self-incongruent) and those that are "self-endorsed" (self-congruent). They claimed that within our model the concept of self-alien goals has no place (indeed, that it has no meaning; chap. 7, p. 5). If self-alien means self-antithetical, this would be true. Our approach would suggest that every goal that's adopted is connected to the person, although the connections can vary from very strong to very weak (recall Fig. 11.1). In this sense, the idea of holding a goal that is purely self-antithetical has no meaning.

On the other hand, Ryan and Deci's use of the term self-alien did not always imply self-antithetical. At one point (p. 2-5) they equated self-alien with "compelled by forces external to the self" and "introjected."

To us, this implies only that the connection of this value to the self within the goal hierarchy is weak. If the term self-alien really does not mean antithetical to the self, our model certainly has a place for it. It's simply a goal that doesn't contribute much to the ideal self.

But let's address the question differently. Does our model have a place for the type of *phenomena* that Ryan and Deci would characterize as reflecting the use of self-alien goals? The answer to this question is clearly yes. The hierarchical model provides an easy way to address even goals that are damaging to the self—goals that tear apart the fabric of the self. Our discussion here focuses mostly on this case, rather than the easily managed case of goals that are simply not closely connected to the self.

An example that Ryan and Deci appealed to, in relation to this theme, is the case of the anorexic. The anorexic is pursuing a goal that can be viewed as self-alien, because pursuit of this goal threatens other important values of the self. Among other things, anorexics are creating a discrepancy with respect to their health, a value linked strongly to the core self (Fig. 11.4). The eating-restraint goal thus conflicts with the health goal. Pursuit of the former is creating problems for the latter. We agree with Ryan and Deci that behavior which conflicts with other important self-relevant goals can be problematic and potentially damaging. As Fig. 11.4 illustrates, this is a direct implication of hierarchical organization.

The hierarchy also indicates why pursuit of goals that are largely self-irrelevant is not a problem unless these pursuits take up so much time and energy that too little is left for self-affirming goals (i.e., too much pursuit of oughts can preempt consideration of ideals). Chasing these minimally important goal does not inherently create incongruities elsewhere. It's only when the pursuit of one goal has the consequence of enlarging discrepancies from other core values of the self (either directly,

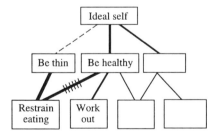

FIG. 11.4. In an anorexic person, conforming to the goal of eating restraint is contributing to the goal of being thin, which is contributing at least minimally to the ideal self. However, conforming to the goal of eating restraint is also having a distinct adverse influence (indicated by the barred line) on another goal that is very strongly related to the ideal self—remaining healthy.

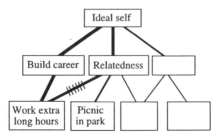

FIG. 11.5. Conflict can arise even when behavioral goals are not self-alien. By working extra long hours in order to further a career aspiration that is very self-actualizing, this woman may at the same time be having a distinct adverse influence (indicated by the barred line) on another goal that is very strongly related to her ideal self—spending time maintaining a sense of relatedness with her family.

or by virtue of extended neglect) that there is a problem (cf. Baumeister, Shapiro, & Tice, 1985; Emmons & King, 1988; Van Hook & Higgins, 1988).

It cannot be the case, however, that conflict per se makes a goal what Ryan and Deci call self-alien. This is because, even among identified and intrinsically valued goals, conflicts arise fairly often. For example, the woman who wants to develop her career (in which she has an intrinsic interest) and also spend time with her family (an activity that fulfills her desires for relatedness) faces a conflict imposed by the limited number of hours in the day and days in the week (Fig. 11.5). Neither of these goals can be called self-alien. But the effort to attain one (e.g., further the career by working extra hours) can interfere with efforts to attain the other (by removing the time available for family activities). Nor are such conflicts between intrinsically valued goals especially rare.

Thus, conflicting with a value of the self is not enough to render a goal alien from the ideal self. What, then, might do so? Perhaps a goal becomes self-alien if its pursuit creates more problems than the benefits it provides.

Why Would People Ever Pursue Goals That Are Truly Self-Alien?

In considering these possibilities, a very important question is why someone would ever pursue a goal whose pursuit causes problems greater than the benefits it provides? Sometimes people approach goals they don't care about, even goals that create conflicts, in order to avoid antigoals. Ryan and Deci mentioned the adolescent who insists on wearing the right designer logo. We're not as sure as they are that he's trying to gain acceptance, rather than staving off rejection, and we don't regard desire for approval and fear of rejection as the same. If it's fear of rejection that lies at the heart of this behavior, the behavior is being coerced by the anti-goal. He may approach this coerced goal even at the cost of conflict elsewhere (perhaps in the form of arguments with his father, who resents paying the extra money).

We don't think that such coercion is the only reason for approaching goals that are self-damaging, however. We would argue that people sometimes approach goals that ultimately create damage within the self for a more straightforward reason: They see an affirmative value in those goals, despite the fact that they're creating a problem elsewhere. This case therefore does not differ structurally from the earlier example of the woman who's trying to balance a career and time with family. It differs (if at all) only in the balance of gains and losses.

What kind of affirmative value are we talking about? It has often been argued that when people are distracted away from self-actualization, it's by the desire to gain acceptance from others. Because acceptance often is conditional, the desire for acceptance causes the person to act in ways that interfere with self-actualization—that slow it down or even actively oppose it (Rogers, 1980). What is rarely emphasized is that this process of interference with self-actualization is rooted in the desire for relatedness—another core value of the self.

That is, the person in this situation implicitly (or explicitly) believes that gaining the acceptance of others will satisfy the need for relatedness. Attaining their acceptance may satisfy this need, but at the potential cost of enlarging discrepancies elsewhere within the self. Even worse, this acceptance may not actually satisfy the need for relatedness after all. The person may expect it to do so and may try to see it as doing so, but a superficial acceptance from others may actually do little or nothing to satisfy this need (even while the self-actualizing tendency remains stifled).

As a concrete example, it's fairly common for adolescents to hang out with bad crowds and do antisocial activities because they crave acceptance from their peers (we assume throughout this example that the goal is attaining acceptance rather than avoiding rejection). If the bad crowd is the only one that will give them attention and acceptance, that's the one they'll try to fit into. This can have adverse consequences for self-actualization. They may ignore their studies (because studying isn't cool), poison their relations with their parents (because parents are this crowd's enemy), and become drastically different from the people they used to be. They may deviate in many ways from aspects of their core self because of their need for relatedness and the belief (perhaps mistaken)

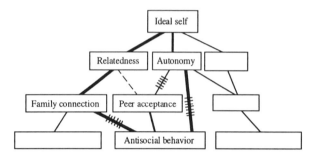

FIG. 11.6. Adolescents sometimes engage in antisocial behavior because it's a way of attaining acceptance from peers. They believe that gaining acceptance from peers will satisfy the need for relatedness. However, if the peer relations are superficial, rather than true friendships, the peer connection won't satisfy that need much (indicated by the dashed line). In the meantime, the antisocial behavior is creating a discrepancy in relations with family members (indicated by the barred line); because the family connection is a strong contributor to satisfaction of the need for relatedness, this disruption works against satisfaction of that need. The exaggerated striving for peer acceptance also creates a discrepancy with respect to the need for autonomy (barred line). Indeed, engaging in the antisocial behavior may create such discrepancies with the autonomy urge more directly (barred line). Thus, activity that's intended to satisfy the need for relatedness (the antisocial behavior) is actually creating important incongruences elsewhere in the self.

that the actions they are engaging in will satisfy their need for relatedness (Fig. 11.6).[9]

If the belief that relatedness can be attained this way is actually erroneous, the person often gradually comes to realize it. Gradually, the goals that matter most to the self (those that are linked most tightly to the core self in the hierarchy) will hold sway. As this happens and as the person abandons the conflict-inducing goals, the self becomes more congruous throughout. (This process, which is consistent with a hierarchical model, can also be seen to be consistent with the process of multiple-constraint satisfaction in a connectionist network of interconnected elements.)

By pointing to the need for relatedless as an important element in this conflictual situation, we have pointed to a reason why a goal that Ryan and Deci might term self-alien (a goal whose pursuit induces conflict with the core values of the self) comes to be adopted at all (an issue that Ryan and Deci didn't address). Nothing in this portrayal seems inconsistent

---

[9]This sort of behavior is not, of course, limited to adolescents. Nonetheless, the focus on peer acceptance at the price of good family relationships seems to blossom during the middle teen years. It may be that the hormonal changes of puberty induce a preferential orientation to relations with individuals who are potential mating partners.

with an experiential-organismic model—indeed, what we've just said essentially reframes the position that was taken consistently by Rogers (1980) about how the need for positive regard can cause people to act in ways that interfere with self-actualization. But by framing the issue in terms of a hierarchy of goal values that contribute to the self, we have done more than simply point out that some goals are self-affirming and others can be self-damaging. We've also pointed out how even self-damaging tendencies can often be rooted in an attempt to attain core values of the self.

What Are the Needs of the True Self?

Ryan and Deci (chap. 7) said that by invoking a hierarchy we have a problem in specifying what the upper level goals are and where they come from and what it means to have some goals as more central than others. This is the same problem they encountered when starting to develop their ideas. They decided that the needs for autonomy and relatedness are fundamental. But why? How sure are they about that? Is the need for autonomy a fundamental human need, or is the apparent primacy of this need a creation of Western culture?

One of the problems many observers have had with self-actualization models is that it's extremely difficult to specify a priori what anyone's true self consists of and thus what kind of behavior is self-actualizing for that person. If an individual's true self incorporates an intrinsic interest in accumulating wealth, for example, who can say that interest isn't part of that person's true self, and that the accumulation of wealth isn't self-actualizing for that person? Indeed, there is evidence that wealth and status can be pursued for either autonomous or controlled reasons (as can community involvement) and that the goals themselves matter less to self-actualization than the reasons underlying their pursuit (Carver & Baird, 1998).

Although it will certainly be disheartening to some people (including ourselves) to consider this possibility, it is not obvious to us why the true self of every person should even be assumed to be rooted in values that affirm human connectedness and excellence. Why, for example, is it not the case that the true self of the sociopath is exactly what it seems to be—exploitive, unconnected, entitled, inimical to society, but supportive and protective of its own autonomous well-being?

The notion of hierarchicality helps us to understand why an activity is self-congruent or self-damaging. The activity is *self-congruent* if engaging in it helps to close gaps at the core of the self. The activity is *self-damaging* if engaging in it enlarges gaps at the core of the self. But even with the notion of hierarchicality as a tool, the question of what needs reside at the core self of a given individual remains at least somewhat open. Ryan and Deci have given us one portrayal of what needs define the core self, but we are less sure than they are about the universality of that portrayal.[10]

Why Is Competence Necessary for an Activity to Relate to the Authentic Self?

The Csikszentmihalyi and Nakamura chapter (chap. 2) and the Ryan and Deci chapter (chap. 7) both placed an emphasis on the notion of the authenticity of the self. These two sets of authors see the authentic self reflected in pursuit of goals that produce positive affect. Indeed, they seem to imply the necessity of experiencing positive affect in order for the true self to be involved.

We have grave concerns about requiring that a person be experiencing positive affect for the experience to be authentic. This criterion seems to merge with the criterion of competence, because you'll feel good when you are competent at something tied to the core self. We've always found it odd that competence per se should be a hallmark of the authentic self. What if a person wants to do something for perfectly authentic and autonomous reasons, but is horrible at it? We can readily see how this person would have trouble having a flow experience while engaged in this activity. But why should this desire (this goal) not be part of the person's authentic self?[11]

We are *not* trying to argue that these organismic theoretical positions reduce to efficacy models. That is, in both the Ryan and Deci and the Csikszentmihalyi and Nakamura approaches, it gains nothing to be efficacious at an activity that's imposed on you, is irrelevant to your true self, or is self-alien. Efficacy is desirable only with regard to values that are authentic. But if the value is authentic, efficacy seems very important indeed. In fact, it seems from what these authors have written that efficacy is one determinant of whether the value *is* authentic. We find that hard to understand.

---

[10]We should be clear here about what we believe. Although we've been raising questions about aspects of Deci and Ryan's theory, we certainly don't regard it as fundamentally misguided. Although we make no claim to have thought of it on our own, we agree with them that needs for relatedness and effectance are intrinsic and fundamental for most people (though we don't know for sure about the sociopath). It's when we move beyond these basics to their divergent potential manifestations that we become less confident about what is universal and what is idiosyncratic.

[11]The experiential approach seems to imply, in this regard, that people become most involved in what they find themselves to be good at. We believe this is true (cf. Carver & Scheier, 1998, chap. 12).

Another View of Competence

Our own view of the tendency toward greater competence is grounded in a principle with echoes of Piaget (1963) and Kelly (1955). We think the human organism continuously strives to make better predictions of events in the world. Better prediction (both as an observer and as an actor) means better outcomes and greater efficiency. We agree with Ryan and Deci that efficiency at attaining a goal that is ultimately self-damaging doesn't help and may even harm the person. Nonetheless, we think the tendency to move toward greater efficiency probably occurs in whatever activities people continue to pursue. We don't regard the tendency toward greater efficiency or competence as a human need, in the same sense as relatedness (or effectance). Rather, it's an operating characteristic of the organism, an aspect of the functioning of our cognitive machinery.

Indeed, the principle of evolving greater efficiency—again, following Piaget—seems to provide a basis for discussing growth (see also Vallacher and Nowak's, chap. 10, p. 9 discussion of ever-continuing integration among disparate systems). Growth, as Piaget (1963) viewed it, rests on processes of organization (integrating simple processes into a more complex whole, which may even have emergent properties) and adaptation (fitting the requirements of the environment). Similarly, some views of consciousness hold that its purpose is to sort out decisions and create default values for perception, thought, and action (Bargh, 1997; Norman & Shallice, 1986; Shallice, 1978). When attention is freed for other use, it gravitates to new or more elaborate decisions. The person's understanding thus evolves to become both more complex and more integrated. As people become capable of handling more and more with minimal thought, they begin to take into account more and more variables at once, thereby stretching themselves and their ability to function yet further (see Carver & Scheier, 1998, chap. 16).

Several of the authors suggested that the sort of model we presented has little regard for growth. We think the preceding discussion illustrates that such a conclusion is incorrect. But let's not stop here. Let's continue a bit further down that path.

Exploration, Curiosity, and Growth

Ryan and Deci (chap. 7) wrote that the cybernetic framework leaves unaddressed issues such as the inherent growth tendencies that the experiential-organismic perspective incorporates, because we don't appreciate the inherent experiential rewards that often energize behaviors such as exploratory, playful, and growth-related behaviors (p. 7-5). An important followup question, which we've rarely seen addressed, is what are those experiential rewards? What makes such activities motivating?

Let's consider a construct that seems not too far from these: curiosity. Loewenstein (1994) argued that curiosity stems from the perception of a gap in knowledge. Following James, Hebb, Piaget, Hunt, and Berlyne (among others), he concluded that curiosity involves a comparison of one's present information against a reference point. Curiosity occurs when the reference point is higher than present knowledge. He argues that people must experience a contrast between these two to experience curiosity. If they experience the contrast, they experience curiosity, which they may then try to satisfy by exploration. This depiction sounds very cybernetic to us.

People are ignorant of many things (i.e., have many such discrepancies in knowledge), but they aren't always curious. Loewenstein argued that whether curiosity emerges depends in part on the size of the discrepancy. Too large a disparity (which raises doubt about closing it) dampens curiosity. In effect, people feel overwhelmed, and they disengage. Indeed, Loewenstein argued that before people expose themselves to a curiosity-inducing situation, they estimate whether their curiosity will ultimately be satisfied. If the chances are too slim, most people won't expose themselves to the situation.

Thus, curiosity reflects an engagement aimed at discrepancy reduction, and avoidance of the unknown represents a disengagement from the discrepancy-reduction effort. This distinction between the curious person and the avoider of the unknown seems to fit our conceptualization of effort and disengagement quite well. Again, although this discussion is far from conclusive, we see every reason to believe that a cybernetic model has a place in it for growth and exploration.

CLOSING COMMENT

In this chapter, we've tried to address several of what we saw as the more important concerns and criticisms that were raised in the preceding commentaries. We regret we could not reply to every issue raised, but something always remains left unsaid when time and space are limited. Our choice of issues to address was based on a desire to render as clear as possible the central themes of the model presented earlier and the relation of those themes to other models of behavior.

We hope that some of what we've written here will serve to fine-tune the impact of the target chapter for readers of this volume, by clarifying points of potential confusion and by extending the themes of that chapter in several directions. As is always the case in an enterprise of this nature, the closing chapter of the volume is an ending to the book, but not an ending to the enterprise. Rather, this is simply another way station in a continuing dynamic process of discourse, persuasion, debate, and investigation. We look forward to further efforts at synthesizing and refining ideas, integrating ideas across conceptual boundaries, and gaining yet greater clarity about the nature of the human experience, on the part of those who are interested (as are we) in the self-regulation of behavior.

ACKNOWLEDGMENT

This work was facilitated by NCI grants CA64710 and CA64711.

REFERENCES

Apter, M. J. (1982). *The experience of motivation: The theory of psychological reversals*. San Diego, CA: Academic Press.

Bargh, J. A. (1997). The automaticity of everyday life. In R. S. Wyer, Jr. (Ed.), *Advances in social cognition* (Vol. 10, pp. 1–61). Mahwah, NJ: Lawrence Erlbaum Associates.

Baumeister, R. F., Shapiro, J. P., & Tice, D. M. (1985). Two kinds of identity crisis. *Journal of Personality, 53*, 407–424.

Carver, C. S., & Baird, E. (1998). The American dream revisited: Is it *what* you want or *why* you want it that matters? *Psychological Science, 9*, 289–292.

Carver, C. S., Blaney, P. H., & Scheier, M. F. (1979). Focus of attention, chronic expectancy, and responses to a feared stimulus. *Journal of Personality and Social Psychology, 37*, 1186–1195.

Carver, C. S., & Scheier, M. F. (1990). Origins and functions of positive and negative affect: A control-process view. *Psychological Review, 97*, 19–35.

Carver, C. S., & Scheier, M. F. (1998). *On the self-regulation of behavior*. New York: Cambridge University Press.

Clark, R. N. (1996). *Control system dynamics*. New York: Cambridge University Press.

Csikszentmihalyi, M. (1996). *Creativity: Flow and the psychology of discovery and invention*. New York: HarperCollins.

DeAngelis, D. L., Post, W. M., & Travis, C. C. (1986). *Positive feedback in natural systems* (*Biomathematics, Vol. 15*). Berlin and New York: Springer-Verlag.

Emmons, R. A., & King, L .A. (1988). Conflict among personal strivings: Immediate and long-term implications for psychological and physical well-being. *Journal of Personality and Social Psychology, 54*, 1040–1048.

Ford, D. H. (1987). *Humans as self-constructing living systems: A developmental perspective on behavior and personality*. Hillsdale, NJ: Lawrence Erlbaum Associates.

Heckhausen, H., & Gollwitzer, P. M. (1987). Thought contents and cognitive functioning in motivational versus volitional states of mind. *Motivation and Emotion, 11*, 101–120.

Higgins, E. T. (1987). Self-discrepancy: A theory relating self and affect. *Psychological Review, 94*, 319–340.

Higgins, E. T. (1996). Ideals, oughts, and regulatory focus: Affect and motivation from distinct pains and pleasures. In P. M. Gollwitzer & J. A. Bargh (Eds.), *The psychology of action: Linking cognition and motivation to behavior* (pp. 91–114). New York: Guilford.

Kelly, G. A. (1955). *The psychology of personal constructs*. New York: Norton.

Loewenstein, G. (1994). The psychology of curiosity: A review and reinterpretation. *Psychological Bulletin, 116*, 75–98.

Maes, P. (1990). Situated agents can have goals. In P. Maes (Ed.), *Designing autonomous agents: Theory and practice from biology to engineering and back* (pp. 49–70). Cambridge, MA: MIT Press.

Martin, L. L., & Tesser, A. (1996). Some ruminative thoughts. In R. S. Wyer, Jr. (Ed.), *Advances in social cognition* (Vol. 9, pp. 1–47). Mahwah, NJ: Lawrence Erlbaum Associates.

Martin, L. L., Ward, D. W., Achee, J. W., & Wyer, R. S., Jr. (1993). Mood as input: People have to interpret the motivational implications of their mood. *Journal of Personality and Social Psychology, 64*, 317–326.

McFarland, D., & Bösser, T. (1993). *Intelligent behavior in animal and robots.* Cambridge, MA: MIT Press.

Melton, R. J. (1995). The role of positive affect in syllogism performance. *Personality and Social Psychology Bulletin, 21*, 788–794.

Miller, J. G. (1978). *Living systems.* New York: McGraw-Hill.

Miller, J. G., & Miller, J. L. (1992). Cybernetics, general systems theory, and living systems theory. In R. L. Levine & H. E. Fitzgerald (Eds.), *Analysis of dynamical psychological systems: Vol. 1. Basic approaches to general systems, dynamic systems, and cybernetics* (pp. 9–34). New York: Plenum.

Mizruchi, M. S. (1991). Urgency, motivation, and group performance: The effect of prior success on current success among professional basketball teams. *Social Psychology Quarterly, 54*, 181–189.

Norman, D. A., & Shallice, T. (1986). Attention to action: Willed and automatic control of behavior. In R. J. Davidson, G. E. Schwartz, & D. Shapiro (Eds.), *Consciousness and self-regulation: Advances in research and theory* (Vol. 4, pp. 1–18). New York: Plenum.

Piaget, J. (1963). *The child's conception of the world.* Paterson, NJ: Littlefield, Adams.

Powers, W. T. (1978). Quantitative analysis of purposive systems: Some spadework at the foundations of scientific psychology. *Psychological Review, 85*, 417–435.

Read, S. J., Vanman, E. J., & Miller, L. C. (1997). Connectionism, parallel constraint satisfaction processes, and Gestalt principles: (Re)introducing cognitive dynamics to social psychology. *Review of Personality and Social Psychology, 1*, 26–53.

Rogers, C. R. (1980). *A way of being.* Boston: Houghton Mifflin.

Shallice, T. (1978). The dominant action system: An information-processing approach to consciousness. In K. S. Pope & J. L. Singer (Eds.), *The stream of consciousness: Scientific investigations into the flow of human experience* (pp. 117–157). New York: Wiley.

Simon, H. A. (1967). Motivational and emotional controls of cognition. *Psychology Review, 74*, 29–39.

Skinner, B. F. (1953). *Science and human behavior.* New York: Macmillan.

Suls, J. M. (1972). Two-stage model for appreciation of jokes and cartoons: Information-processing analysis. In J. H. Goldstein & P. E. McGhee (Eds.), *The psychology of humor* (pp. 81–100). San Diego, CA: Academic Press.

Thagard, P. (1989). Explanatory coherence. *Behavioral and Brain Sciences, 12*, 435–467.

Van Hook, E., & Higgins, E. T. (1988). Self-related problems beyond the self-concept: Motivational consequences of discrepant self-guides. *Journal of Personality and Social Psychology, 55*, 625–633.

Wiener, N. (1948). *Cybernetics: Control and communication in the animal and the machine.* Cambridge, MA: MIT Press.

Wyer, R. S., Jr., & Collins, J. E., II. (1992). A theory of humor elicitation. *Psychological Review, 99*, 663–688.

Author Index

Subject Index